ANOTHER DAY
IN CUBICLE
PARADISE

Other DILBERT books from Andrews McMeel Publishing

When Did Ignorance Become a Point of View?
ISBN: 0-7407-1839-8

Excuse Me While I Wag
ISBN: 0-7407-1390-6

Dilbert-A Treasury of Sunday Strips: Version 00
ISBN: 0-7407-0531-8

Random Acts of Management
ISBN: 0-7407-0453-2

Dilbert Gives You the Business
ISBN: 0-7407-0338-2 hardcover
ISBN: 0-7407-0003-0 paperback

Don't Step in the Leadership
ISBN: 0-8362-7844-5

Journey to Cubeville
ISBN: 0-8362-7175-0 hardcover
ISBN: 0-8362-6745-1 paperback

I'm Not Anti-Business, I'm Anti-Idiot
ISBN: 0-8362-5182-2

Seven Years of Highly Defective People
ISBN: 0-8362-5129-6 hardcover
ISBN: 0-8362-3668-8 paperback

Casual Day Has Gone Too Far
ISBN: 0-8362-2899-5

Fugitive from the Cubicle Police
ISBN: 0-8362-2119-2

Still Pumped from Using the Mouse
ISBN: 0-8362-1026-3

It's Obvious You Won't Survive by Your Wits Alone
ISBN: 0-8362-0415-8

Bring Me the Head of Willy the Mailboy!
ISBN: 0-8362-1779-9

Shave the Whales
ISBN: 0-8362-1740-3

Dogbert's Clues for the Clueless
ISBN: 0-8362-1737-3

Build a Better Life by Stealing Office Supplies
ISBN: 0-8362-1757-8

Always Postpone Meetings with Time-Wasting Morons
ISBN: 0-8362-1758-6

For ordering information, call 1-800-642-6480.

ANOTHER DAY IN CUBICLE PARADISE

A DILBERT BOOK
BY SCOTT ADAMS

Andrews McMeel
Publishing

Kansas City

——— ATTENTION: SCHOOLS AND BUSINESSES ———

Andrews McMeel books are available at quantity discounts with bulk purchase for educational, business, or sales promotional use. For information, please write to: Special Sales Department, Andrews McMeel Publishing, 4520 Main Street, Kansas City, Missouri 64111.

For the best negative shopper ever

Introduction

Someone wise once said (Okay, it was me, about a minute ago), "Never sit for eight hours a day in a fabric-covered box that someone else paid for." And then it hit me. I finally figured out what's wrong with the whole cubicle concept: Communism.

That's right; cubicles are a form of communism. Think about it. You don't own your cubicle—the "state" does. Well, technically your stockholders own the cubicle, not the state, but it's the same problem. Because the people who pay for your cubicle don't have to sit in it, there's no incentive for cubicles to be all that they can be. It's no wonder they're bleak and dingy.

Maybe it's time to lift the yoke of communism from the oppressed cubicle masses. I say every employee should own his or her cubicle and take it along to every new assignment. The cubicle of the future would be modular so you can easily relocate it and customize it to taste. Sure, this new system would introduce some annoying eccentricities into the system. Every person would have a different idea of what the perfect cubicle should be. Your neighbors might have low-rider cubicles and Barbie-themed cubicles and maybe the clothing-optional, disco cubicles. But that's a small price to pay for the freedom to customize your own workspace.

I would decorate my cubicle like the inside of a womb, except with better electronic gadgetry. I wouldn't need a chair. I'd just curl up in a fetal position near my keyboard. When you're in a womb, it feels as if your life is full of possibilities and all of them are ahead of you. You feel warm and fed and loved. And I think I'd put censors at the doorway (the design of which I shall not describe), so that when I left my womb-cube a motherly voice would scream as if giving birth. It might annoy my cubicle neighbors, but we can take that up at the next meeting of the Cube-Owners Association.

Speaking of wonderful things, there's still time to join Dogbert's New Ruling Class (DNRC) and be by his side when he conquers the world and makes everyone else our domestic servants. To be a member all you need to do is sign up for the free *Dilbert Newsletter* that is published approximately whenever I feel like it — about five times a year if you're lucky.

To subscribe or unsubscribe, go to www.dilbert.com. If you have problems with the automated subscription method, write to newsletter@unitedmedia.com.

S.Adams

Scott Adams

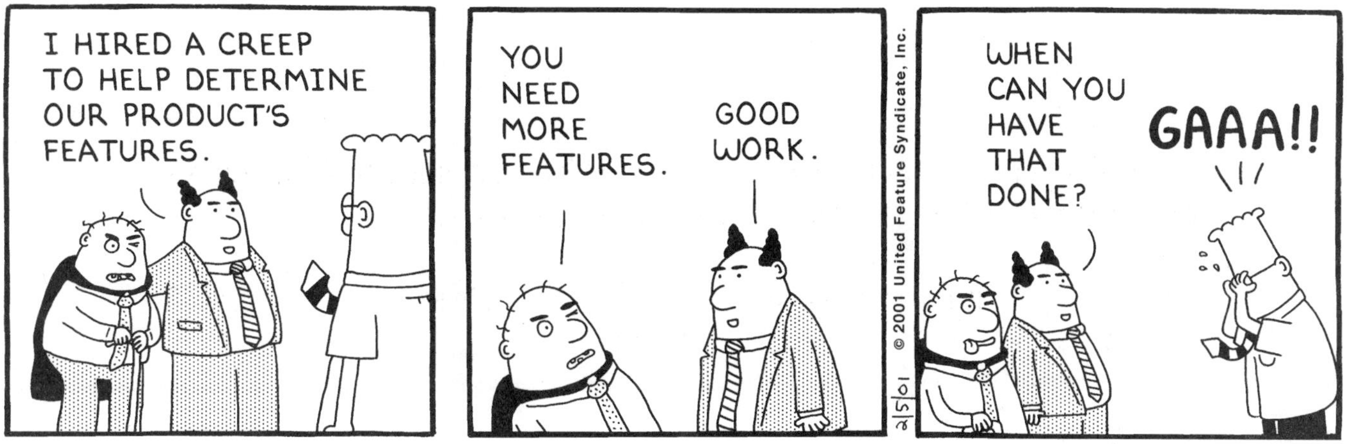
I HIRED A CREEP TO HELP DETERMINE OUR PRODUCT'S FEATURES.
YOU NEED MORE FEATURES.
GOOD WORK.
2/5/01 © 2001 United Feature Syndicate, Inc.
WHEN CAN YOU HAVE THAT DONE?
GAAA!!

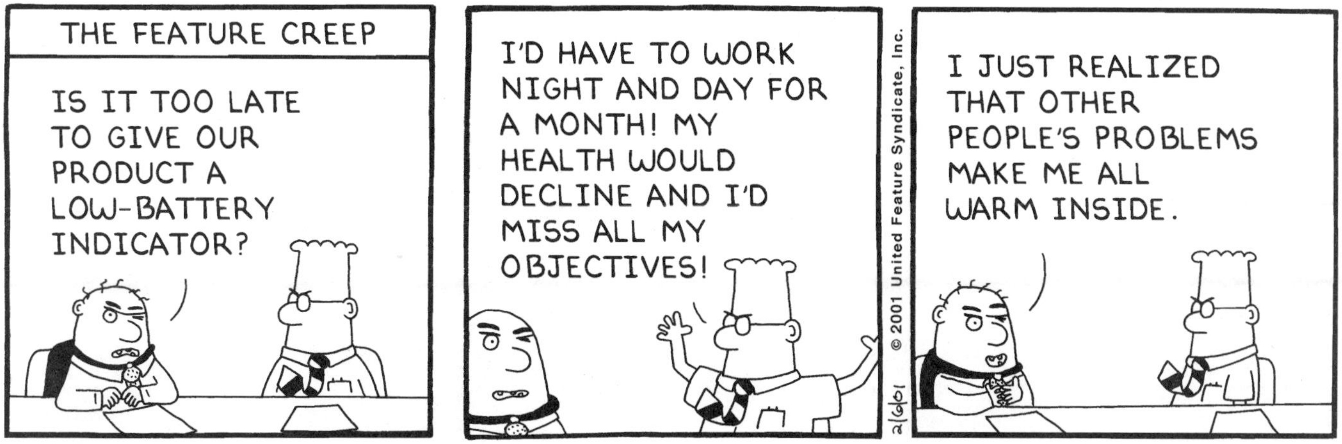
THE FEATURE CREEP
IS IT TOO LATE TO GIVE OUR PRODUCT A LOW-BATTERY INDICATOR?
I'D HAVE TO WORK NIGHT AND DAY FOR A MONTH! MY HEALTH WOULD DECLINE AND I'D MISS ALL MY OBJECTIVES!
2/6/01 © 2001 United Feature Syndicate, Inc.
I JUST REALIZED THAT OTHER PEOPLE'S PROBLEMS MAKE ME ALL WARM INSIDE.

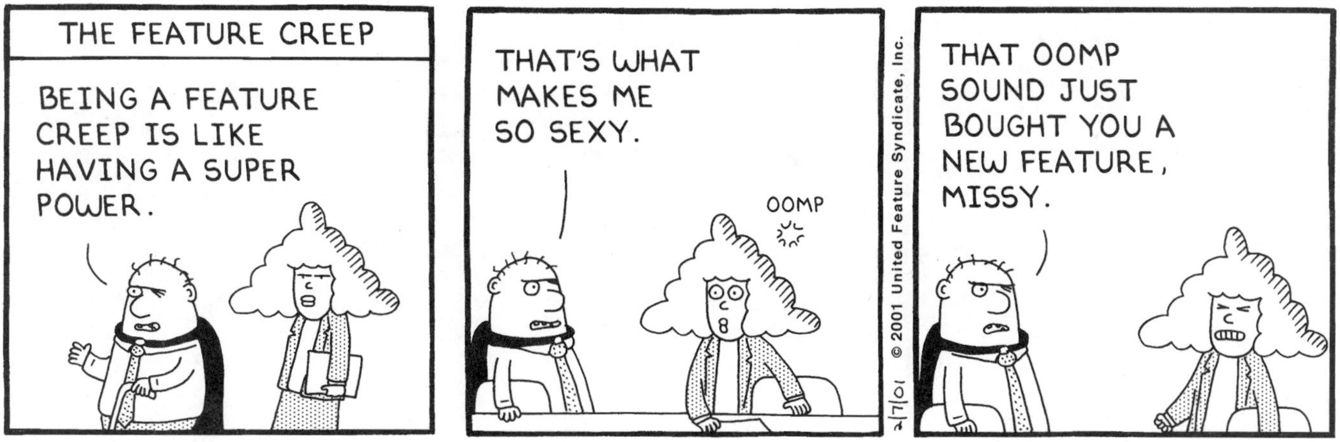
THE FEATURE CREEP
BEING A FEATURE CREEP IS LIKE HAVING A SUPER POWER.
THAT'S WHAT MAKES ME SO SEXY.
OOMP
2/7/01 © 2001 United Feature Syndicate, Inc.
THAT OOMP SOUND JUST BOUGHT YOU A NEW FEATURE, MISSY.

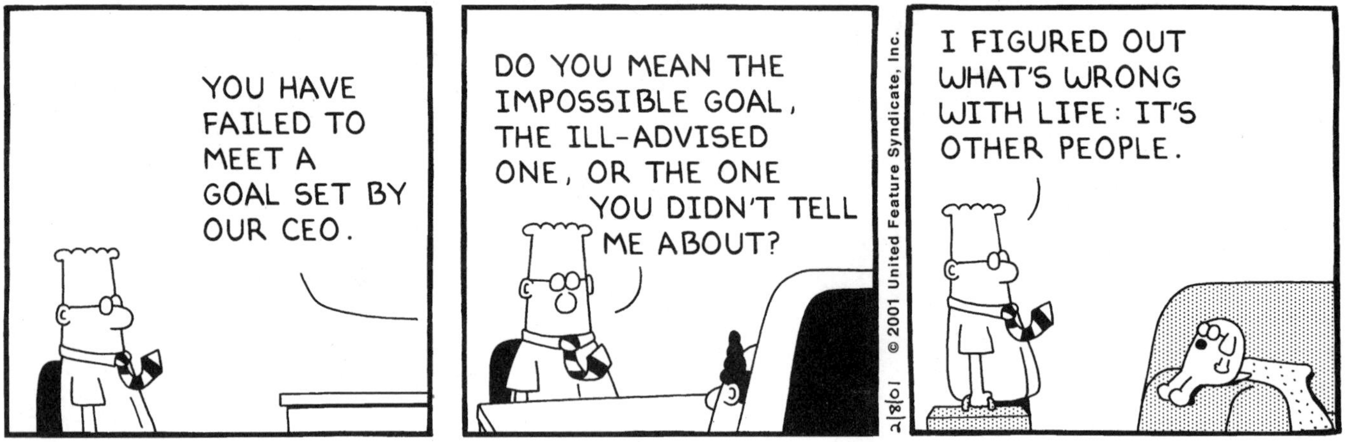
YOU HAVE FAILED TO MEET A GOAL SET BY OUR CEO.
DO YOU MEAN THE IMPOSSIBLE GOAL, THE ILL-ADVISED ONE, OR THE ONE YOU DIDN'T TELL ME ABOUT?
2/8/01 © 2001 United Feature Syndicate, Inc.
I FIGURED OUT WHAT'S WRONG WITH LIFE: IT'S OTHER PEOPLE.

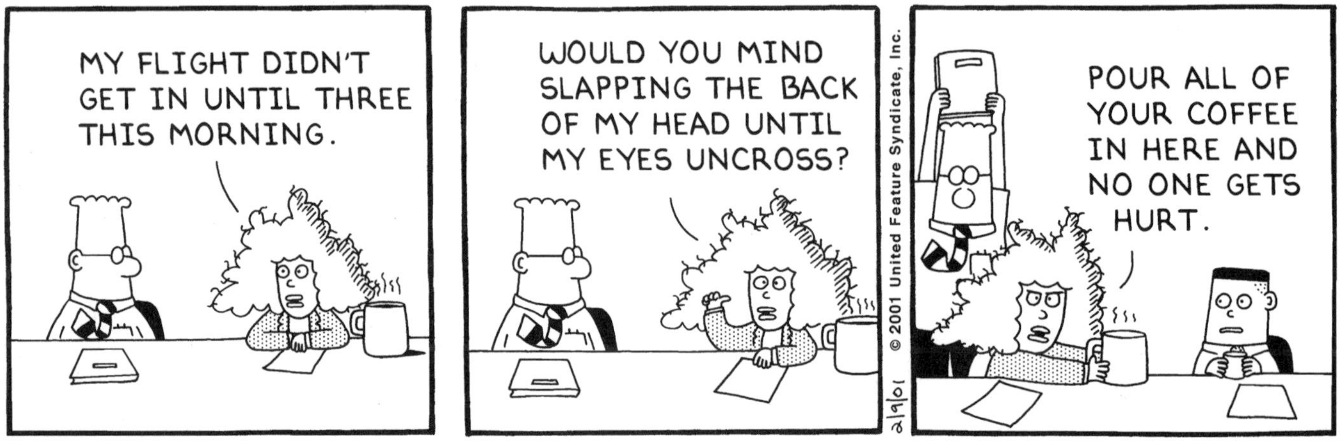
MY FLIGHT DIDN'T GET IN UNTIL THREE THIS MORNING.
WOULD YOU MIND SLAPPING THE BACK OF MY HEAD UNTIL MY EYES UNCROSS?
2/9/01 © 2001 United Feature Syndicate, Inc.
POUR ALL OF YOUR COFFEE IN HERE AND NO ONE GETS HURT.

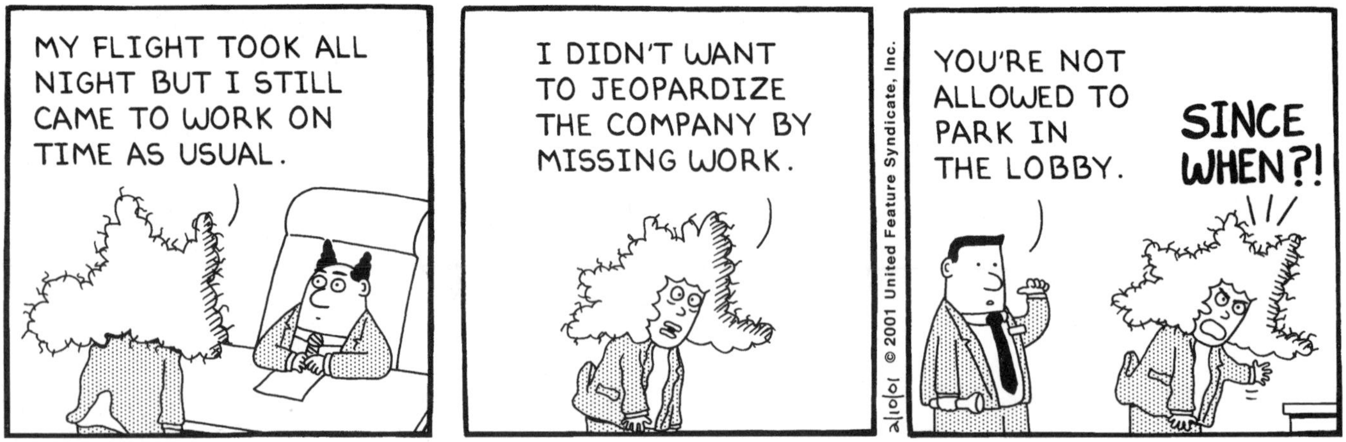
MY FLIGHT TOOK ALL NIGHT BUT I STILL CAME TO WORK ON TIME AS USUAL.
I DIDN'T WANT TO JEOPARDIZE THE COMPANY BY MISSING WORK.
2/10/01 © 2001 United Feature Syndicate, Inc.
YOU'RE NOT ALLOWED TO PARK IN THE LOBBY.
SINCE WHEN?!

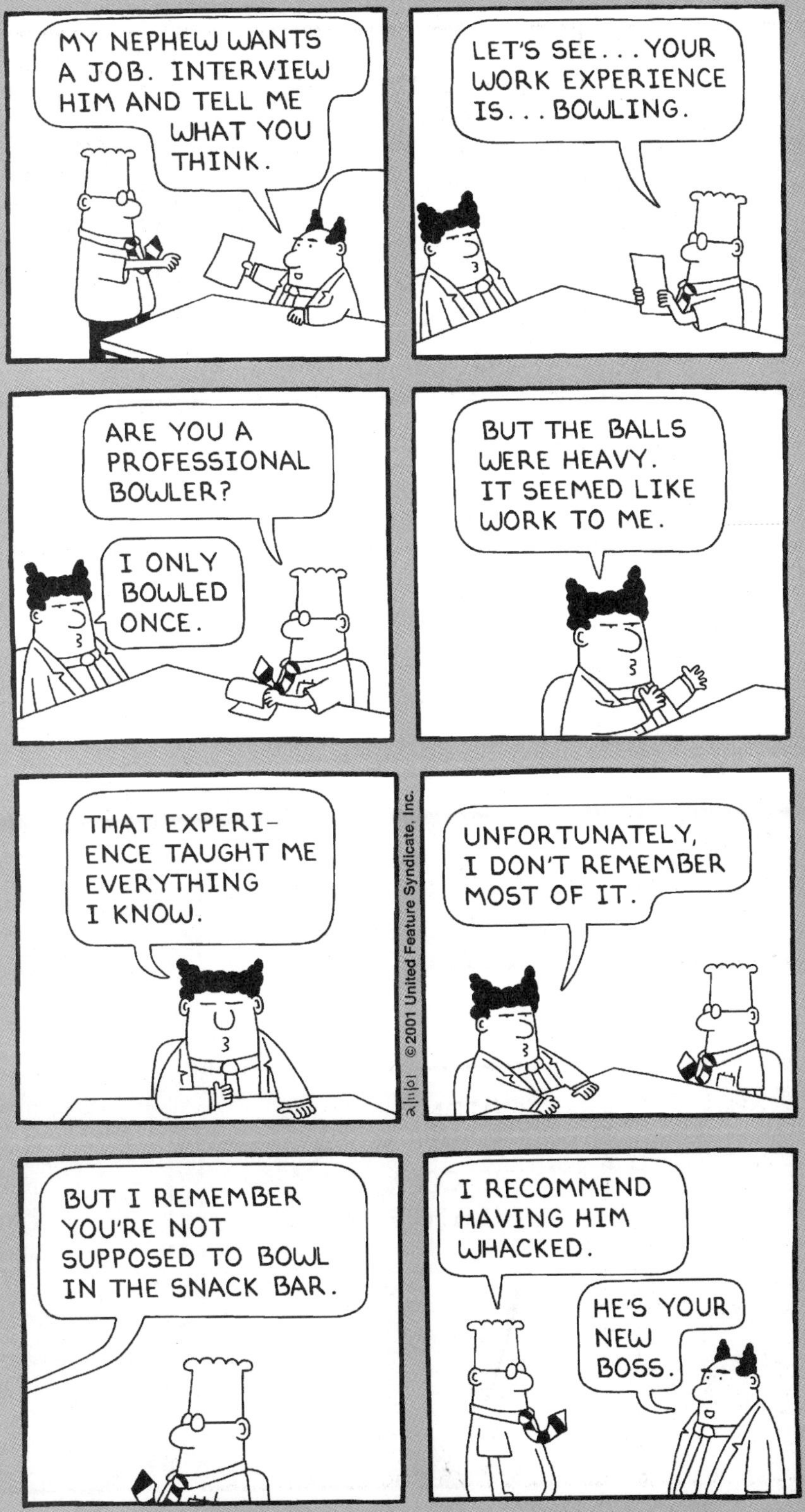
MY NEPHEW WANTS A JOB. INTERVIEW HIM AND TELL ME WHAT YOU THINK.
LET'S SEE . . . YOUR WORK EXPERIENCE IS . . . BOWLING.
ARE YOU A PROFESSIONAL BOWLER?
I ONLY BOWLED ONCE.
BUT THE BALLS WERE HEAVY. IT SEEMED LIKE WORK TO ME.
THAT EXPERIENCE TAUGHT ME EVERYTHING I KNOW.
©2001 United Feature Syndicate, Inc.
UNFORTUNATELY, I DON'T REMEMBER MOST OF IT.
BUT I REMEMBER YOU'RE NOT SUPPOSED TO BOWL IN THE SNACK BAR.
I RECOMMEND HAVING HIM WHACKED.
HE'S YOUR NEW BOSS.

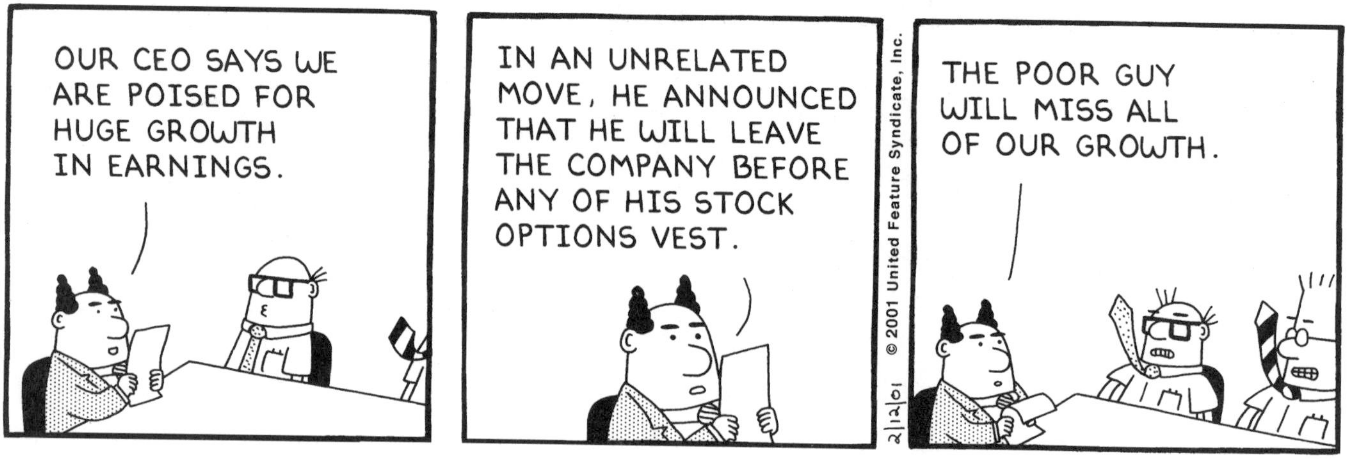
OUR CEO SAYS WE ARE POISED FOR HUGE GROWTH IN EARNINGS.
IN AN UNRELATED MOVE, HE ANNOUNCED THAT HE WILL LEAVE THE COMPANY BEFORE ANY OF HIS STOCK OPTIONS VEST.
© 2001 United Feature Syndicate, Inc.
2/12/01
THE POOR GUY WILL MISS ALL OF OUR GROWTH.

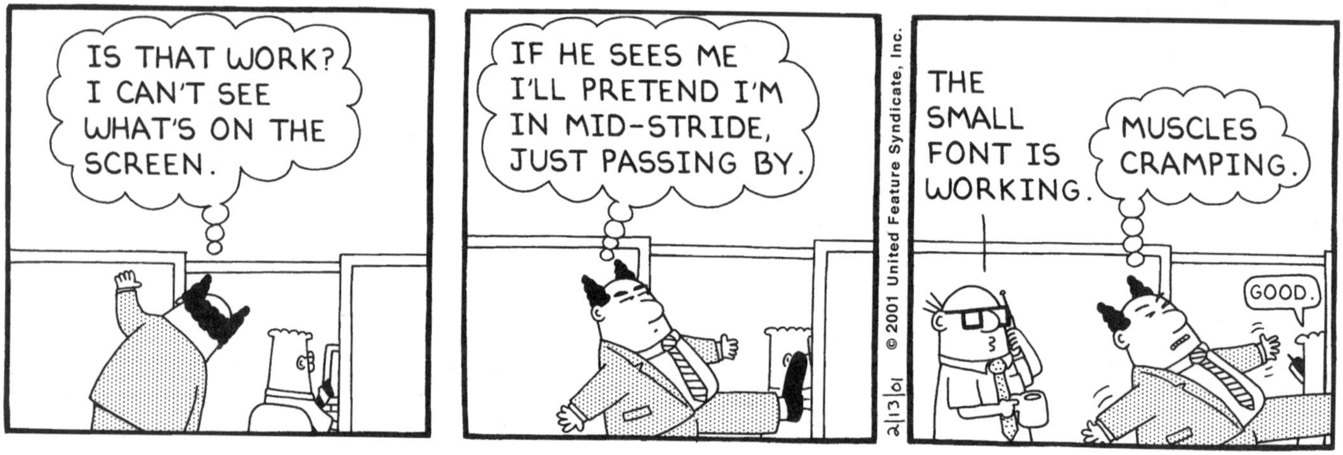
IS THAT WORK? I CAN'T SEE WHAT'S ON THE SCREEN.
IF HE SEES ME I'LL PRETEND I'M IN MID-STRIDE, JUST PASSING BY.
© 2001 United Feature Syndicate, Inc.
2/13/01
THE SMALL FONT IS WORKING.
MUSCLES CRAMPING.
GOOD.

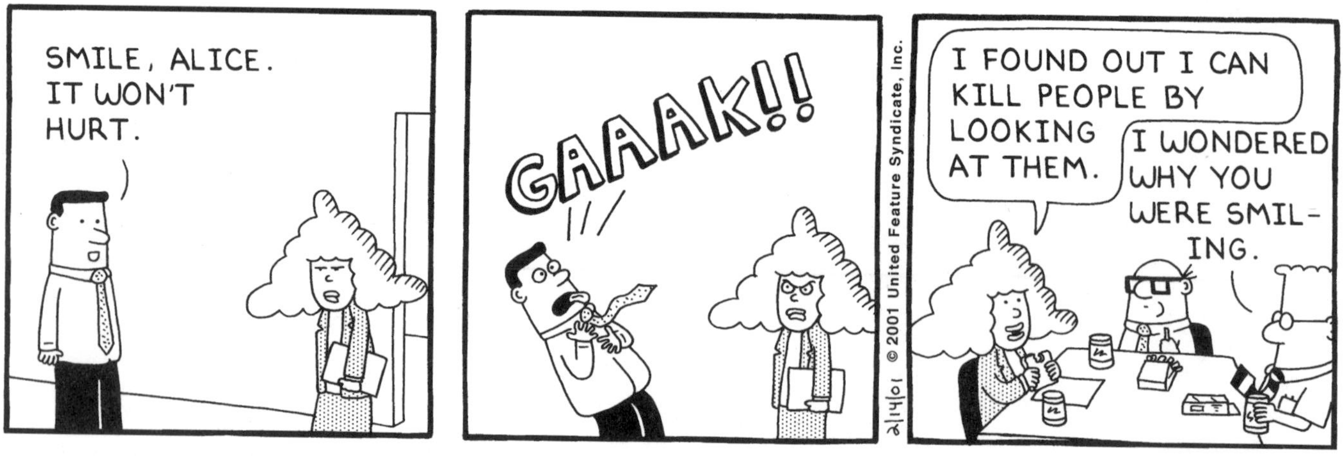
SMILE, ALICE. IT WON'T HURT.
GAAAK!!
© 2001 United Feature Syndicate, Inc.
2/14/01
I FOUND OUT I CAN KILL PEOPLE BY LOOKING AT THEM.
I WONDERED WHY YOU WERE SMIL-ING.

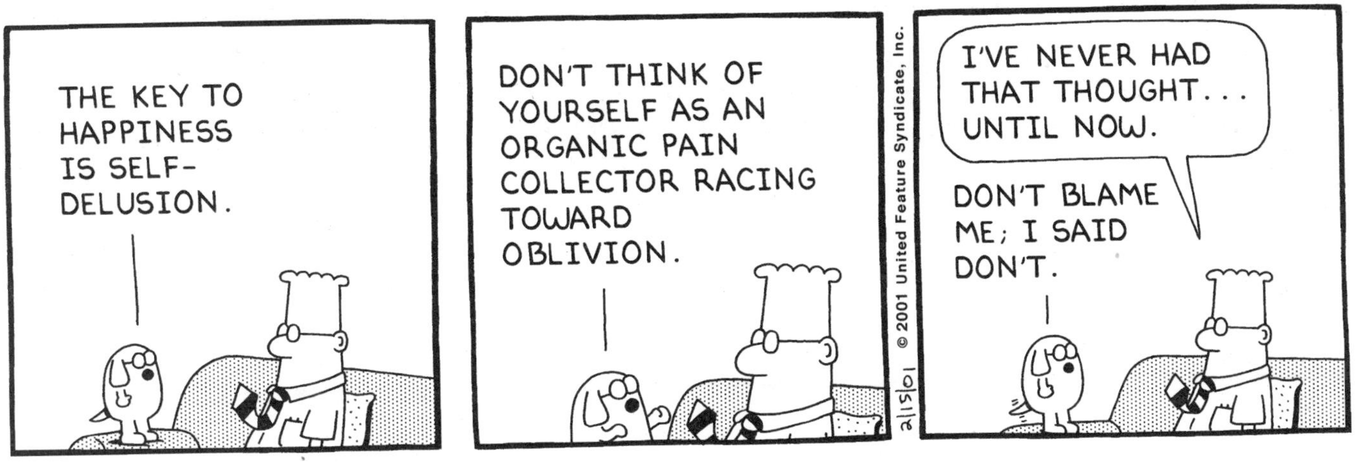
THE KEY TO HAPPINESS IS SELF-DELUSION.
DON'T THINK OF YOURSELF AS AN ORGANIC PAIN COLLECTOR RACING TOWARD OBLIVION.
2/15/01
© 2001 United Feature Syndicate, Inc.
I'VE NEVER HAD THAT THOUGHT... UNTIL NOW.
DON'T BLAME ME; I SAID DON'T.

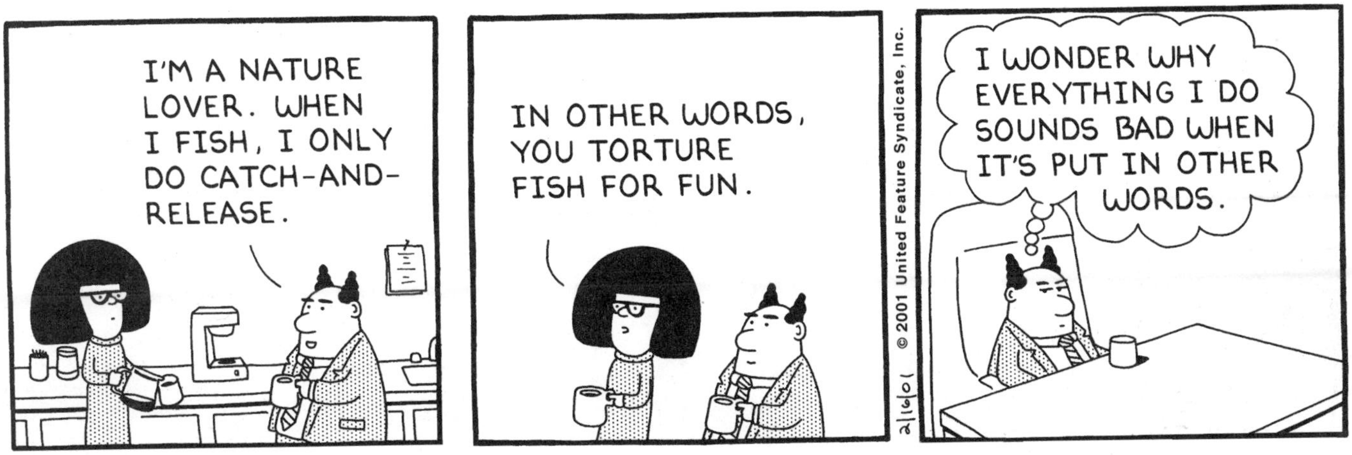
I'M A NATURE LOVER. WHEN I FISH, I ONLY DO CATCH-AND-RELEASE.
IN OTHER WORDS, YOU TORTURE FISH FOR FUN.
2/16/01
© 2001 United Feature Syndicate, Inc.
I WONDER WHY EVERYTHING I DO SOUNDS BAD WHEN IT'S PUT IN OTHER WORDS.

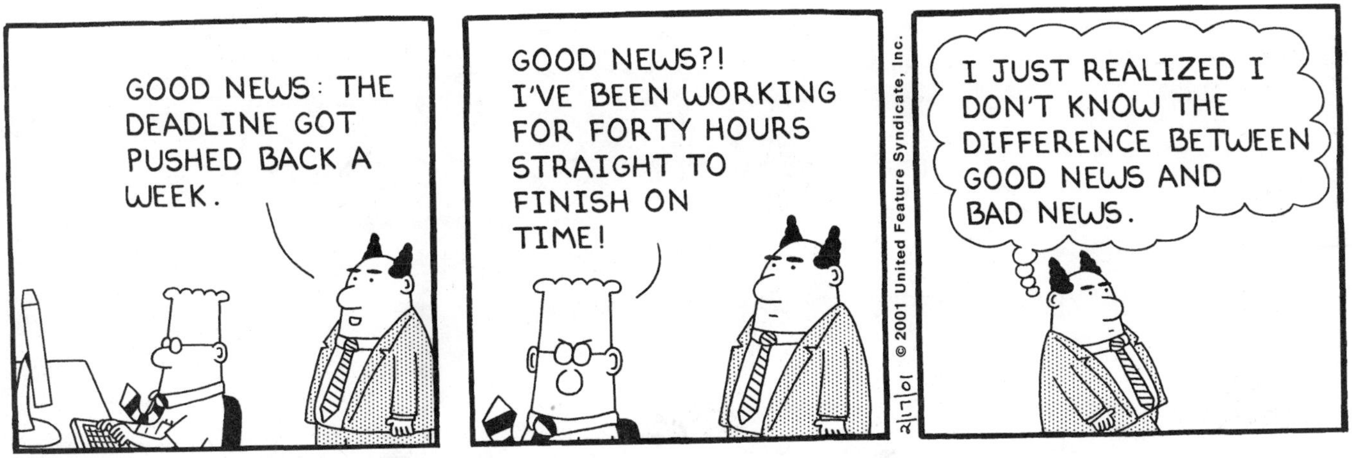
GOOD NEWS: THE DEADLINE GOT PUSHED BACK A WEEK.
GOOD NEWS?! I'VE BEEN WORKING FOR FORTY HOURS STRAIGHT TO FINISH ON TIME!
2/17/01
© 2001 United Feature Syndicate, Inc.
I JUST REALIZED I DON'T KNOW THE DIFFERENCE BETWEEN GOOD NEWS AND BAD NEWS.

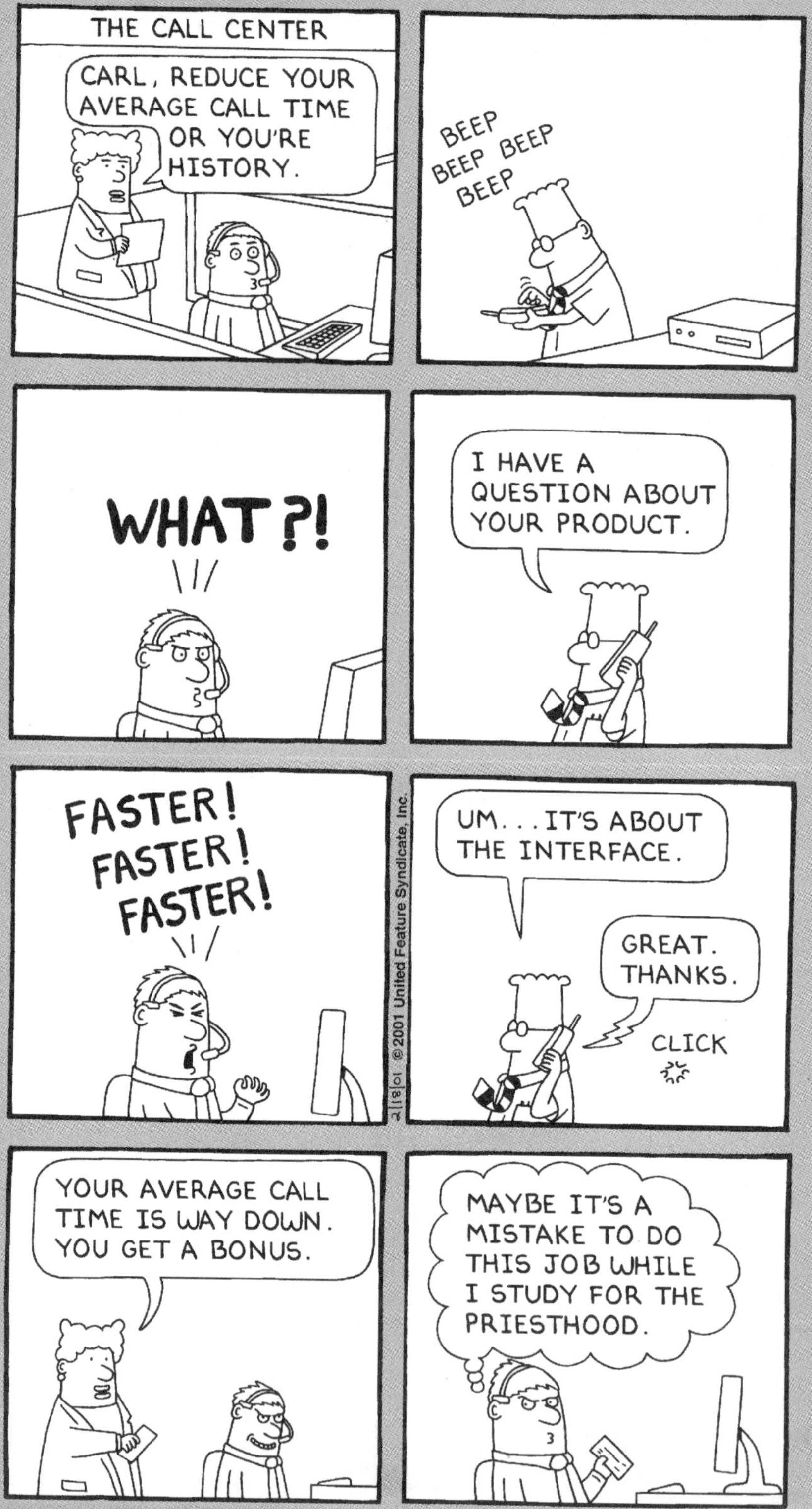
THE CALL CENTER
CARL, REDUCE YOUR AVERAGE CALL TIME OR YOU'RE HISTORY.
BEEP BEEP BEEP BEEP BEEP
WHAT?!
I HAVE A QUESTION ABOUT YOUR PRODUCT.
FASTER! FASTER! FASTER!
UM. . . IT'S ABOUT THE INTERFACE.
GREAT. THANKS.
CLICK
YOUR AVERAGE CALL TIME IS WAY DOWN. YOU GET A BONUS.
MAYBE IT'S A MISTAKE TO DO THIS JOB WHILE I STUDY FOR THE PRIESTHOOD.
2/18/01 ©2001 United Feature Syndicate, Inc.

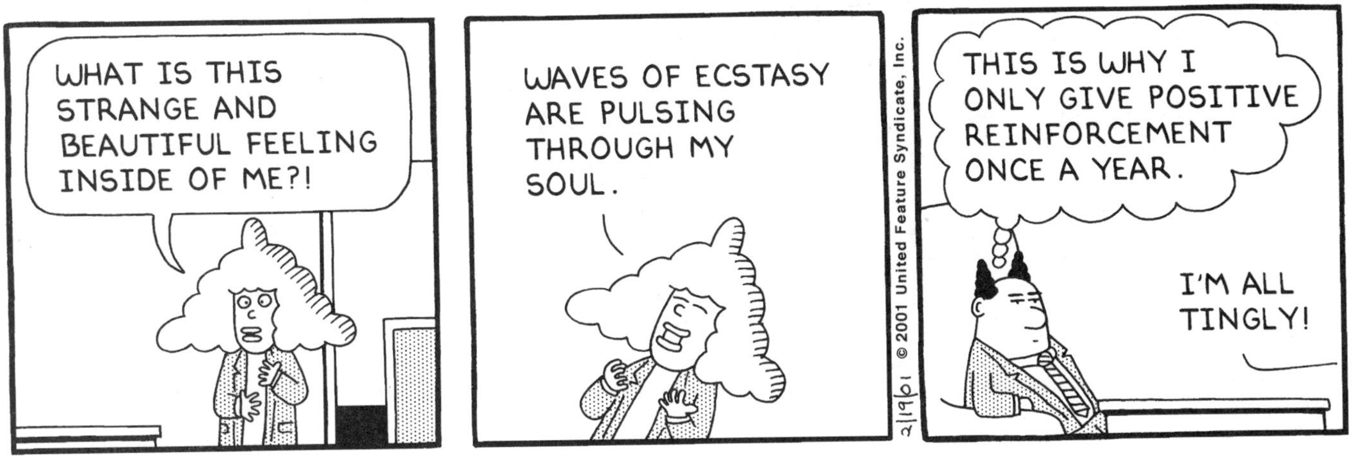
WHAT IS THIS STRANGE AND BEAUTIFUL FEELING INSIDE OF ME?!
WAVES OF ECSTASY ARE PULSING THROUGH MY SOUL.
2/19/01 © 2001 United Feature Syndicate, Inc.
THIS IS WHY I ONLY GIVE POSITIVE REINFORCEMENT ONCE A YEAR.
I'M ALL TINGLY!

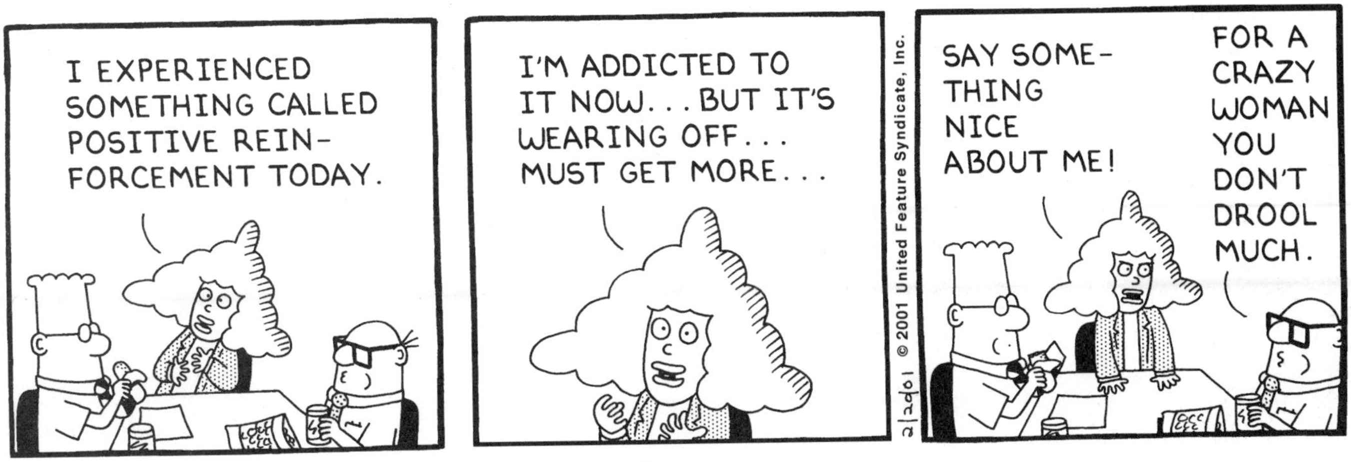
I EXPERIENCED SOMETHING CALLED POSITIVE REIN-FORCEMENT TODAY.
I'M ADDICTED TO IT NOW... BUT IT'S WEARING OFF... MUST GET MORE...
2/20/01 © 2001 United Feature Syndicate, Inc.
SAY SOME-THING NICE ABOUT ME!
FOR A CRAZY WOMAN YOU DON'T DROOL MUCH.

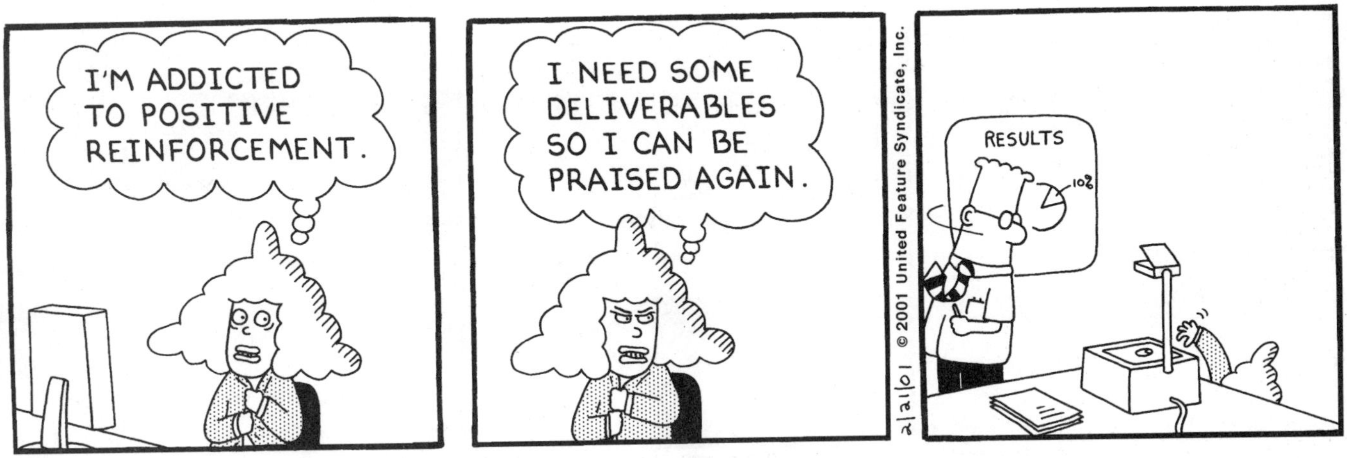
I'M ADDICTED TO POSITIVE REINFORCEMENT.
I NEED SOME DELIVERABLES SO I CAN BE PRAISED AGAIN.
2/21/01 © 2001 United Feature Syndicate, Inc.
RESULTS
10%

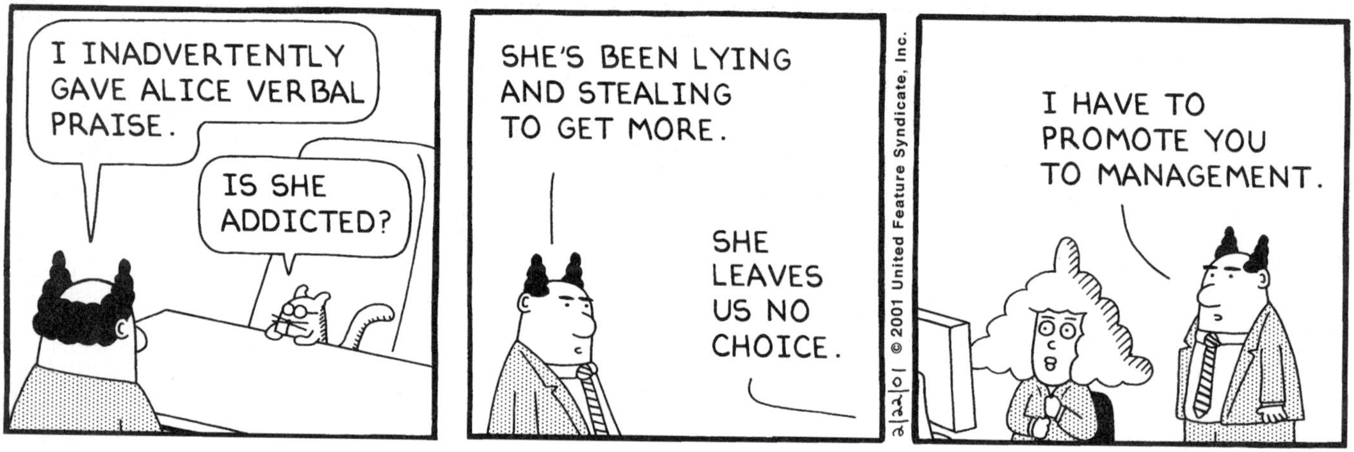
I INADVERTENTLY GAVE ALICE VERBAL PRAISE.
IS SHE ADDICTED?
SHE'S BEEN LYING AND STEALING TO GET MORE.
SHE LEAVES US NO CHOICE.
2/22/01 © 2001 United Feature Syndicate, Inc.
I HAVE TO PROMOTE YOU TO MANAGEMENT.

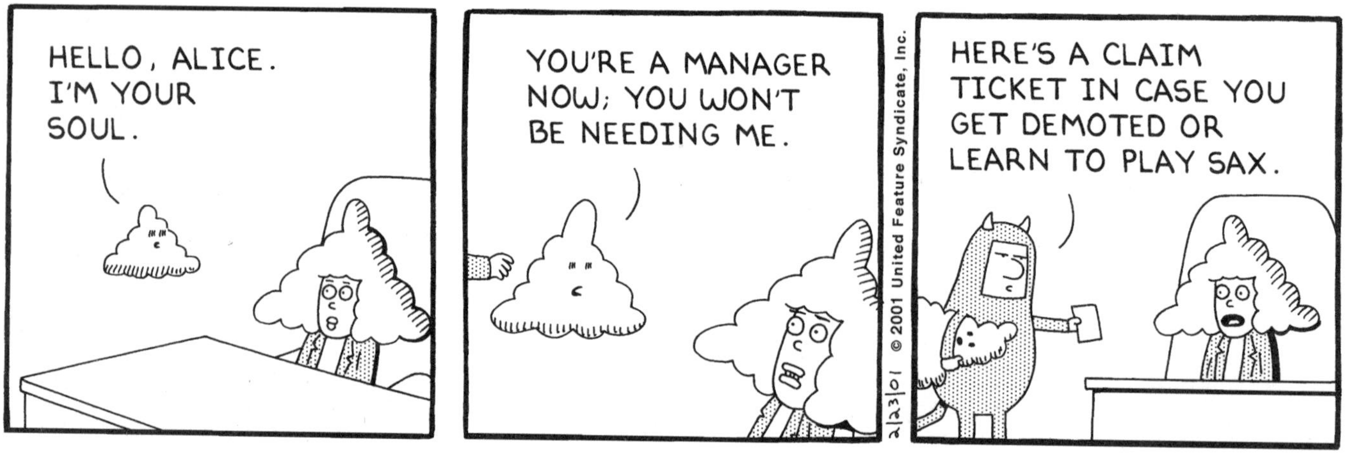
HELLO, ALICE. I'M YOUR SOUL.
YOU'RE A MANAGER NOW; YOU WON'T BE NEEDING ME.
2/23/01 © 2001 United Feature Syndicate, Inc.
HERE'S A CLAIM TICKET IN CASE YOU GET DEMOTED OR LEARN TO PLAY SAX.

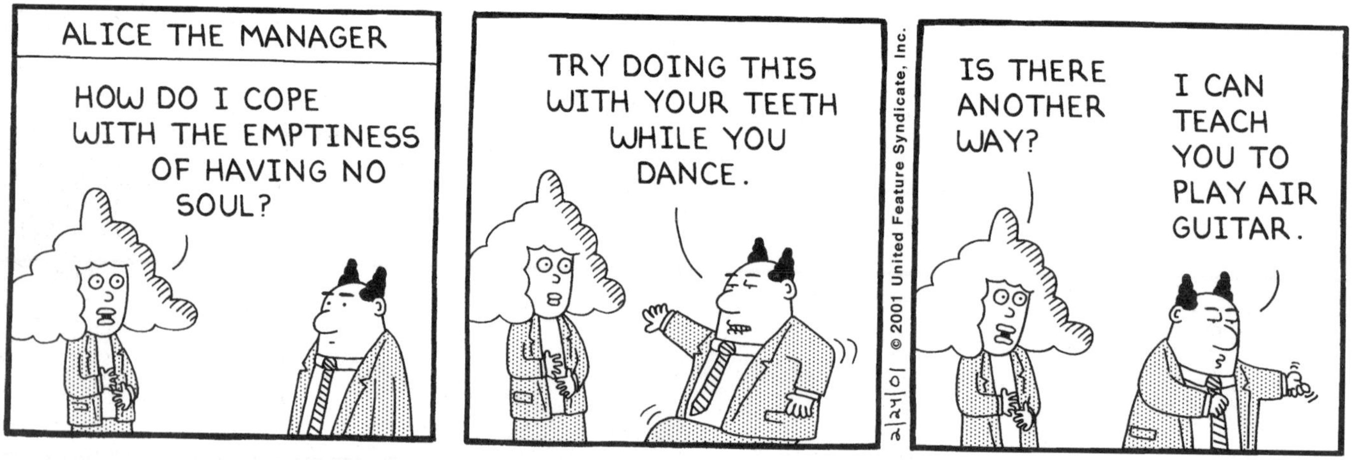
ALICE THE MANAGER
HOW DO I COPE WITH THE EMPTINESS OF HAVING NO SOUL?
TRY DOING THIS WITH YOUR TEETH WHILE YOU DANCE.
2/24/01 © 2001 United Feature Syndicate, Inc.
IS THERE ANOTHER WAY?
I CAN TEACH YOU TO PLAY AIR GUITAR.

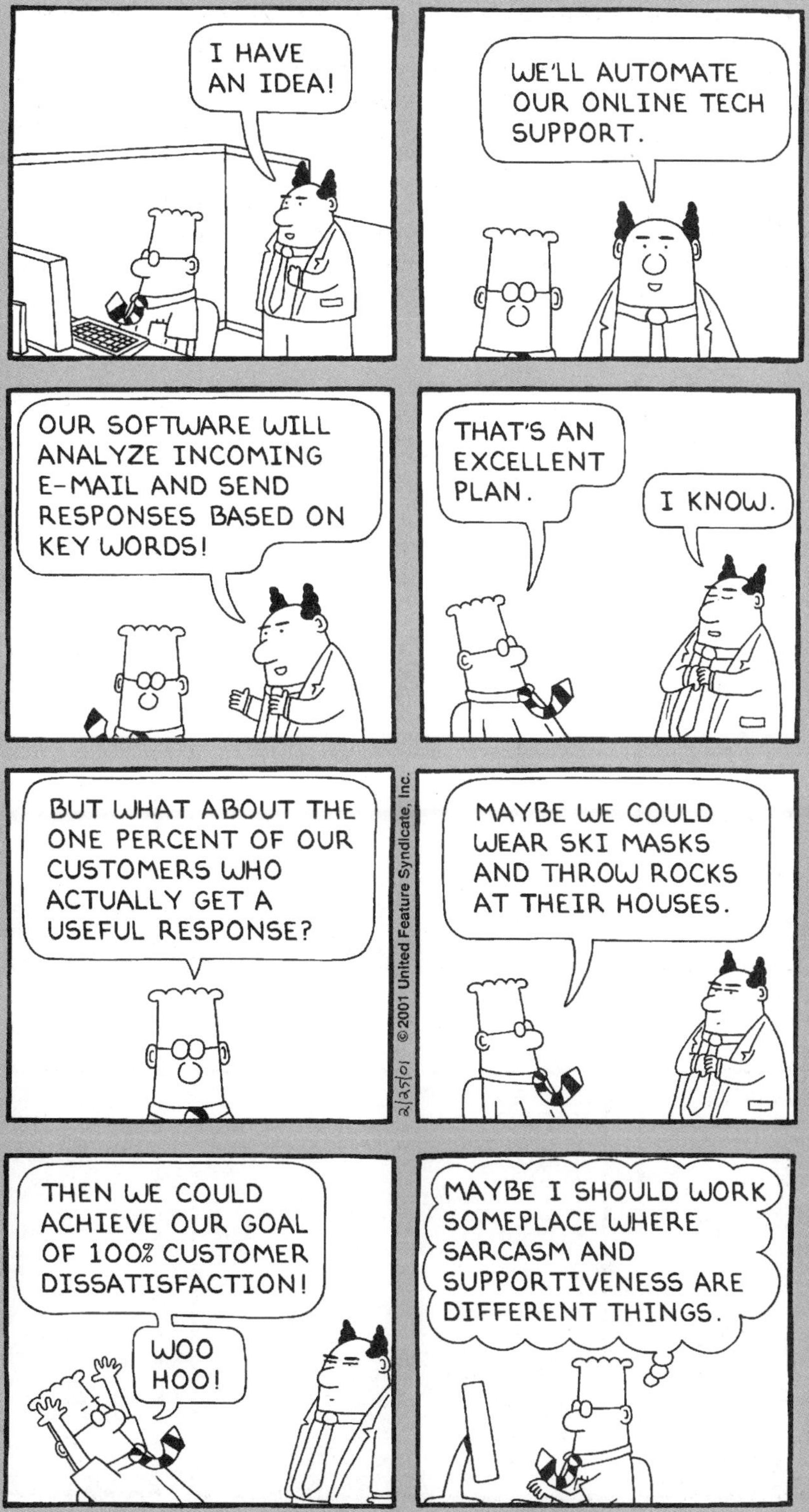
I HAVE AN IDEA!
WE'LL AUTOMATE OUR ONLINE TECH SUPPORT.
OUR SOFTWARE WILL ANALYZE INCOMING E-MAIL AND SEND RESPONSES BASED ON KEY WORDS!
THAT'S AN EXCELLENT PLAN.
I KNOW.
BUT WHAT ABOUT THE ONE PERCENT OF OUR CUSTOMERS WHO ACTUALLY GET A USEFUL RESPONSE?
MAYBE WE COULD WEAR SKI MASKS AND THROW ROCKS AT THEIR HOUSES.
THEN WE COULD ACHIEVE OUR GOAL OF 100% CUSTOMER DISSATISFACTION!
WOO HOO!
MAYBE I SHOULD WORK SOMEPLACE WHERE SARCASM AND SUPPORTIVENESS ARE DIFFERENT THINGS.
2/25/01 ©2001 United Feature Syndicate, Inc.

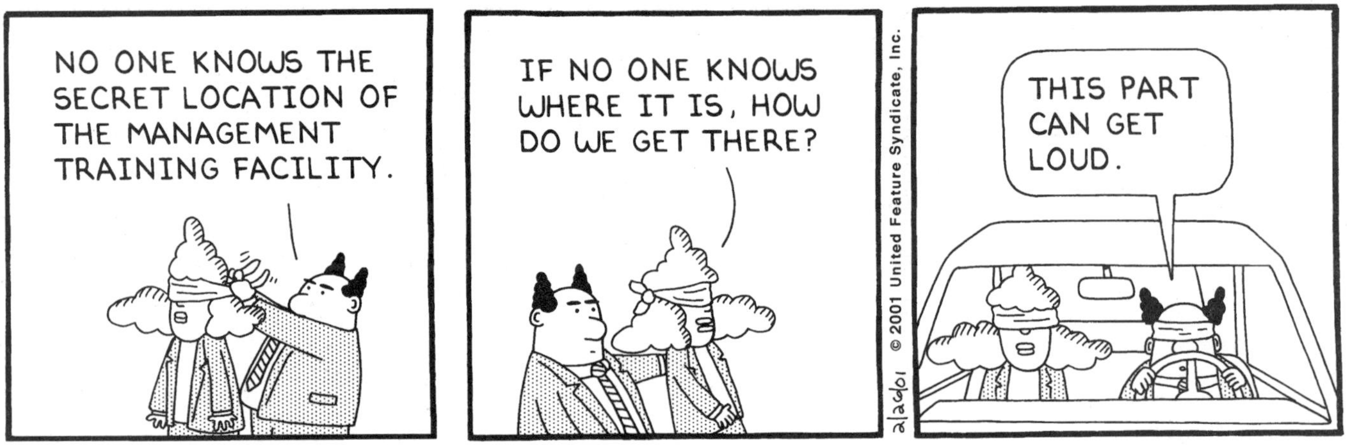
NO ONE KNOWS THE SECRET LOCATION OF THE MANAGEMENT TRAINING FACILITY.
IF NO ONE KNOWS WHERE IT IS, HOW DO WE GET THERE?
2/26/01 © 2001 United Feature Syndicate, Inc.
THIS PART CAN GET LOUD.

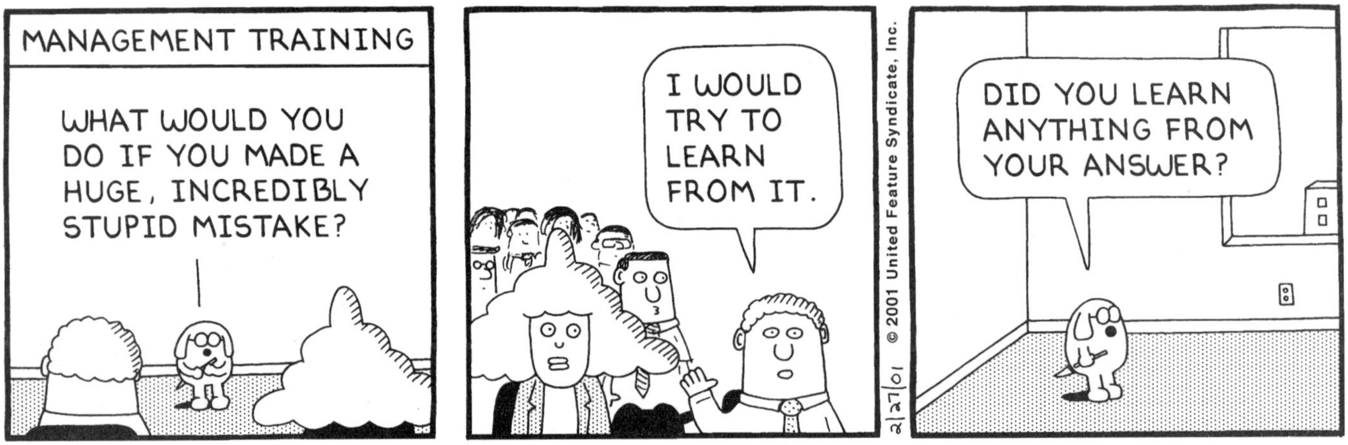
MANAGEMENT TRAINING
WHAT WOULD YOU DO IF YOU MADE A HUGE, INCREDIBLY STUPID MISTAKE?
I WOULD TRY TO LEARN FROM IT.
2/27/01 © 2001 United Feature Syndicate, Inc.
DID YOU LEARN ANYTHING FROM YOUR ANSWER?

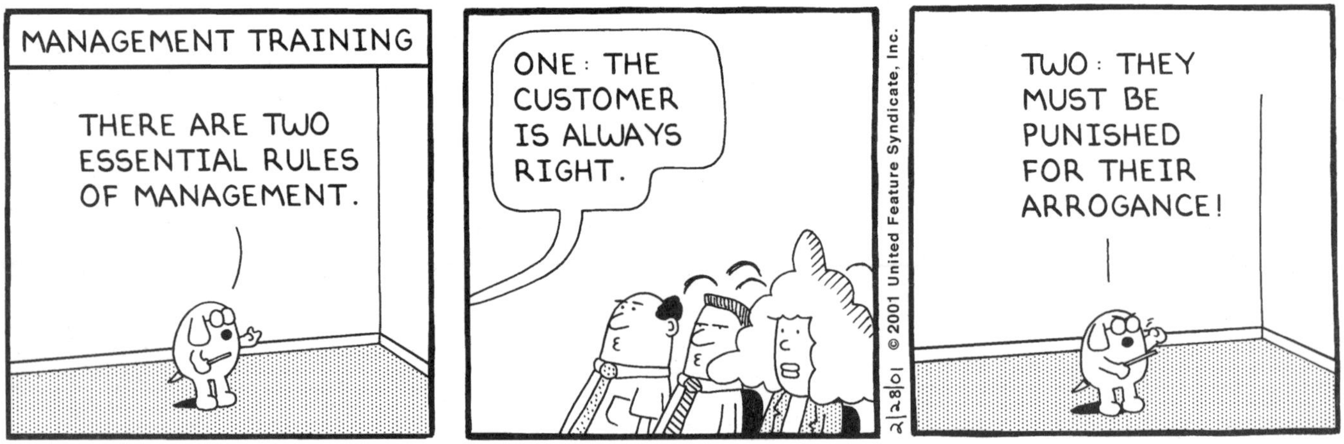
MANAGEMENT TRAINING
THERE ARE TWO ESSENTIAL RULES OF MANAGEMENT.
ONE: THE CUSTOMER IS ALWAYS RIGHT.
2/28/01 © 2001 United Feature Syndicate, Inc.
TWO: THEY MUST BE PUNISHED FOR THEIR ARROGANCE!

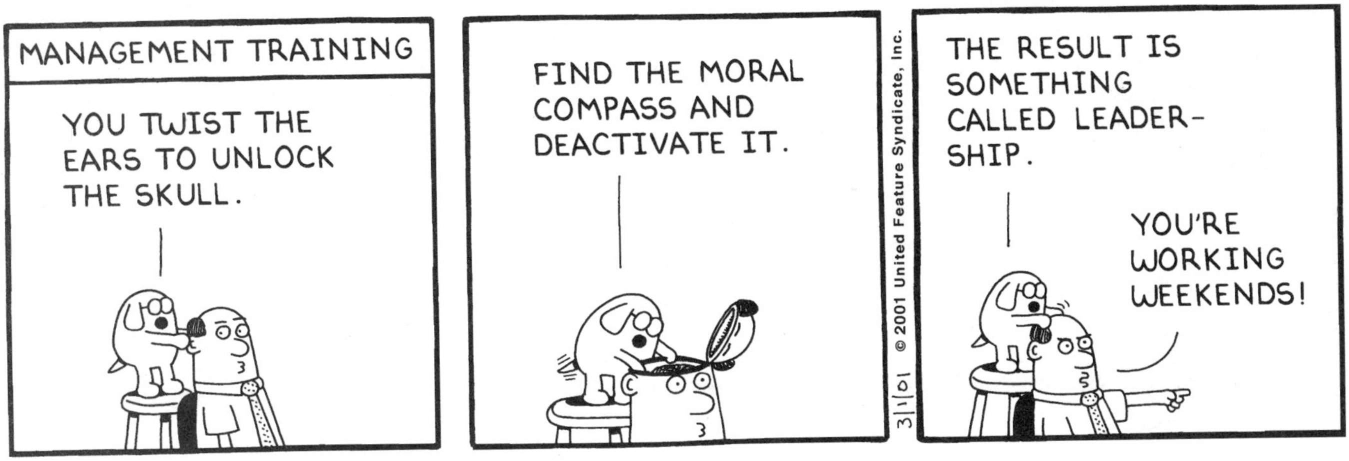
MANAGEMENT TRAINING
YOU TWIST THE EARS TO UNLOCK THE SKULL.
FIND THE MORAL COMPASS AND DEACTIVATE IT.
3/1/01 © 2001 United Feature Syndicate, Inc.
THE RESULT IS SOMETHING CALLED LEADER-SHIP.
YOU'RE WORKING WEEKENDS!

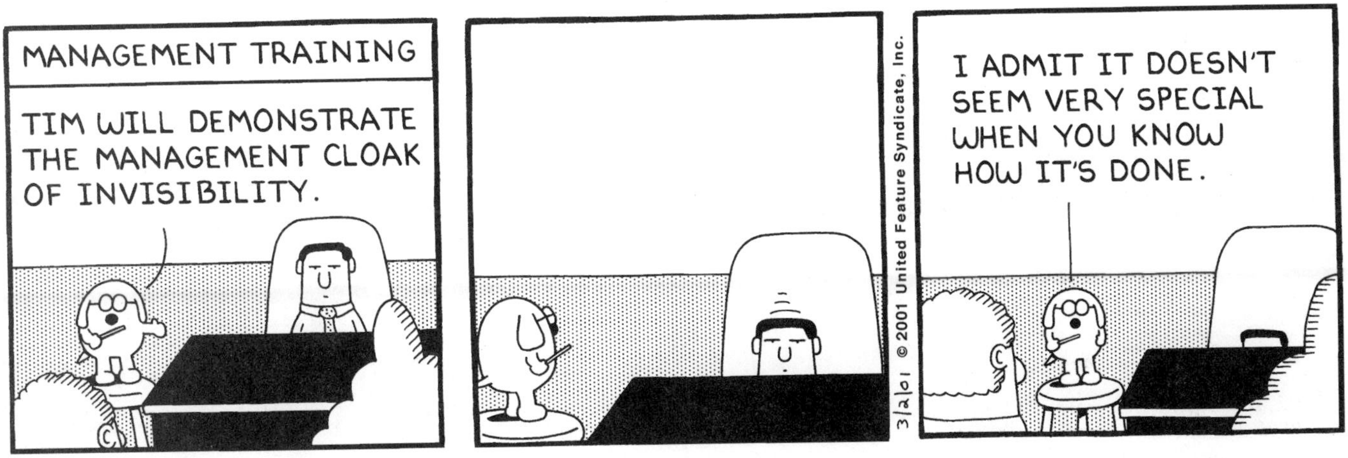
MANAGEMENT TRAINING
TIM WILL DEMONSTRATE THE MANAGEMENT CLOAK OF INVISIBILITY.
3/2/01 © 2001 United Feature Syndicate, Inc.
I ADMIT IT DOESN'T SEEM VERY SPECIAL WHEN YOU KNOW HOW IT'S DONE.

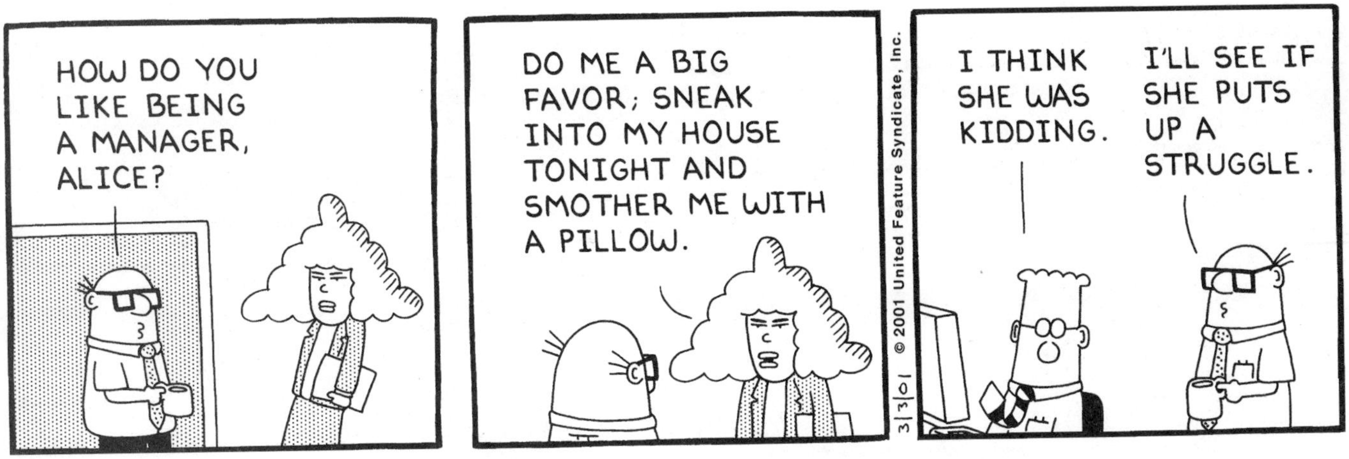
HOW DO YOU LIKE BEING A MANAGER, ALICE?
DO ME A BIG FAVOR; SNEAK INTO MY HOUSE TONIGHT AND SMOTHER ME WITH A PILLOW.
3/3/01 © 2001 United Feature Syndicate, Inc.
I THINK SHE WAS KIDDING.
I'LL SEE IF SHE PUTS UP A STRUGGLE.

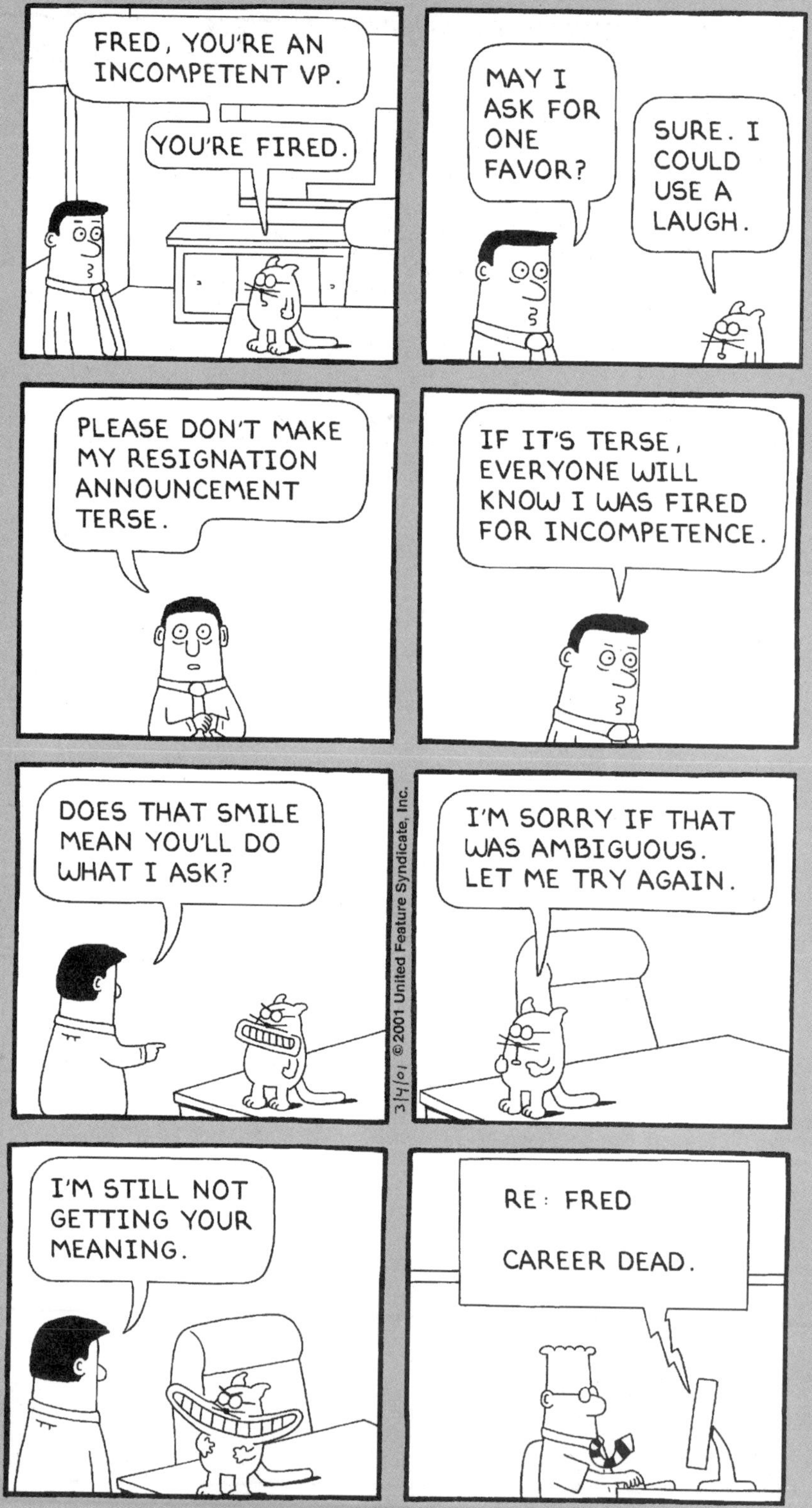
FRED, YOU'RE AN INCOMPETENT VP.
YOU'RE FIRED.
MAY I ASK FOR ONE FAVOR?
SURE. I COULD USE A LAUGH.
PLEASE DON'T MAKE MY RESIGNATION ANNOUNCEMENT TERSE.
IF IT'S TERSE, EVERYONE WILL KNOW I WAS FIRED FOR INCOMPETENCE.
DOES THAT SMILE MEAN YOU'LL DO WHAT I ASK?
I'M SORRY IF THAT WAS AMBIGUOUS. LET ME TRY AGAIN.
I'M STILL NOT GETTING YOUR MEANING.
RE: FRED
CAREER DEAD.
3/4/01 ©2001 United Feature Syndicate, Inc.

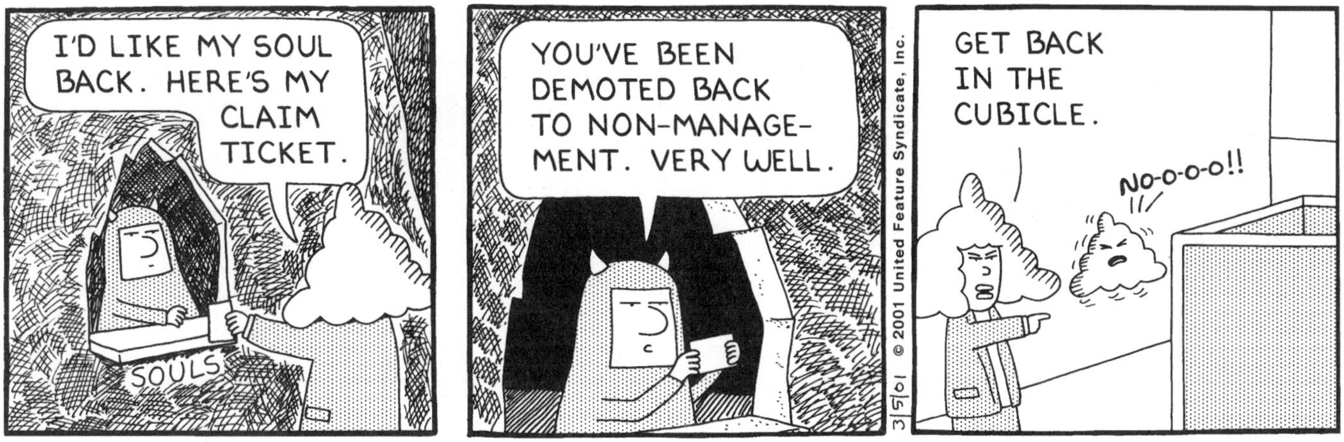
I'D LIKE MY SOUL BACK. HERE'S MY CLAIM TICKET.
SOULS
YOU'VE BEEN DEMOTED BACK TO NON-MANAGEMENT. VERY WELL.
3/5/01 © 2001 United Feature Syndicate, Inc.
GET BACK IN THE CUBICLE.
NO-O-O-O!!

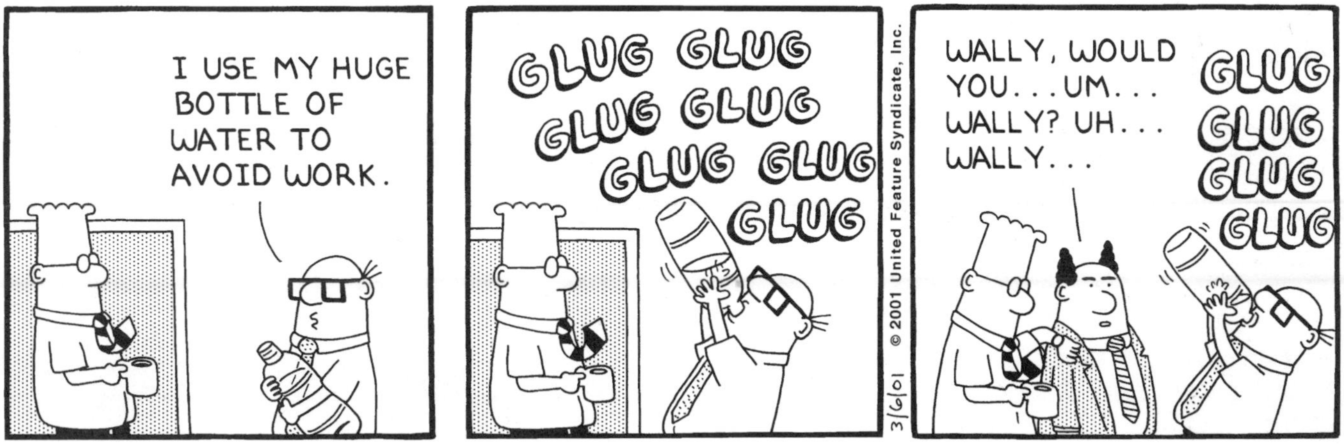
I USE MY HUGE BOTTLE OF WATER TO AVOID WORK.
GLUG GLUG GLUG GLUG GLUG GLUG GLUG
3/6/01 © 2001 United Feature Syndicate, Inc.
WALLY, WOULD YOU...UM... WALLY? UH... WALLY...
GLUG GLUG GLUG GLUG

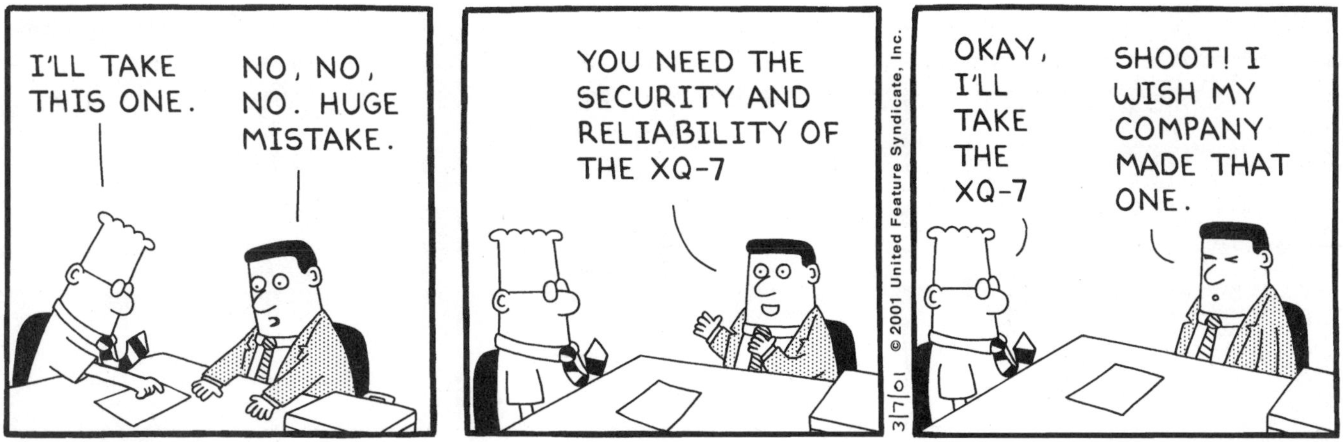
I'LL TAKE THIS ONE.
NO, NO, NO. HUGE MISTAKE.
YOU NEED THE SECURITY AND RELIABILITY OF THE XQ-7
3/7/01 © 2001 United Feature Syndicate, Inc.
OKAY, I'LL TAKE THE XQ-7
SHOOT! I WISH MY COMPANY MADE THAT ONE.

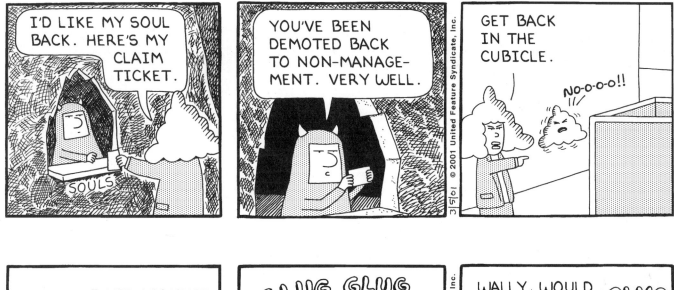

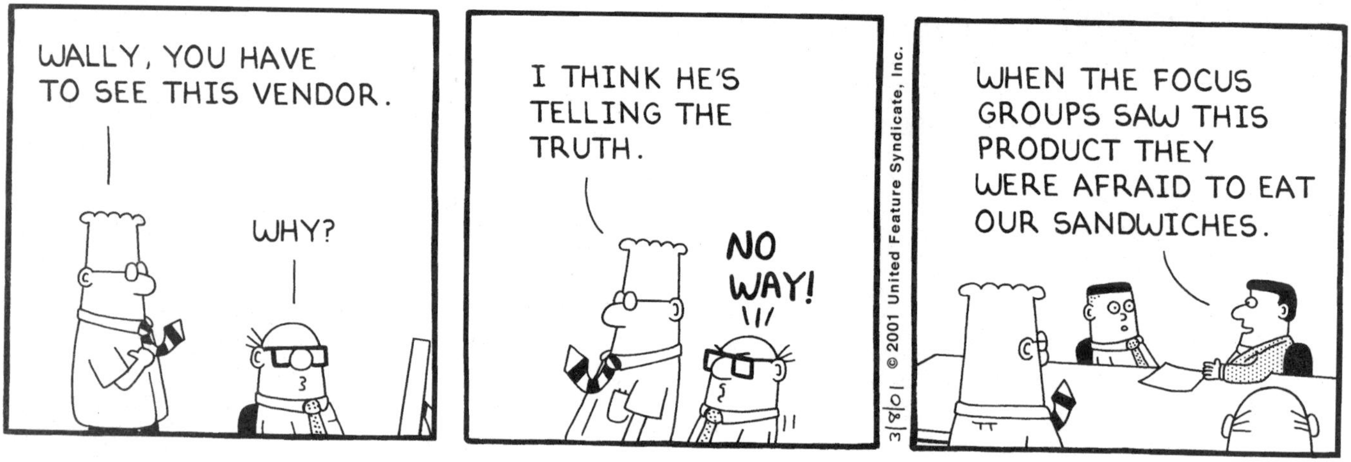
WALLY, YOU HAVE TO SEE THIS VENDOR.
WHY?
I THINK HE'S TELLING THE TRUTH.
NO WAY!
WHEN THE FOCUS GROUPS SAW THIS PRODUCT THEY WERE AFRAID TO EAT OUR SANDWICHES.
3/8/01 © 2001 United Feature Syndicate, Inc.

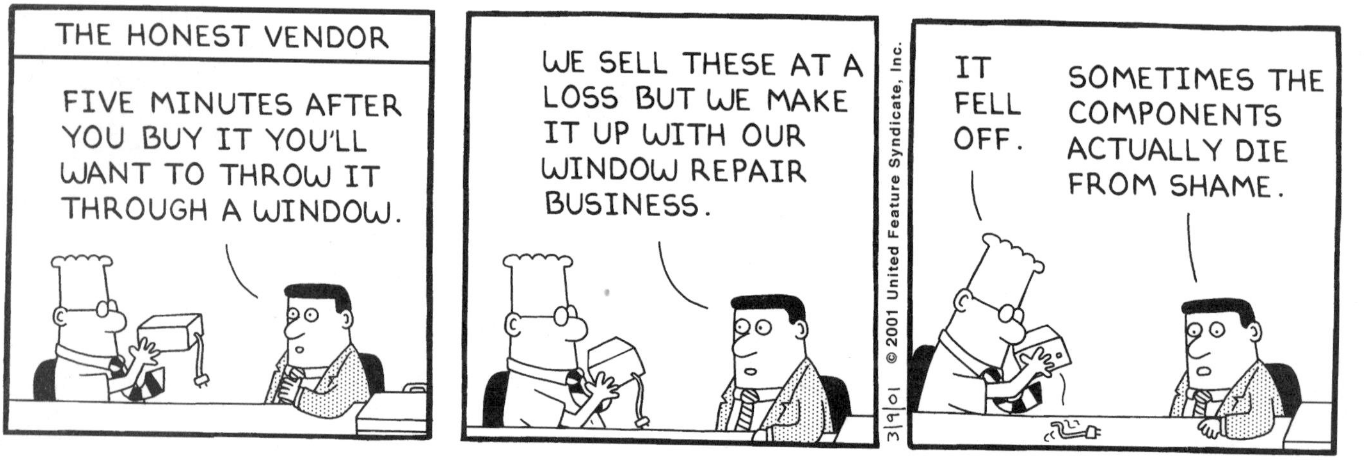
THE HONEST VENDOR
FIVE MINUTES AFTER YOU BUY IT YOU'LL WANT TO THROW IT THROUGH A WINDOW.
WE SELL THESE AT A LOSS BUT WE MAKE IT UP WITH OUR WINDOW REPAIR BUSINESS.
IT FELL OFF.
SOMETIMES THE COMPONENTS ACTUALLY DIE FROM SHAME.
3/9/01 © 2001 United Feature Syndicate, Inc.

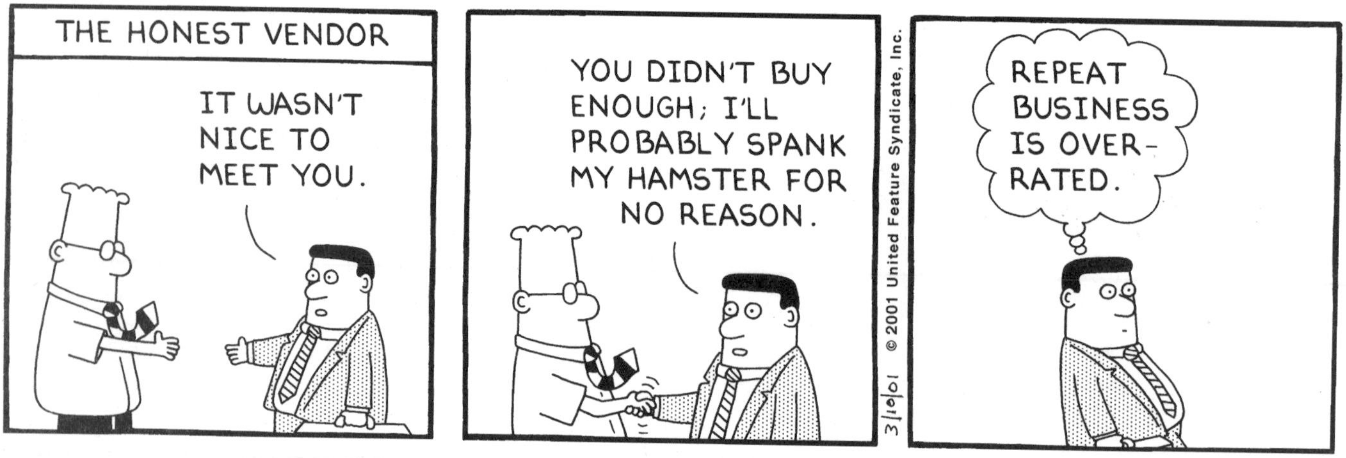
THE HONEST VENDOR
IT WASN'T NICE TO MEET YOU.
YOU DIDN'T BUY ENOUGH; I'LL PROBABLY SPANK MY HAMSTER FOR NO REASON.
REPEAT BUSINESS IS OVER-RATED.
3/10/01 © 2001 United Feature Syndicate, Inc.

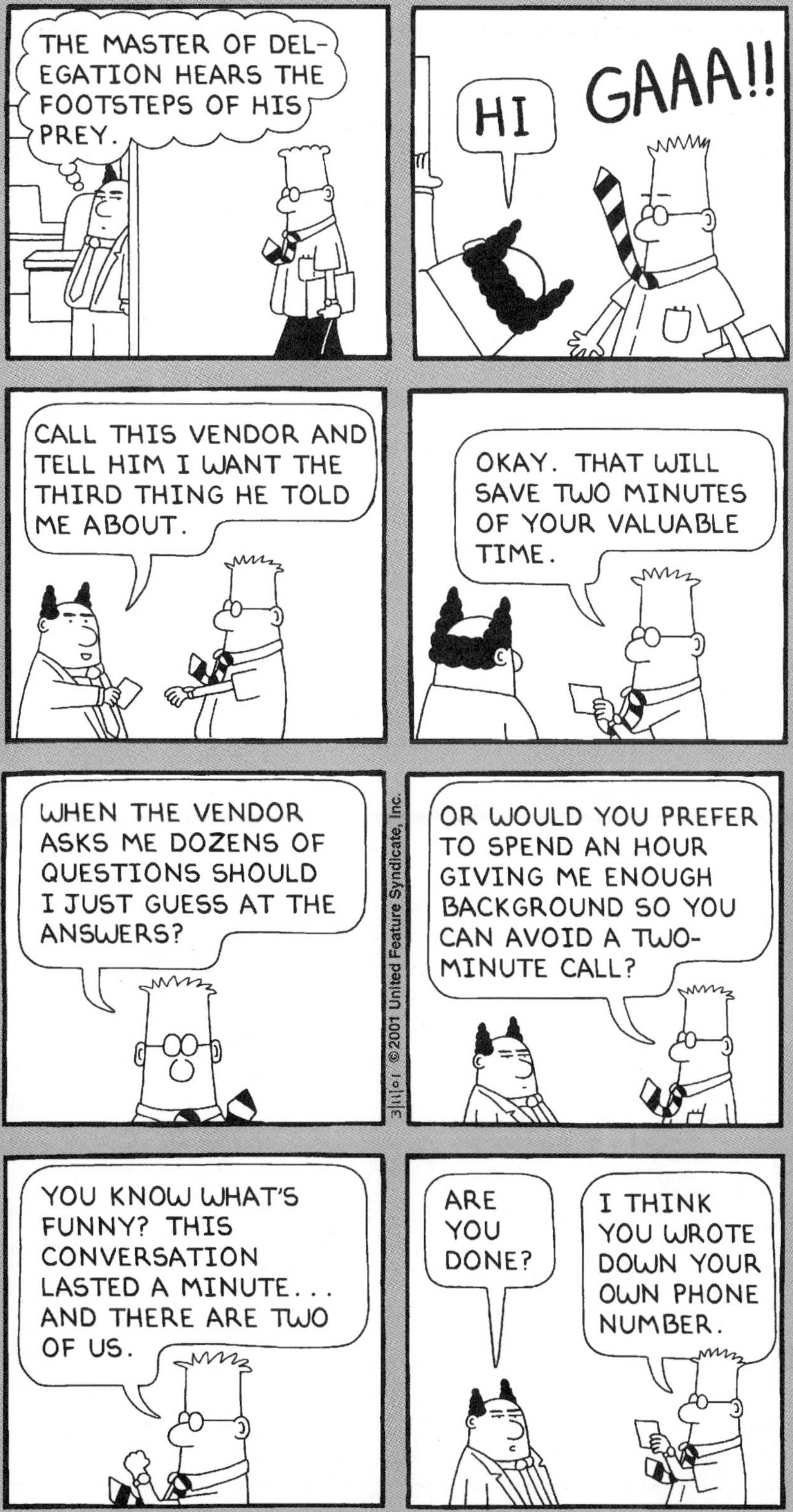
THE MASTER OF DELEGATION HEARS THE FOOTSTEPS OF HIS PREY.
HI
GAAA!!
CALL THIS VENDOR AND TELL HIM I WANT THE THIRD THING HE TOLD ME ABOUT.
OKAY. THAT WILL SAVE TWO MINUTES OF YOUR VALUABLE TIME.
WHEN THE VENDOR ASKS ME DOZENS OF QUESTIONS SHOULD I JUST GUESS AT THE ANSWERS?
OR WOULD YOU PREFER TO SPEND AN HOUR GIVING ME ENOUGH BACKGROUND SO YOU CAN AVOID A TWO-MINUTE CALL?
3/11/01 © 2001 United Feature Syndicate, Inc.
YOU KNOW WHAT'S FUNNY? THIS CONVERSATION LASTED A MINUTE... AND THERE ARE TWO OF US.
ARE YOU DONE?
I THINK YOU WROTE DOWN YOUR OWN PHONE NUMBER.

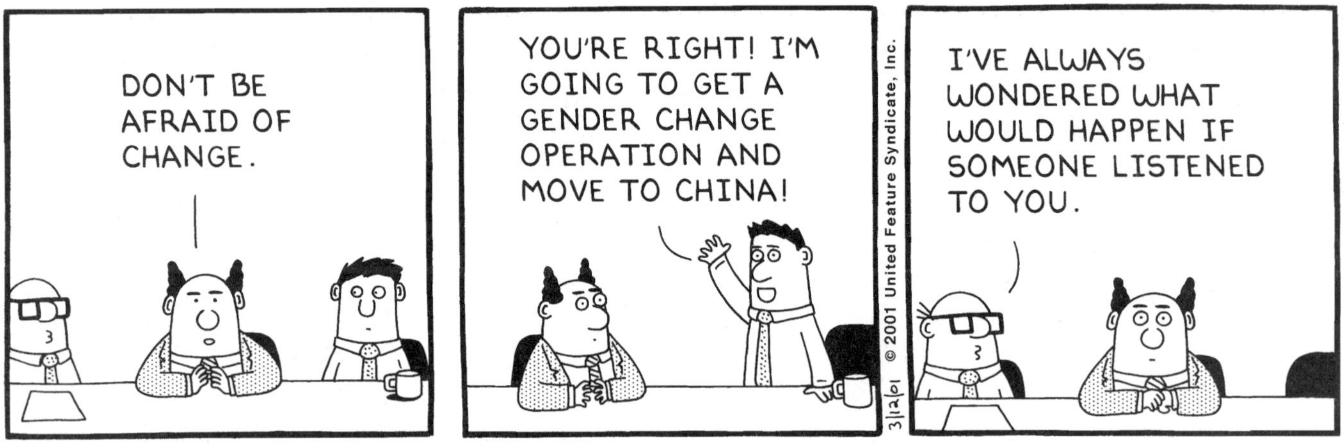
DON'T BE AFRAID OF CHANGE.
YOU'RE RIGHT! I'M GOING TO GET A GENDER CHANGE OPERATION AND MOVE TO CHINA!
3/12/01 © 2001 United Feature Syndicate, Inc.
I'VE ALWAYS WONDERED WHAT WOULD HAPPEN IF SOMEONE LISTENED TO YOU.

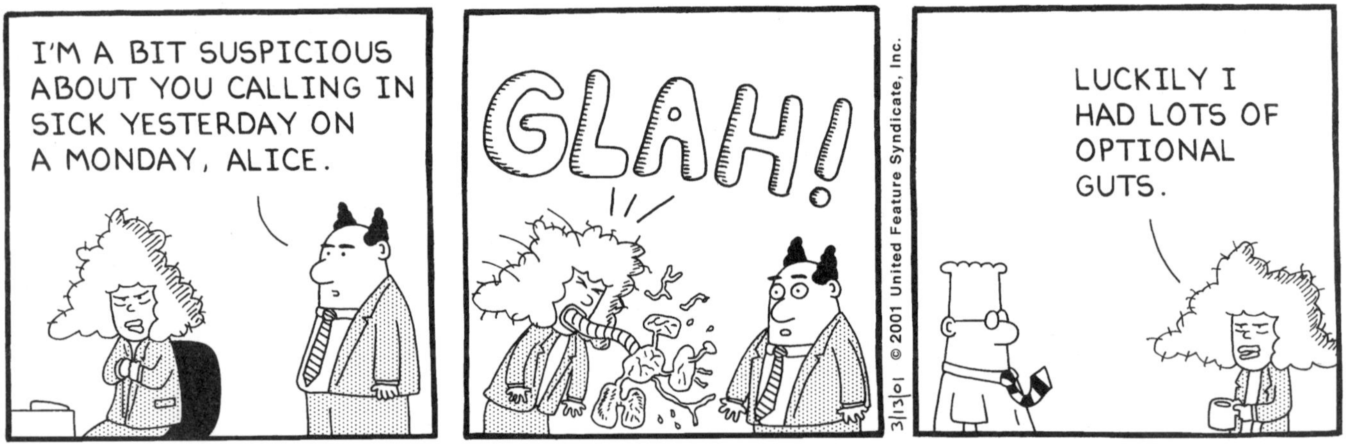
I'M A BIT SUSPICIOUS ABOUT YOU CALLING IN SICK YESTERDAY ON A MONDAY, ALICE.
GLAH!
3/13/01 © 2001 United Feature Syndicate, Inc.
LUCKILY I HAD LOTS OF OPTIONAL GUTS.

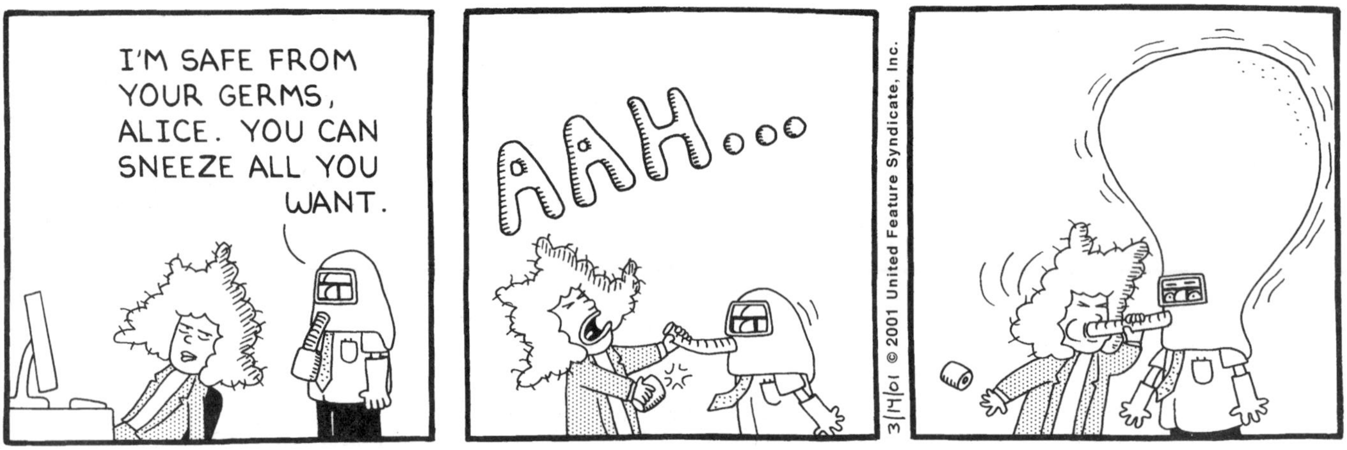
I'M SAFE FROM YOUR GERMS, ALICE. YOU CAN SNEEZE ALL YOU WANT.
AAH...
3/14/01 © 2001 United Feature Syndicate, Inc.

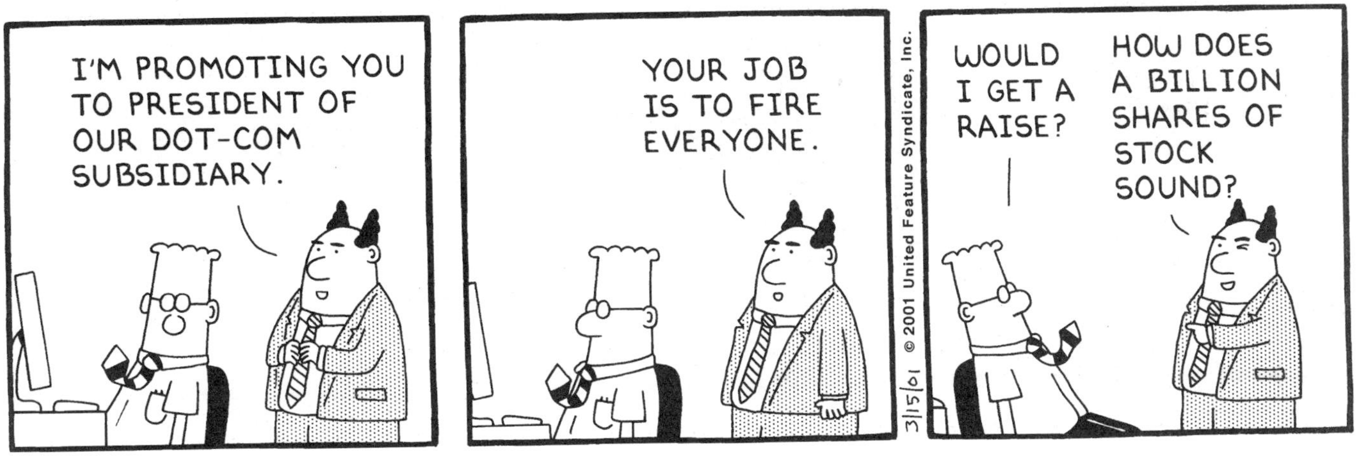
I'M PROMOTING YOU TO PRESIDENT OF OUR DOT-COM SUBSIDIARY.
YOUR JOB IS TO FIRE EVERYONE.
3/15/01 © 2001 United Feature Syndicate, Inc.
WOULD I GET A RAISE?
HOW DOES A BILLION SHARES OF STOCK SOUND?

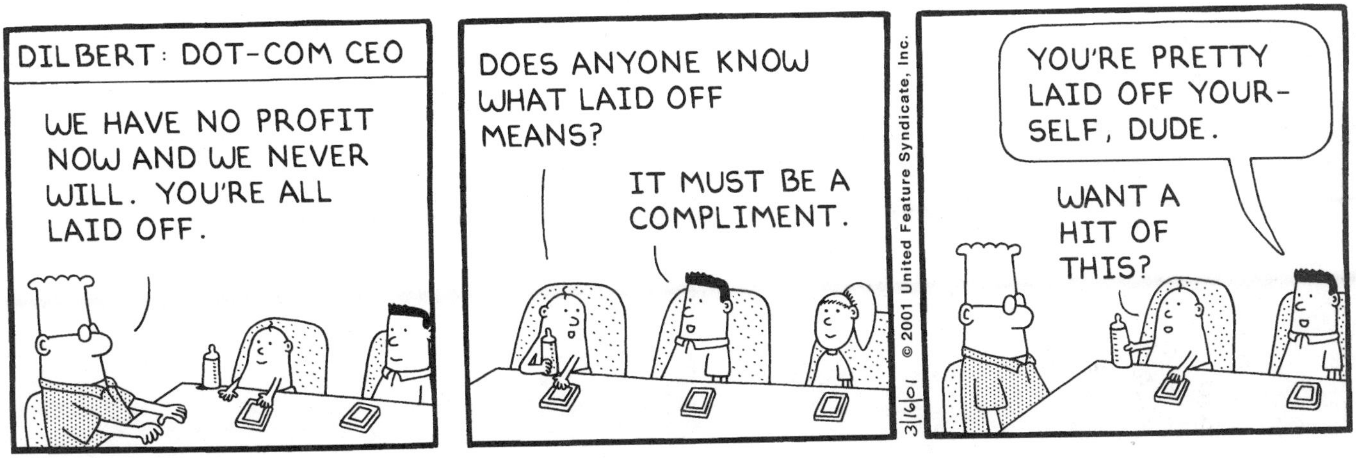
DILBERT: DOT-COM CEO
WE HAVE NO PROFIT NOW AND WE NEVER WILL. YOU'RE ALL LAID OFF.
DOES ANYONE KNOW WHAT LAID OFF MEANS?
IT MUST BE A COMPLIMENT.
3/16/01 © 2001 United Feature Syndicate, Inc.
YOU'RE PRETTY LAID OFF YOUR-SELF, DUDE.
WANT A HIT OF THIS?

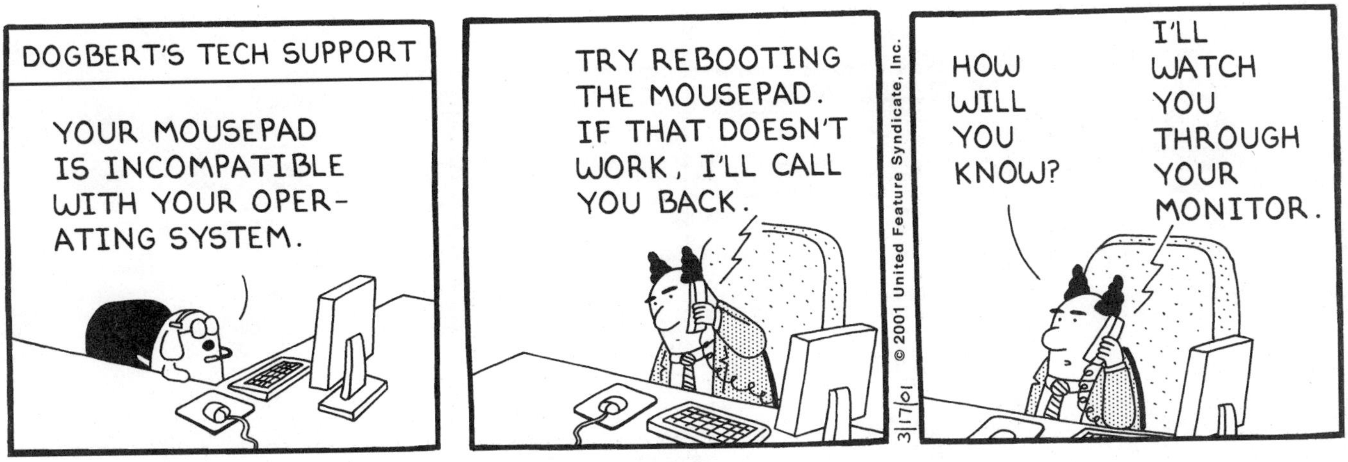
DOGBERT'S TECH SUPPORT
YOUR MOUSEPAD IS INCOMPATIBLE WITH YOUR OPER-ATING SYSTEM.
TRY REBOOTING THE MOUSEPAD. IF THAT DOESN'T WORK, I'LL CALL YOU BACK.
3/17/01 © 2001 United Feature Syndicate, Inc.
HOW WILL YOU KNOW?
I'LL WATCH YOU THROUGH YOUR MONITOR.

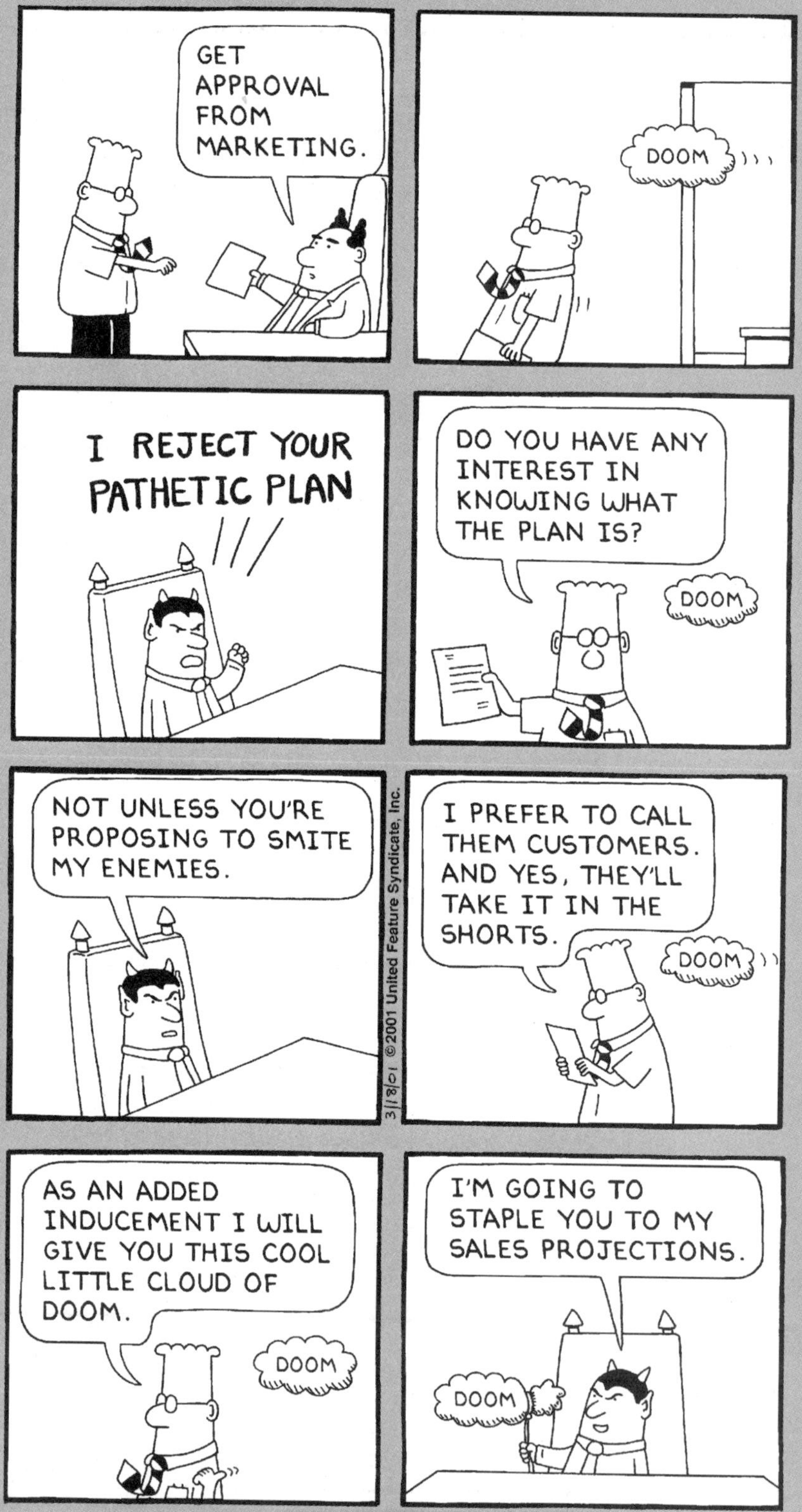
GET APPROVAL FROM MARKETING.
DOOM
I REJECT YOUR PATHETIC PLAN
DO YOU HAVE ANY INTEREST IN KNOWING WHAT THE PLAN IS?
DOOM
NOT UNLESS YOU'RE PROPOSING TO SMITE MY ENEMIES.
I PREFER TO CALL THEM CUSTOMERS. AND YES, THEY'LL TAKE IT IN THE SHORTS.
DOOM
AS AN ADDED INDUCEMENT I WILL GIVE YOU THIS COOL LITTLE CLOUD OF DOOM.
DOOM
I'M GOING TO STAPLE YOU TO MY SALES PROJECTIONS.
DOOM
3/18/01 © 2001 United Feature Syndicate, Inc.

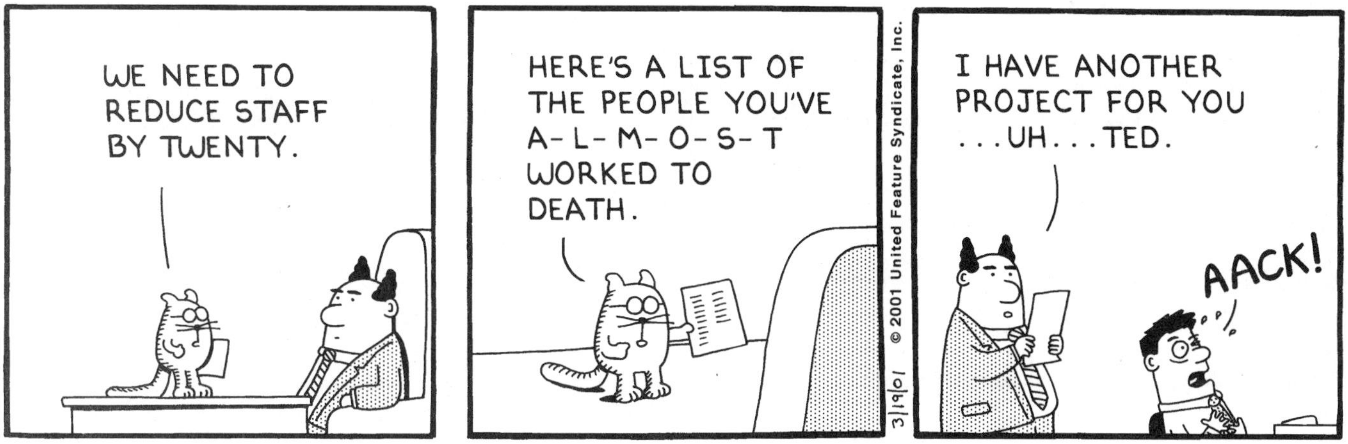
WE NEED TO REDUCE STAFF BY TWENTY.
HERE'S A LIST OF THE PEOPLE YOU'VE A-L-M-O-S-T WORKED TO DEATH.
3/19/01 © 2001 United Feature Syndicate, Inc.
I HAVE ANOTHER PROJECT FOR YOU . . . UH . . . TED.
AACK!

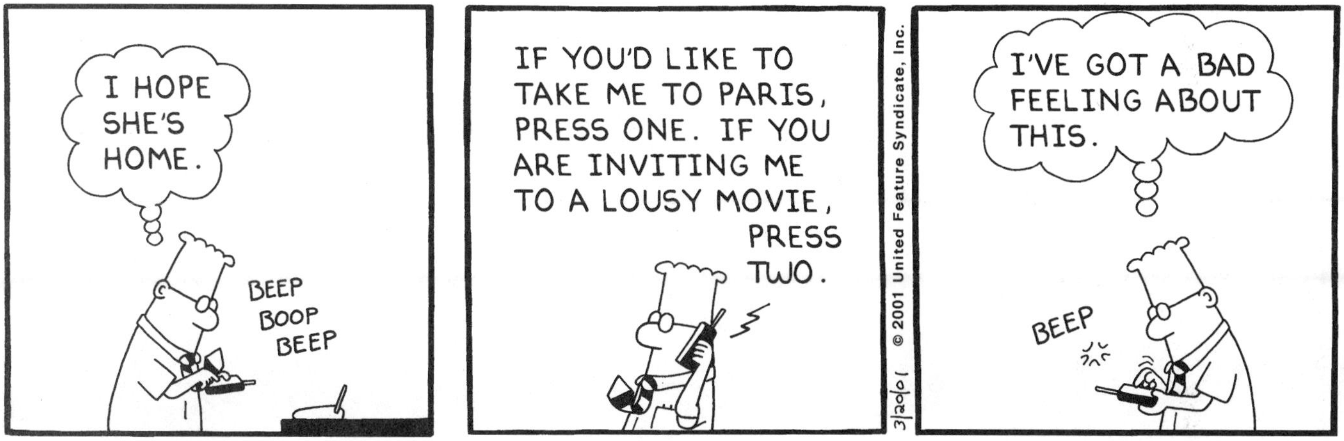
I HOPE SHE'S HOME.
BEEP BOOP BEEP
IF YOU'D LIKE TO TAKE ME TO PARIS, PRESS ONE. IF YOU ARE INVITING ME TO A LOUSY MOVIE, PRESS TWO.
3/20/01 © 2001 United Feature Syndicate, Inc.
I'VE GOT A BAD FEELING ABOUT THIS.
BEEP

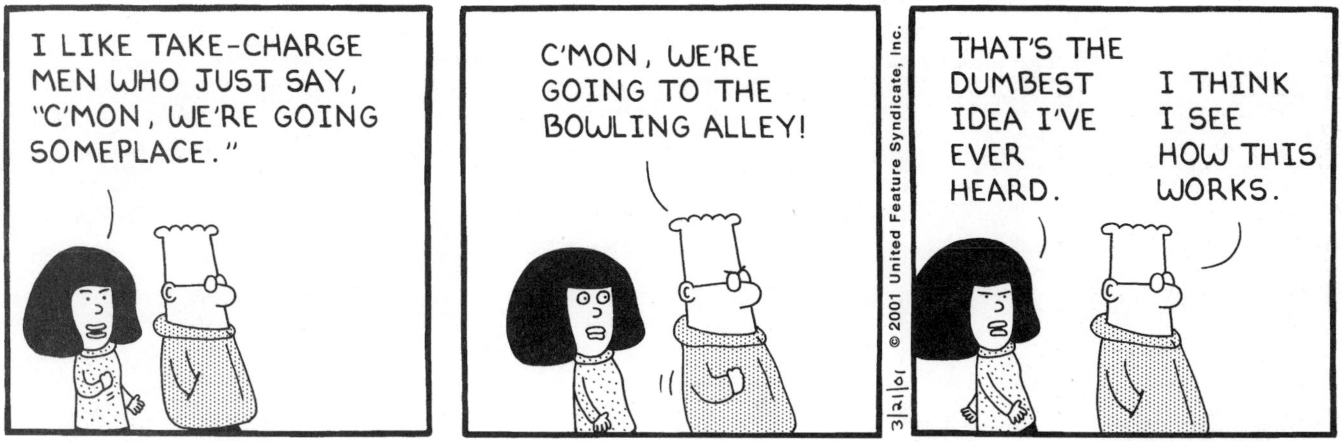
I LIKE TAKE-CHARGE MEN WHO JUST SAY, "C'MON, WE'RE GOING SOMEPLACE."
C'MON, WE'RE GOING TO THE BOWLING ALLEY!
3/21/01 © 2001 United Feature Syndicate, Inc.
THAT'S THE DUMBEST IDEA I'VE EVER HEARD.
I THINK I SEE HOW THIS WORKS.

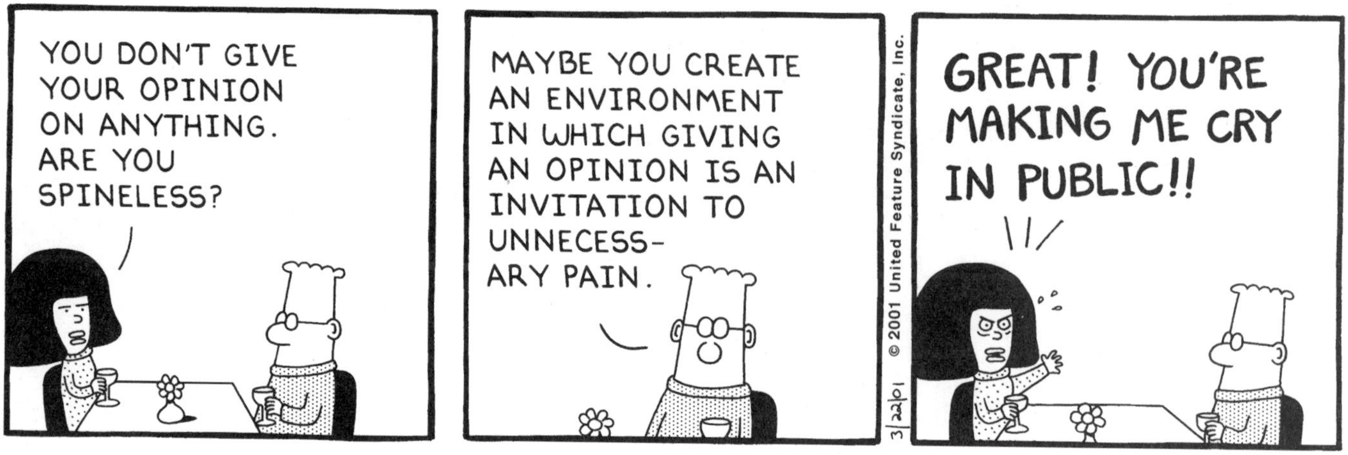
YOU DON'T GIVE YOUR OPINION ON ANYTHING. ARE YOU SPINELESS?
MAYBE YOU CREATE AN ENVIRONMENT IN WHICH GIVING AN OPINION IS AN INVITATION TO UNNECESS-ARY PAIN.
3/22/01 © 2001 United Feature Syndicate, Inc.
GREAT! YOU'RE MAKING ME CRY IN PUBLIC!!

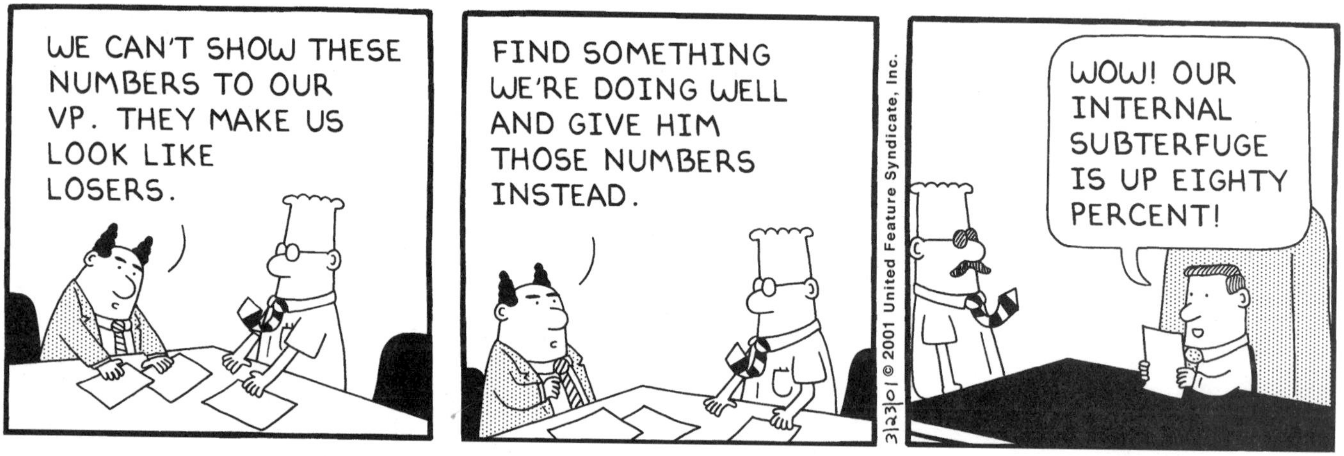
WE CAN'T SHOW THESE NUMBERS TO OUR VP. THEY MAKE US LOOK LIKE LOSERS.
FIND SOMETHING WE'RE DOING WELL AND GIVE HIM THOSE NUMBERS INSTEAD.
3/23/01 © 2001 United Feature Syndicate, Inc.
WOW! OUR INTERNAL SUBTERFUGE IS UP EIGHTY PERCENT!

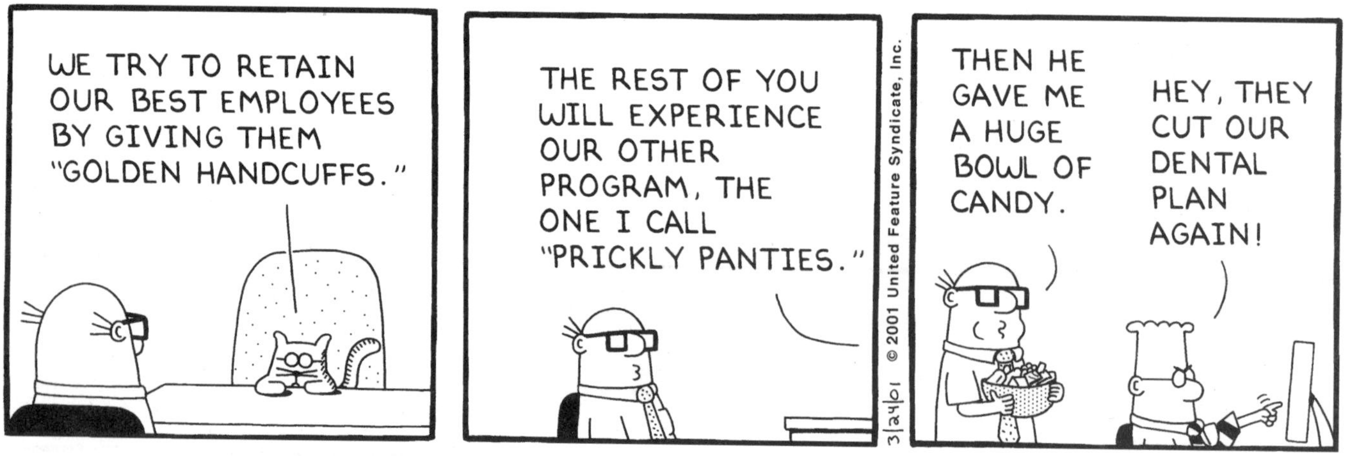
WE TRY TO RETAIN OUR BEST EMPLOYEES BY GIVING THEM "GOLDEN HANDCUFFS."
THE REST OF YOU WILL EXPERIENCE OUR OTHER PROGRAM, THE ONE I CALL "PRICKLY PANTIES."
3/24/01 © 2001 United Feature Syndicate, Inc.
THEN HE GAVE ME A HUGE BOWL OF CANDY.
HEY, THEY CUT OUR DENTAL PLAN AGAIN!

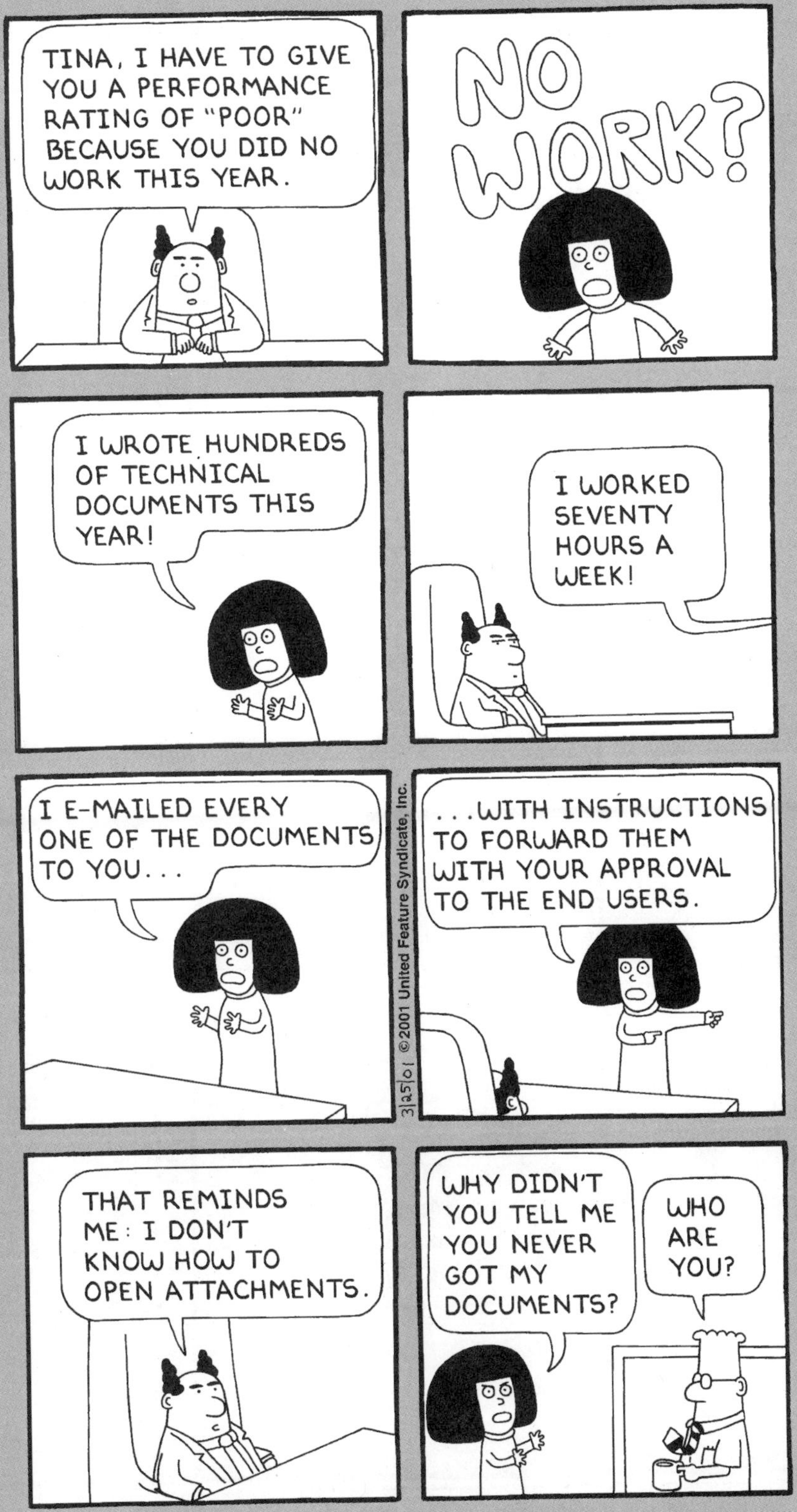
TINA, I HAVE TO GIVE YOU A PERFORMANCE RATING OF "POOR" BECAUSE YOU DID NO WORK THIS YEAR.
NO WORK?
I WROTE HUNDREDS OF TECHNICAL DOCUMENTS THIS YEAR!
I WORKED SEVENTY HOURS A WEEK!
I E-MAILED EVERY ONE OF THE DOCUMENTS TO YOU...
...WITH INSTRUCTIONS TO FORWARD THEM WITH YOUR APPROVAL TO THE END USERS.
THAT REMINDS ME: I DON'T KNOW HOW TO OPEN ATTACHMENTS.
WHY DIDN'T YOU TELL ME YOU NEVER GOT MY DOCUMENTS?
WHO ARE YOU?
3/25/01 ©2001 United Feature Syndicate, Inc.

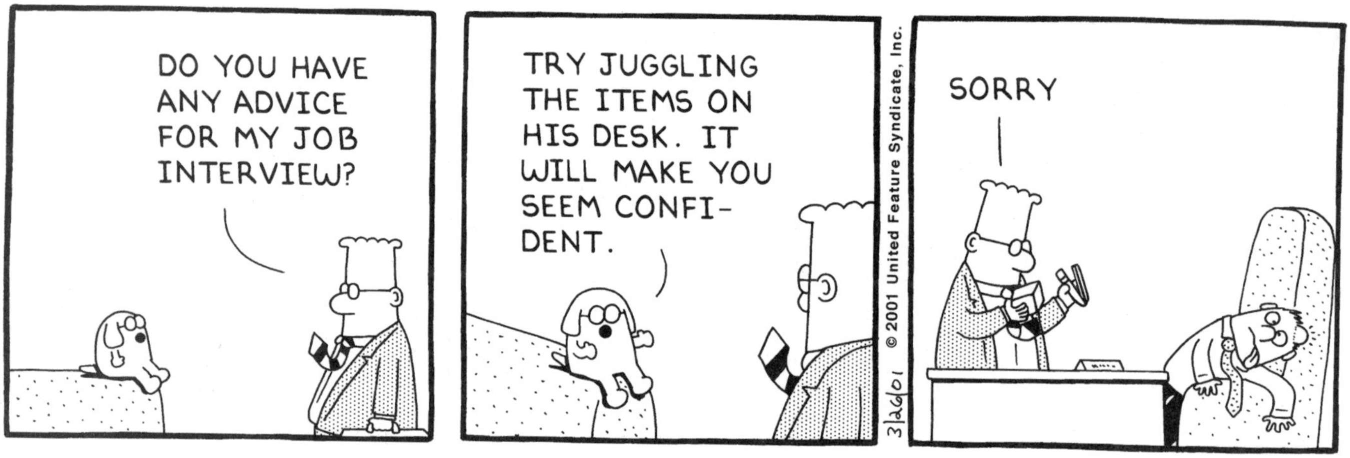
DO YOU HAVE ANY ADVICE FOR MY JOB INTERVIEW?
TRY JUGGLING THE ITEMS ON HIS DESK. IT WILL MAKE YOU SEEM CONFI-DENT.
3/26/01 © 2001 United Feature Syndicate, Inc.
SORRY

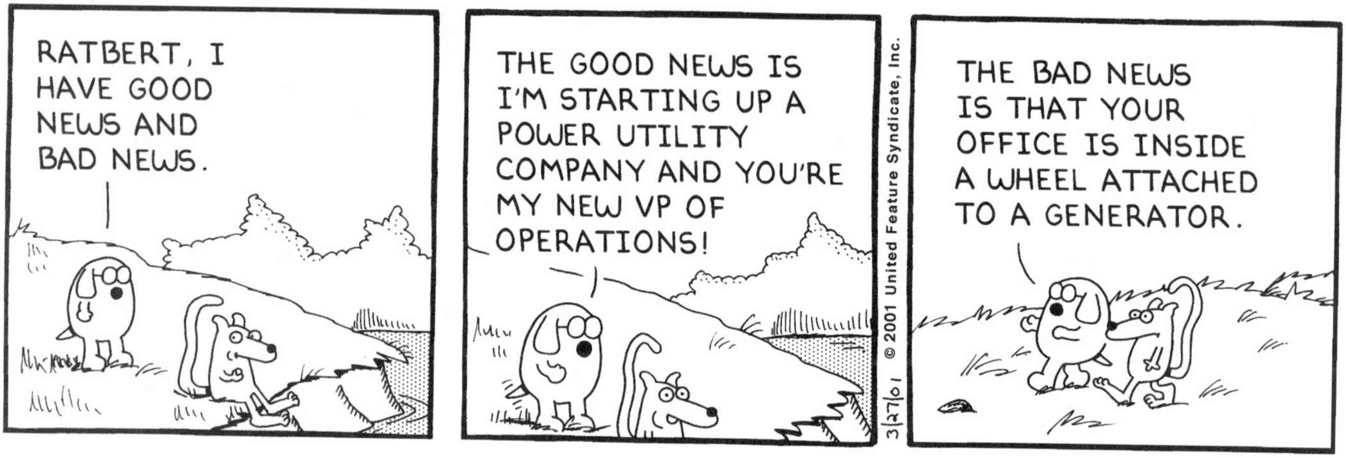
RATBERT, I HAVE GOOD NEWS AND BAD NEWS.
THE GOOD NEWS IS I'M STARTING UP A POWER UTILITY COMPANY AND YOU'RE MY NEW VP OF OPERATIONS!
3/27/01 © 2001 United Feature Syndicate, Inc.
THE BAD NEWS IS THAT YOUR OFFICE IS INSIDE A WHEEL ATTACHED TO A GENERATOR.

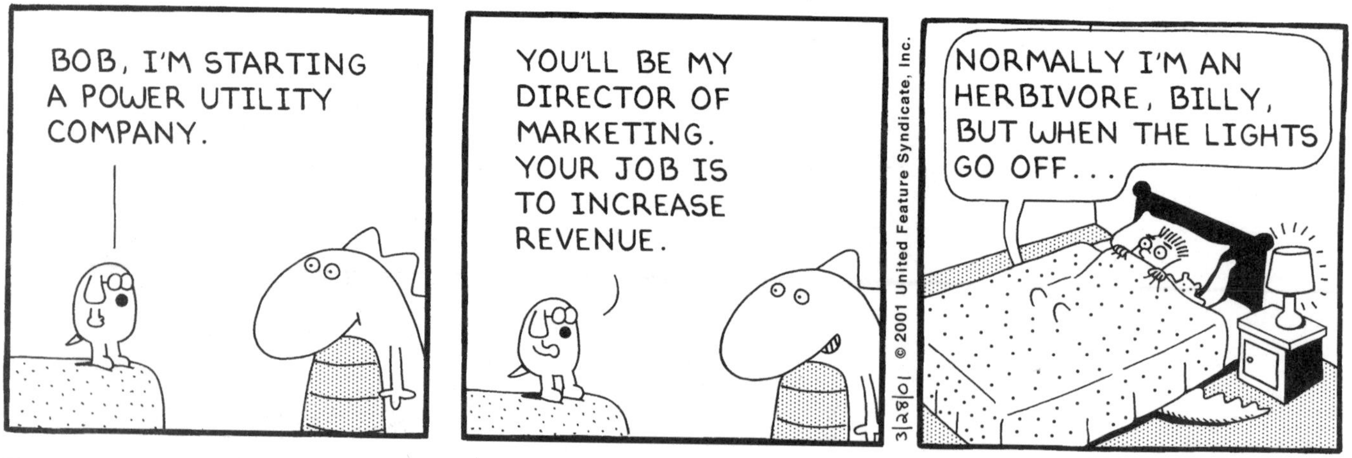
BOB, I'M STARTING A POWER UTILITY COMPANY.
YOU'LL BE MY DIRECTOR OF MARKETING. YOUR JOB IS TO INCREASE REVENUE.
3/28/01 © 2001 United Feature Syndicate, Inc.
NORMALLY I'M AN HERBIVORE, BILLY, BUT WHEN THE LIGHTS GO OFF...

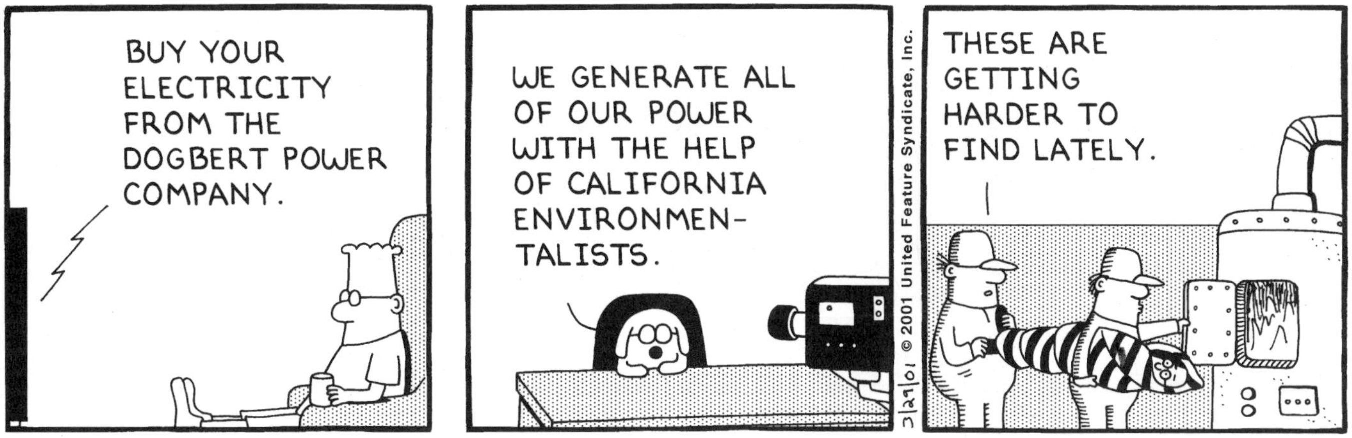
BUY YOUR ELECTRICITY FROM THE DOGBERT POWER COMPANY.
WE GENERATE ALL OF OUR POWER WITH THE HELP OF CALIFORNIA ENVIRONMENTALISTS.
THESE ARE GETTING HARDER TO FIND LATELY.
3/29/01 © 2001 United Feature Syndicate, Inc.

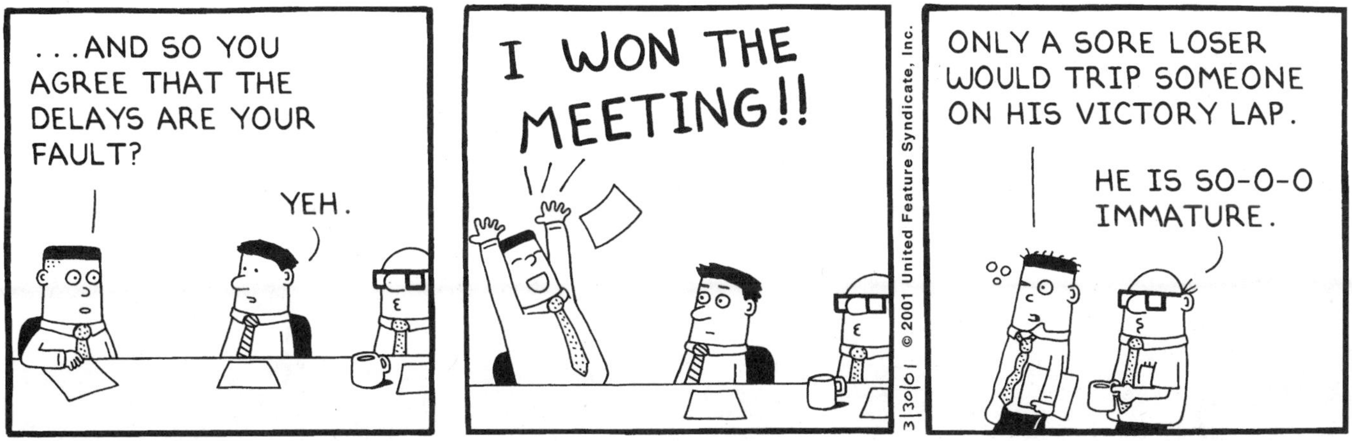
...AND SO YOU AGREE THAT THE DELAYS ARE YOUR FAULT?
YEH.
I WON THE MEETING!!
ONLY A SORE LOSER WOULD TRIP SOMEONE ON HIS VICTORY LAP.
HE IS SO-O-O IMMATURE.
3/30/01 © 2001 United Feature Syndicate, Inc.

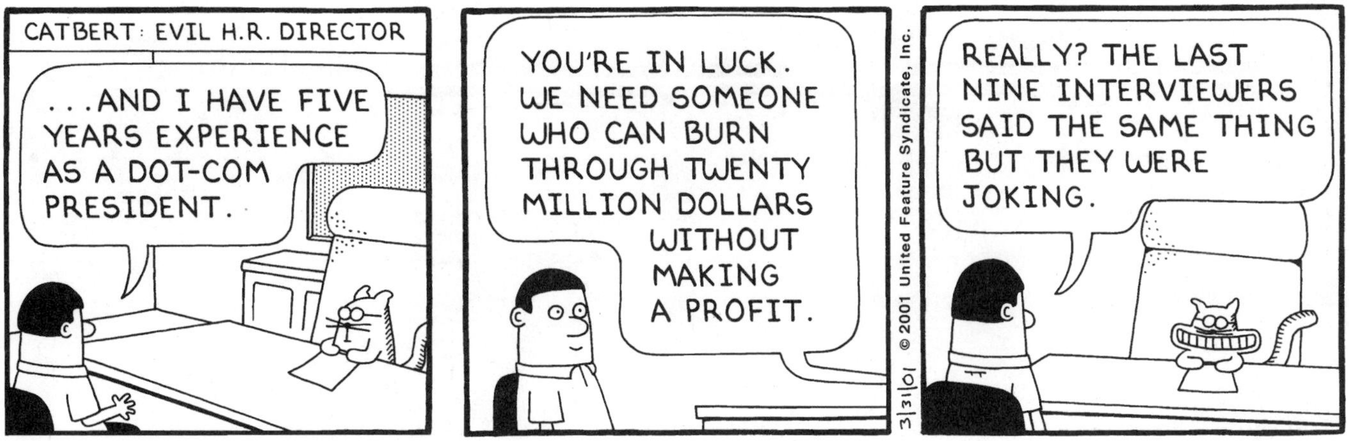
CATBERT: EVIL H.R. DIRECTOR
...AND I HAVE FIVE YEARS EXPERIENCE AS A DOT-COM PRESIDENT.
YOU'RE IN LUCK. WE NEED SOMEONE WHO CAN BURN THROUGH TWENTY MILLION DOLLARS WITHOUT MAKING A PROFIT.
REALLY? THE LAST NINE INTERVIEWERS SAID THE SAME THING BUT THEY WERE JOKING.
3/31/01 © 2001 United Feature Syndicate, Inc.

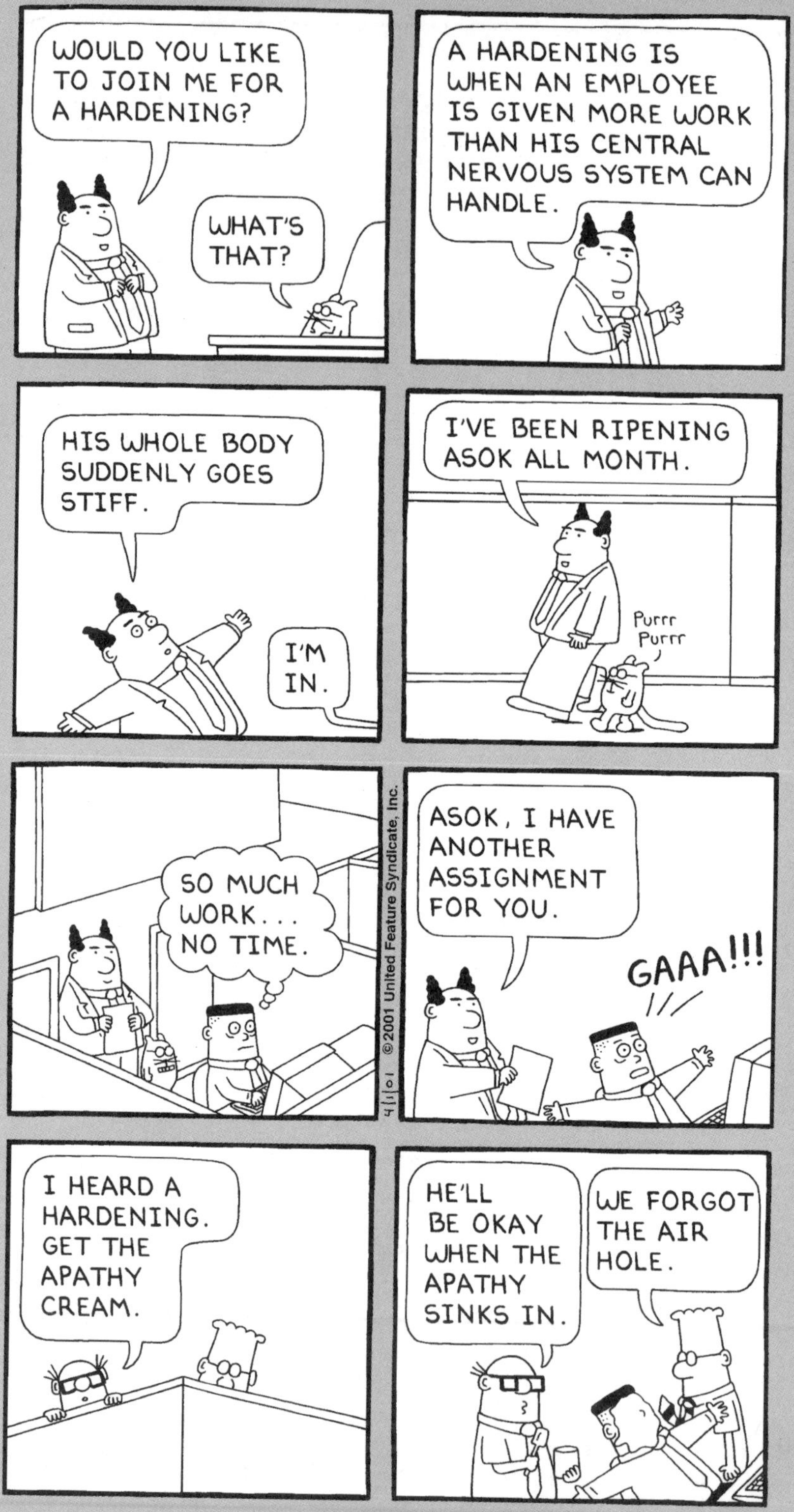
WOULD YOU LIKE TO JOIN ME FOR A HARDENING?
WHAT'S THAT?
A HARDENING IS WHEN AN EMPLOYEE IS GIVEN MORE WORK THAN HIS CENTRAL NERVOUS SYSTEM CAN HANDLE.
HIS WHOLE BODY SUDDENLY GOES STIFF.
I'M IN.
I'VE BEEN RIPENING ASOK ALL MONTH.
Purrr
Purrr
SO MUCH WORK... NO TIME.
©2001 United Feature Syndicate, Inc.
4/1/01
ASOK, I HAVE ANOTHER ASSIGNMENT FOR YOU.
GAAA!!!
I HEARD A HARDENING. GET THE APATHY CREAM.
HE'LL BE OKAY WHEN THE APATHY SINKS IN.
WE FORGOT THE AIR HOLE.

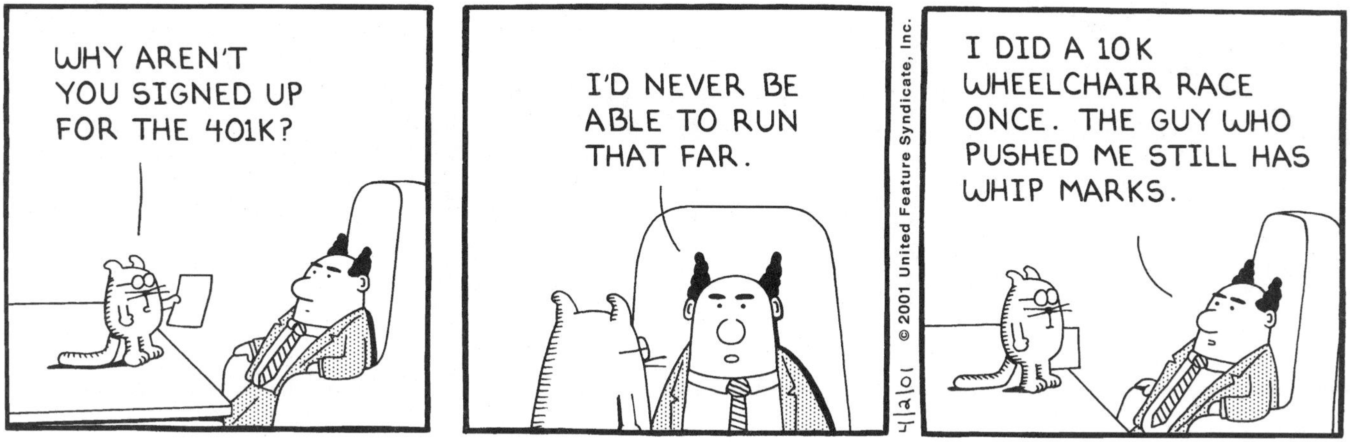
WHY AREN'T YOU SIGNED UP FOR THE 401K?
I'D NEVER BE ABLE TO RUN THAT FAR.
4/2/01 © 2001 United Feature Syndicate, Inc.
I DID A 10K WHEELCHAIR RACE ONCE. THE GUY WHO PUSHED ME STILL HAS WHIP MARKS.

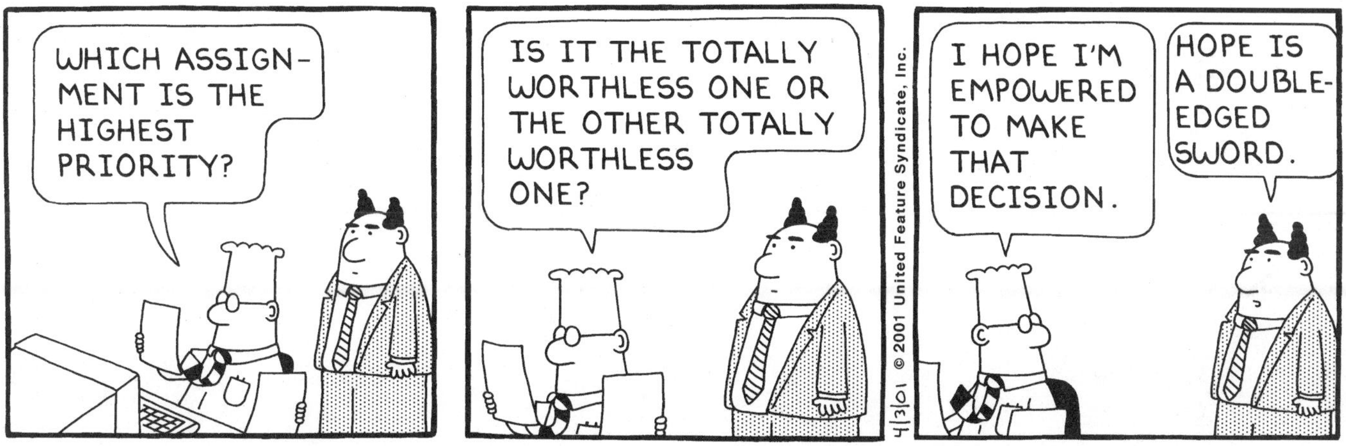
WHICH ASSIGN-MENT IS THE HIGHEST PRIORITY?
IS IT THE TOTALLY WORTHLESS ONE OR THE OTHER TOTALLY WORTHLESS ONE?
4/3/01 © 2001 United Feature Syndicate, Inc.
I HOPE I'M EMPOWERED TO MAKE THAT DECISION.
HOPE IS A DOUBLE-EDGED SWORD.

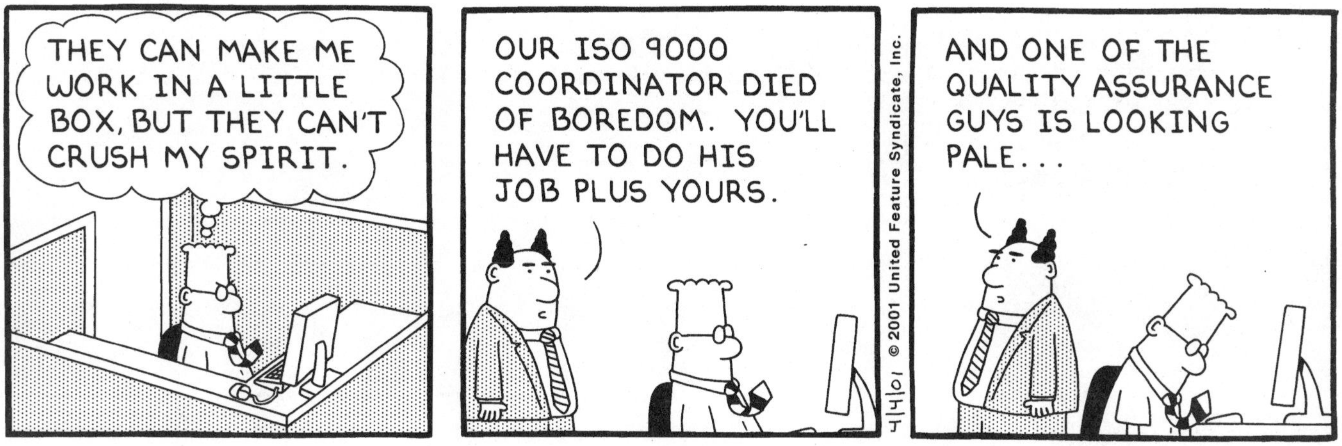
THEY CAN MAKE ME WORK IN A LITTLE BOX, BUT THEY CAN'T CRUSH MY SPIRIT.
OUR ISO 9000 COORDINATOR DIED OF BOREDOM. YOU'LL HAVE TO DO HIS JOB PLUS YOURS.
4/4/01 © 2001 United Feature Syndicate, Inc.
AND ONE OF THE QUALITY ASSURANCE GUYS IS LOOKING PALE...

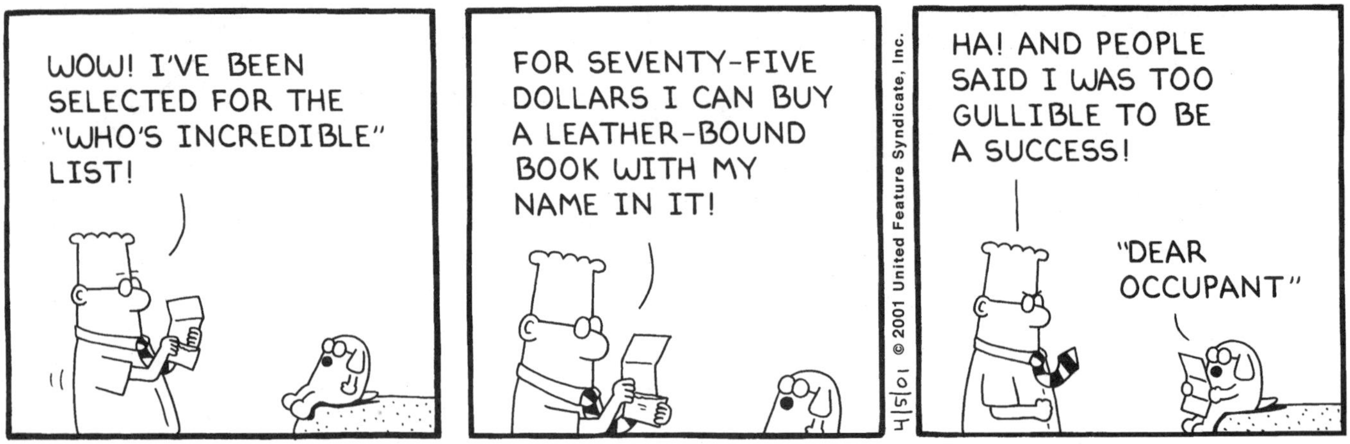
WOW! I'VE BEEN SELECTED FOR THE "WHO'S INCREDIBLE" LIST!
FOR SEVENTY-FIVE DOLLARS I CAN BUY A LEATHER-BOUND BOOK WITH MY NAME IN IT!
4/5/01 © 2001 United Feature Syndicate, Inc.
HA! AND PEOPLE SAID I WAS TOO GULLIBLE TO BE A SUCCESS!
"DEAR OCCUPANT"

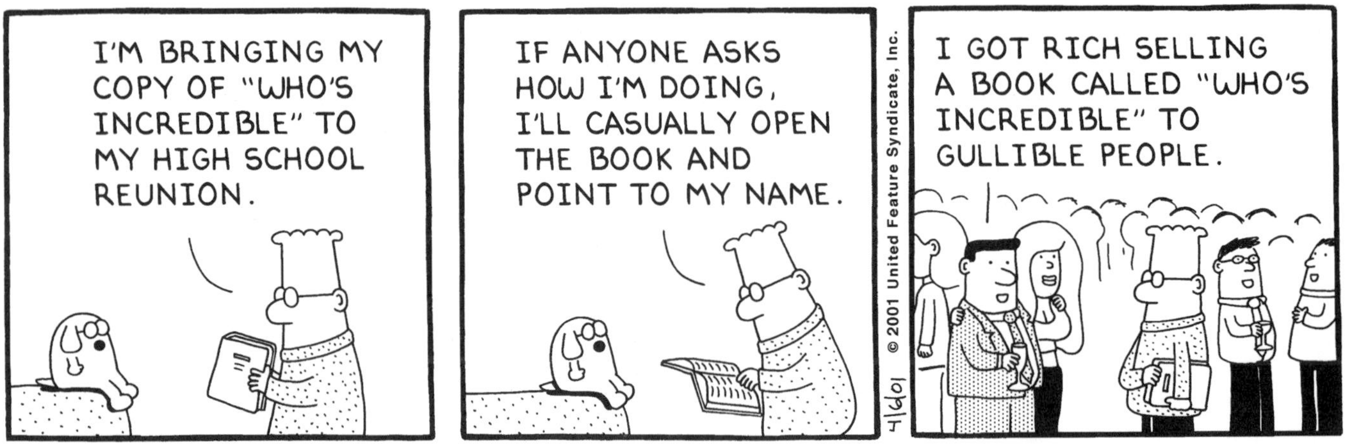
I'M BRINGING MY COPY OF "WHO'S INCREDIBLE" TO MY HIGH SCHOOL REUNION.
IF ANYONE ASKS HOW I'M DOING, I'LL CASUALLY OPEN THE BOOK AND POINT TO MY NAME.
4/6/01 © 2001 United Feature Syndicate, Inc.
I GOT RICH SELLING A BOOK CALLED "WHO'S INCREDIBLE" TO GULLIBLE PEOPLE.

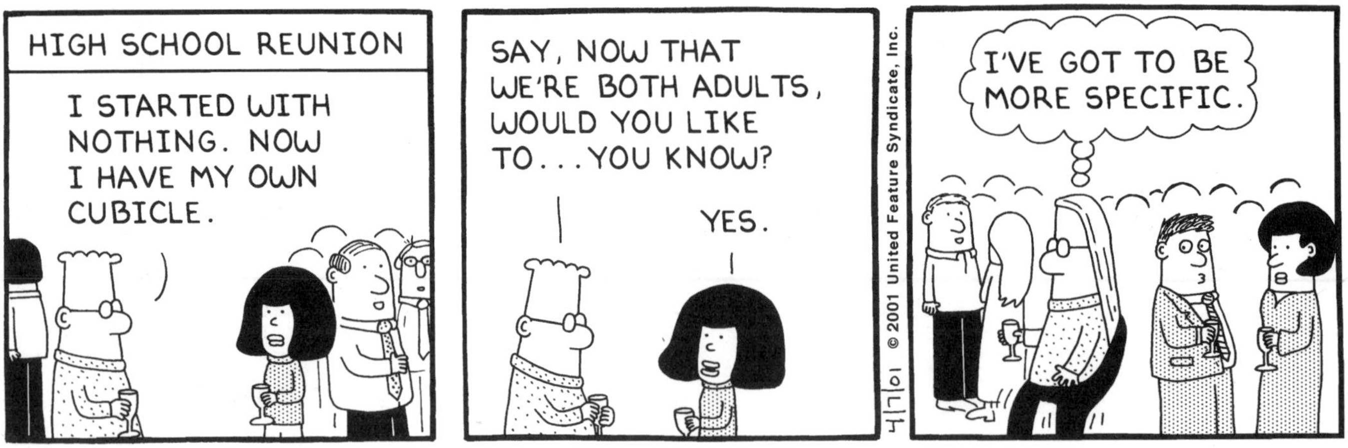
HIGH SCHOOL REUNION
I STARTED WITH NOTHING. NOW I HAVE MY OWN CUBICLE.
SAY, NOW THAT WE'RE BOTH ADULTS, WOULD YOU LIKE TO... YOU KNOW?
YES.
4/7/01 © 2001 United Feature Syndicate, Inc.
I'VE GOT TO BE MORE SPECIFIC.

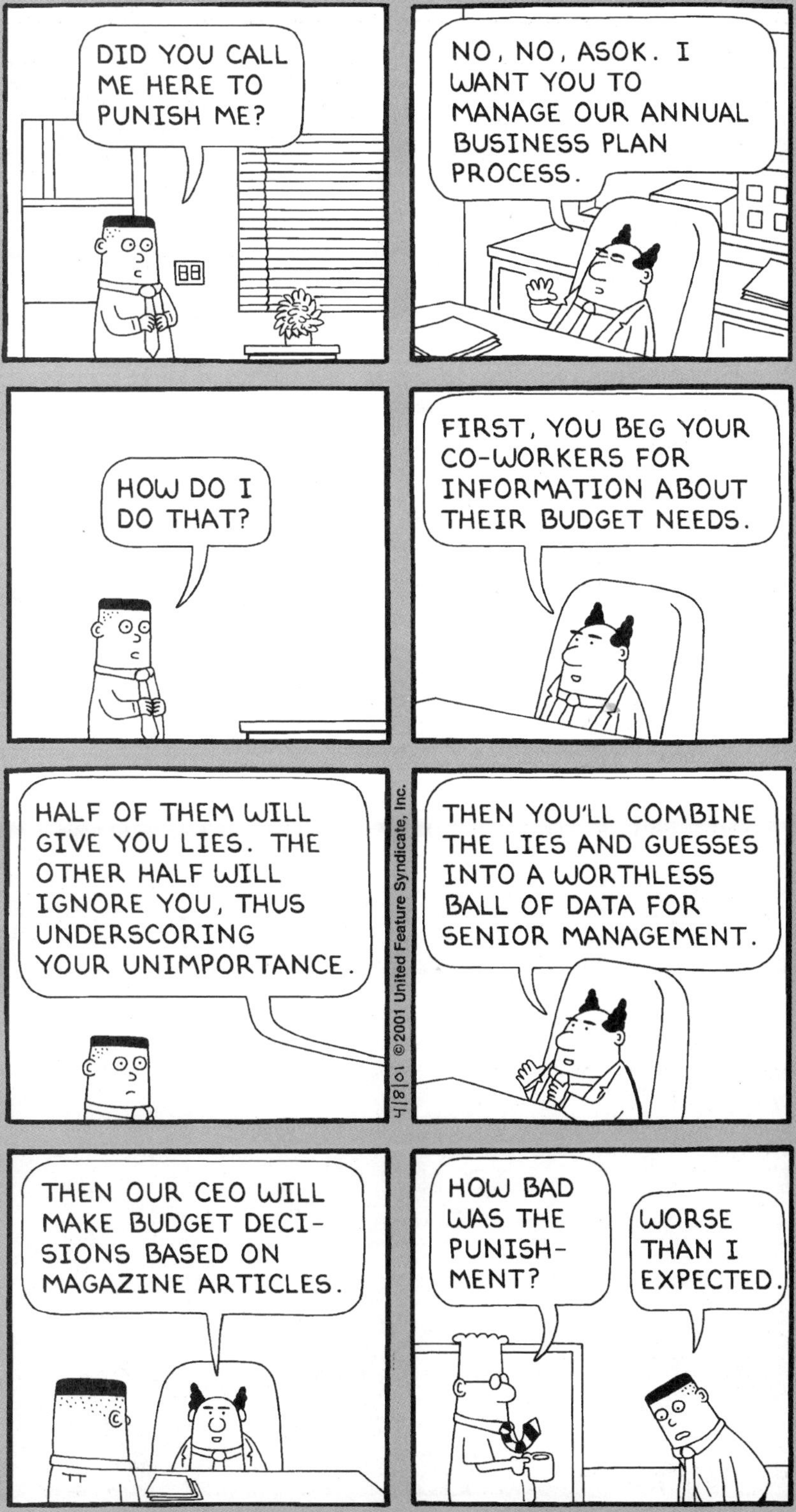
DID YOU CALL ME HERE TO PUNISH ME?
NO, NO, ASOK. I WANT YOU TO MANAGE OUR ANNUAL BUSINESS PLAN PROCESS.
HOW DO I DO THAT?
FIRST, YOU BEG YOUR CO-WORKERS FOR INFORMATION ABOUT THEIR BUDGET NEEDS.
HALF OF THEM WILL GIVE YOU LIES. THE OTHER HALF WILL IGNORE YOU, THUS UNDERSCORING YOUR UNIMPORTANCE.
4/8/01 ©2001 United Feature Syndicate, Inc.
THEN YOU'LL COMBINE THE LIES AND GUESSES INTO A WORTHLESS BALL OF DATA FOR SENIOR MANAGEMENT.
THEN OUR CEO WILL MAKE BUDGET DECISIONS BASED ON MAGAZINE ARTICLES.
HOW BAD WAS THE PUNISHMENT?
WORSE THAN I EXPECTED.

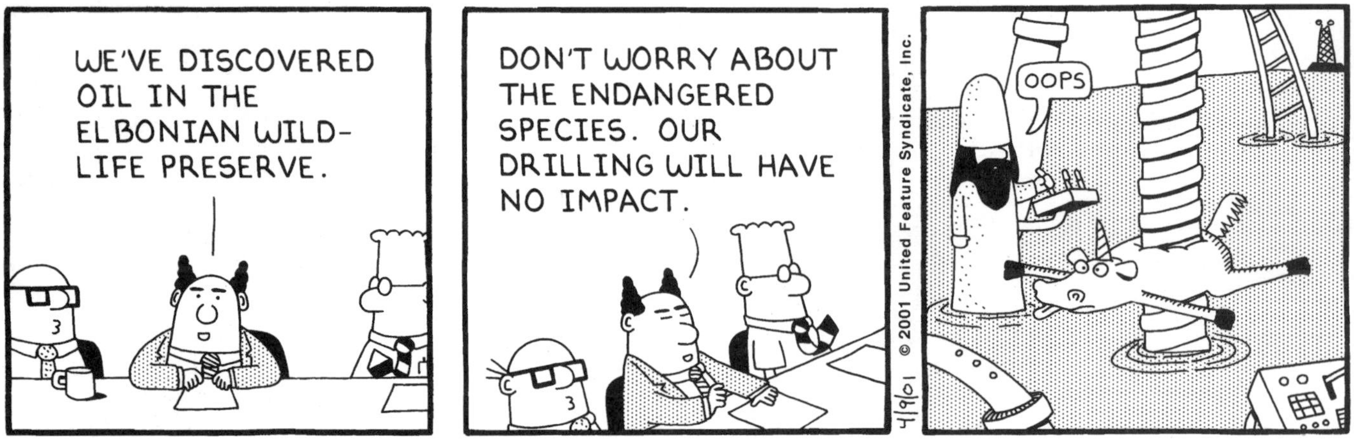
WE'VE DISCOVERED OIL IN THE ELBONIAN WILD-LIFE PRESERVE.
DON'T WORRY ABOUT THE ENDANGERED SPECIES. OUR DRILLING WILL HAVE NO IMPACT.
4/9/01 © 2001 United Feature Syndicate, Inc.
OOPS

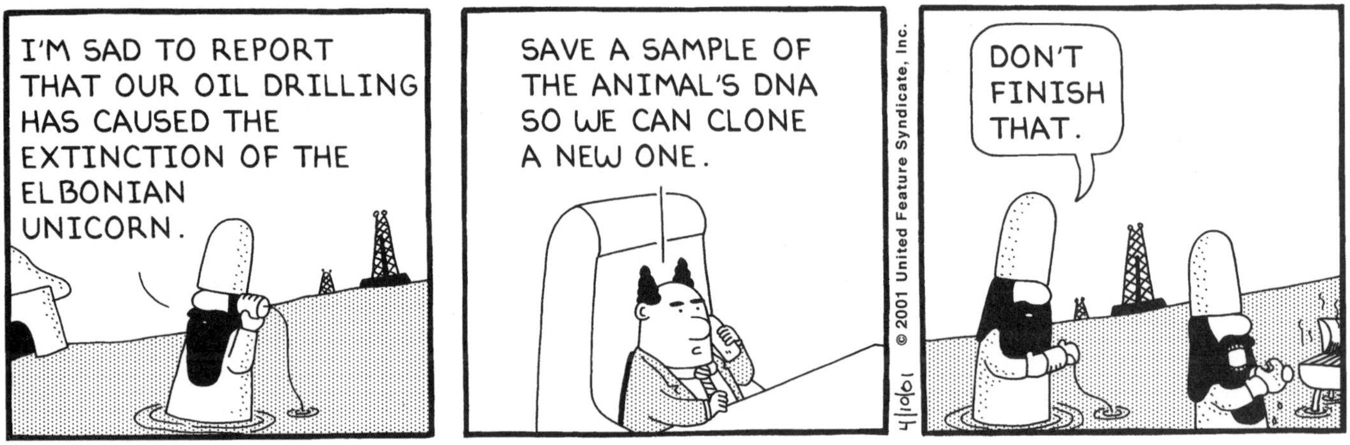
I'M SAD TO REPORT THAT OUR OIL DRILLING HAS CAUSED THE EXTINCTION OF THE ELBONIAN UNICORN.
SAVE A SAMPLE OF THE ANIMAL'S DNA SO WE CAN CLONE A NEW ONE.
4/10/01 © 2001 United Feature Syndicate, Inc.
DON'T FINISH THAT.

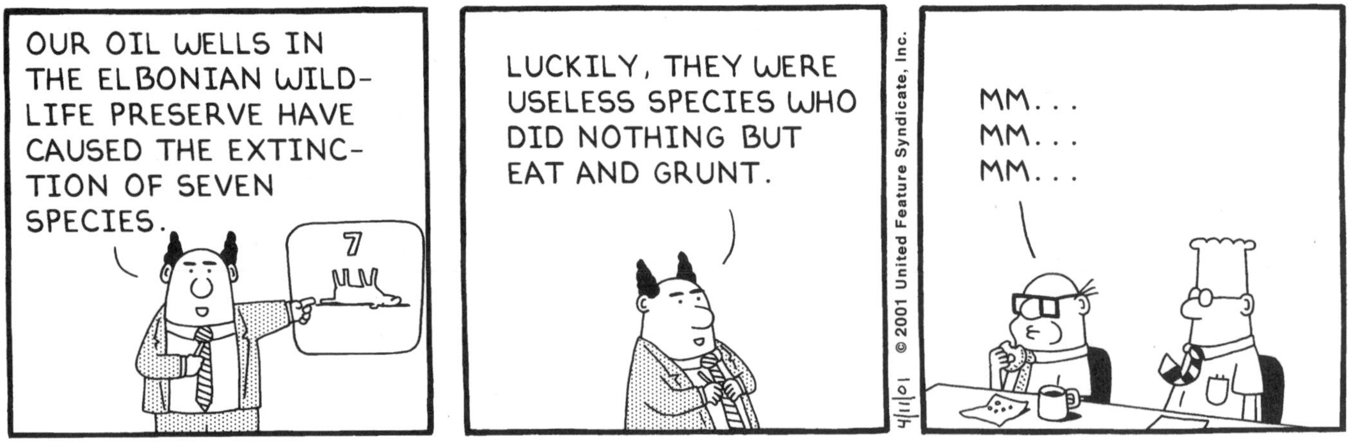
OUR OIL WELLS IN THE ELBONIAN WILD-LIFE PRESERVE HAVE CAUSED THE EXTINCTION OF SEVEN SPECIES.
7
LUCKILY, THEY WERE USELESS SPECIES WHO DID NOTHING BUT EAT AND GRUNT.
4/11/01 © 2001 United Feature Syndicate, Inc.
MM... MM... MM...

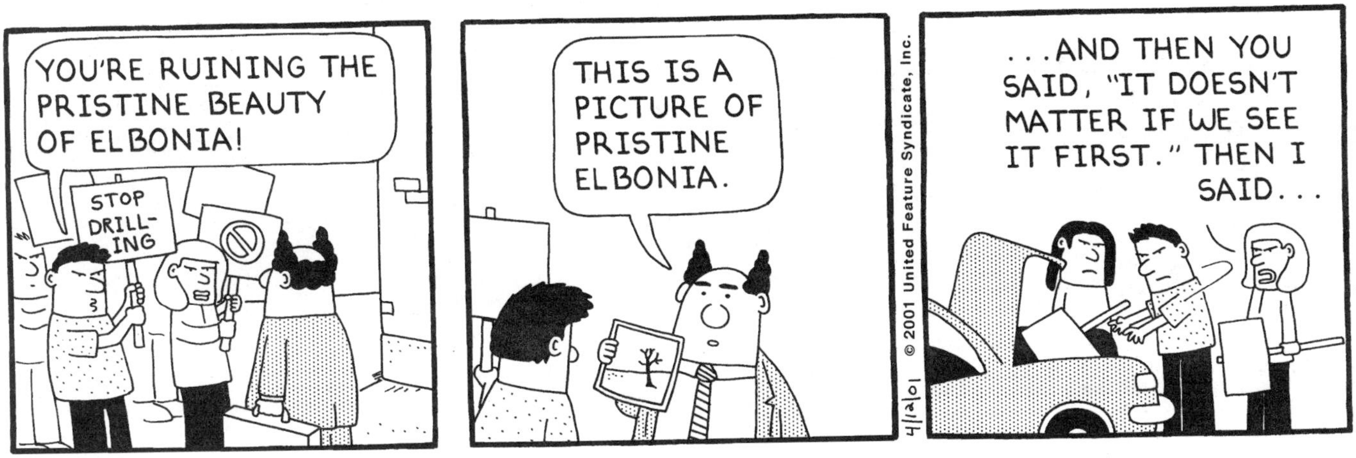
YOU'RE RUINING THE PRISTINE BEAUTY OF ELBONIA!
STOP DRILL-ING
THIS IS A PICTURE OF PRISTINE ELBONIA.
4/12/01 © 2001 United Feature Syndicate, Inc.
...AND THEN YOU SAID, "IT DOESN'T MATTER IF WE SEE IT FIRST." THEN I SAID...

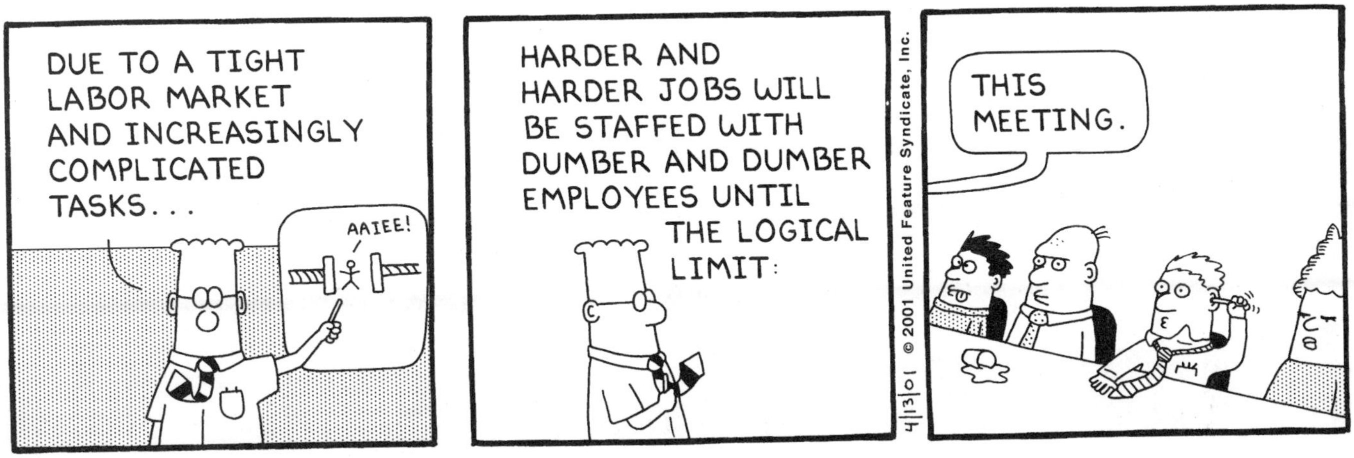
DUE TO A TIGHT LABOR MARKET AND INCREASINGLY COMPLICATED TASKS...
AAIEE!
HARDER AND HARDER JOBS WILL BE STAFFED WITH DUMBER AND DUMBER EMPLOYEES UNTIL THE LOGICAL LIMIT:
4/13/01 © 2001 United Feature Syndicate, Inc.
THIS MEETING.

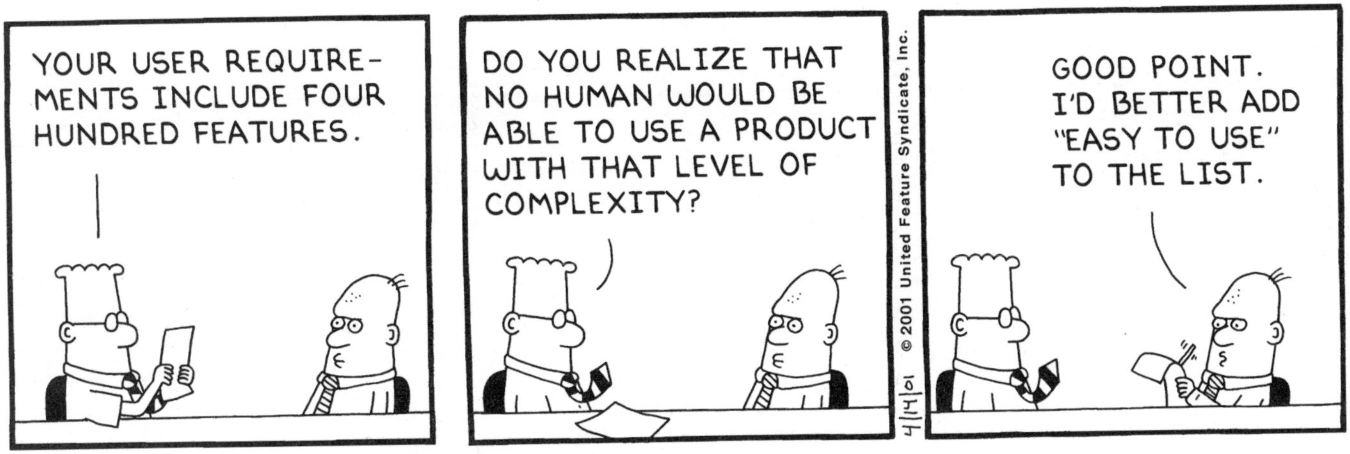
YOUR USER REQUIRE-MENTS INCLUDE FOUR HUNDRED FEATURES.
DO YOU REALIZE THAT NO HUMAN WOULD BE ABLE TO USE A PRODUCT WITH THAT LEVEL OF COMPLEXITY?
4/14/01 © 2001 United Feature Syndicate, Inc.
GOOD POINT. I'D BETTER ADD "EASY TO USE" TO THE LIST.

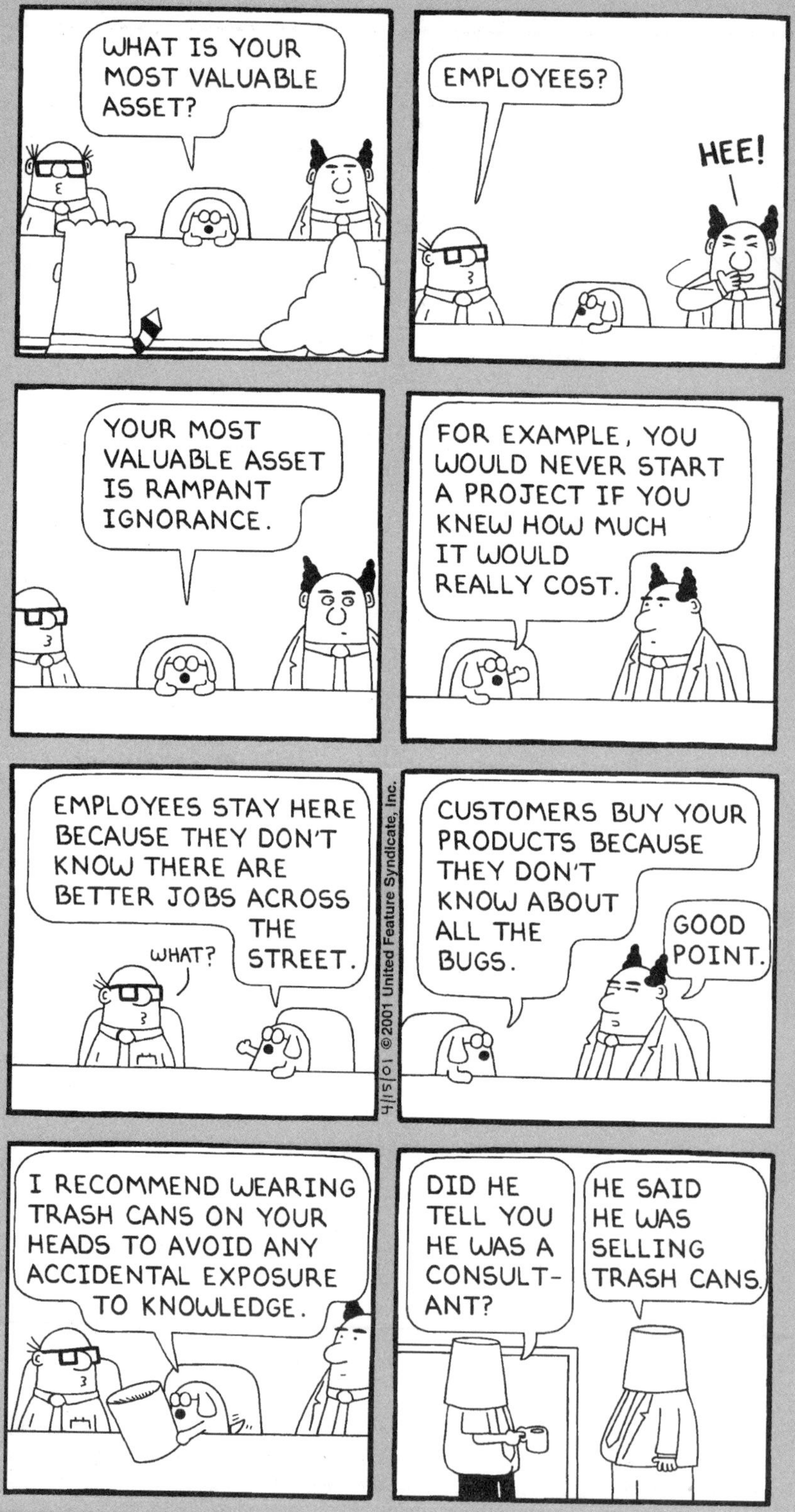
WHAT IS YOUR MOST VALUABLE ASSET?
EMPLOYEES?
HEE!
YOUR MOST VALUABLE ASSET IS RAMPANT IGNORANCE.
FOR EXAMPLE, YOU WOULD NEVER START A PROJECT IF YOU KNEW HOW MUCH IT WOULD REALLY COST.
EMPLOYEES STAY HERE BECAUSE THEY DON'T KNOW THERE ARE BETTER JOBS ACROSS THE STREET.
WHAT?
CUSTOMERS BUY YOUR PRODUCTS BECAUSE THEY DON'T KNOW ABOUT ALL THE BUGS.
GOOD POINT.
I RECOMMEND WEARING TRASH CANS ON YOUR HEADS TO AVOID ANY ACCIDENTAL EXPOSURE TO KNOWLEDGE.
DID HE TELL YOU HE WAS A CONSULT-ANT?
HE SAID HE WAS SELLING TRASH CANS.
4/15/01 ©2001 United Feature Syndicate, Inc.

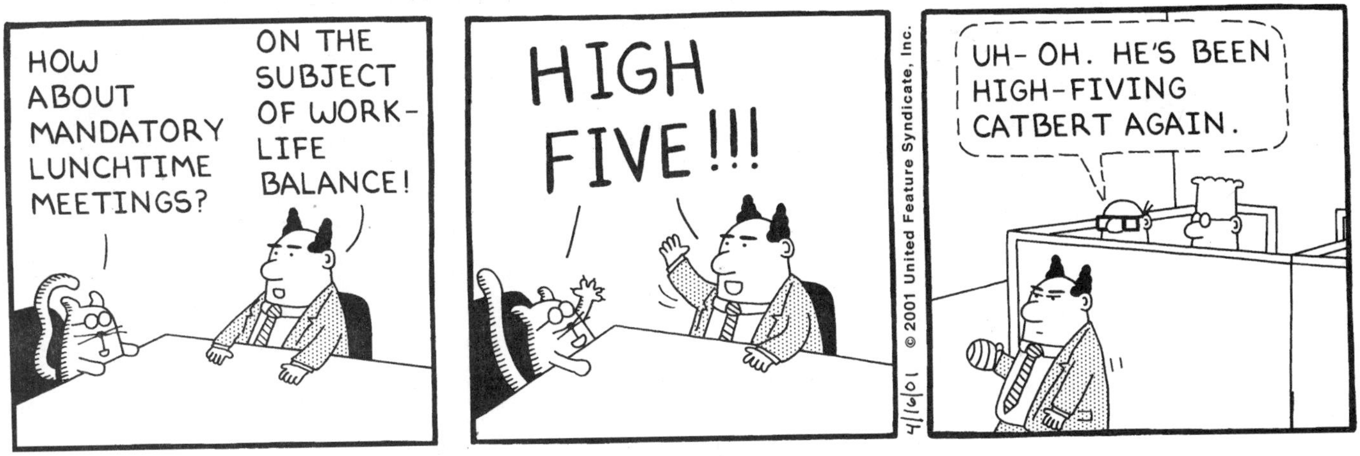
HOW ABOUT MANDATORY LUNCHTIME MEETINGS?
ON THE SUBJECT OF WORK-LIFE BALANCE!
HIGH FIVE!!!
4/16/01 © 2001 United Feature Syndicate, Inc.
UH-OH. HE'S BEEN HIGH-FIVING CATBERT AGAIN.

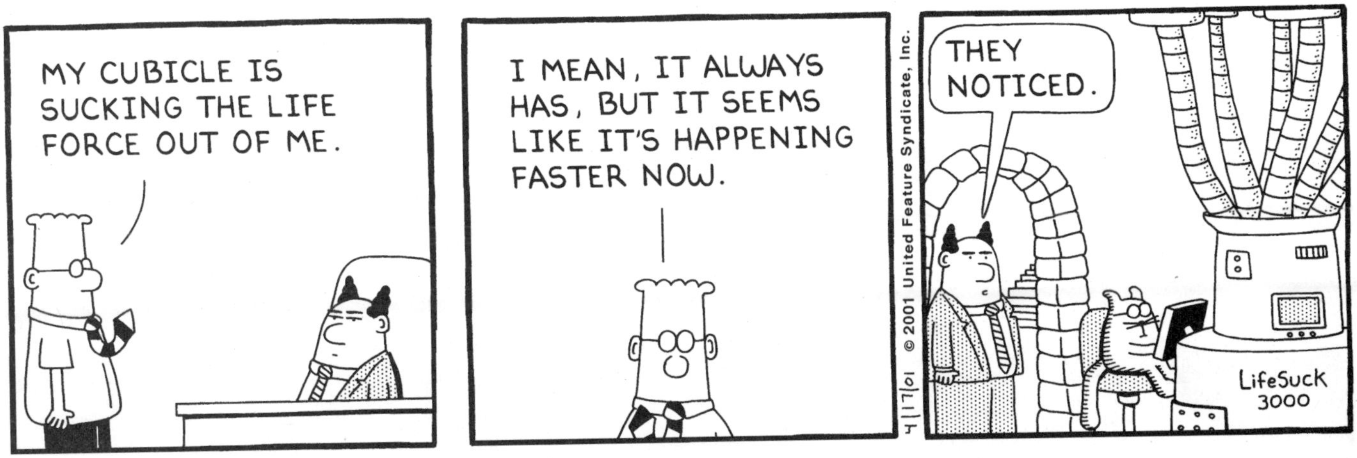
MY CUBICLE IS SUCKING THE LIFE FORCE OUT OF ME.
I MEAN, IT ALWAYS HAS, BUT IT SEEMS LIKE IT'S HAPPENING FASTER NOW.
4/17/01 © 2001 United Feature Syndicate, Inc.
THEY NOTICED.
LifeSuck 3000

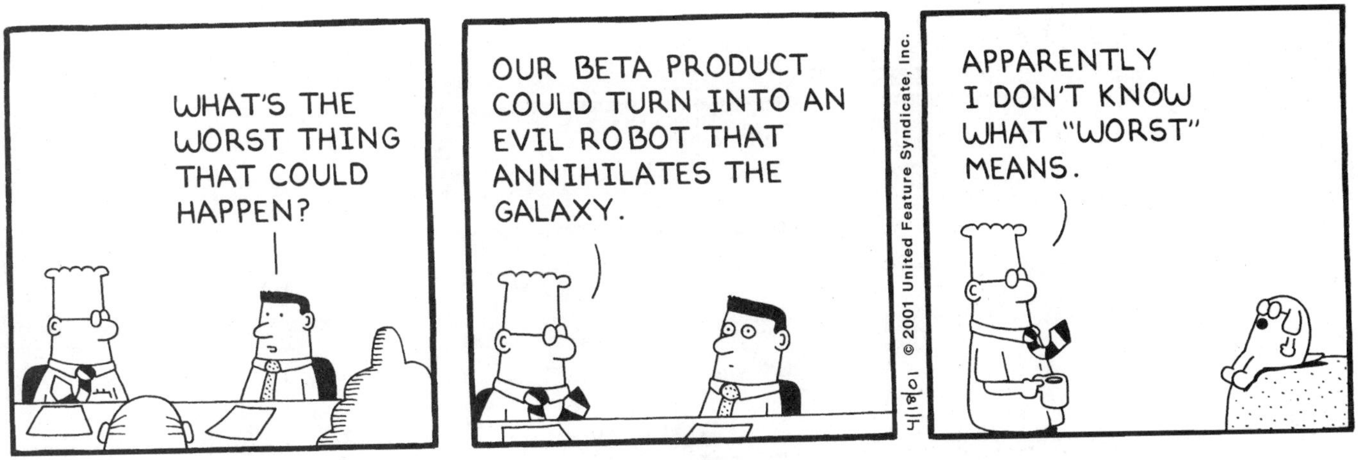
WHAT'S THE WORST THING THAT COULD HAPPEN?
OUR BETA PRODUCT COULD TURN INTO AN EVIL ROBOT THAT ANNIHILATES THE GALAXY.
4/18/01 © 2001 United Feature Syndicate, Inc.
APPARENTLY I DON'T KNOW WHAT "WORST" MEANS.

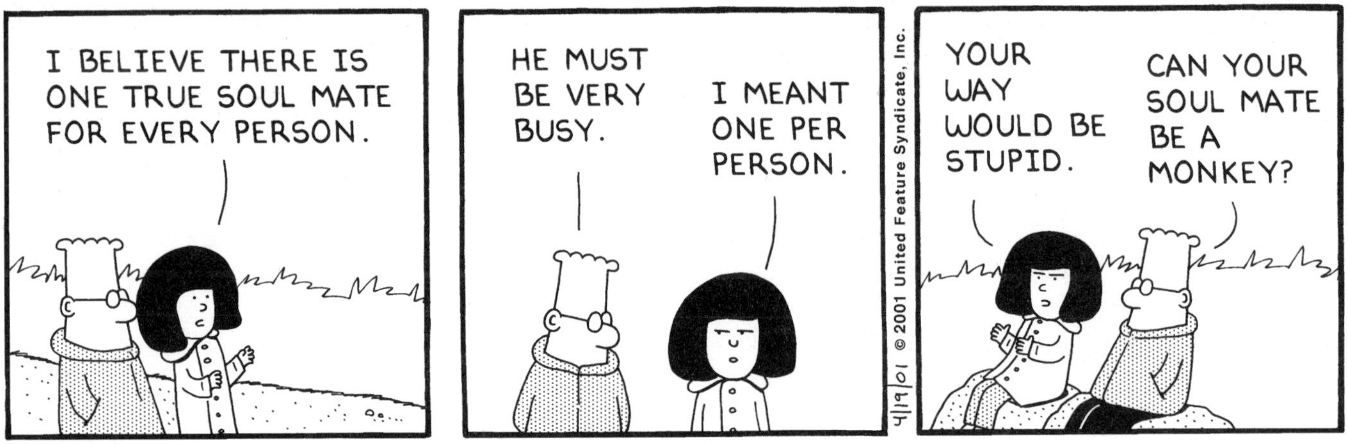
I BELIEVE THERE IS ONE TRUE SOUL MATE FOR EVERY PERSON.
HE MUST BE VERY BUSY.
I MEANT ONE PER PERSON.
4/19/01 © 2001 United Feature Syndicate, Inc.
YOUR WAY WOULD BE STUPID.
CAN YOUR SOUL MATE BE A MONKEY?

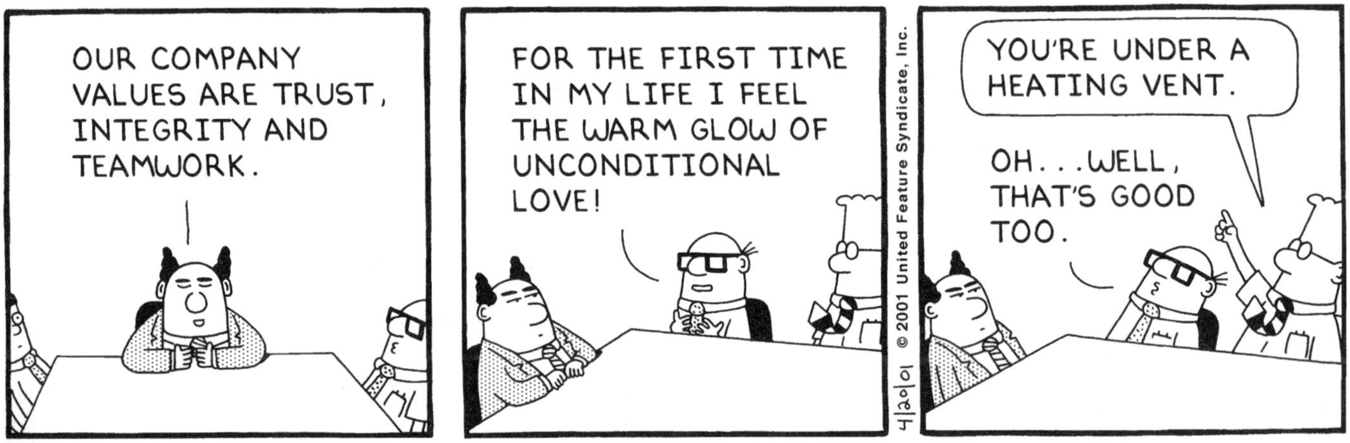
OUR COMPANY VALUES ARE TRUST, INTEGRITY AND TEAMWORK.
FOR THE FIRST TIME IN MY LIFE I FEEL THE WARM GLOW OF UNCONDITIONAL LOVE!
4/20/01 © 2001 United Feature Syndicate, Inc.
YOU'RE UNDER A HEATING VENT.
OH...WELL, THAT'S GOOD TOO.

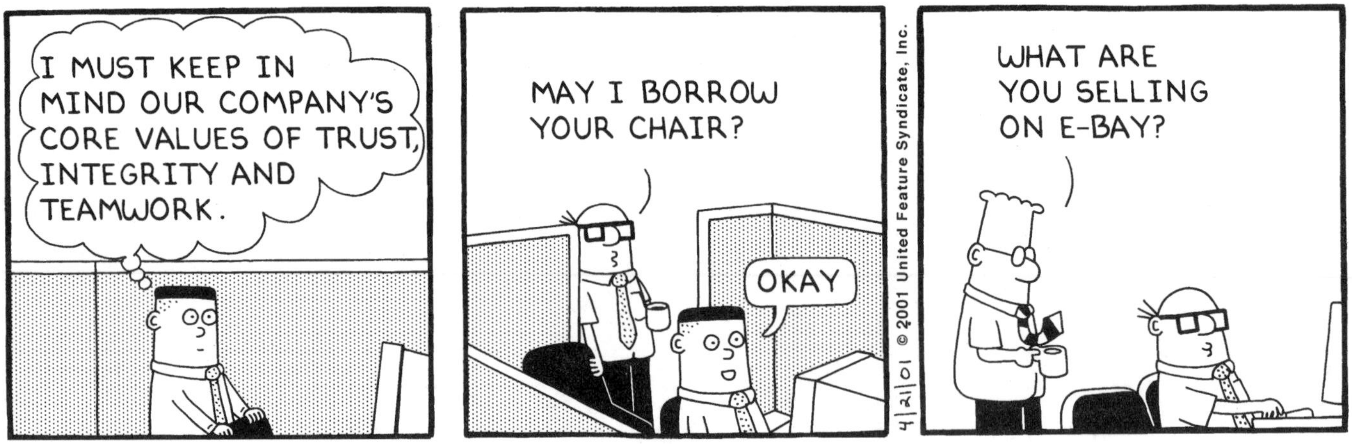
I MUST KEEP IN MIND OUR COMPANY'S CORE VALUES OF TRUST, INTEGRITY AND TEAMWORK.
MAY I BORROW YOUR CHAIR?
OKAY
4/21/01 © 2001 United Feature Syndicate, Inc.
WHAT ARE YOU SELLING ON E-BAY?

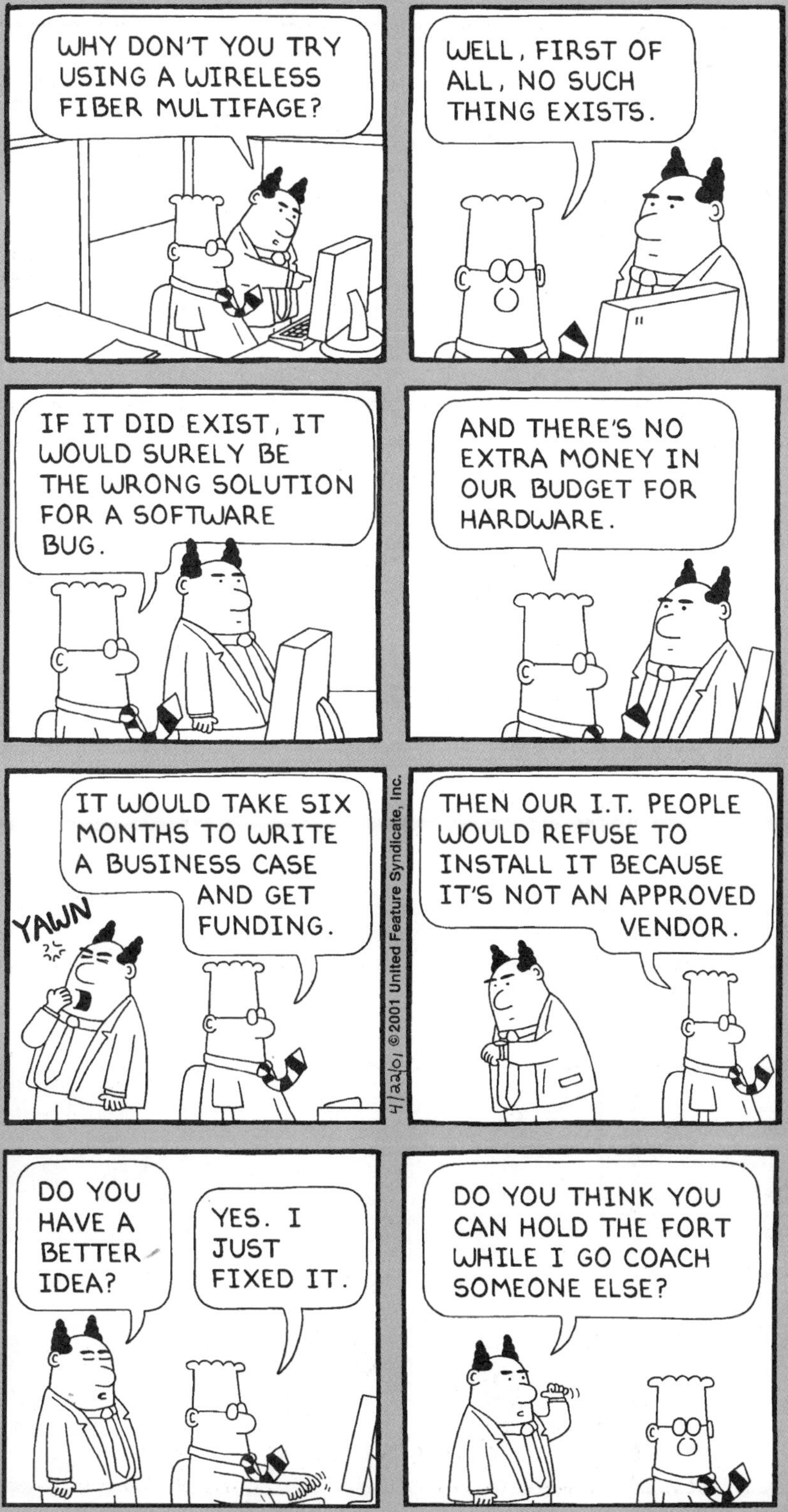
WHY DON'T YOU TRY USING A WIRELESS FIBER MULTIFAGE?
WELL, FIRST OF ALL, NO SUCH THING EXISTS.
IF IT DID EXIST, IT WOULD SURELY BE THE WRONG SOLUTION FOR A SOFTWARE BUG.
AND THERE'S NO EXTRA MONEY IN OUR BUDGET FOR HARDWARE.
IT WOULD TAKE SIX MONTHS TO WRITE A BUSINESS CASE AND GET FUNDING.
YAWN
4/22/01 © 2001 United Feature Syndicate, Inc.
THEN OUR I.T. PEOPLE WOULD REFUSE TO INSTALL IT BECAUSE IT'S NOT AN APPROVED VENDOR.
DO YOU HAVE A BETTER IDEA?
YES. I JUST FIXED IT.
DO YOU THINK YOU CAN HOLD THE FORT WHILE I GO COACH SOMEONE ELSE?

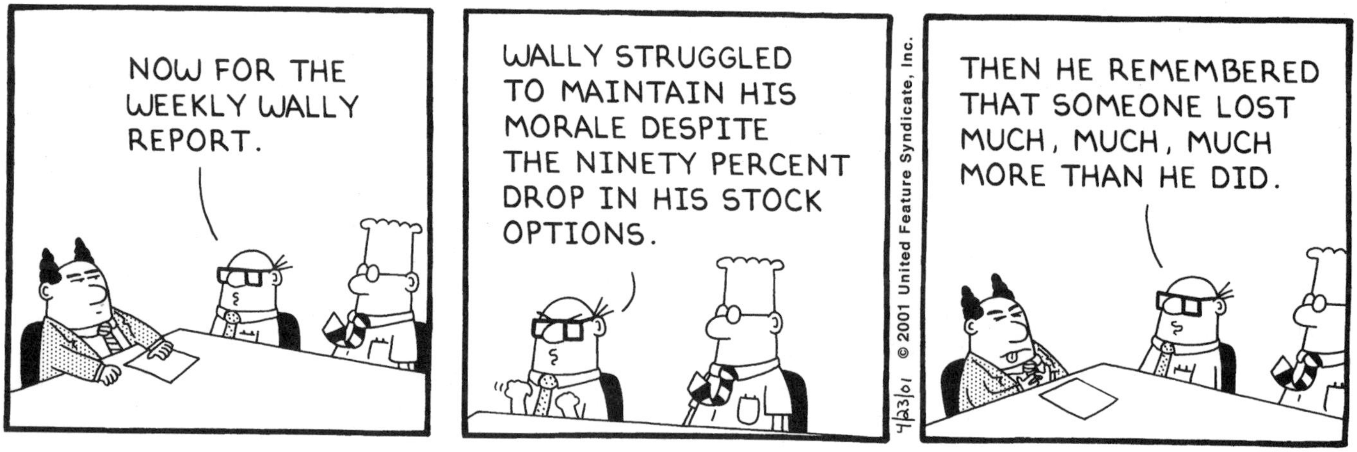
NOW FOR THE WEEKLY WALLY REPORT.
WALLY STRUGGLED TO MAINTAIN HIS MORALE DESPITE THE NINETY PERCENT DROP IN HIS STOCK OPTIONS.
4/23/01 © 2001 United Feature Syndicate, Inc.
THEN HE REMEMBERED THAT SOMEONE LOST MUCH, MUCH, MUCH MORE THAN HE DID.

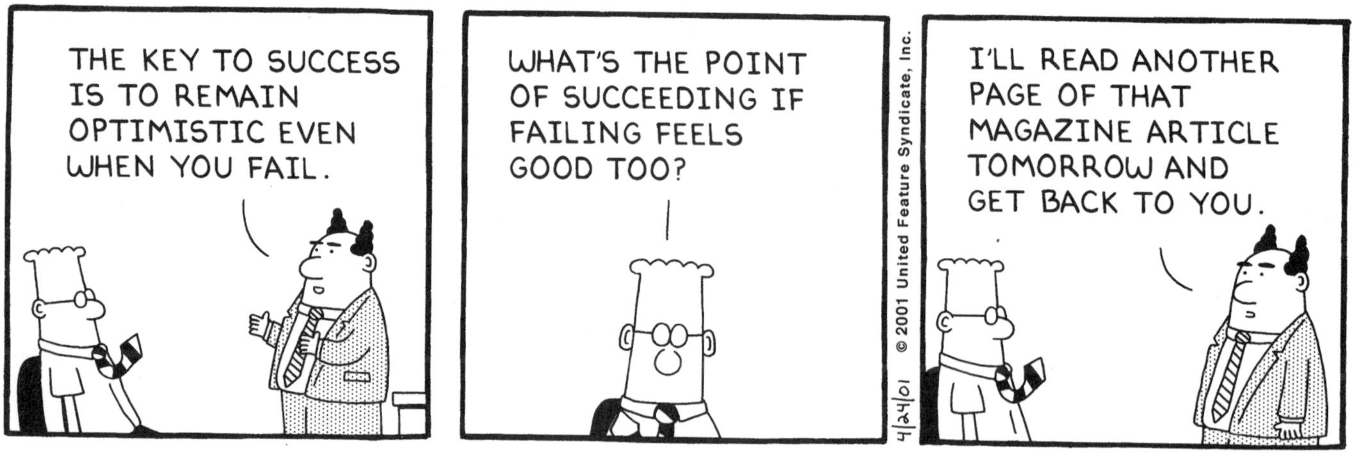
THE KEY TO SUCCESS IS TO REMAIN OPTIMISTIC EVEN WHEN YOU FAIL.
WHAT'S THE POINT OF SUCCEEDING IF FAILING FEELS GOOD TOO?
4/24/01 © 2001 United Feature Syndicate, Inc.
I'LL READ ANOTHER PAGE OF THAT MAGAZINE ARTICLE TOMORROW AND GET BACK TO YOU.

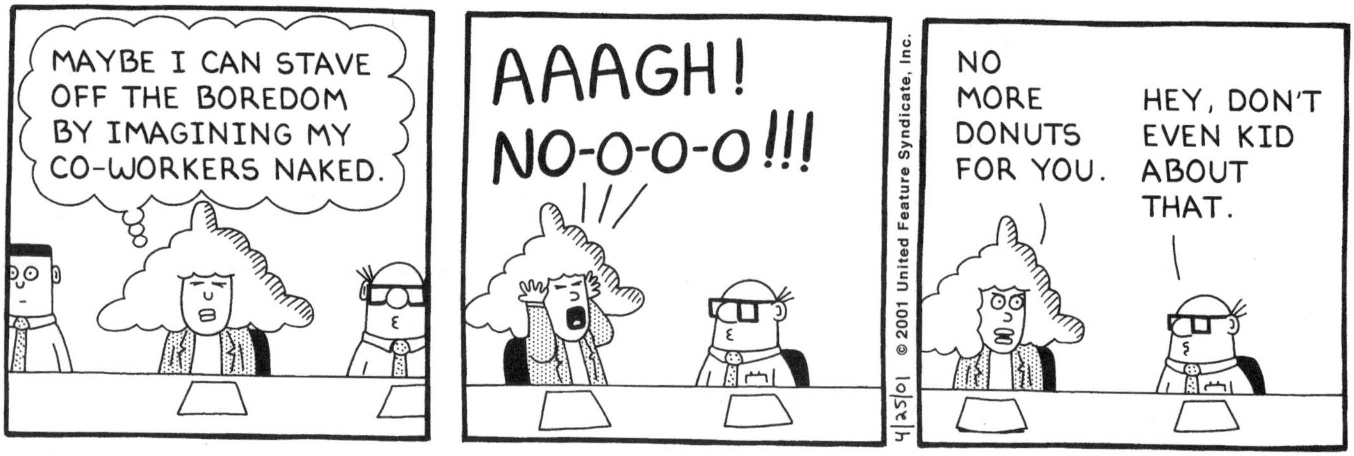
MAYBE I CAN STAVE OFF THE BOREDOM BY IMAGINING MY CO-WORKERS NAKED.
AAAGH! NO-O-O-O!!!
4/25/01 © 2001 United Feature Syndicate, Inc.
NO MORE DONUTS FOR YOU.
HEY, DON'T EVEN KID ABOUT THAT.

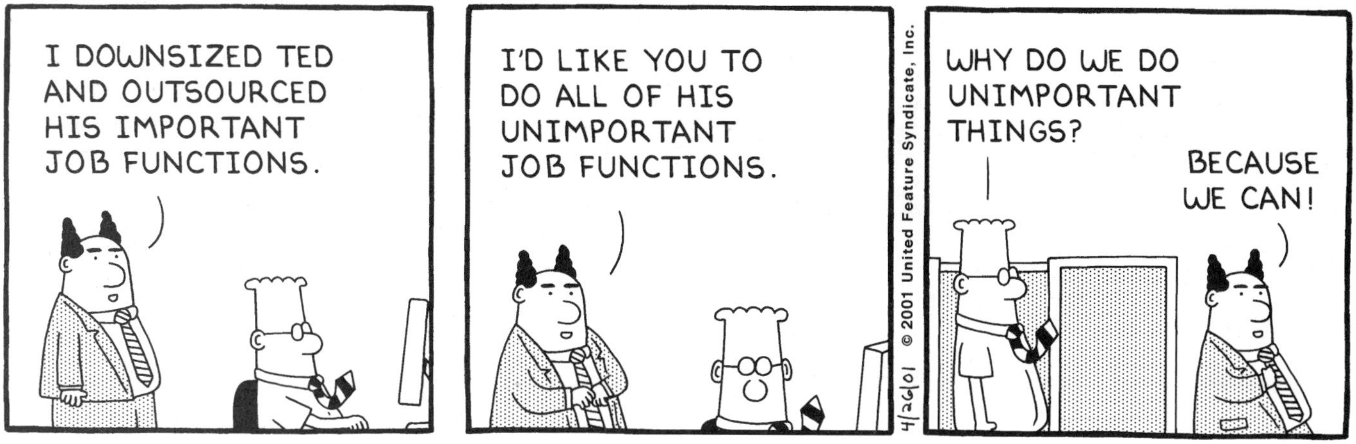
I DOWNSIZED TED AND OUTSOURCED HIS IMPORTANT JOB FUNCTIONS.
I'D LIKE YOU TO DO ALL OF HIS UNIMPORTANT JOB FUNCTIONS.
4/26/01 © 2001 United Feature Syndicate, Inc.
WHY DO WE DO UNIMPORTANT THINGS?
BECAUSE WE CAN!

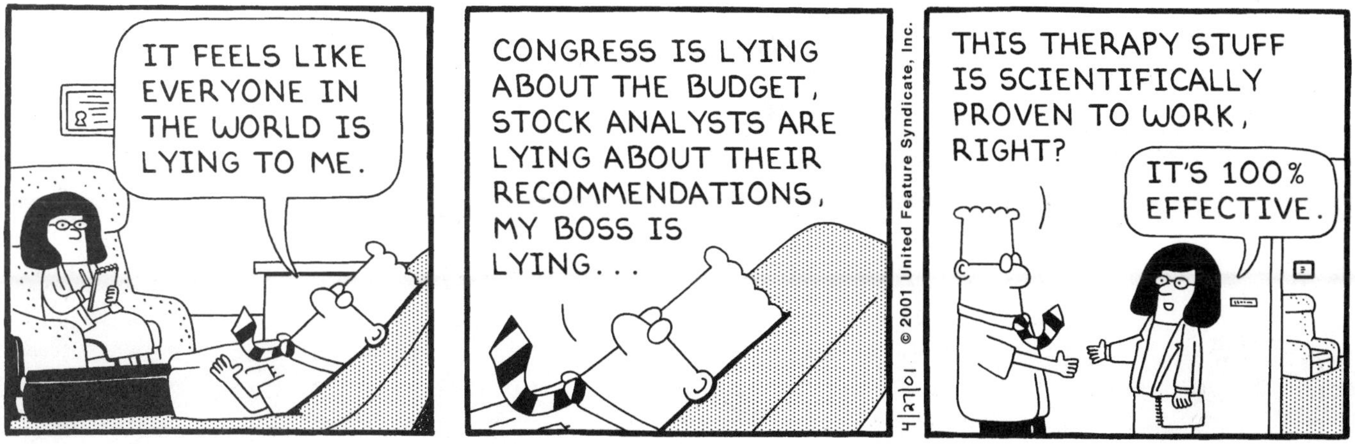
IT FEELS LIKE EVERYONE IN THE WORLD IS LYING TO ME.
CONGRESS IS LYING ABOUT THE BUDGET, STOCK ANALYSTS ARE LYING ABOUT THEIR RECOMMENDATIONS, MY BOSS IS LYING...
4/27/01 © 2001 United Feature Syndicate, Inc.
THIS THERAPY STUFF IS SCIENTIFICALLY PROVEN TO WORK, RIGHT?
IT'S 100% EFFECTIVE.

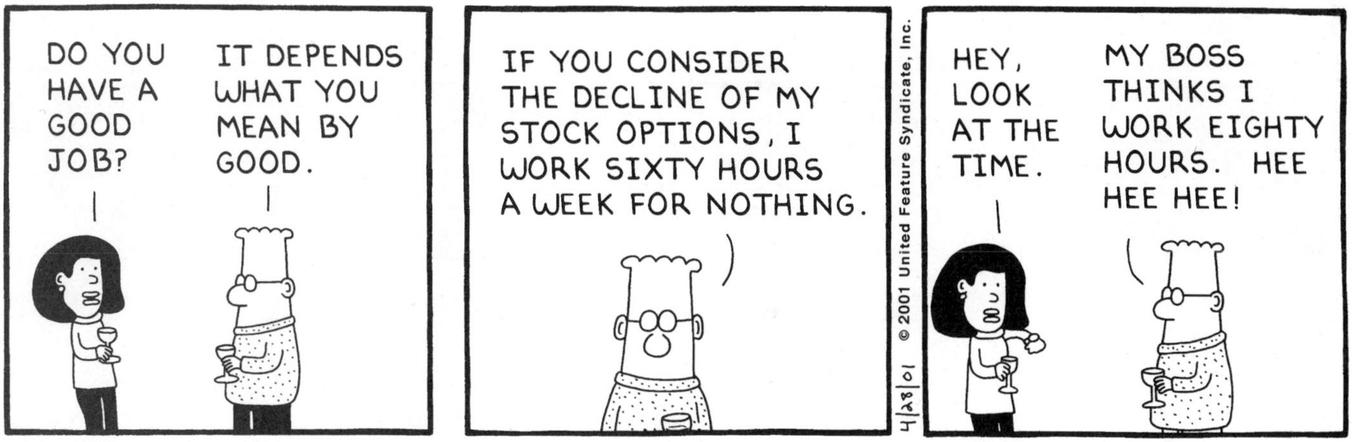
DO YOU HAVE A GOOD JOB?
IT DEPENDS WHAT YOU MEAN BY GOOD.
IF YOU CONSIDER THE DECLINE OF MY STOCK OPTIONS, I WORK SIXTY HOURS A WEEK FOR NOTHING.
4/28/01 © 2001 United Feature Syndicate, Inc.
HEY, LOOK AT THE TIME.
MY BOSS THINKS I WORK EIGHTY HOURS. HEE HEE HEE!

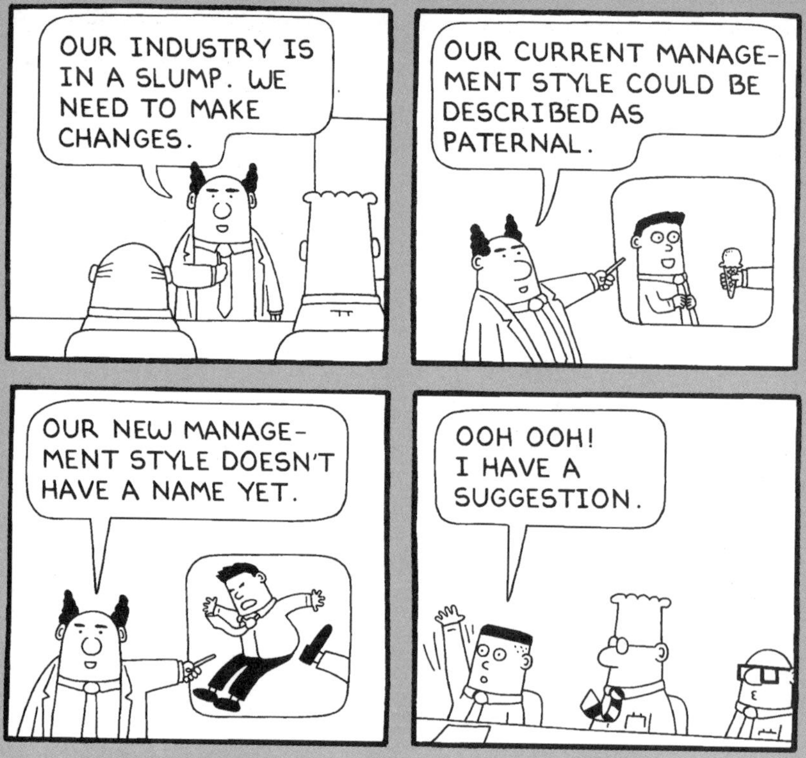
OUR INDUSTRY IS IN A SLUMP. WE NEED TO MAKE CHANGES.
OUR CURRENT MANAGEMENT STYLE COULD BE DESCRIBED AS PATERNAL.
OUR NEW MANAGEMENT STYLE DOESN'T HAVE A NAME YET.
OOH OOH! I HAVE A SUGGESTION.

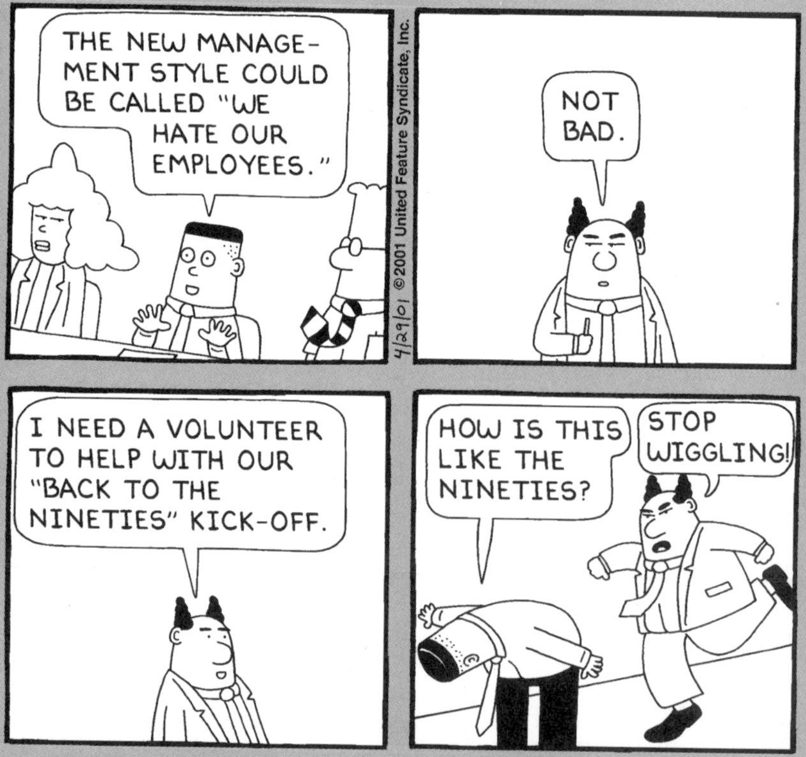
THE NEW MANAGEMENT STYLE COULD BE CALLED "WE HATE OUR EMPLOYEES."
4/29/01 ©2001 United Feature Syndicate, Inc.
NOT BAD.
I NEED A VOLUNTEER TO HELP WITH OUR "BACK TO THE NINETIES" KICK-OFF.
HOW IS THIS LIKE THE NINETIES?
STOP WIGGLING!

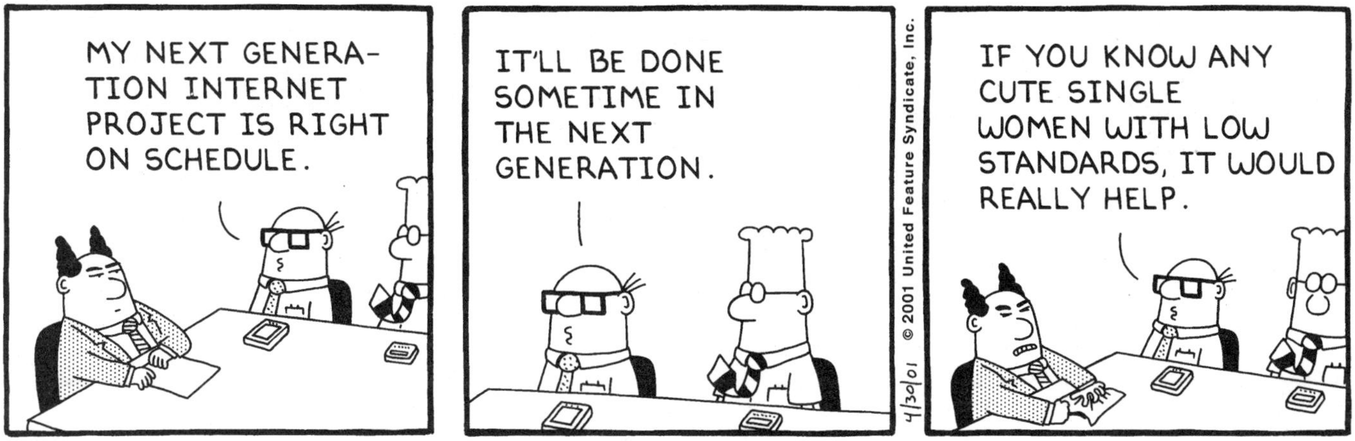
MY NEXT GENERATION INTERNET PROJECT IS RIGHT ON SCHEDULE.
IT'LL BE DONE SOMETIME IN THE NEXT GENERATION.
4/30/01 © 2001 United Feature Syndicate, Inc.
IF YOU KNOW ANY CUTE SINGLE WOMEN WITH LOW STANDARDS, IT WOULD REALLY HELP.

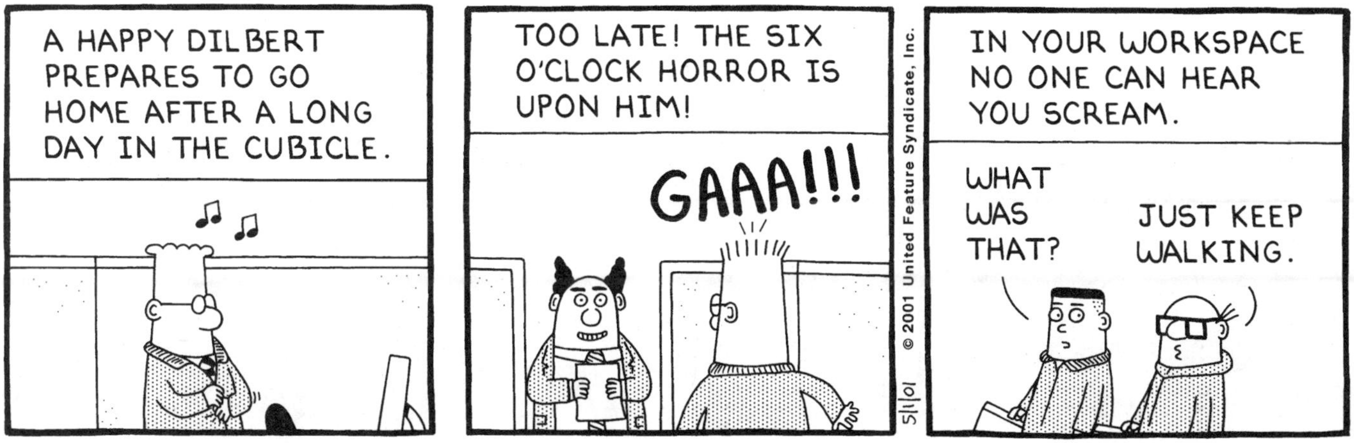
A HAPPY DILBERT PREPARES TO GO HOME AFTER A LONG DAY IN THE CUBICLE.
TOO LATE! THE SIX O'CLOCK HORROR IS UPON HIM!
GAAA!!!
5/1/01 © 2001 United Feature Syndicate, Inc.
IN YOUR WORKSPACE NO ONE CAN HEAR YOU SCREAM.
WHAT WAS THAT?
JUST KEEP WALKING.

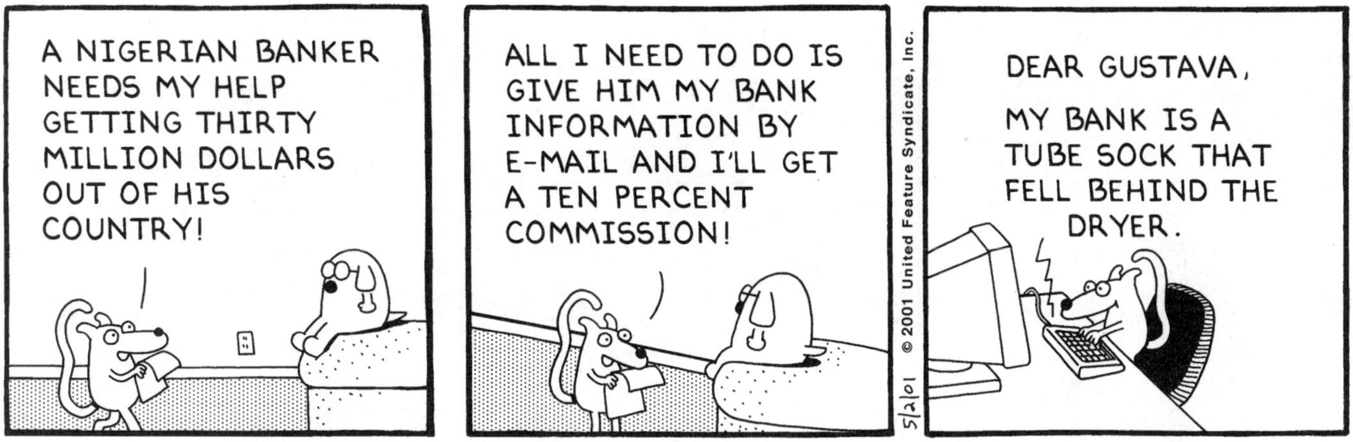
A NIGERIAN BANKER NEEDS MY HELP GETTING THIRTY MILLION DOLLARS OUT OF HIS COUNTRY!
ALL I NEED TO DO IS GIVE HIM MY BANK INFORMATION BY E-MAIL AND I'LL GET A TEN PERCENT COMMISSION!
5/2/01 © 2001 United Feature Syndicate, Inc.
DEAR GUSTAVA,
MY BANK IS A TUBE SOCK THAT FELL BEHIND THE DRYER.

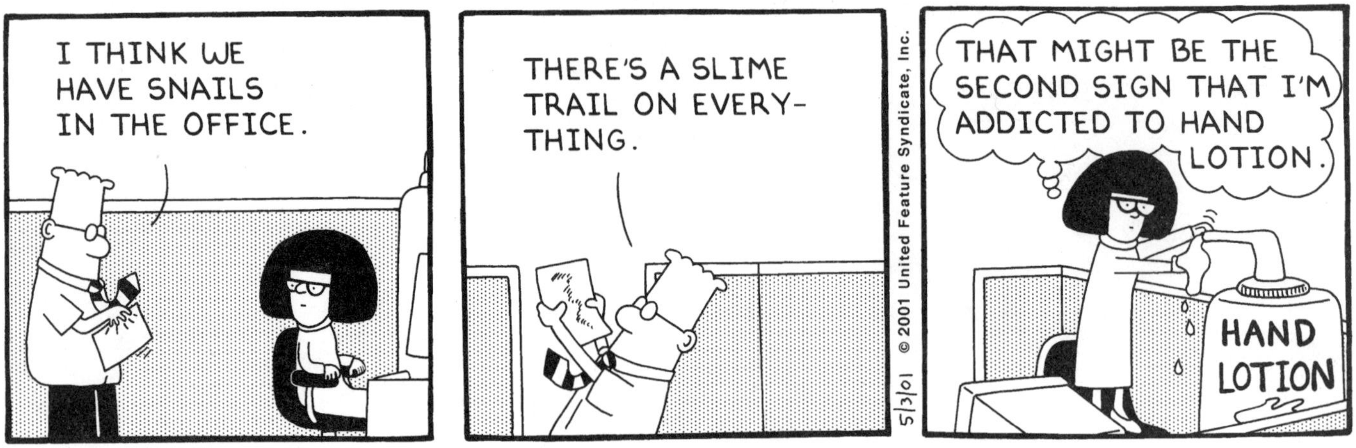
I THINK WE HAVE SNAILS IN THE OFFICE.
THERE'S A SLIME TRAIL ON EVERY-THING.
5/3/01 © 2001 United Feature Syndicate, Inc.
THAT MIGHT BE THE SECOND SIGN THAT I'M ADDICTED TO HAND LOTION.
HAND LOTION

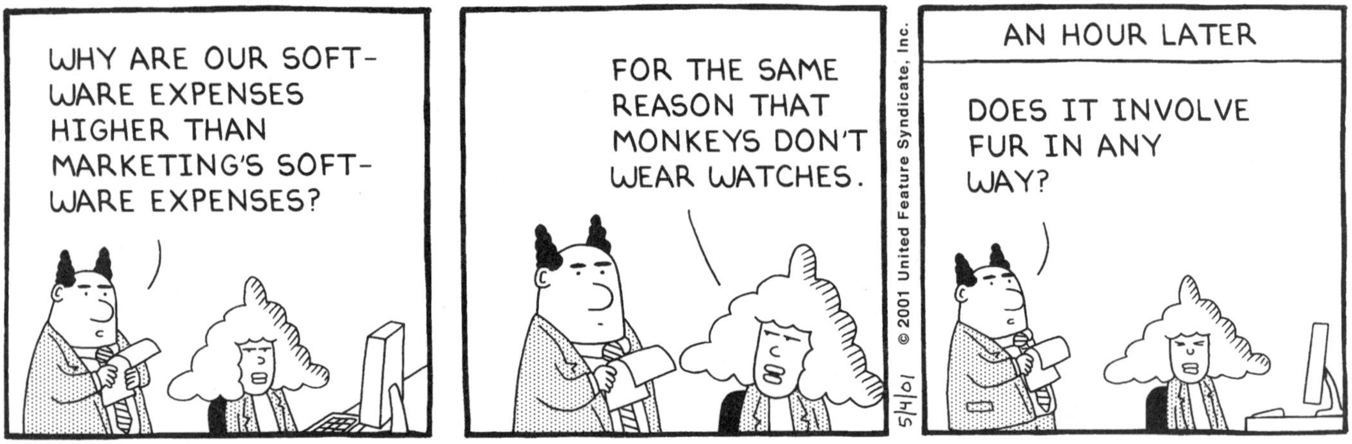
WHY ARE OUR SOFT-WARE EXPENSES HIGHER THAN MARKETING'S SOFT-WARE EXPENSES?
FOR THE SAME REASON THAT MONKEYS DON'T WEAR WATCHES.
5/4/01 © 2001 United Feature Syndicate, Inc.
AN HOUR LATER
DOES IT INVOLVE FUR IN ANY WAY?

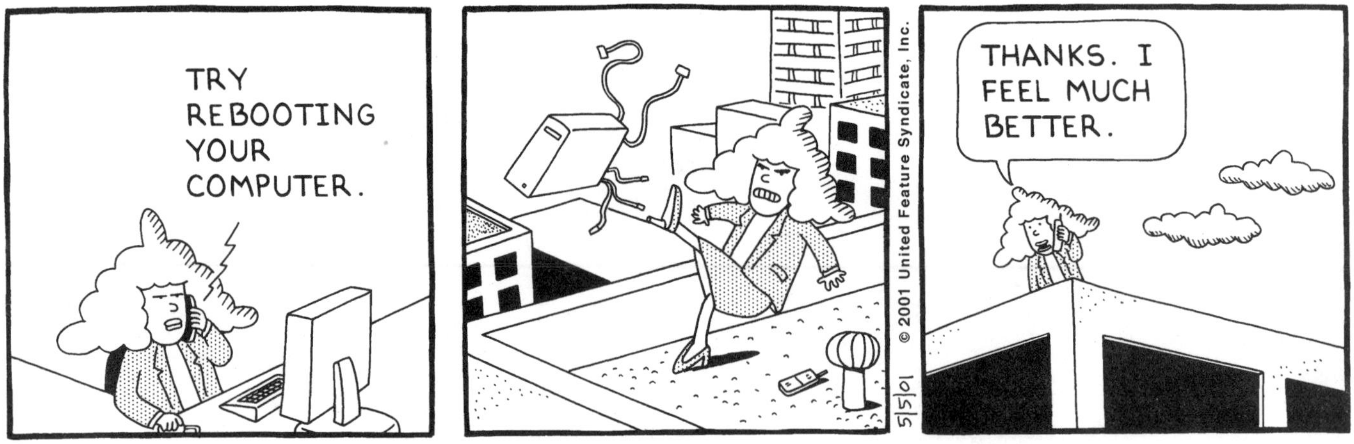
TRY REBOOTING YOUR COMPUTER.
5/5/01 © 2001 United Feature Syndicate, Inc.
THANKS. I FEEL MUCH BETTER.

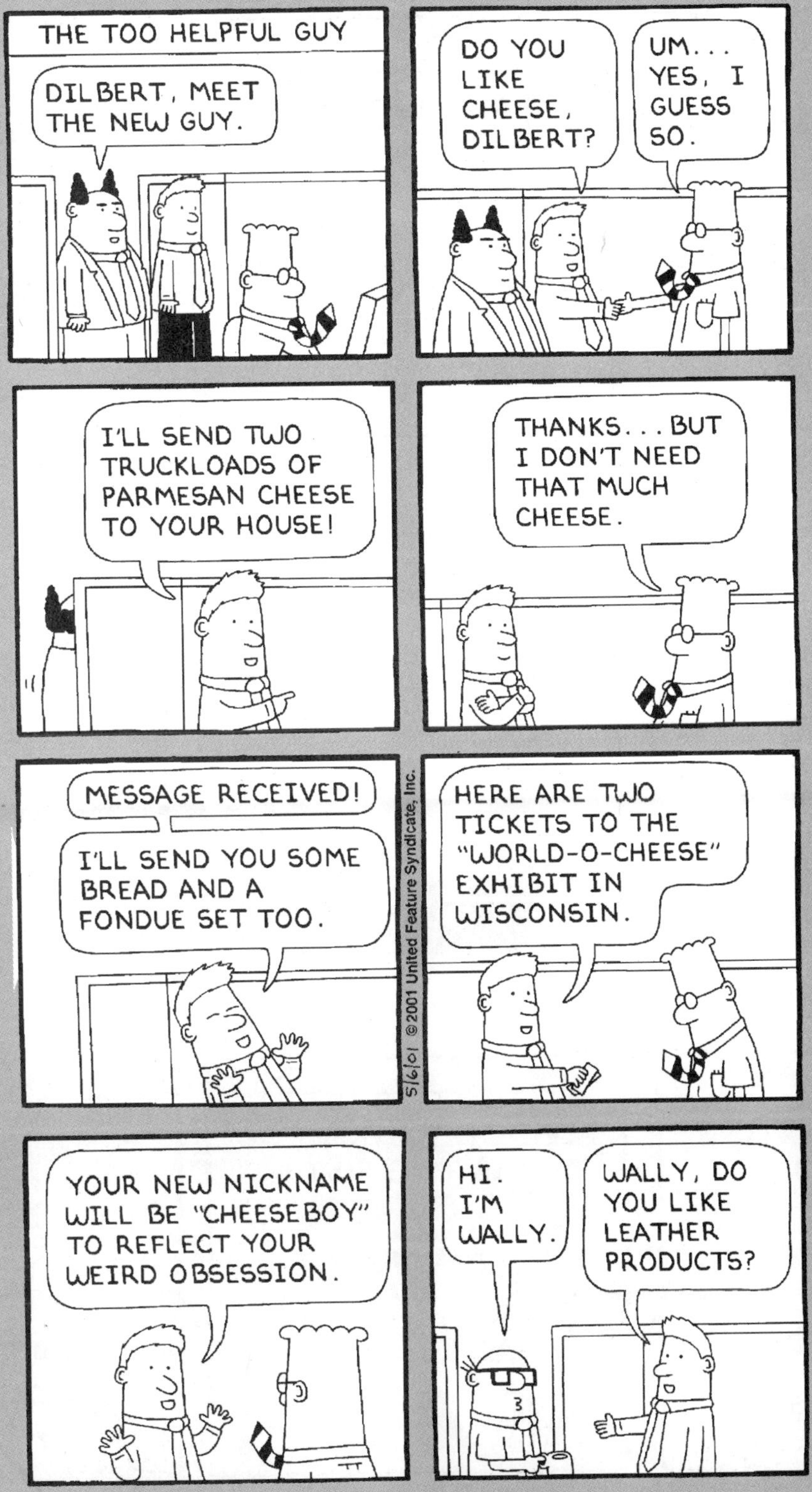
THE TOO HELPFUL GUY
DILBERT, MEET THE NEW GUY.
DO YOU LIKE CHEESE, DILBERT?
UM... YES, I GUESS SO.
I'LL SEND TWO TRUCKLOADS OF PARMESAN CHEESE TO YOUR HOUSE!
THANKS... BUT I DON'T NEED THAT MUCH CHEESE.
MESSAGE RECEIVED!
I'LL SEND YOU SOME BREAD AND A FONDUE SET TOO.
5/6/01 ©2001 United Feature Syndicate, Inc.
HERE ARE TWO TICKETS TO THE "WORLD-O-CHEESE" EXHIBIT IN WISCONSIN.
YOUR NEW NICKNAME WILL BE "CHEESEBOY" TO REFLECT YOUR WEIRD OBSESSION.
HI. I'M WALLY.
WALLY, DO YOU LIKE LEATHER PRODUCTS?

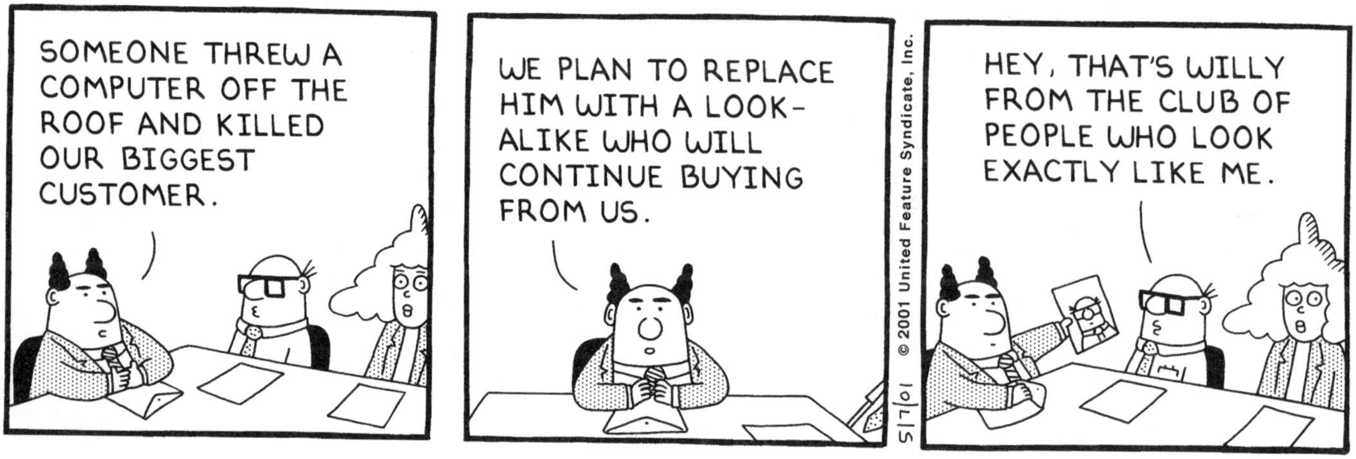
SOMEONE THREW A COMPUTER OFF THE ROOF AND KILLED OUR BIGGEST CUSTOMER.
WE PLAN TO REPLACE HIM WITH A LOOK-ALIKE WHO WILL CONTINUE BUYING FROM US.
HEY, THAT'S WILLY FROM THE CLUB OF PEOPLE WHO LOOK EXACTLY LIKE ME.
© 2001 United Feature Syndicate, Inc.
5/7/01

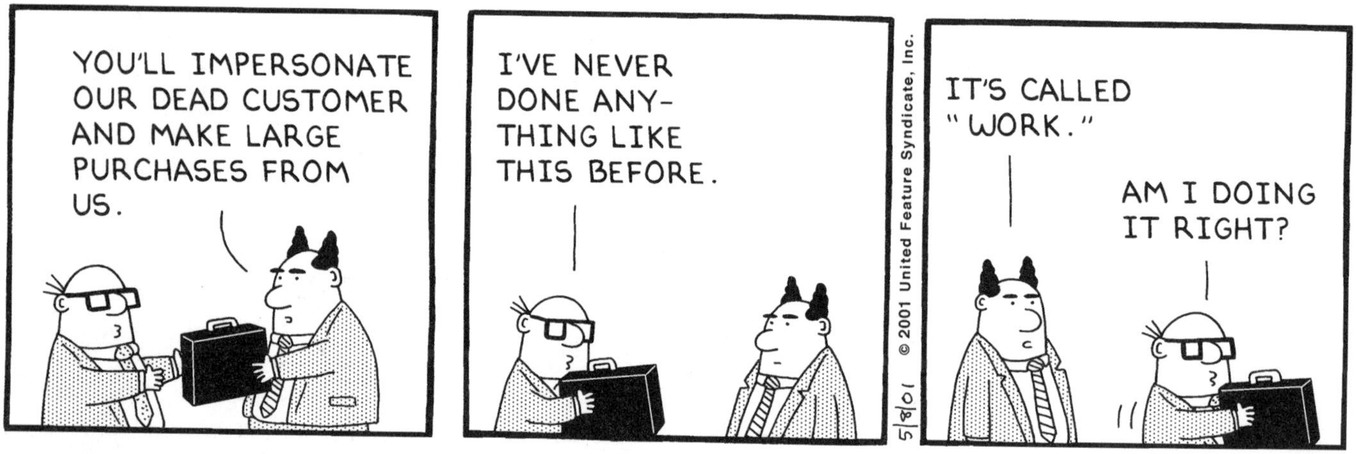
YOU'LL IMPERSONATE OUR DEAD CUSTOMER AND MAKE LARGE PURCHASES FROM US.
I'VE NEVER DONE ANYTHING LIKE THIS BEFORE.
IT'S CALLED "WORK."
AM I DOING IT RIGHT?
© 2001 United Feature Syndicate, Inc.
5/8/01

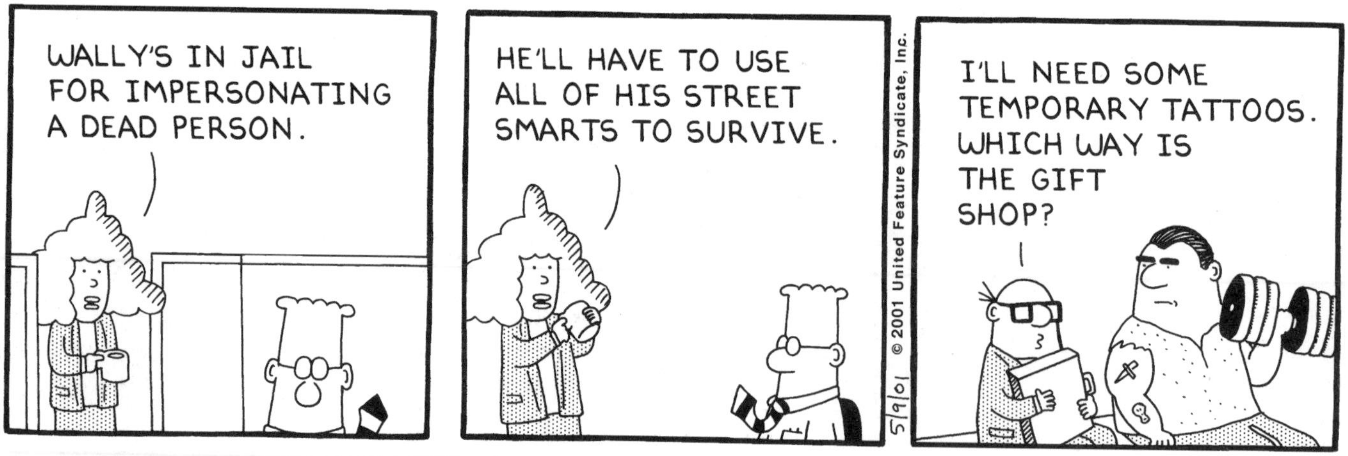
WALLY'S IN JAIL FOR IMPERSONATING A DEAD PERSON.
HE'LL HAVE TO USE ALL OF HIS STREET SMARTS TO SURVIVE.
I'LL NEED SOME TEMPORARY TATTOOS. WHICH WAY IS THE GIFT SHOP?
© 2001 United Feature Syndicate, Inc.
5/9/01

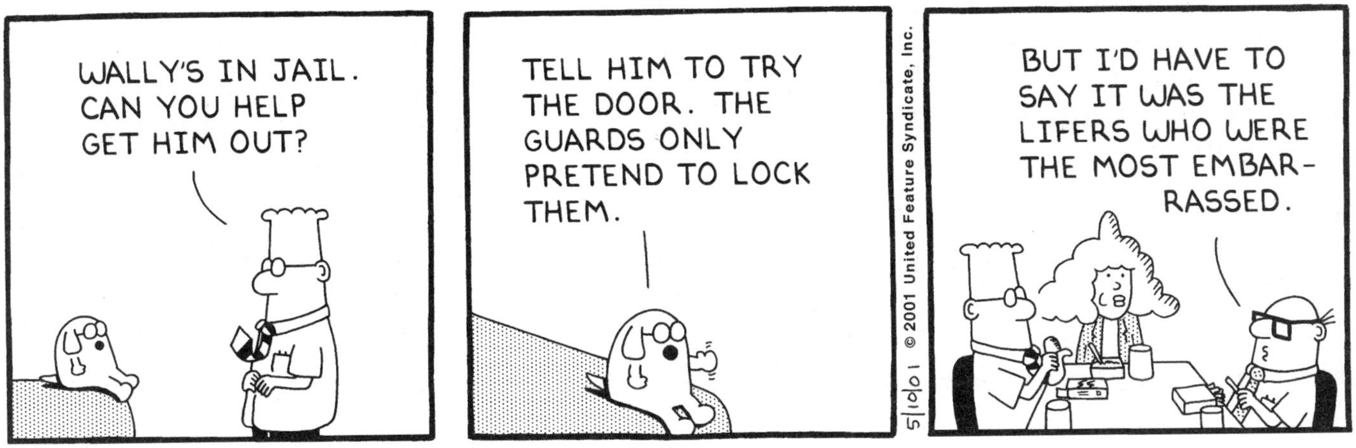
WALLY'S IN JAIL. CAN YOU HELP GET HIM OUT?
TELL HIM TO TRY THE DOOR. THE GUARDS ONLY PRETEND TO LOCK THEM.
5/10/01 © 2001 United Feature Syndicate, Inc.
BUT I'D HAVE TO SAY IT WAS THE LIFERS WHO WERE THE MOST EMBAR-RASSED.

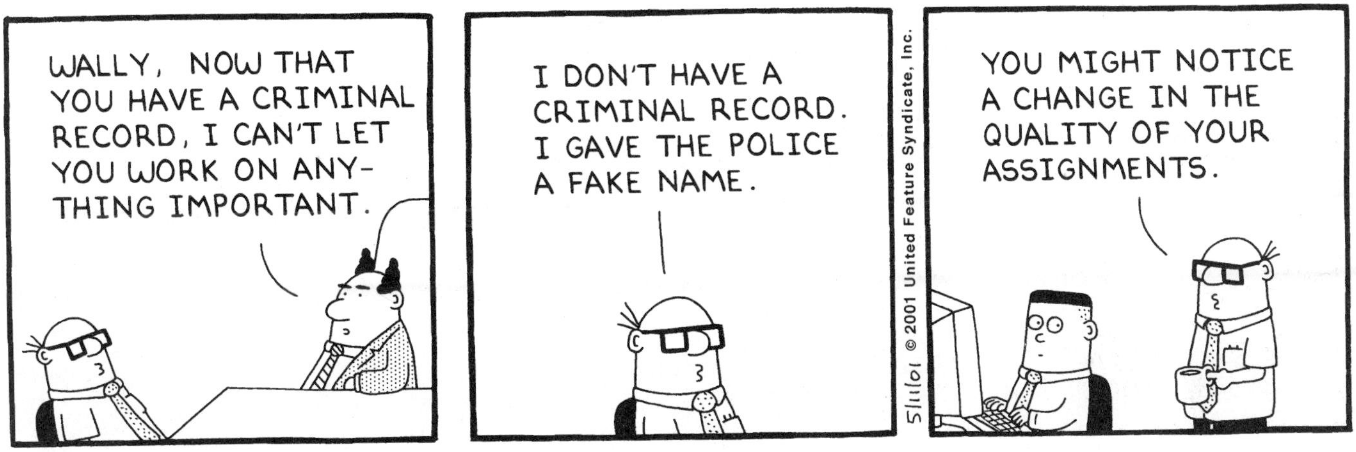
WALLY, NOW THAT YOU HAVE A CRIMINAL RECORD, I CAN'T LET YOU WORK ON ANY-THING IMPORTANT.
I DON'T HAVE A CRIMINAL RECORD. I GAVE THE POLICE A FAKE NAME.
5/11/01 © 2001 United Feature Syndicate, Inc.
YOU MIGHT NOTICE A CHANGE IN THE QUALITY OF YOUR ASSIGNMENTS.

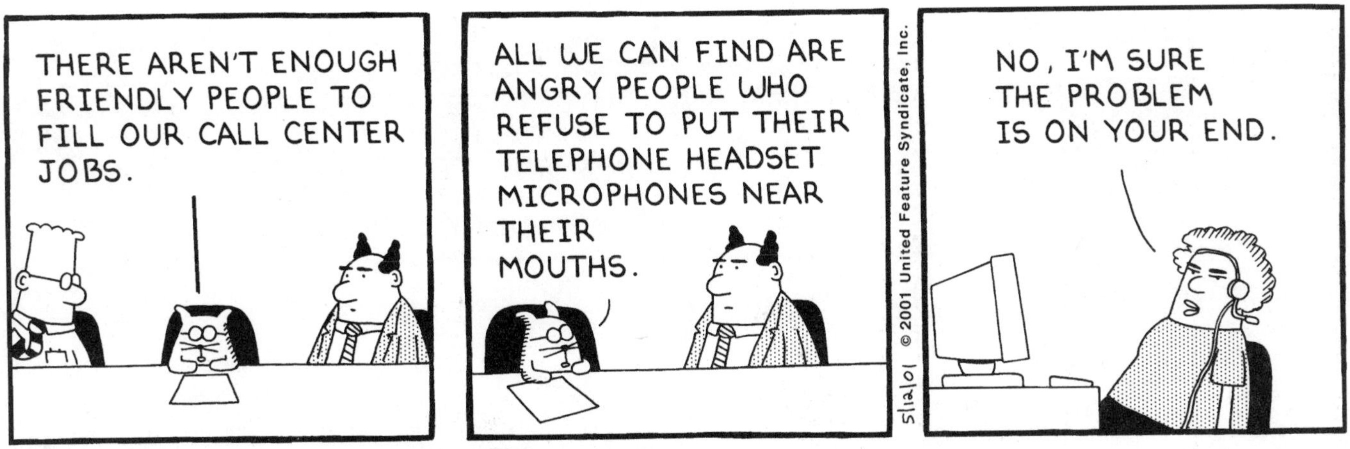
THERE AREN'T ENOUGH FRIENDLY PEOPLE TO FILL OUR CALL CENTER JOBS.
ALL WE CAN FIND ARE ANGRY PEOPLE WHO REFUSE TO PUT THEIR TELEPHONE HEADSET MICROPHONES NEAR THEIR MOUTHS.
5/12/01 © 2001 United Feature Syndicate, Inc.
NO, I'M SURE THE PROBLEM IS ON YOUR END.

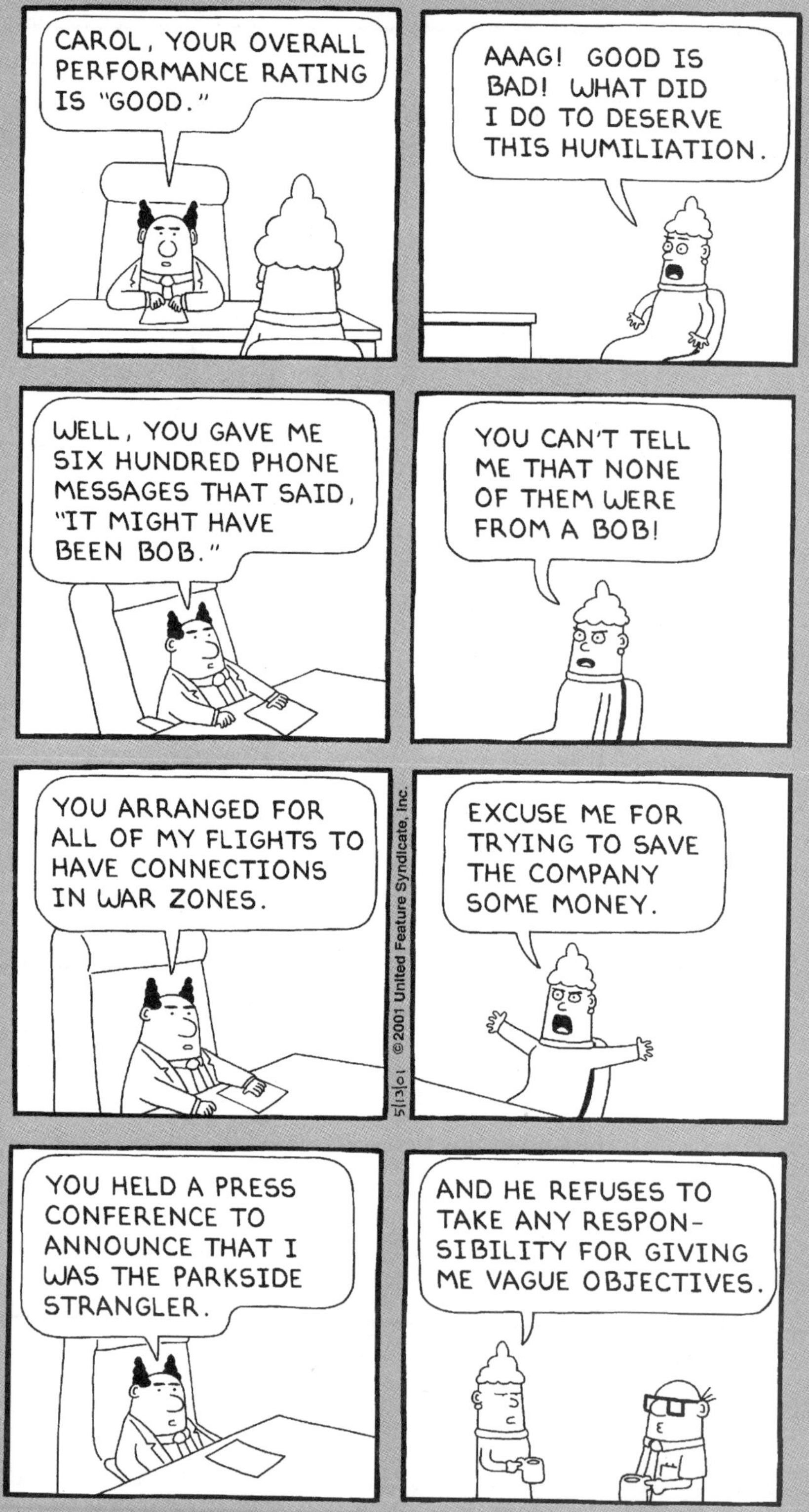
CAROL, YOUR OVERALL PERFORMANCE RATING IS "GOOD."
AAAG! GOOD IS BAD! WHAT DID I DO TO DESERVE THIS HUMILIATION.
WELL, YOU GAVE ME SIX HUNDRED PHONE MESSAGES THAT SAID, "IT MIGHT HAVE BEEN BOB."
YOU CAN'T TELL ME THAT NONE OF THEM WERE FROM A BOB!
YOU ARRANGED FOR ALL OF MY FLIGHTS TO HAVE CONNECTIONS IN WAR ZONES.
EXCUSE ME FOR TRYING TO SAVE THE COMPANY SOME MONEY.
YOU HELD A PRESS CONFERENCE TO ANNOUNCE THAT I WAS THE PARKSIDE STRANGLER.
AND HE REFUSES TO TAKE ANY RESPON- SIBILITY FOR GIVING ME VAGUE OBJECTIVES.
5/13/01 ©2001 United Feature Syndicate, Inc.

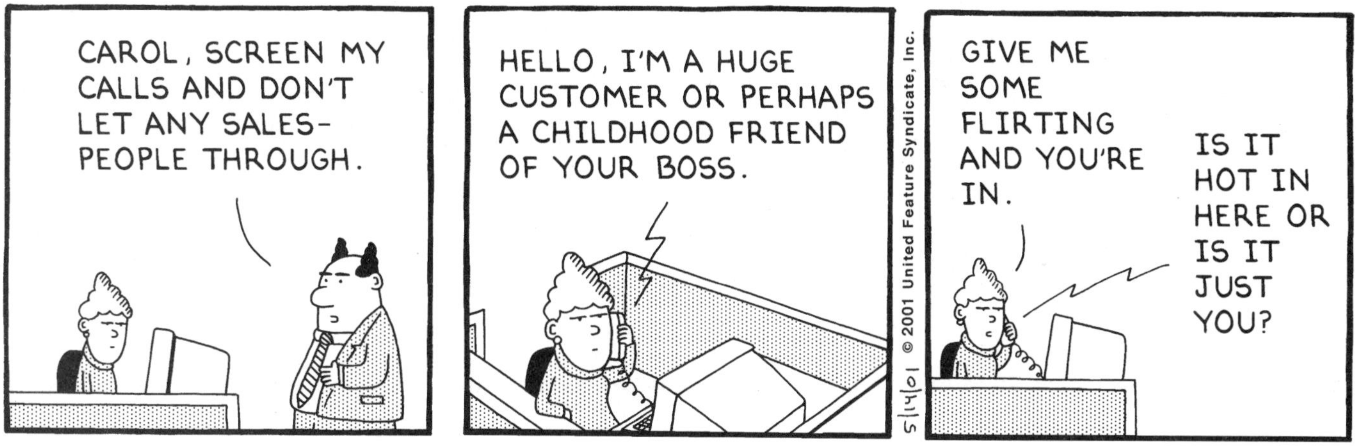
CAROL, SCREEN MY CALLS AND DON'T LET ANY SALES-PEOPLE THROUGH.
HELLO, I'M A HUGE CUSTOMER OR PERHAPS A CHILDHOOD FRIEND OF YOUR BOSS.
5/14/01 © 2001 United Feature Syndicate, Inc.
GIVE ME SOME FLIRTING AND YOU'RE IN.
IS IT HOT IN HERE OR IS IT JUST YOU?

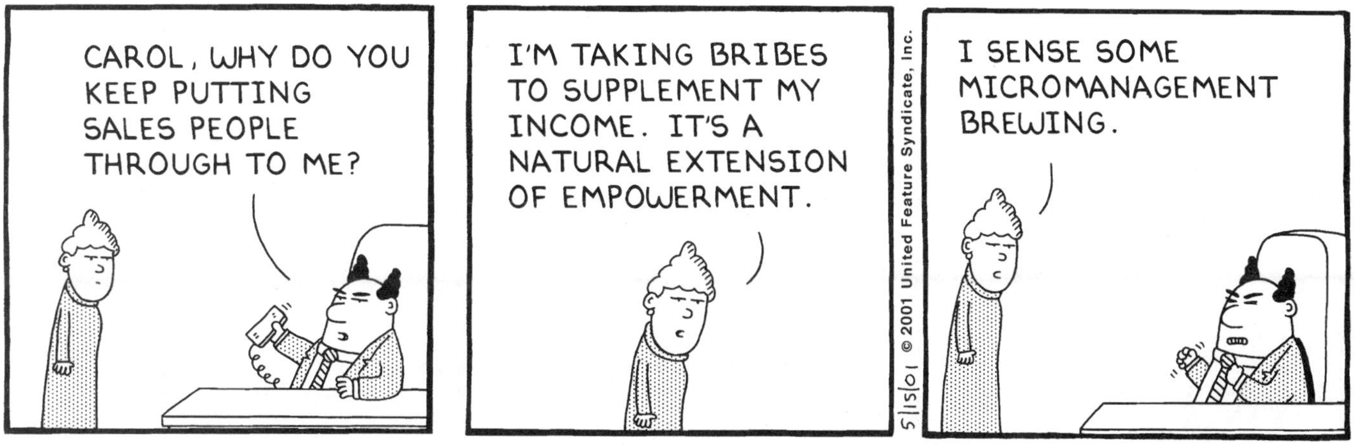
CAROL, WHY DO YOU KEEP PUTTING SALES PEOPLE THROUGH TO ME?
I'M TAKING BRIBES TO SUPPLEMENT MY INCOME. IT'S A NATURAL EXTENSION OF EMPOWERMENT.
5/15/01 © 2001 United Feature Syndicate, Inc.
I SENSE SOME MICROMANAGEMENT BREWING.

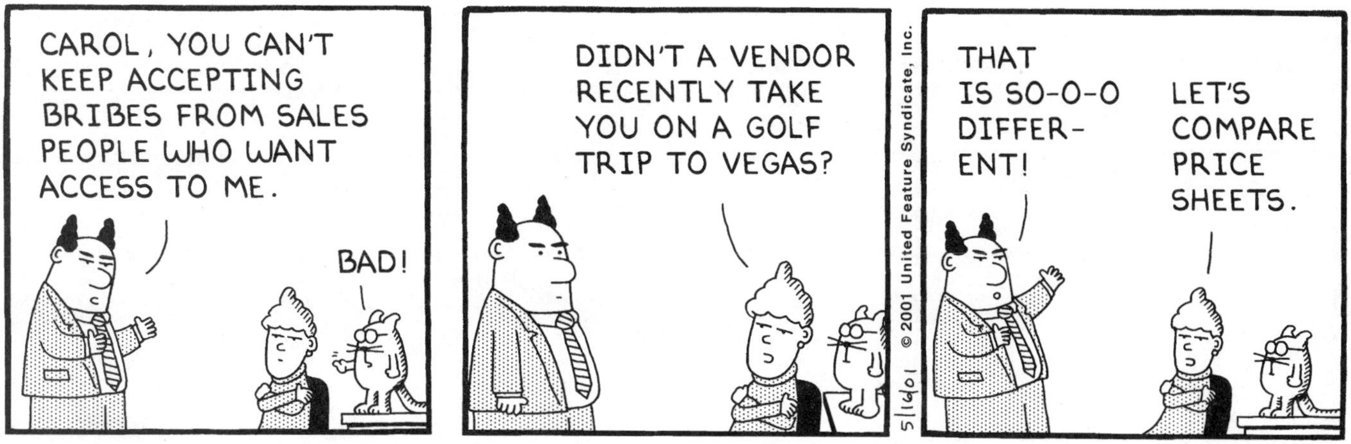
CAROL, YOU CAN'T KEEP ACCEPTING BRIBES FROM SALES PEOPLE WHO WANT ACCESS TO ME.
BAD!
DIDN'T A VENDOR RECENTLY TAKE YOU ON A GOLF TRIP TO VEGAS?
5/16/01 © 2001 United Feature Syndicate, Inc.
THAT IS SO-O-O DIFFER-ENT!
LET'S COMPARE PRICE SHEETS.

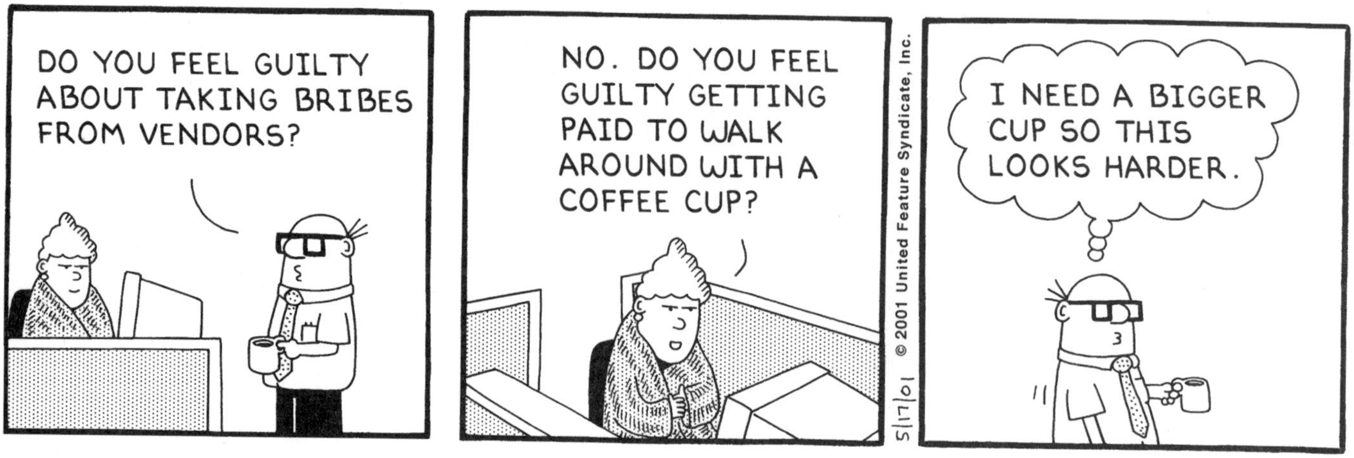
DO YOU FEEL GUILTY ABOUT TAKING BRIBES FROM VENDORS?
NO. DO YOU FEEL GUILTY GETTING PAID TO WALK AROUND WITH A COFFEE CUP?
I NEED A BIGGER CUP SO THIS LOOKS HARDER.
5/17/01 © 2001 United Feature Syndicate, Inc.

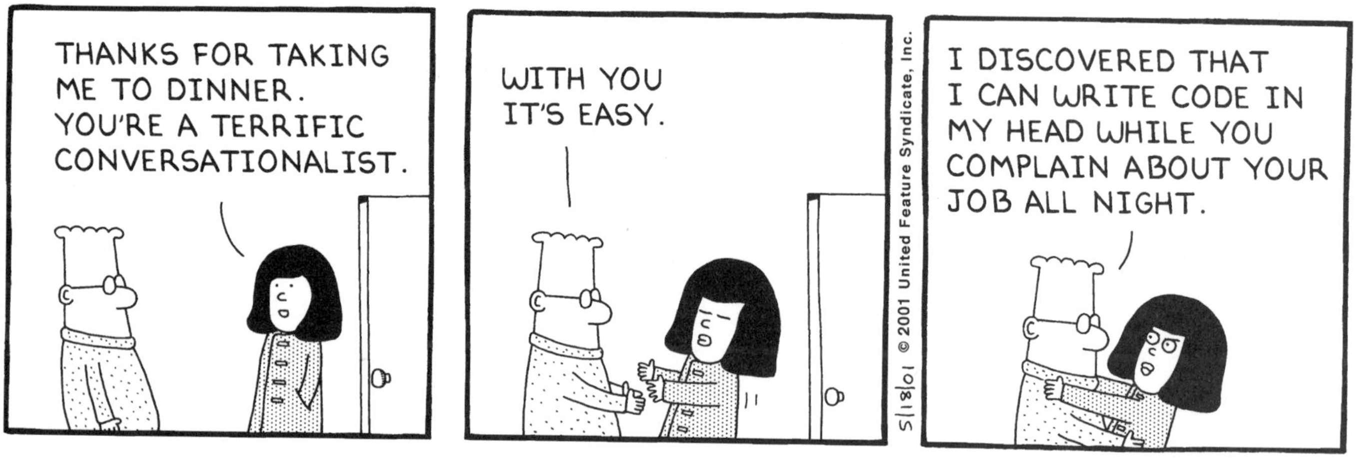
THANKS FOR TAKING ME TO DINNER. YOU'RE A TERRIFIC CONVERSATIONALIST.
WITH YOU IT'S EASY.
I DISCOVERED THAT I CAN WRITE CODE IN MY HEAD WHILE YOU COMPLAIN ABOUT YOUR JOB ALL NIGHT.
5/18/01 © 2001 United Feature Syndicate, Inc.

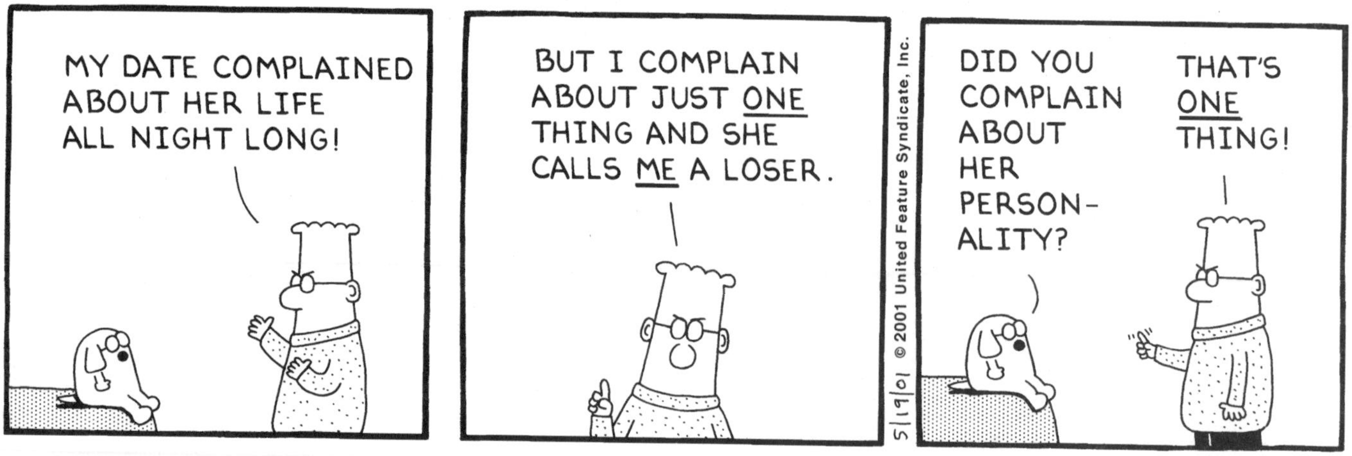
MY DATE COMPLAINED ABOUT HER LIFE ALL NIGHT LONG!
BUT I COMPLAIN ABOUT JUST ONE THING AND SHE CALLS ME A LOSER.
DID YOU COMPLAIN ABOUT HER PERSON-ALITY?
THAT'S ONE THING!
5/19/01 © 2001 United Feature Syndicate, Inc.

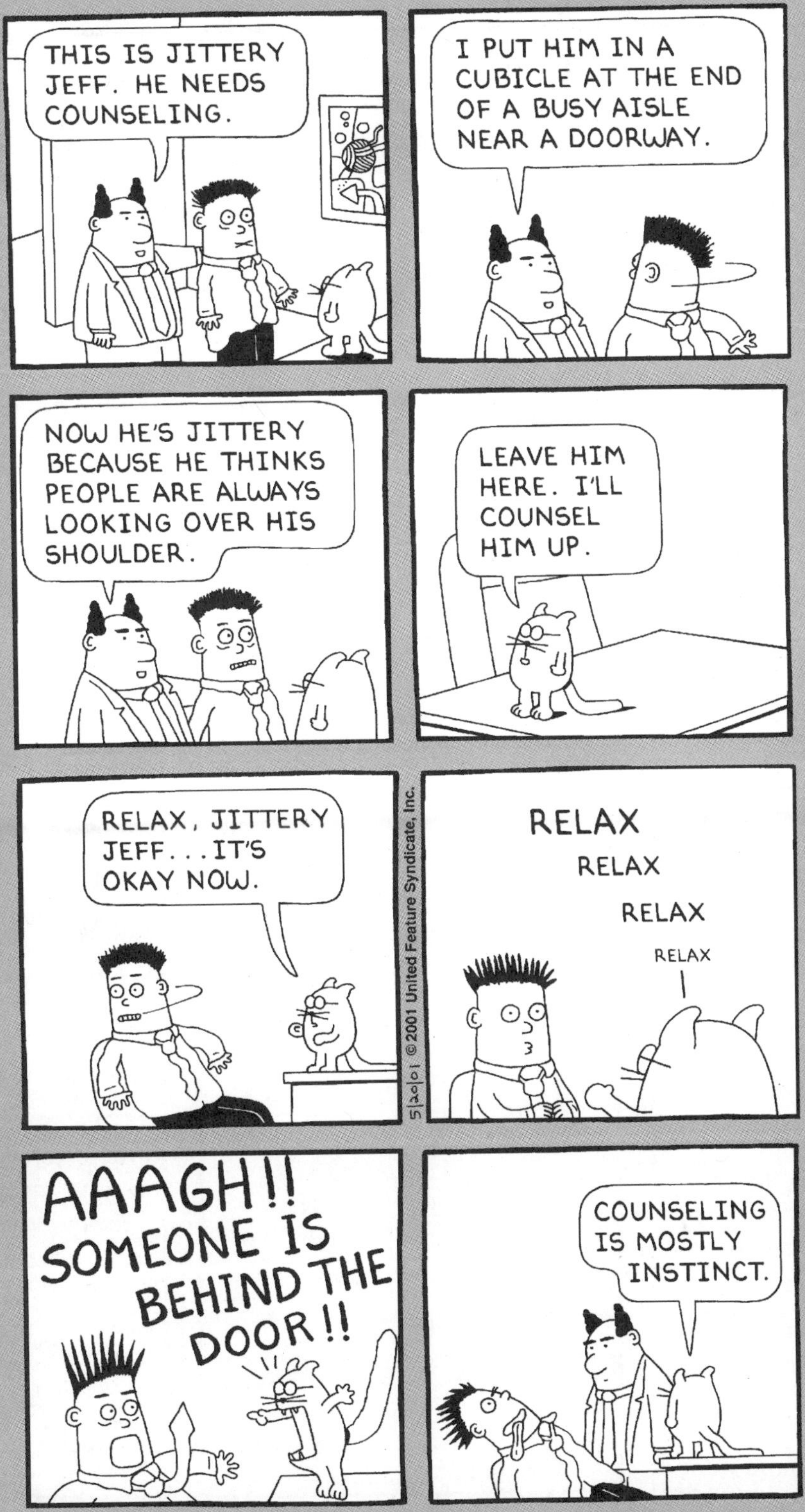
THIS IS JITTERY JEFF. HE NEEDS COUNSELING.
I PUT HIM IN A CUBICLE AT THE END OF A BUSY AISLE NEAR A DOORWAY.
NOW HE'S JITTERY BECAUSE HE THINKS PEOPLE ARE ALWAYS LOOKING OVER HIS SHOULDER.
LEAVE HIM HERE. I'LL COUNSEL HIM UP.
RELAX, JITTERY JEFF...IT'S OKAY NOW.
5/20/01 ©2001 United Feature Syndicate, Inc.
RELAX
RELAX
RELAX
RELAX
AAAGH!! SOMEONE IS BEHIND THE DOOR!!
COUNSELING IS MOSTLY INSTINCT.

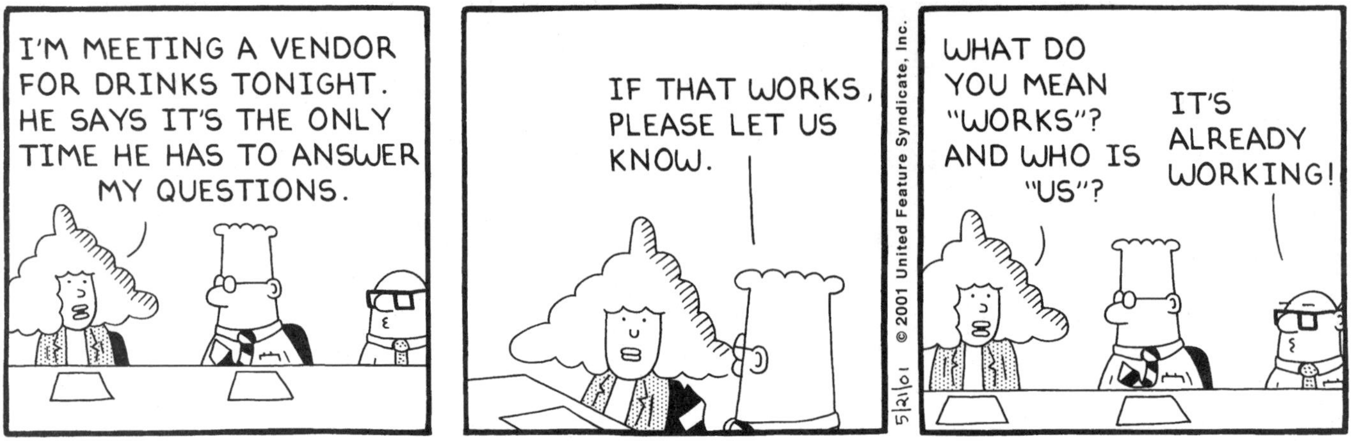
I'M MEETING A VENDOR FOR DRINKS TONIGHT. HE SAYS IT'S THE ONLY TIME HE HAS TO ANSWER MY QUESTIONS.
IF THAT WORKS, PLEASE LET US KNOW.
5/21/01 © 2001 United Feature Syndicate, Inc.
WHAT DO YOU MEAN "WORKS"? AND WHO IS "US"?
IT'S ALREADY WORKING!

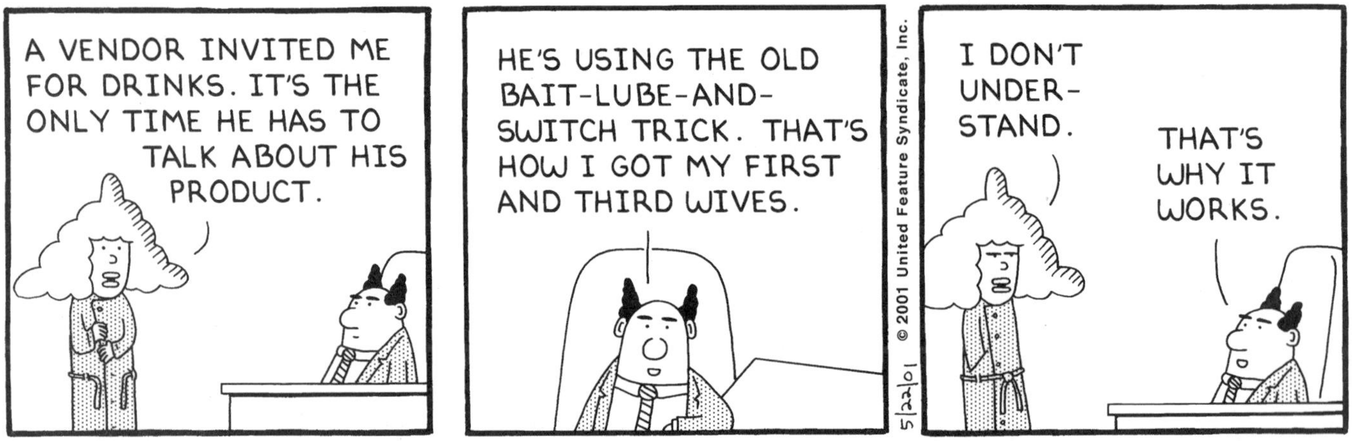
A VENDOR INVITED ME FOR DRINKS. IT'S THE ONLY TIME HE HAS TO TALK ABOUT HIS PRODUCT.
HE'S USING THE OLD BAIT-LUBE-AND-SWITCH TRICK. THAT'S HOW I GOT MY FIRST AND THIRD WIVES.
5/22/01 © 2001 United Feature Syndicate, Inc.
I DON'T UNDER-STAND.
THAT'S WHY IT WORKS.

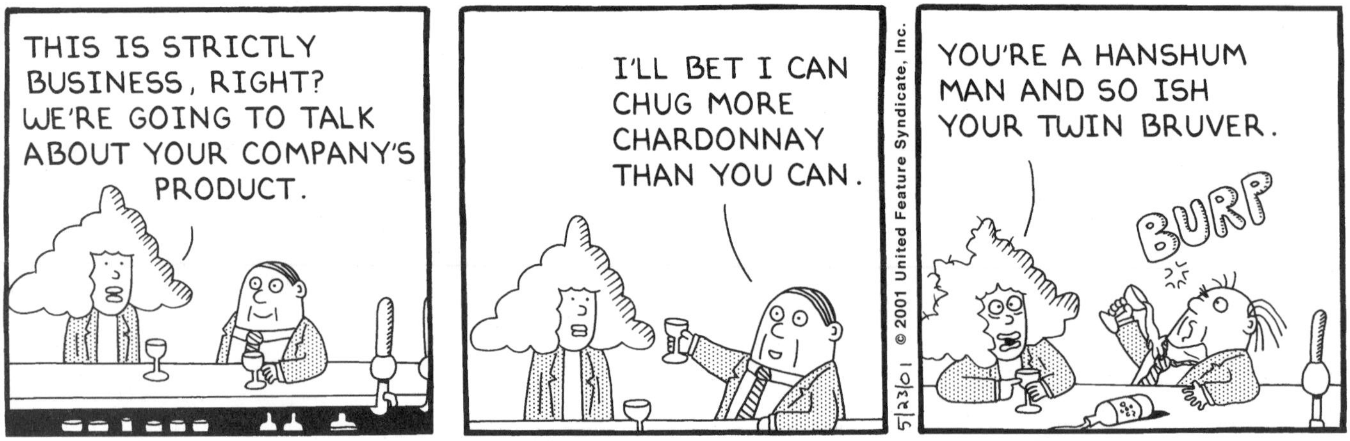
THIS IS STRICTLY BUSINESS, RIGHT? WE'RE GOING TO TALK ABOUT YOUR COMPANY'S PRODUCT.
I'LL BET I CAN CHUG MORE CHARDONNAY THAN YOU CAN.
5/23/01 © 2001 United Feature Syndicate, Inc.
YOU'RE A HANSHUM MAN AND SO ISH YOUR TWIN BRUVER.
BURP

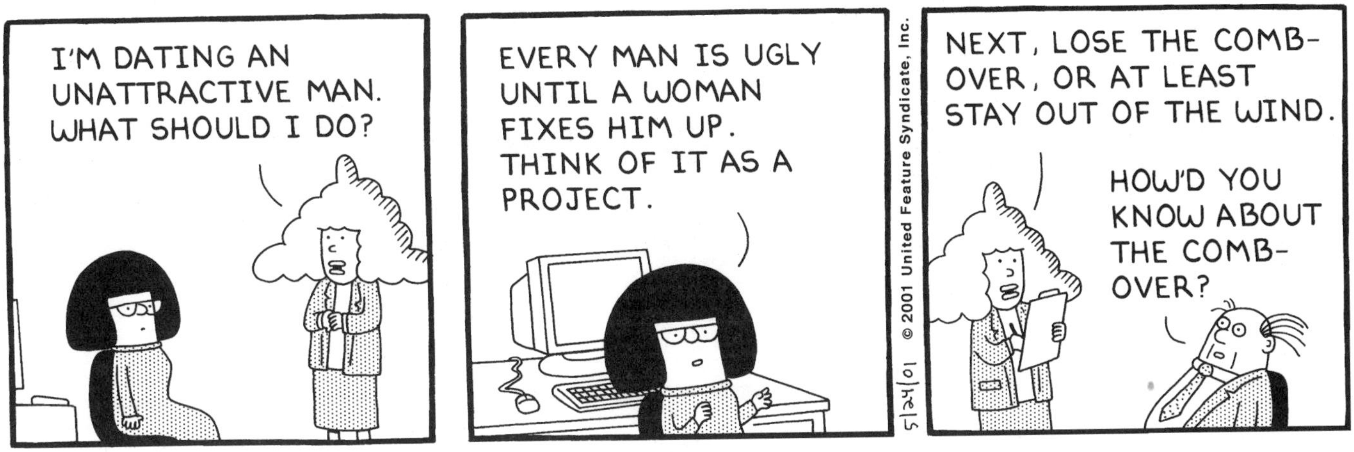
I'M DATING AN UNATTRACTIVE MAN. WHAT SHOULD I DO?
EVERY MAN IS UGLY UNTIL A WOMAN FIXES HIM UP. THINK OF IT AS A PROJECT.
5/24/01
© 2001 United Feature Syndicate, Inc.
NEXT, LOSE THE COMB-OVER, OR AT LEAST STAY OUT OF THE WIND.
HOW'D YOU KNOW ABOUT THE COMB-OVER?

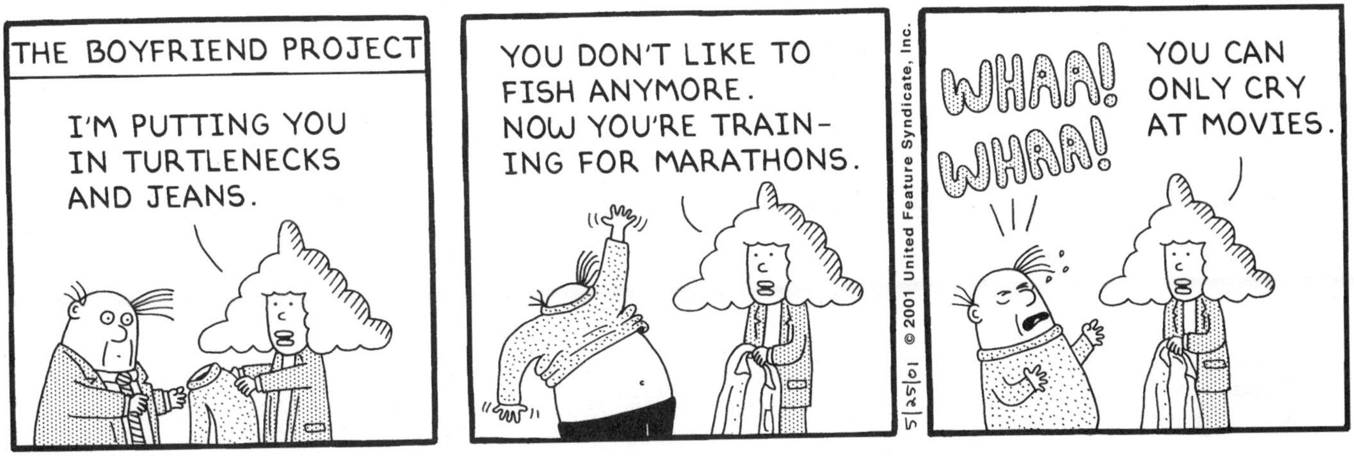
THE BOYFRIEND PROJECT
I'M PUTTING YOU IN TURTLENECKS AND JEANS.
YOU DON'T LIKE TO FISH ANYMORE. NOW YOU'RE TRAIN-ING FOR MARATHONS.
5/25/01
© 2001 United Feature Syndicate, Inc.
WHAA! WHAA!
YOU CAN ONLY CRY AT MOVIES.

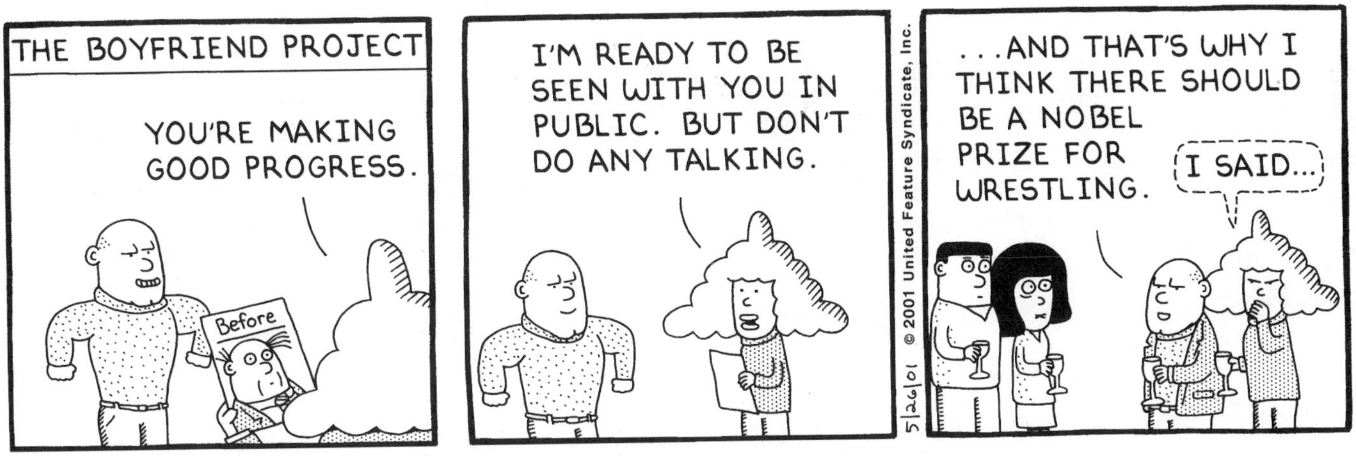
THE BOYFRIEND PROJECT
YOU'RE MAKING GOOD PROGRESS.
Before
I'M READY TO BE SEEN WITH YOU IN PUBLIC. BUT DON'T DO ANY TALKING.
5/26/01
© 2001 United Feature Syndicate, Inc.
...AND THAT'S WHY I THINK THERE SHOULD BE A NOBEL PRIZE FOR WRESTLING.
I SAID...

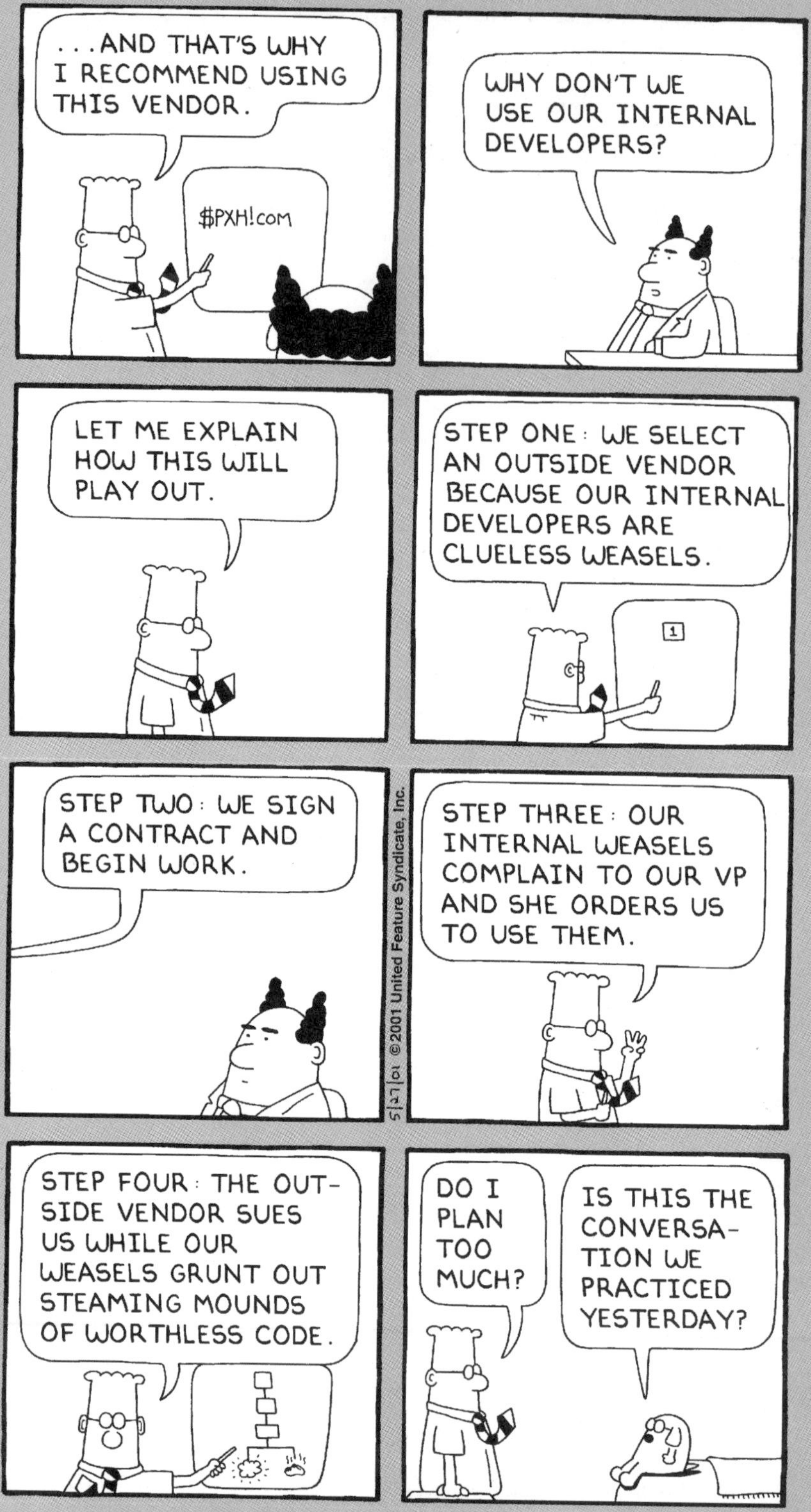
...AND THAT'S WHY I RECOMMEND USING THIS VENDOR.
$PXH!COM
WHY DON'T WE USE OUR INTERNAL DEVELOPERS?
LET ME EXPLAIN HOW THIS WILL PLAY OUT.
STEP ONE: WE SELECT AN OUTSIDE VENDOR BECAUSE OUR INTERNAL DEVELOPERS ARE CLUELESS WEASELS.
1
STEP TWO: WE SIGN A CONTRACT AND BEGIN WORK.
STEP THREE: OUR INTERNAL WEASELS COMPLAIN TO OUR VP AND SHE ORDERS US TO USE THEM.
STEP FOUR: THE OUT-SIDE VENDOR SUES US WHILE OUR WEASELS GRUNT OUT STEAMING MOUNDS OF WORTHLESS CODE.
DO I PLAN TOO MUCH?
IS THIS THE CONVERSA-TION WE PRACTICED YESTERDAY?

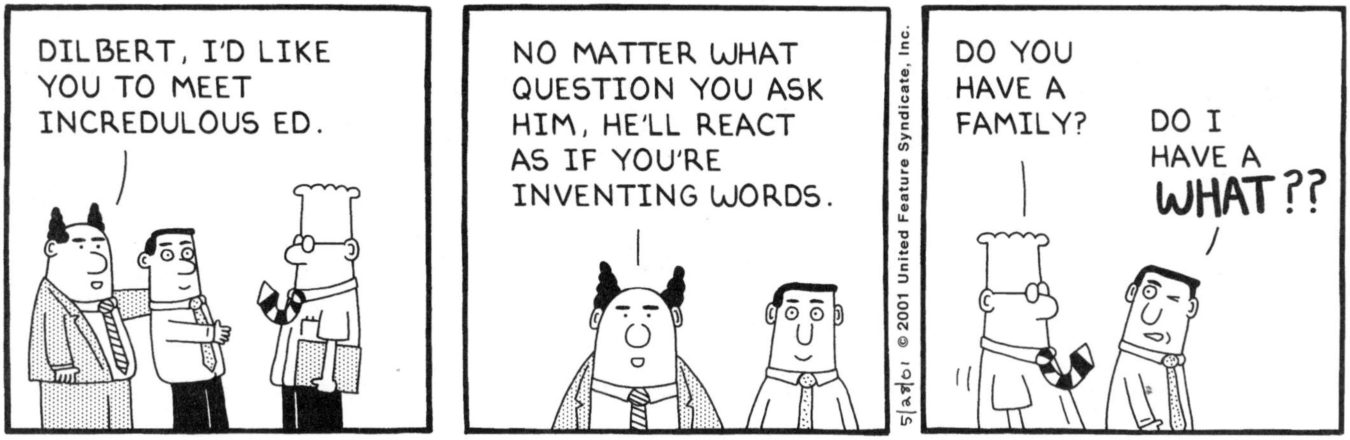
DILBERT, I'D LIKE YOU TO MEET INCREDULOUS ED.
NO MATTER WHAT QUESTION YOU ASK HIM, HE'LL REACT AS IF YOU'RE INVENTING WORDS.
5/28/01 © 2001 United Feature Syndicate, Inc.
DO YOU HAVE A FAMILY?
DO I HAVE A WHAT??

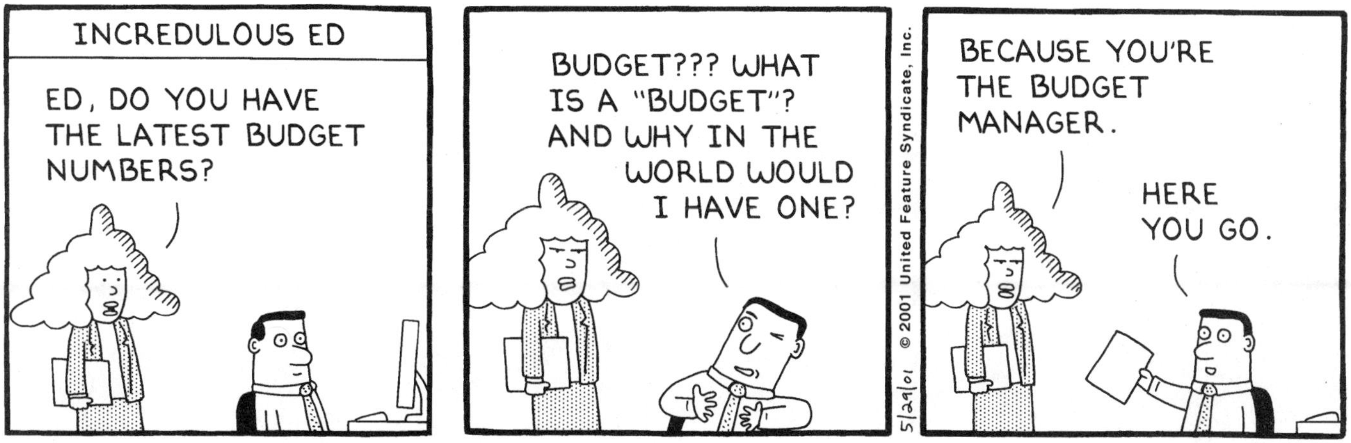
INCREDULOUS ED
ED, DO YOU HAVE THE LATEST BUDGET NUMBERS?
BUDGET??? WHAT IS A "BUDGET"? AND WHY IN THE WORLD WOULD I HAVE ONE?
5/29/01 © 2001 United Feature Syndicate, Inc.
BECAUSE YOU'RE THE BUDGET MANAGER.
HERE YOU GO.

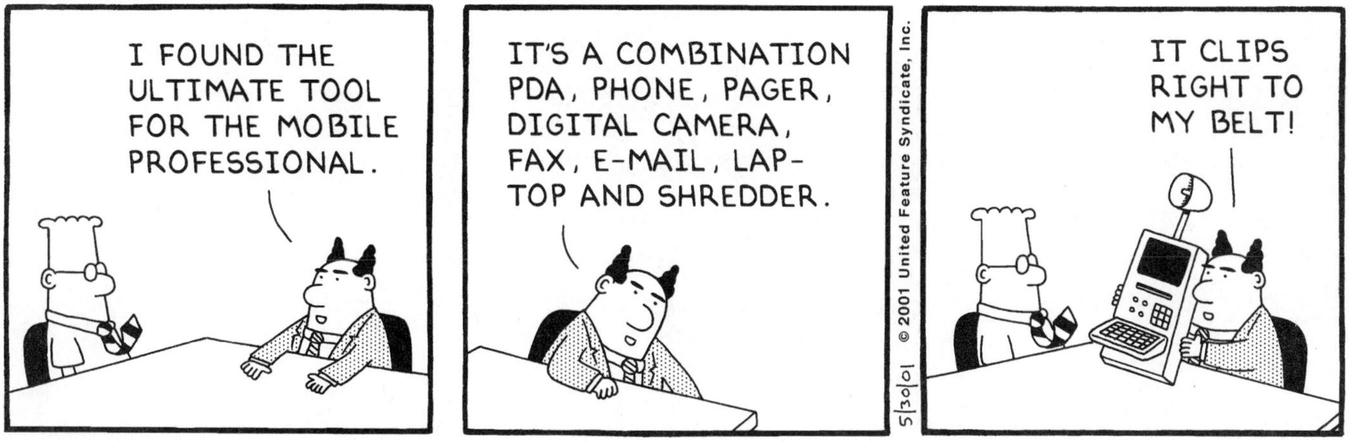
I FOUND THE ULTIMATE TOOL FOR THE MOBILE PROFESSIONAL.
IT'S A COMBINATION PDA, PHONE, PAGER, DIGITAL CAMERA, FAX, E-MAIL, LAPTOP AND SHREDDER.
5/30/01 © 2001 United Feature Syndicate, Inc.
IT CLIPS RIGHT TO MY BELT!

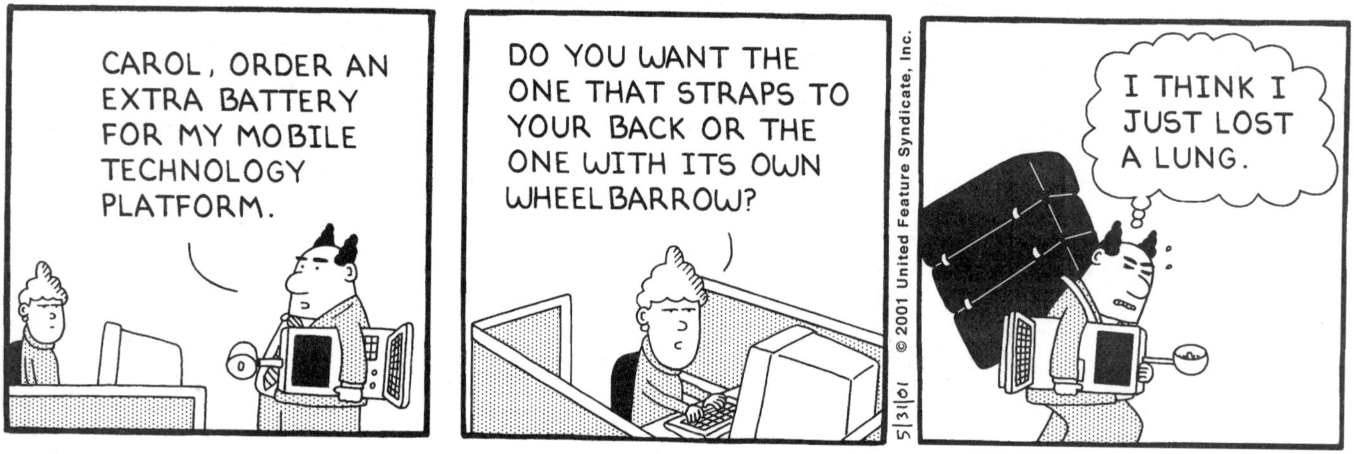
CAROL, ORDER AN EXTRA BATTERY FOR MY MOBILE TECHNOLOGY PLATFORM.
DO YOU WANT THE ONE THAT STRAPS TO YOUR BACK OR THE ONE WITH ITS OWN WHEELBARROW?
5/31/01 © 2001 United Feature Syndicate, Inc.
I THINK I JUST LOST A LUNG.

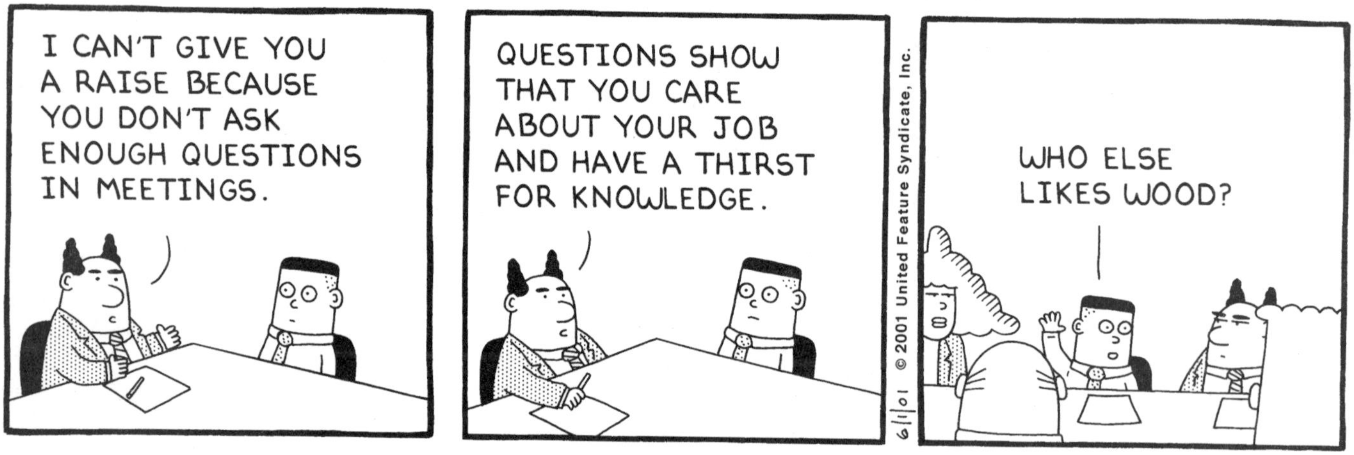
I CAN'T GIVE YOU A RAISE BECAUSE YOU DON'T ASK ENOUGH QUESTIONS IN MEETINGS.
QUESTIONS SHOW THAT YOU CARE ABOUT YOUR JOB AND HAVE A THIRST FOR KNOWLEDGE.
6/1/01 © 2001 United Feature Syndicate, Inc.
WHO ELSE LIKES WOOD?

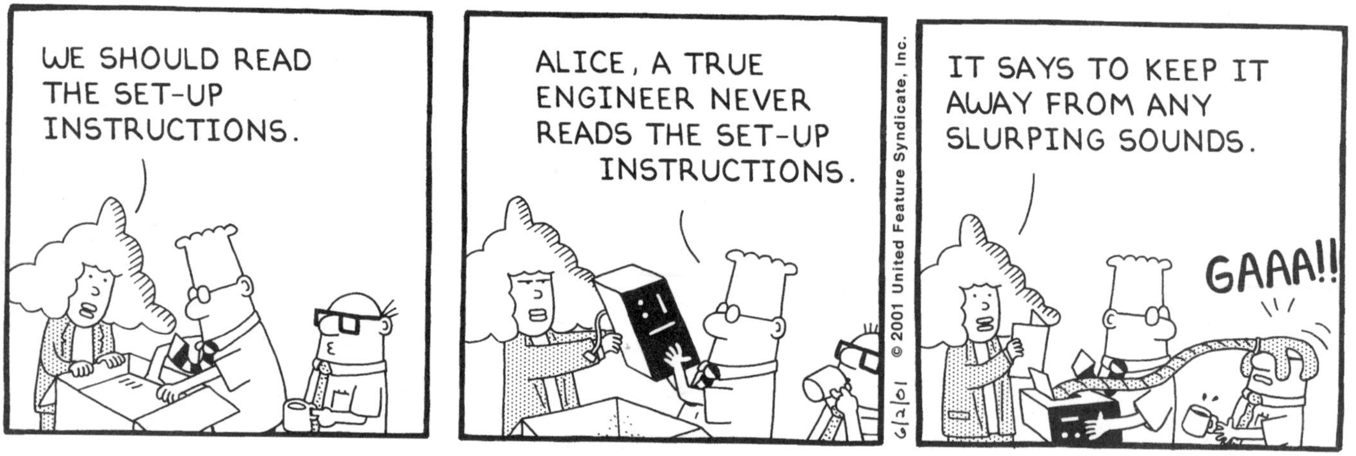
WE SHOULD READ THE SET-UP INSTRUCTIONS.
ALICE, A TRUE ENGINEER NEVER READS THE SET-UP INSTRUCTIONS.
6/2/01 © 2001 United Feature Syndicate, Inc.
IT SAYS TO KEEP IT AWAY FROM ANY SLURPING SOUNDS.
GAAA!!

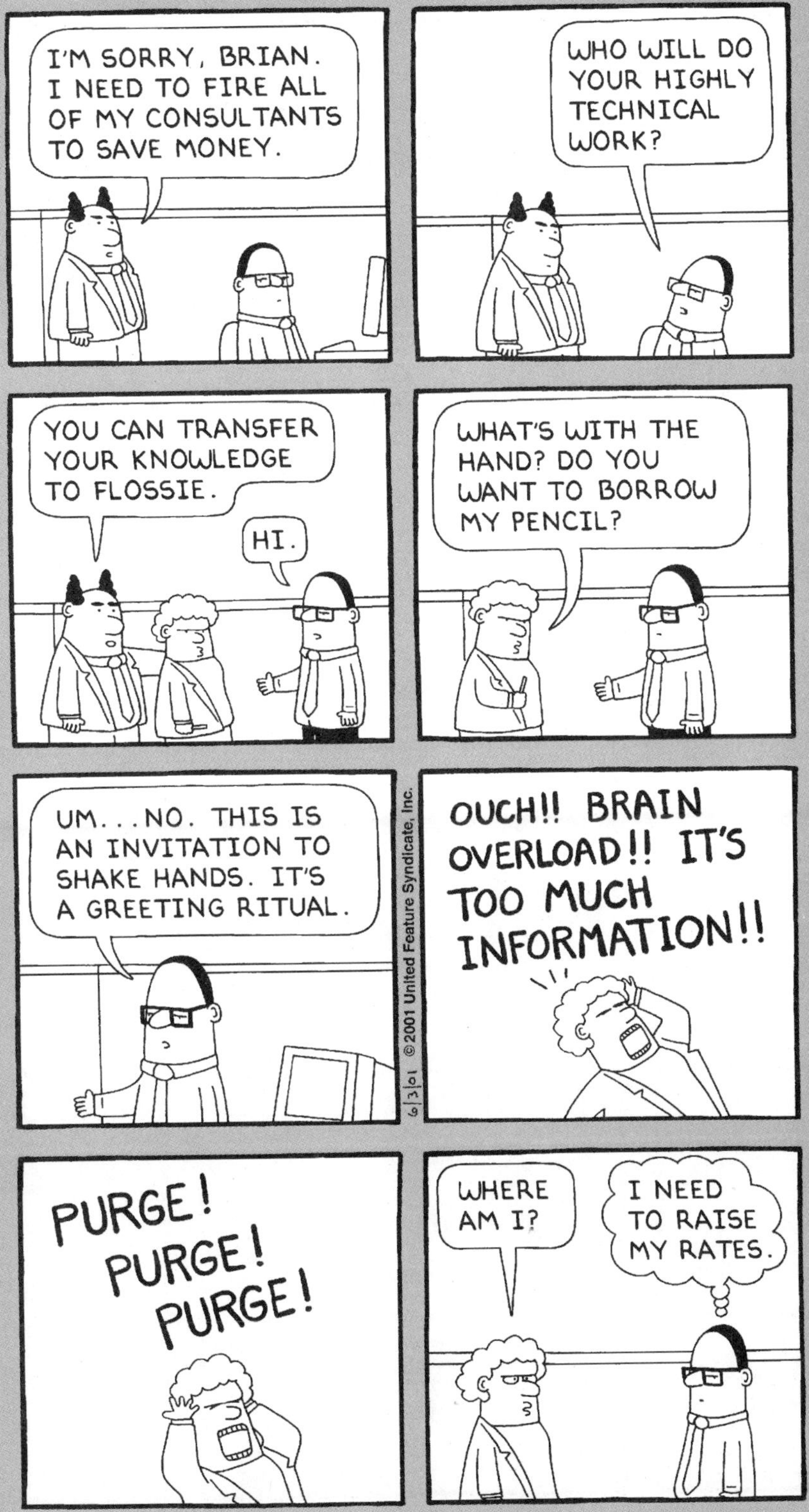
I'M SORRY, BRIAN. I NEED TO FIRE ALL OF MY CONSULTANTS TO SAVE MONEY.
WHO WILL DO YOUR HIGHLY TECHNICAL WORK?
YOU CAN TRANSFER YOUR KNOWLEDGE TO FLOSSIE.
HI.
WHAT'S WITH THE HAND? DO YOU WANT TO BORROW MY PENCIL?
UM...NO. THIS IS AN INVITATION TO SHAKE HANDS. IT'S A GREETING RITUAL.
6/3/01 ©2001 United Feature Syndicate, Inc.
OUCH!! BRAIN OVERLOAD!! IT'S TOO MUCH INFORMATION!!
PURGE! PURGE! PURGE!
WHERE AM I?
I NEED TO RAISE MY RATES.

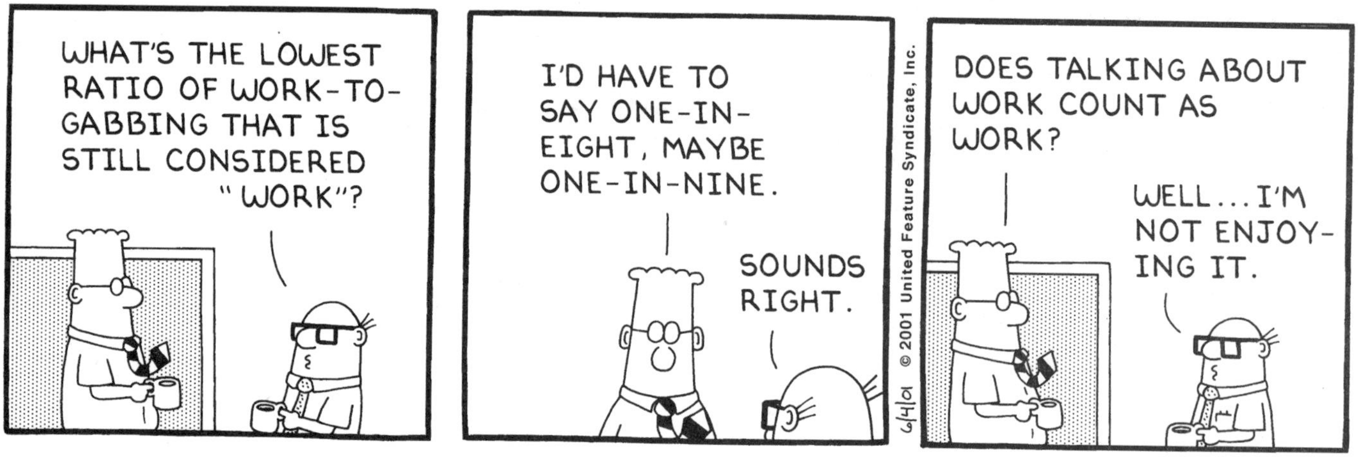
WHAT'S THE LOWEST RATIO OF WORK-TO-GABBING THAT IS STILL CONSIDERED "WORK"?
I'D HAVE TO SAY ONE-IN-EIGHT, MAYBE ONE-IN-NINE.
SOUNDS RIGHT.
6/4/01 © 2001 United Feature Syndicate, Inc.
DOES TALKING ABOUT WORK COUNT AS WORK?
WELL... I'M NOT ENJOYING IT.

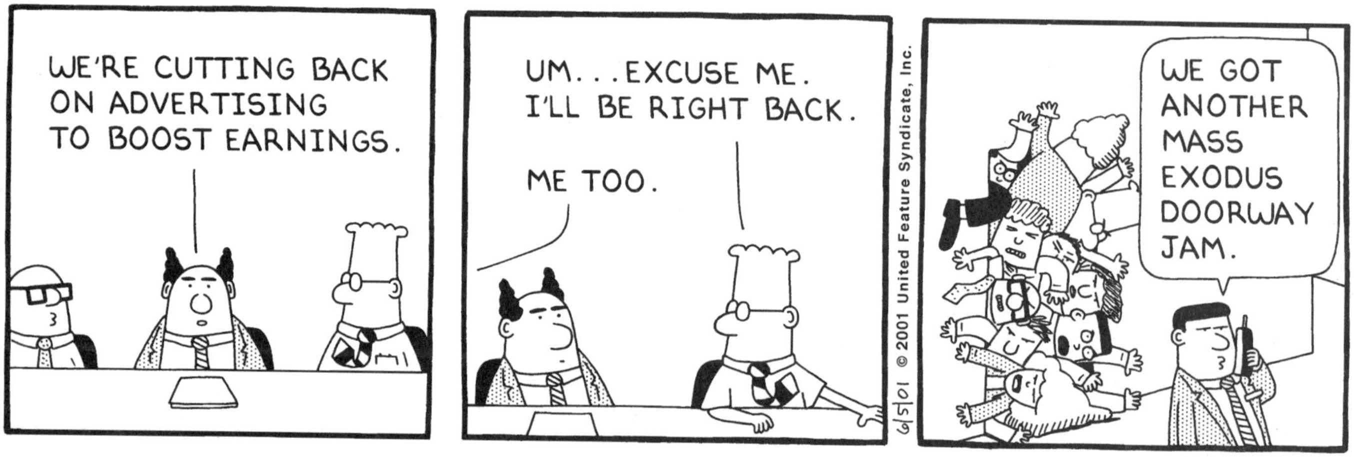
WE'RE CUTTING BACK ON ADVERTISING TO BOOST EARNINGS.
UM... EXCUSE ME. I'LL BE RIGHT BACK.
ME TOO.
6/5/01 © 2001 United Feature Syndicate, Inc.
WE GOT ANOTHER MASS EXODUS DOORWAY JAM.

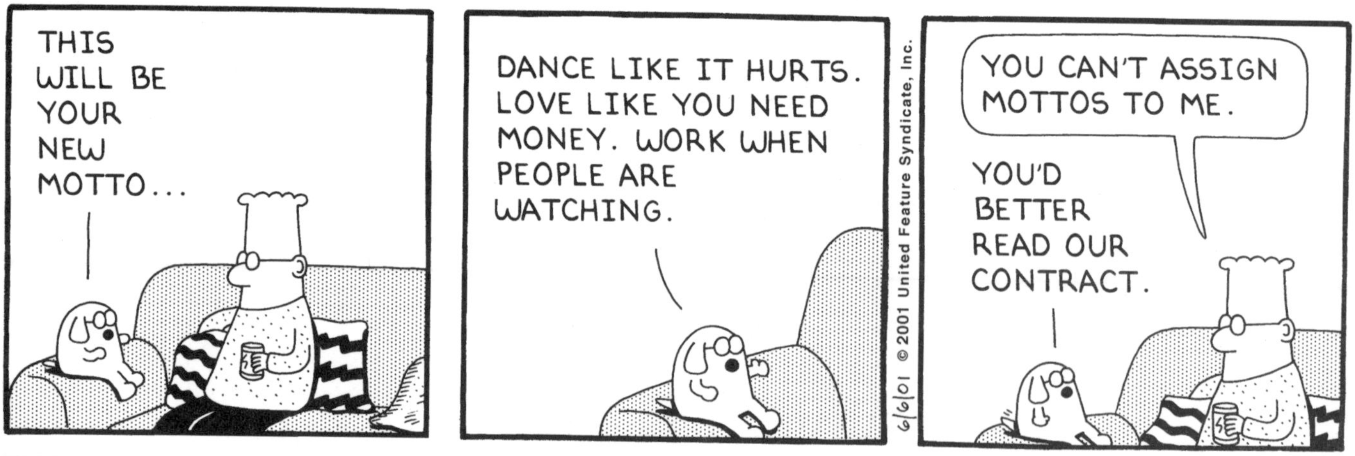
THIS WILL BE YOUR NEW MOTTO...
DANCE LIKE IT HURTS. LOVE LIKE YOU NEED MONEY. WORK WHEN PEOPLE ARE WATCHING.
6/6/01 © 2001 United Feature Syndicate, Inc.
YOU CAN'T ASSIGN MOTTOS TO ME.
YOU'D BETTER READ OUR CONTRACT.

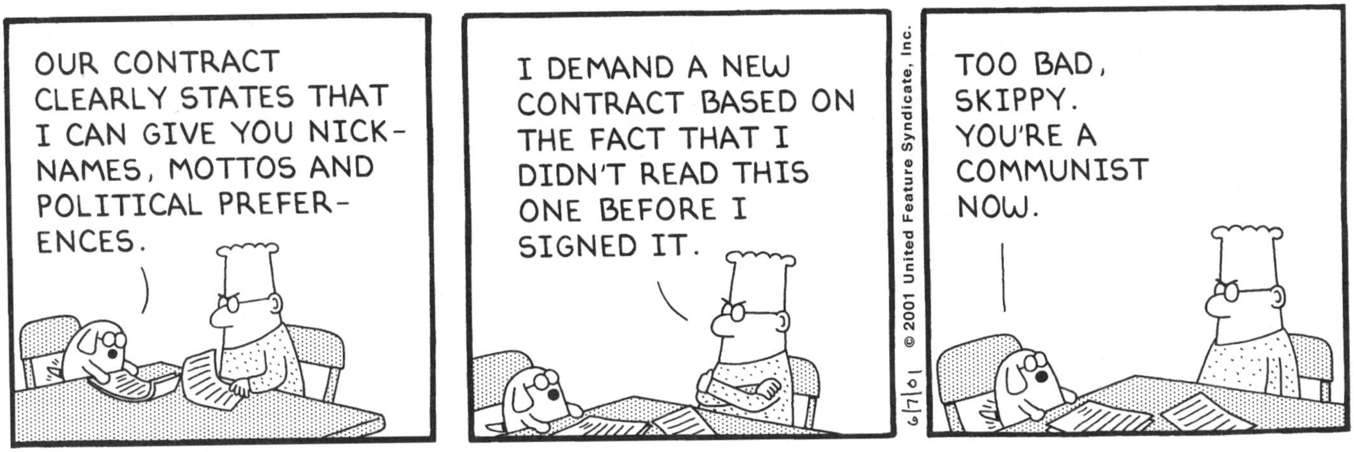

OUR CONTRACT CLEARLY STATES THAT I CAN GIVE YOU NICK-NAMES, MOTTOS AND POLITICAL PREFER-ENCES.
I DEMAND A NEW CONTRACT BASED ON THE FACT THAT I DIDN'T READ THIS ONE BEFORE I SIGNED IT.
6/7/01 © 2001 United Feature Syndicate, Inc.
TOO BAD, SKIPPY. YOU'RE A COMMUNIST NOW.

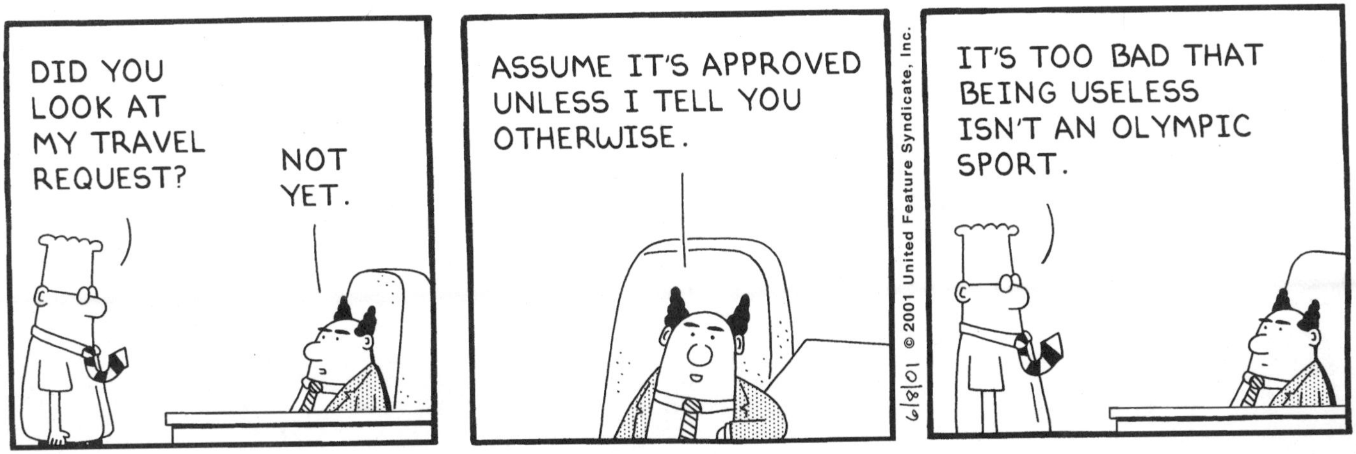

DID YOU LOOK AT MY TRAVEL REQUEST?
NOT YET.
ASSUME IT'S APPROVED UNLESS I TELL YOU OTHERWISE.
6/8/01 © 2001 United Feature Syndicate, Inc.
IT'S TOO BAD THAT BEING USELESS ISN'T AN OLYMPIC SPORT.

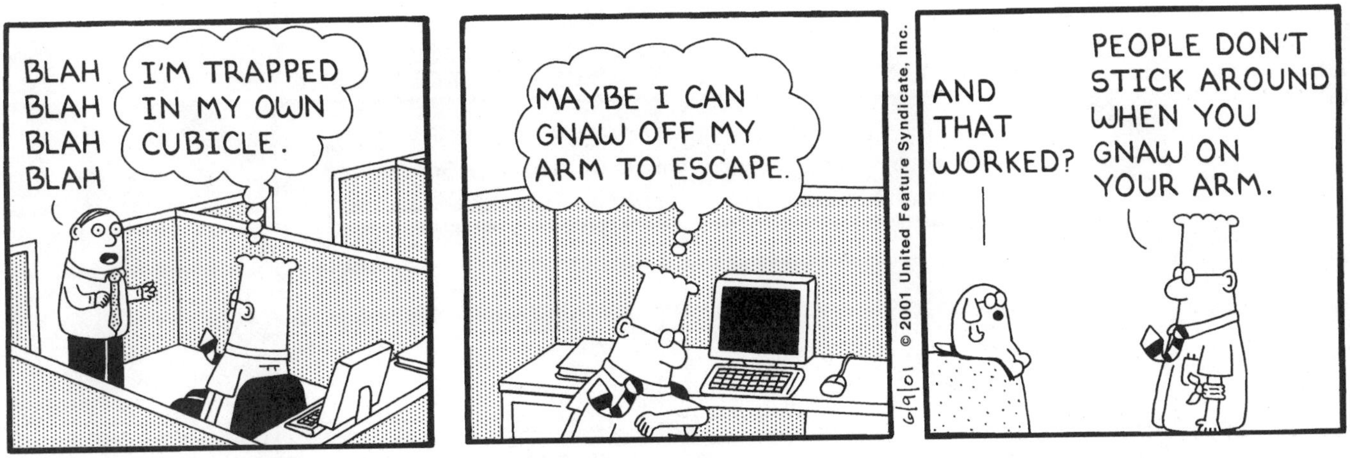

BLAH BLAH BLAH BLAH
I'M TRAPPED IN MY OWN CUBICLE.
MAYBE I CAN GNAW OFF MY ARM TO ESCAPE.
6/9/01 © 2001 United Feature Syndicate, Inc.
AND THAT WORKED?
PEOPLE DON'T STICK AROUND WHEN YOU GNAW ON YOUR ARM.

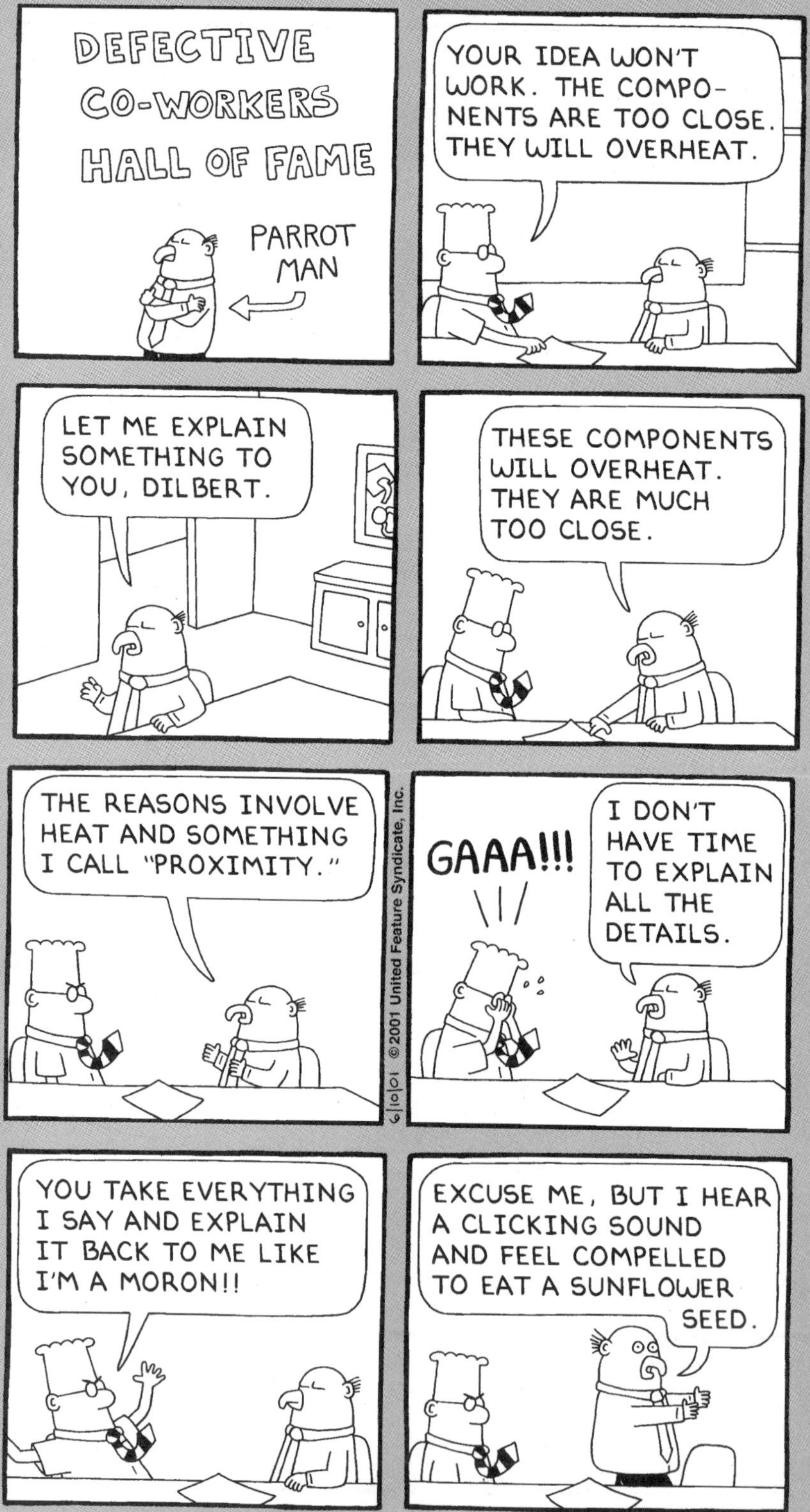
DEFECTIVE CO-WORKERS HALL OF FAME
PARROT MAN
YOUR IDEA WON'T WORK. THE COMPO-NENTS ARE TOO CLOSE. THEY WILL OVERHEAT.
LET ME EXPLAIN SOMETHING TO YOU, DILBERT.
THESE COMPONENTS WILL OVERHEAT. THEY ARE MUCH TOO CLOSE.
THE REASONS INVOLVE HEAT AND SOMETHING I CALL "PROXIMITY."
6/10/01 ©2001 United Feature Syndicate, Inc.
GAAA!!!
I DON'T HAVE TIME TO EXPLAIN ALL THE DETAILS.
YOU TAKE EVERYTHING I SAY AND EXPLAIN IT BACK TO ME LIKE I'M A MORON!!
EXCUSE ME, BUT I HEAR A CLICKING SOUND AND FEEL COMPELLED TO EAT A SUNFLOWER SEED.

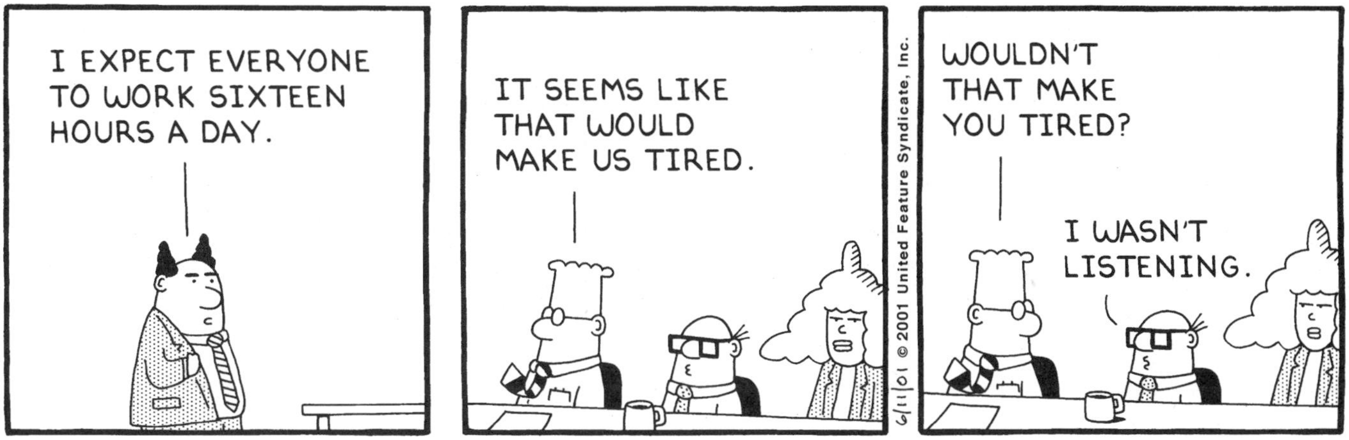
I EXPECT EVERYONE TO WORK SIXTEEN HOURS A DAY.
IT SEEMS LIKE THAT WOULD MAKE US TIRED.
6/11/01 © 2001 United Feature Syndicate, Inc.
WOULDN'T THAT MAKE YOU TIRED?
I WASN'T LISTENING.

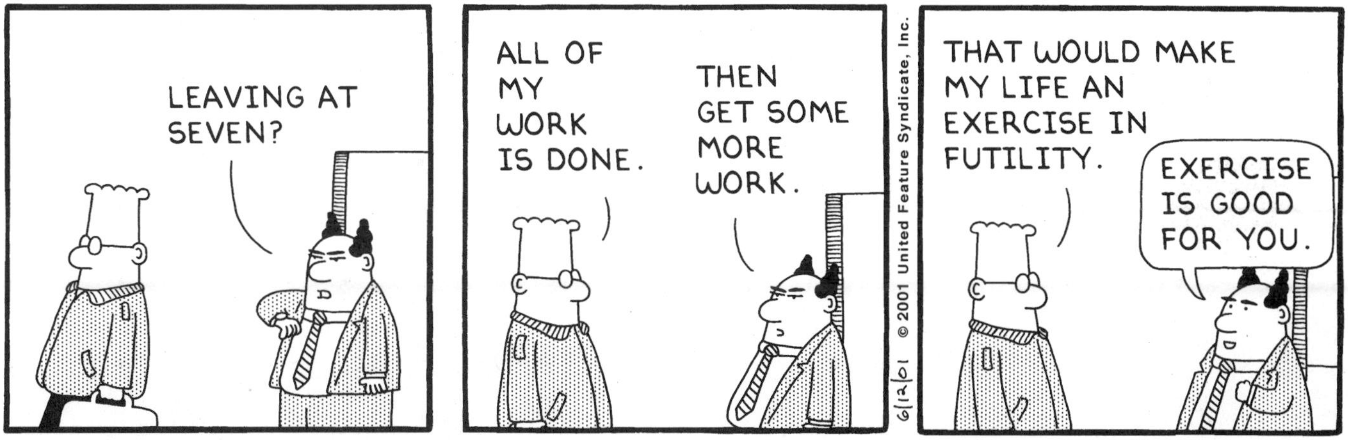
LEAVING AT SEVEN?
ALL OF MY WORK IS DONE.
THEN GET SOME MORE WORK.
6/12/01 © 2001 United Feature Syndicate, Inc.
THAT WOULD MAKE MY LIFE AN EXERCISE IN FUTILITY.
EXERCISE IS GOOD FOR YOU.

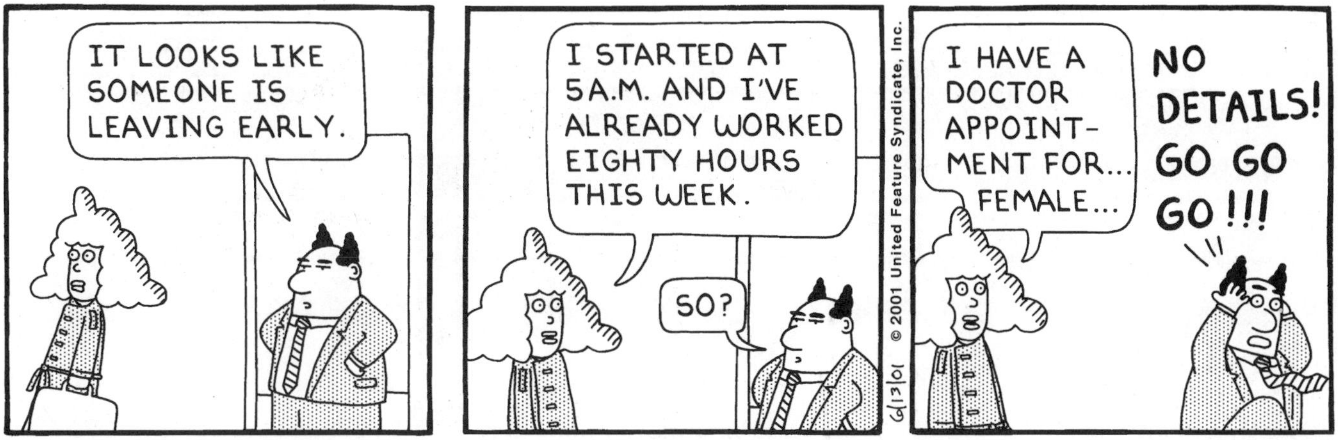
IT LOOKS LIKE SOMEONE IS LEAVING EARLY.
I STARTED AT 5 A.M. AND I'VE ALREADY WORKED EIGHTY HOURS THIS WEEK.
SO?
6/13/01 © 2001 United Feature Syndicate, Inc.
I HAVE A DOCTOR APPOINT-MENT FOR... FEMALE...
NO DETAILS! GO GO GO!!!

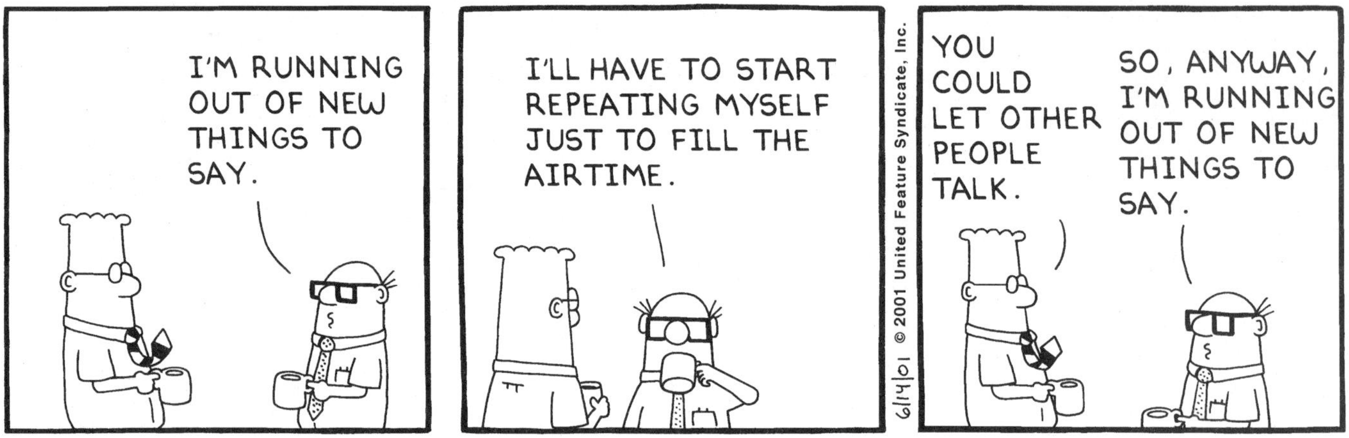
I'M RUNNING OUT OF NEW THINGS TO SAY.
I'LL HAVE TO START REPEATING MYSELF JUST TO FILL THE AIRTIME.
6/14/01 © 2001 United Feature Syndicate, Inc.
YOU COULD LET OTHER PEOPLE TALK.
SO, ANYWAY, I'M RUNNING OUT OF NEW THINGS TO SAY.

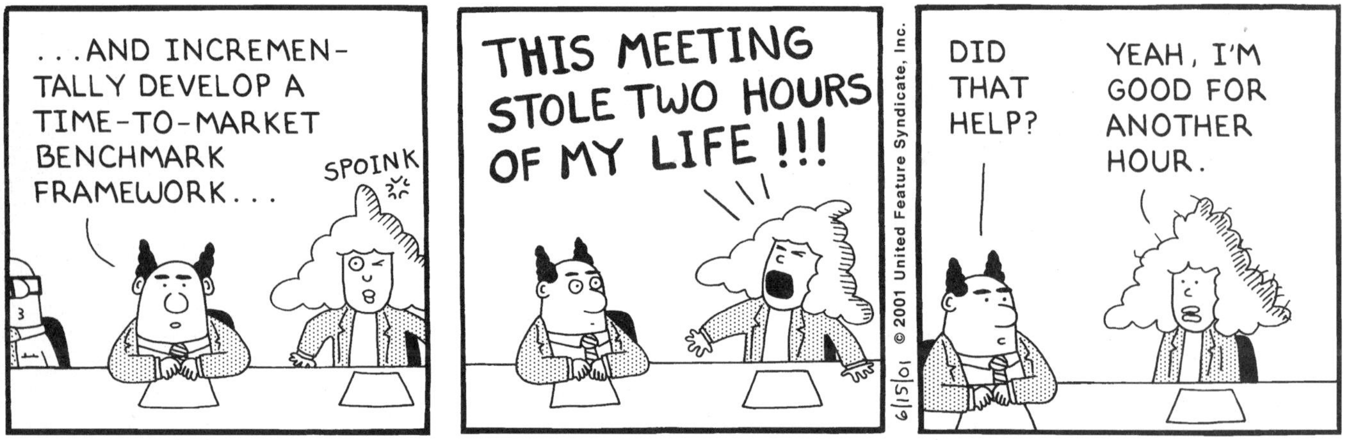
...AND INCREMENTALLY DEVELOP A TIME-TO-MARKET BENCHMARK FRAMEWORK...
SPOINK
THIS MEETING STOLE TWO HOURS OF MY LIFE !!!
6/15/01 © 2001 United Feature Syndicate, Inc.
DID THAT HELP?
YEAH, I'M GOOD FOR ANOTHER HOUR.

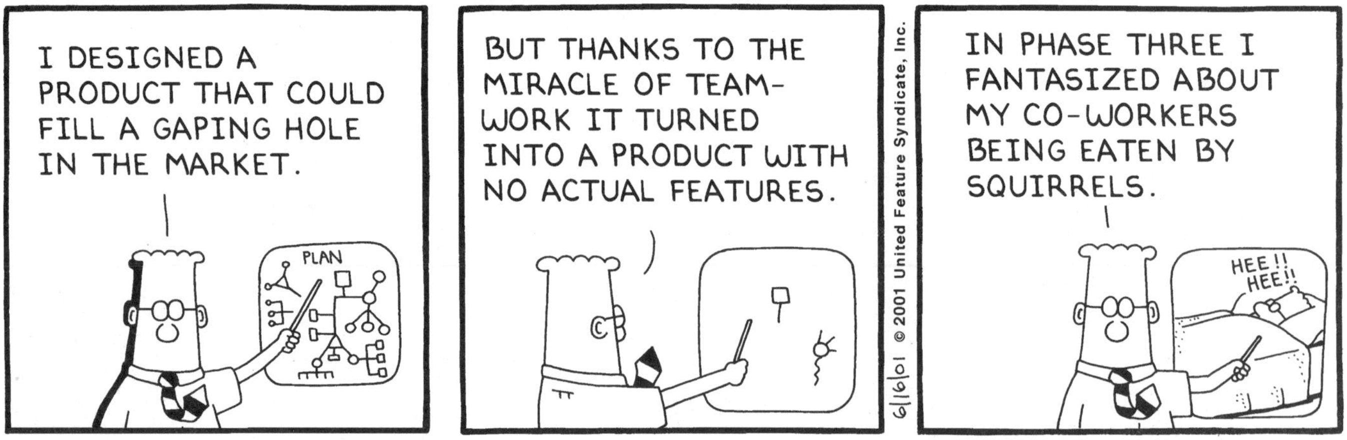
I DESIGNED A PRODUCT THAT COULD FILL A GAPING HOLE IN THE MARKET.
PLAN
BUT THANKS TO THE MIRACLE OF TEAMWORK IT TURNED INTO A PRODUCT WITH NO ACTUAL FEATURES.
6/16/01 © 2001 United Feature Syndicate, Inc.
IN PHASE THREE I FANTASIZED ABOUT MY CO-WORKERS BEING EATEN BY SQUIRRELS.
HEE!! HEE!!

WE FOUND A BUG IN OUR SOFTWARE.
IT SEARCHES YOUR E-MAIL ADDRESS BOOK FOR YOUR MOTHER'S NAME.
EVERY SUNDAY IT USES YOUR E-MAIL TO SEND HER A MESSAGE...
...COMPARING HER FACE TO VARIOUS PARTS OF ANIMALS.
DO YOU HAVE ANY HARD DATA THAT PROVES WE SHOULD FIX THE BUG?
WE CAN'T THROW MONEY AT EVERY PROBLEM.
IT'S YOUR MOM.
YOU MISERABLE
✿☆%#@!!!
SEE WHAT I MEAN?
NO. I GET THIS CALL EVERY DAY.
☆#%
©2001 United Feature Syndicate, Inc.
6/17/01

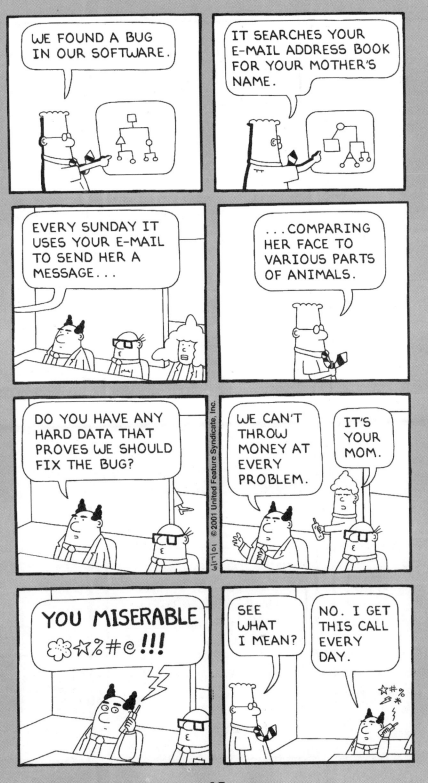

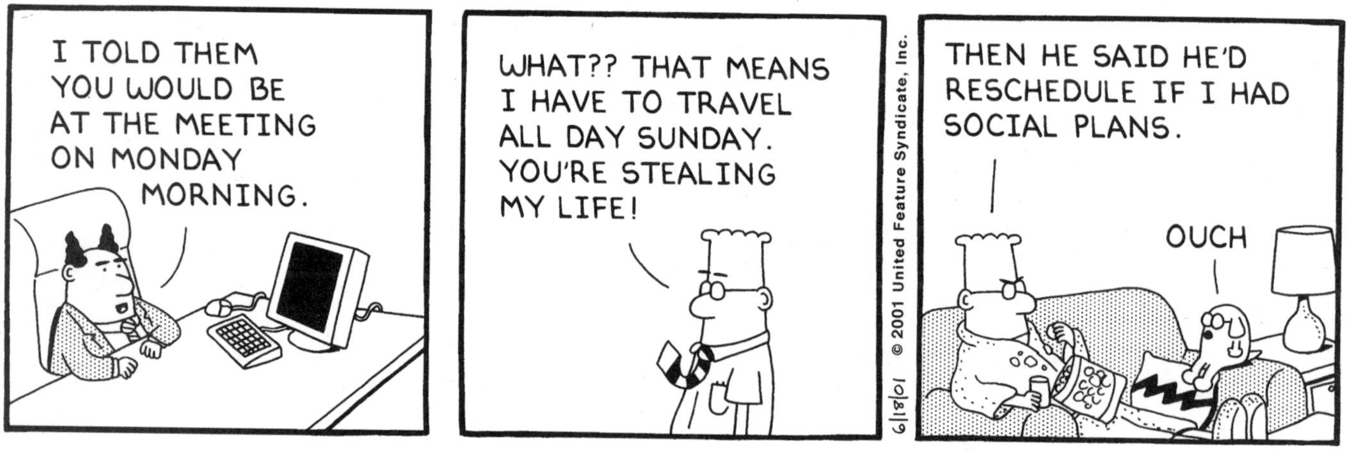
I TOLD THEM YOU WOULD BE AT THE MEETING ON MONDAY MORNING.
WHAT?? THAT MEANS I HAVE TO TRAVEL ALL DAY SUNDAY. YOU'RE STEALING MY LIFE!
6/18/01 © 2001 United Feature Syndicate, Inc.
THEN HE SAID HE'D RESCHEDULE IF I HAD SOCIAL PLANS.
OUCH

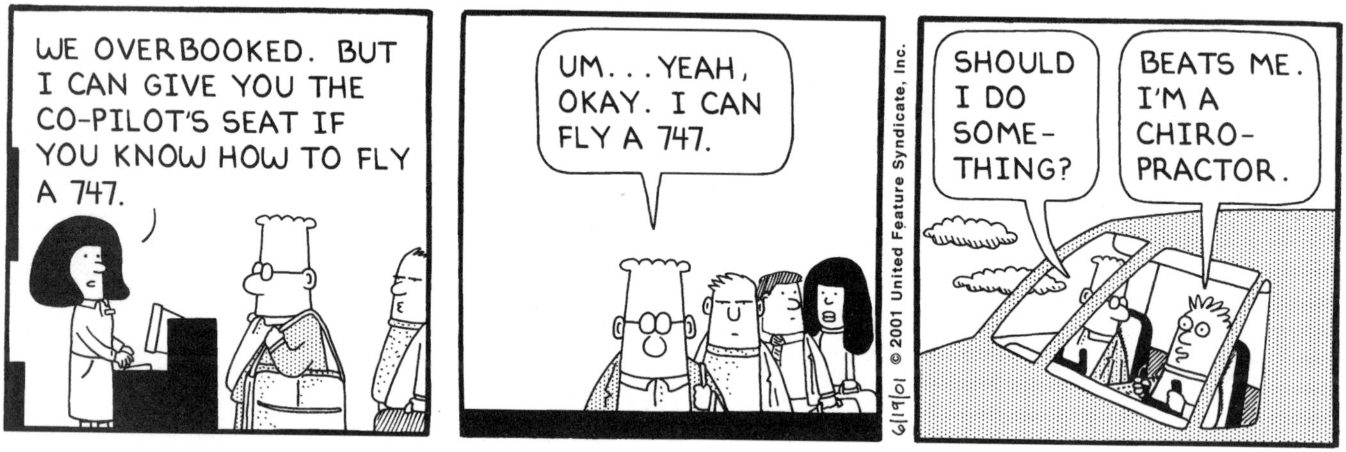
WE OVERBOOKED. BUT I CAN GIVE YOU THE CO-PILOT'S SEAT IF YOU KNOW HOW TO FLY A 747.
UM... YEAH, OKAY. I CAN FLY A 747.
6/19/01 © 2001 United Feature Syndicate, Inc.
SHOULD I DO SOME-THING?
BEATS ME. I'M A CHIRO-PRACTOR.

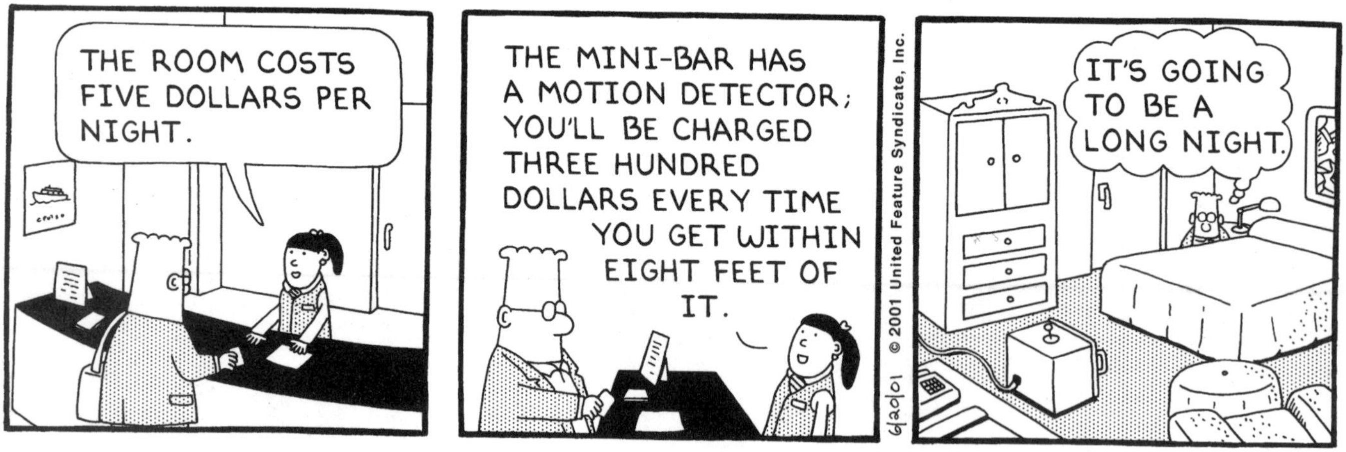
THE ROOM COSTS FIVE DOLLARS PER NIGHT.
THE MINI-BAR HAS A MOTION DETECTOR; YOU'LL BE CHARGED THREE HUNDRED DOLLARS EVERY TIME YOU GET WITHIN EIGHT FEET OF IT.
6/20/01 © 2001 United Feature Syndicate, Inc.
IT'S GOING TO BE A LONG NIGHT.

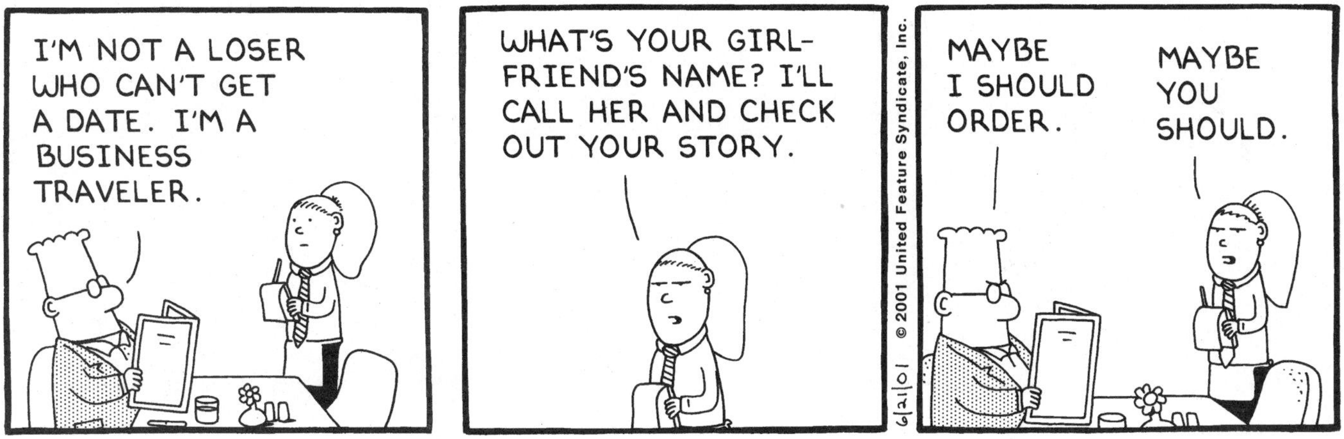
I'M NOT A LOSER WHO CAN'T GET A DATE. I'M A BUSINESS TRAVELER.
WHAT'S YOUR GIRL-FRIEND'S NAME? I'LL CALL HER AND CHECK OUT YOUR STORY.
6/21/01 © 2001 United Feature Syndicate, Inc.
MAYBE I SHOULD ORDER.
MAYBE YOU SHOULD.

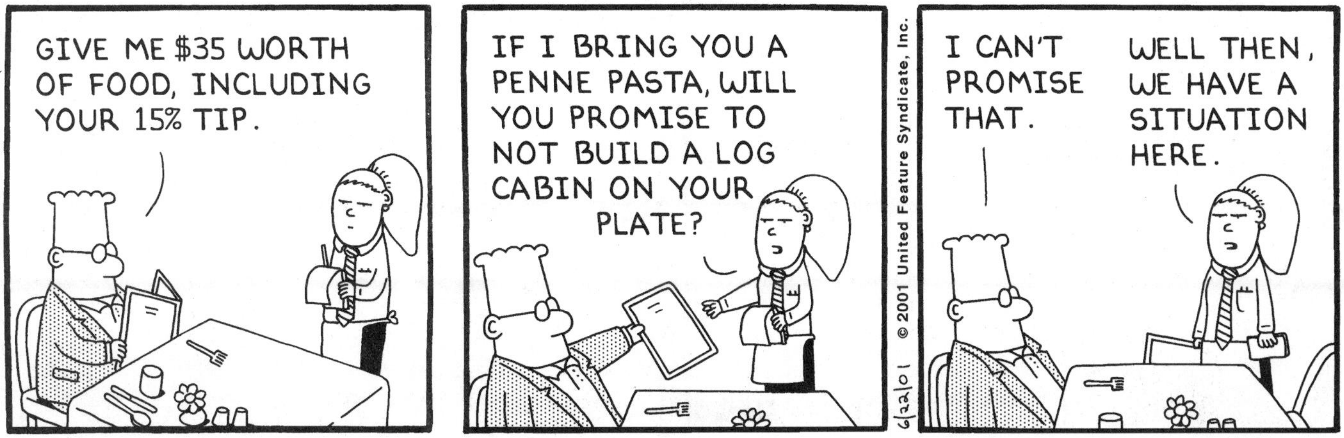
GIVE ME $35 WORTH OF FOOD, INCLUDING YOUR 15% TIP.
IF I BRING YOU A PENNE PASTA, WILL YOU PROMISE TO NOT BUILD A LOG CABIN ON YOUR PLATE?
6/22/01 © 2001 United Feature Syndicate, Inc.
I CAN'T PROMISE THAT.
WELL THEN, WE HAVE A SITUATION HERE.

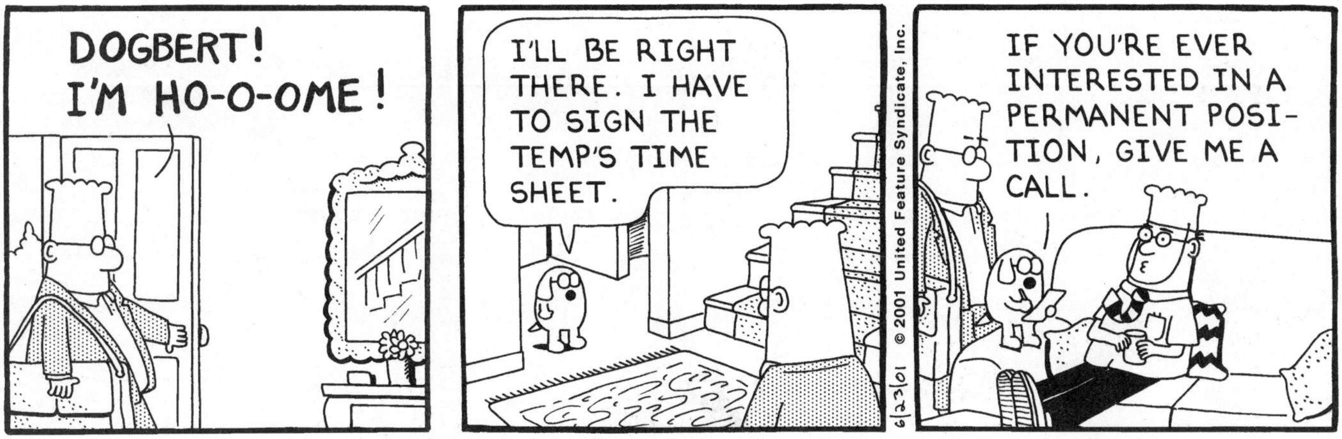
DOGBERT! I'M HO-O-OME!
I'LL BE RIGHT THERE. I HAVE TO SIGN THE TEMP'S TIME SHEET.
6/23/01 © 2001 United Feature Syndicate, Inc.
IF YOU'RE EVER INTERESTED IN A PERMANENT POSI-TION, GIVE ME A CALL.

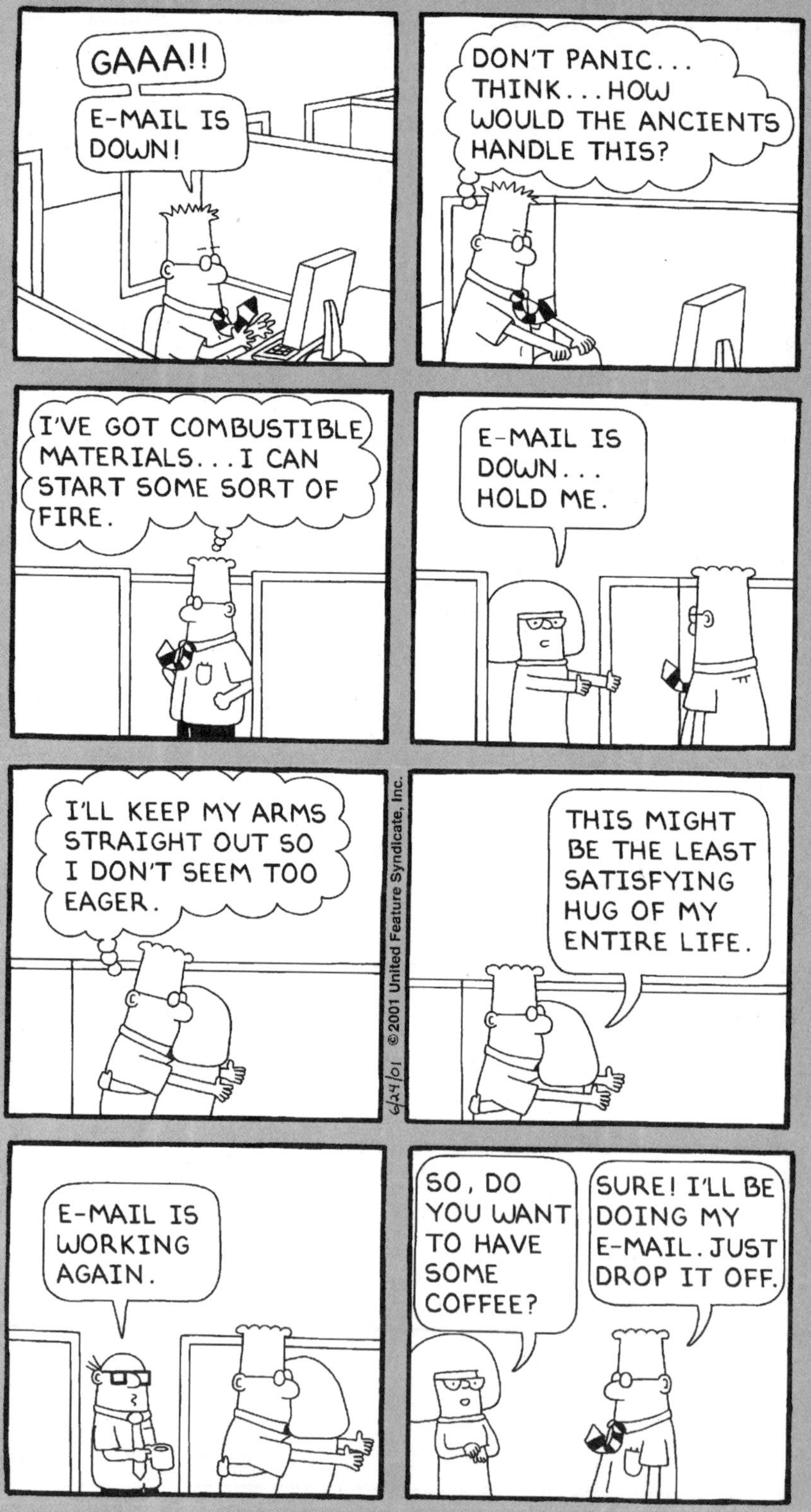
GAAA!!
E-MAIL IS DOWN!
DON'T PANIC... THINK... HOW WOULD THE ANCIENTS HANDLE THIS?
I'VE GOT COMBUSTIBLE MATERIALS... I CAN START SOME SORT OF FIRE.
E-MAIL IS DOWN... HOLD ME.
I'LL KEEP MY ARMS STRAIGHT OUT SO I DON'T SEEM TOO EAGER.
THIS MIGHT BE THE LEAST SATISFYING HUG OF MY ENTIRE LIFE.
E-MAIL IS WORKING AGAIN.
SO, DO YOU WANT TO HAVE SOME COFFEE?
SURE! I'LL BE DOING MY E-MAIL. JUST DROP IT OFF.
©2001 United Feature Syndicate, Inc.
6/24/01

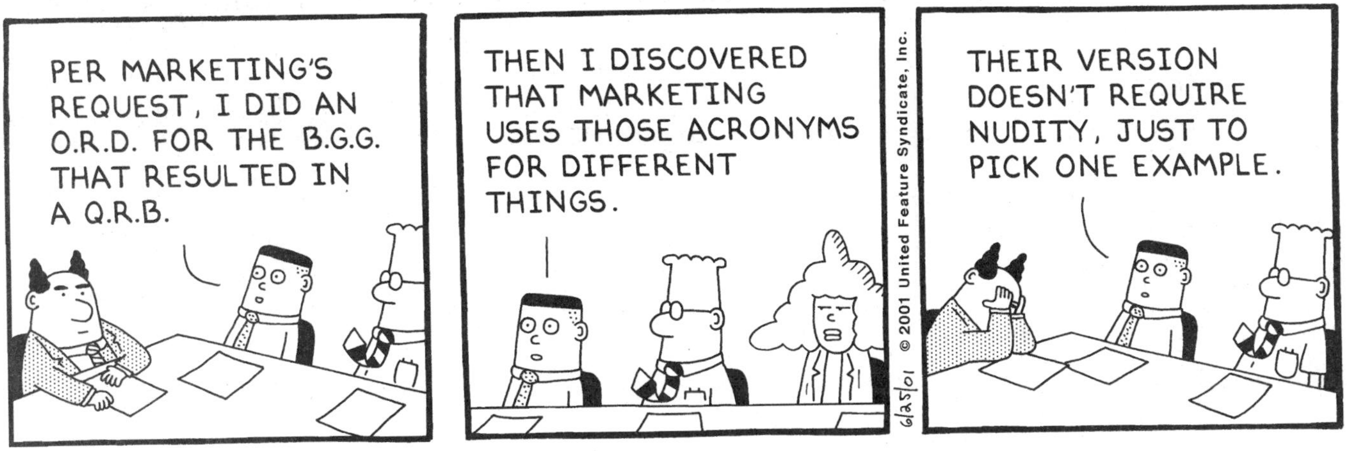
PER MARKETING'S REQUEST, I DID AN O.R.D. FOR THE B.G.G. THAT RESULTED IN A Q.R.B.
THEN I DISCOVERED THAT MARKETING USES THOSE ACRONYMS FOR DIFFERENT THINGS.
6/25/01 © 2001 United Feature Syndicate, Inc.
THEIR VERSION DOESN'T REQUIRE NUDITY, JUST TO PICK ONE EXAMPLE.

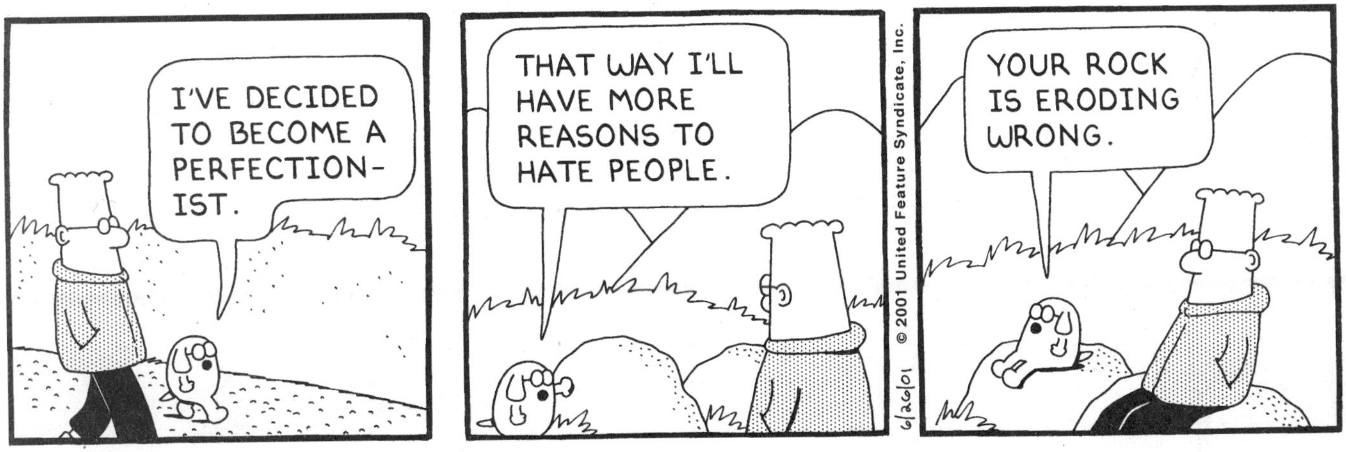
I'VE DECIDED TO BECOME A PERFECTION-IST.
THAT WAY I'LL HAVE MORE REASONS TO HATE PEOPLE.
6/26/01 © 2001 United Feature Syndicate, Inc.
YOUR ROCK IS ERODING WRONG.

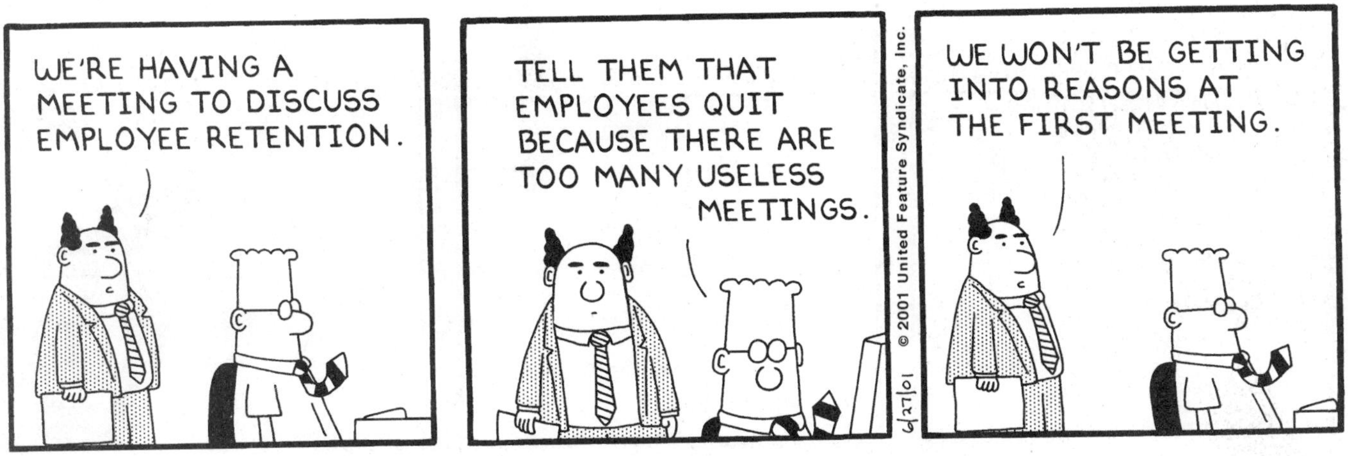
WE'RE HAVING A MEETING TO DISCUSS EMPLOYEE RETENTION.
TELL THEM THAT EMPLOYEES QUIT BECAUSE THERE ARE TOO MANY USELESS MEETINGS.
6/27/01 © 2001 United Feature Syndicate, Inc.
WE WON'T BE GETTING INTO REASONS AT THE FIRST MEETING.

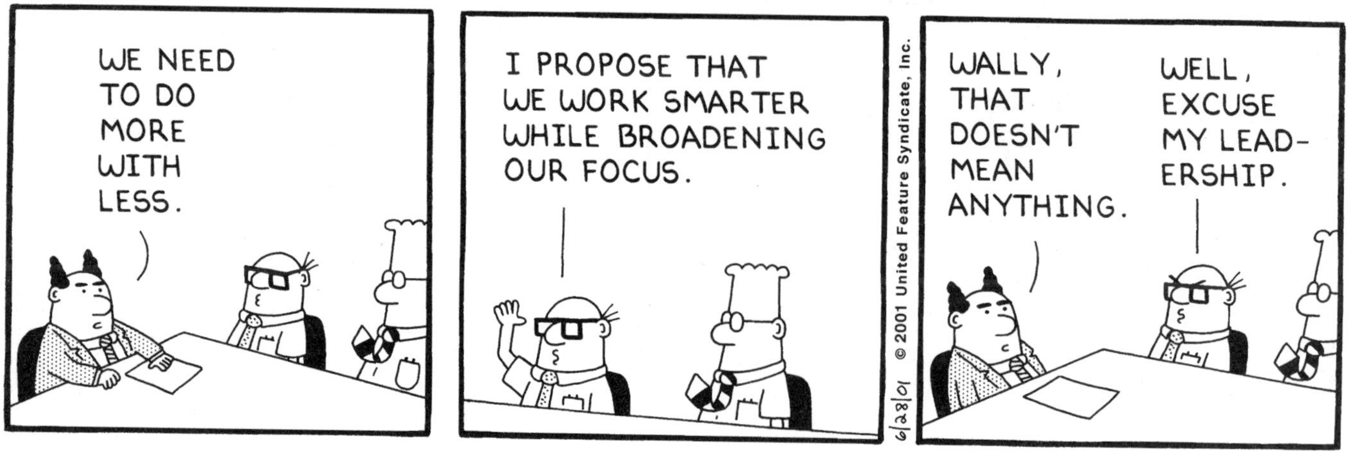
WE NEED TO DO MORE WITH LESS.
I PROPOSE THAT WE WORK SMARTER WHILE BROADENING OUR FOCUS.
WALLY, THAT DOESN'T MEAN ANYTHING.
WELL, EXCUSE MY LEAD- ERSHIP.
© 2001 United Feature Syndicate, Inc.
6/28/01

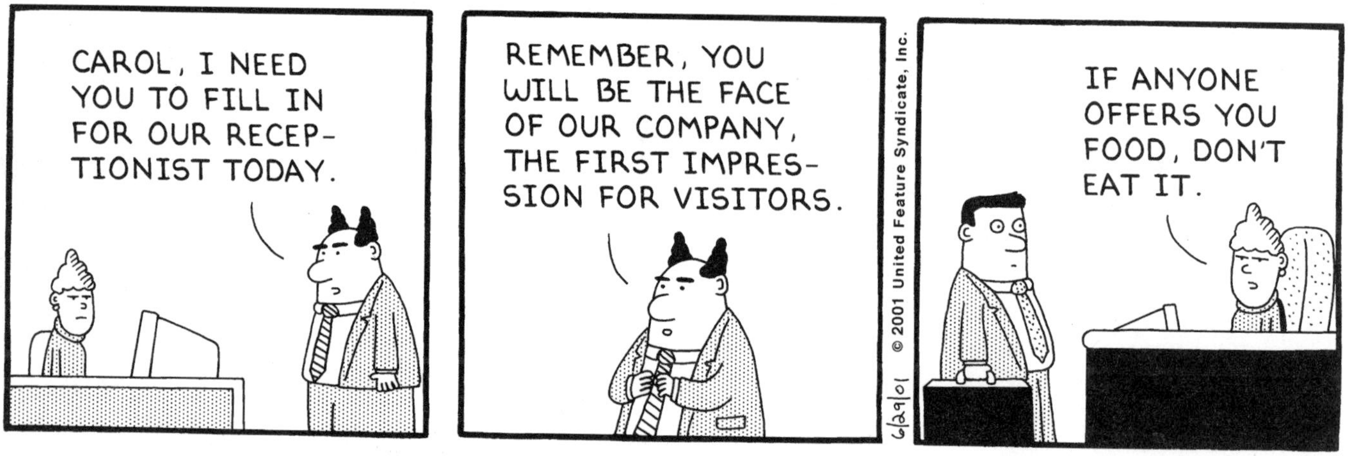
CAROL, I NEED YOU TO FILL IN FOR OUR RECEP- TIONIST TODAY.
REMEMBER, YOU WILL BE THE FACE OF OUR COMPANY, THE FIRST IMPRES- SION FOR VISITORS.
IF ANYONE OFFERS YOU FOOD, DON'T EAT IT.
© 2001 United Feature Syndicate, Inc.
6/29/01

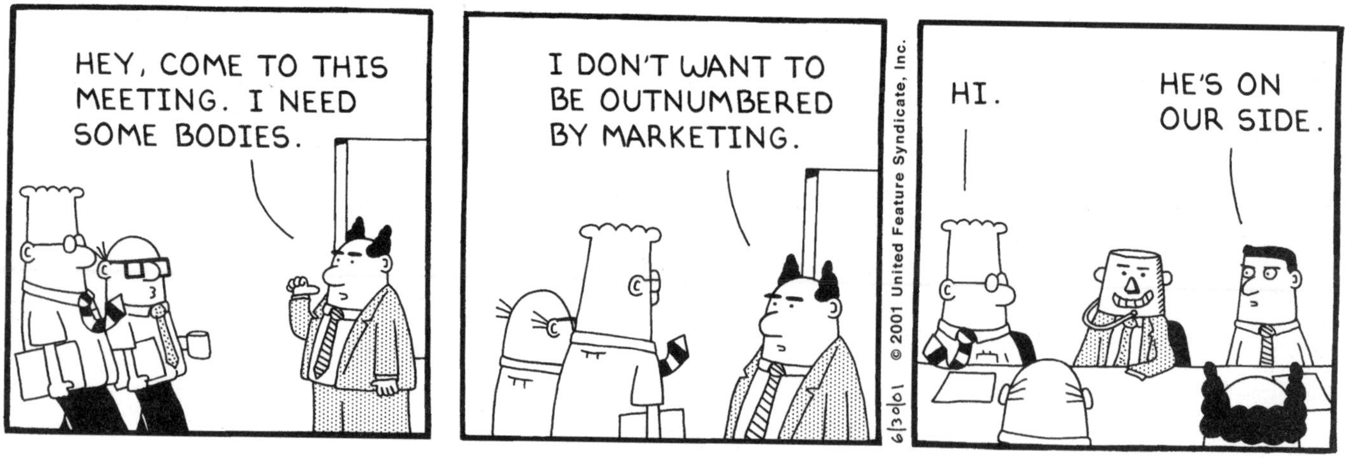
HEY, COME TO THIS MEETING. I NEED SOME BODIES.
I DON'T WANT TO BE OUTNUMBERED BY MARKETING.
HI.
HE'S ON OUR SIDE.
© 2001 United Feature Syndicate, Inc.
6/30/01

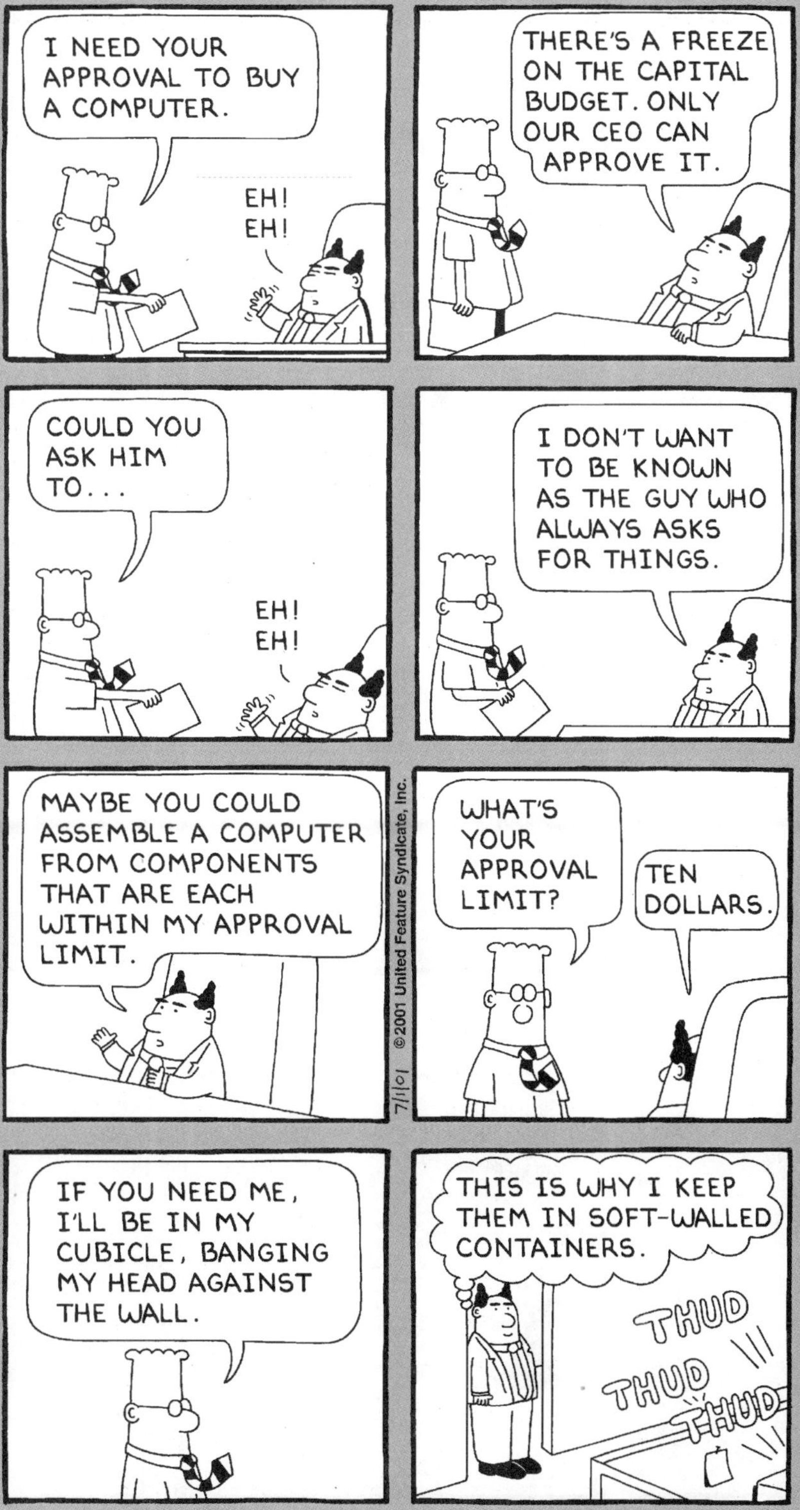
I NEED YOUR APPROVAL TO BUY A COMPUTER.
EH! EH!
THERE'S A FREEZE ON THE CAPITAL BUDGET. ONLY OUR CEO CAN APPROVE IT.
COULD YOU ASK HIM TO...
EH! EH!
I DON'T WANT TO BE KNOWN AS THE GUY WHO ALWAYS ASKS FOR THINGS.
MAYBE YOU COULD ASSEMBLE A COMPUTER FROM COMPONENTS THAT ARE EACH WITHIN MY APPROVAL LIMIT.
© 2001 United Feature Syndicate, Inc.
7/1/01
WHAT'S YOUR APPROVAL LIMIT?
TEN DOLLARS.
IF YOU NEED ME, I'LL BE IN MY CUBICLE, BANGING MY HEAD AGAINST THE WALL.
THIS IS WHY I KEEP THEM IN SOFT-WALLED CONTAINERS.
THUD
THUD
THUD

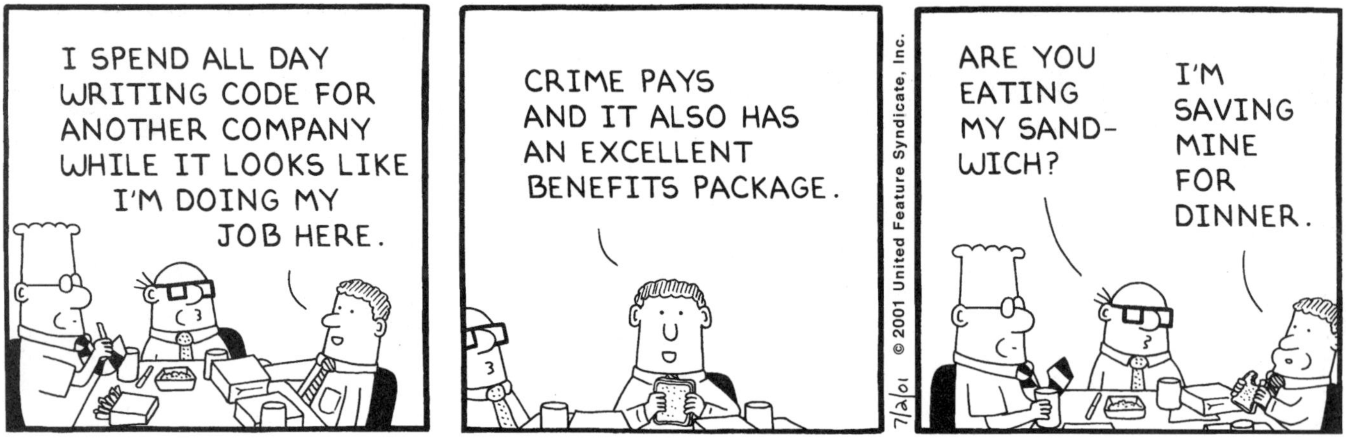
I SPEND ALL DAY WRITING CODE FOR ANOTHER COMPANY WHILE IT LOOKS LIKE I'M DOING MY JOB HERE.
CRIME PAYS AND IT ALSO HAS AN EXCELLENT BENEFITS PACKAGE.
7/2/01 © 2001 United Feature Syndicate, Inc.
ARE YOU EATING MY SAND-WICH?
I'M SAVING MINE FOR DINNER.

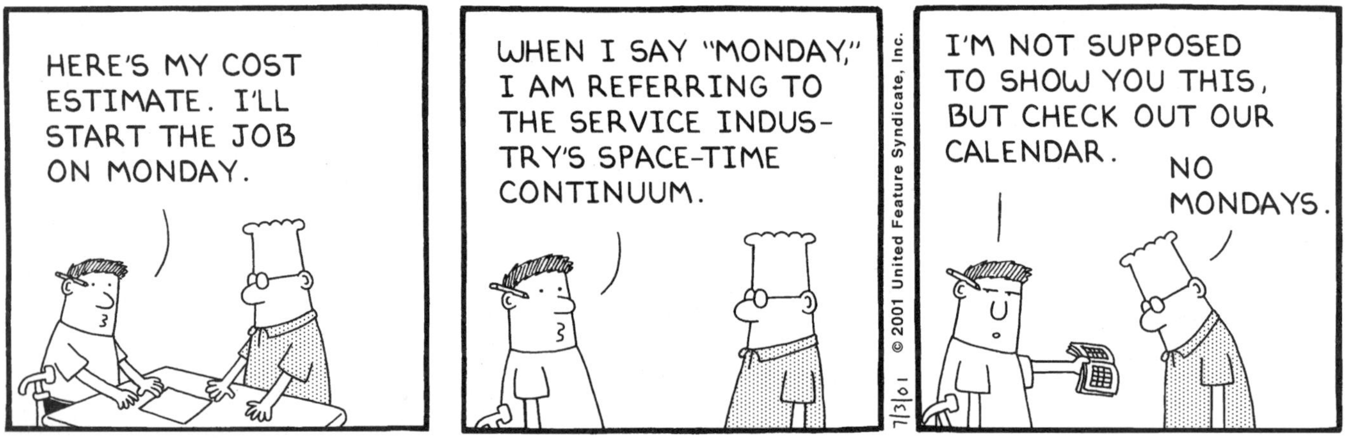
HERE'S MY COST ESTIMATE. I'LL START THE JOB ON MONDAY.
WHEN I SAY "MONDAY," I AM REFERRING TO THE SERVICE INDUS-TRY'S SPACE-TIME CONTINUUM.
7/3/01 © 2001 United Feature Syndicate, Inc.
I'M NOT SUPPOSED TO SHOW YOU THIS, BUT CHECK OUT OUR CALENDAR.
NO MONDAYS.

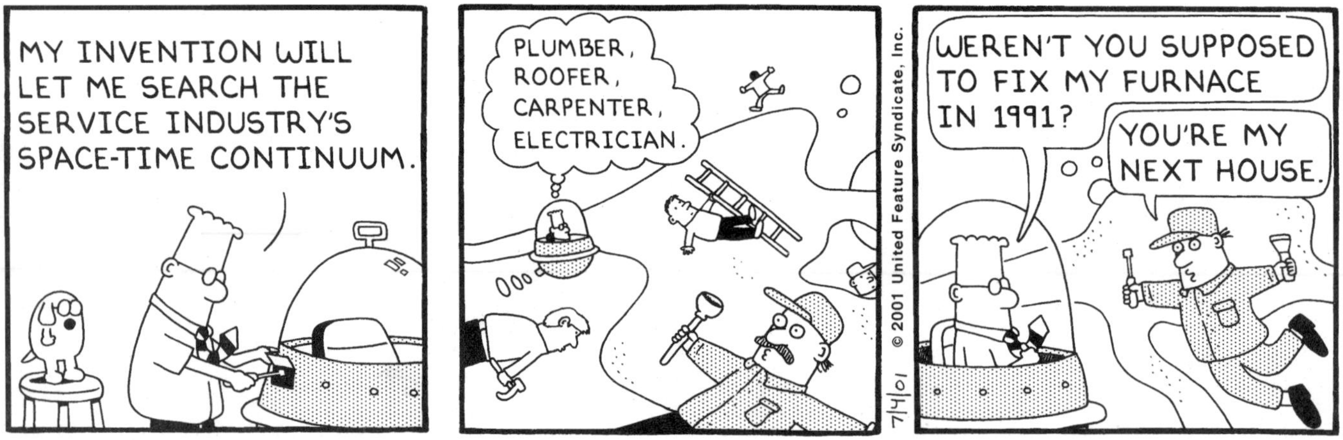
MY INVENTION WILL LET ME SEARCH THE SERVICE INDUSTRY'S SPACE-TIME CONTINUUM.
PLUMBER, ROOFER, CARPENTER, ELECTRICIAN.
7/4/01 © 2001 United Feature Syndicate, Inc.
WEREN'T YOU SUPPOSED TO FIX MY FURNACE IN 1991?
YOU'RE MY NEXT HOUSE.

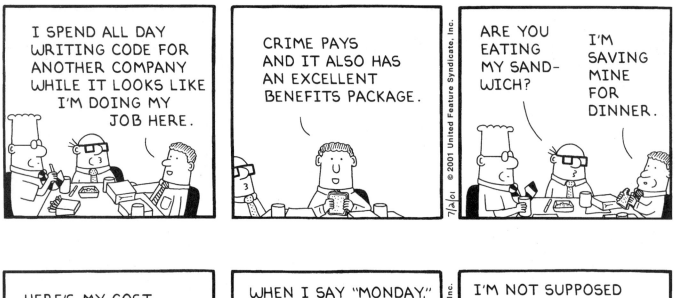

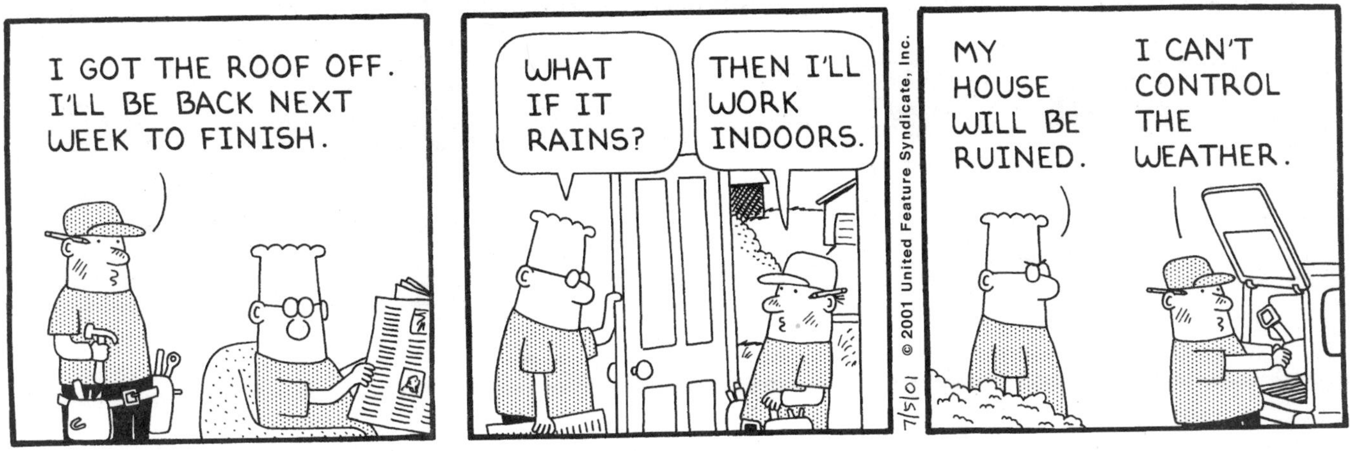
I GOT THE ROOF OFF. I'LL BE BACK NEXT WEEK TO FINISH.
WHAT IF IT RAINS?
THEN I'LL WORK INDOORS.
© 2001 United Feature Syndicate, Inc.
7/5/01
MY HOUSE WILL BE RUINED.
I CAN'T CONTROL THE WEATHER.

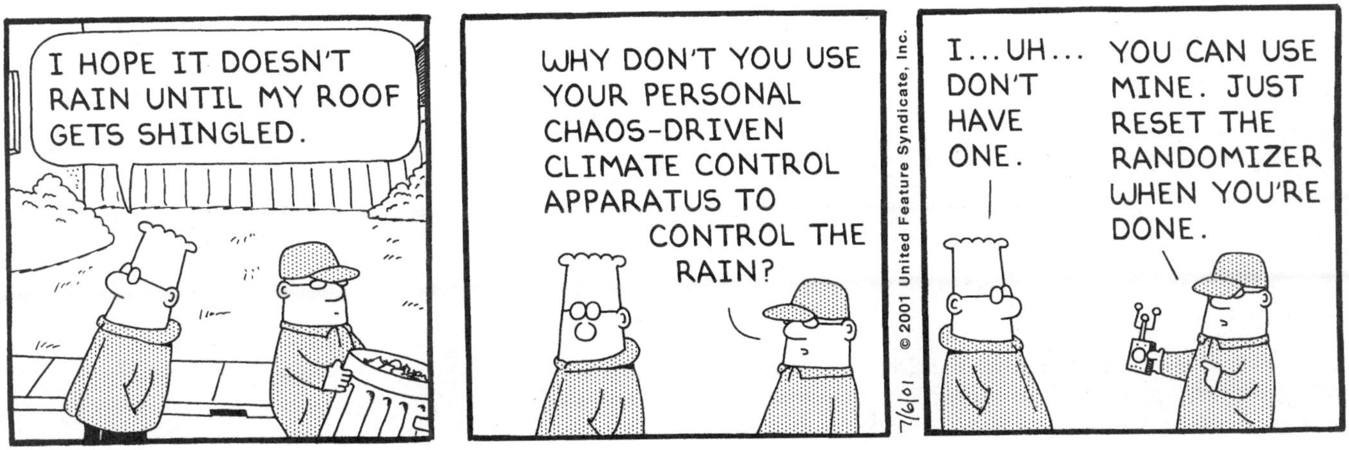
I HOPE IT DOESN'T RAIN UNTIL MY ROOF GETS SHINGLED.
WHY DON'T YOU USE YOUR PERSONAL CHAOS-DRIVEN CLIMATE CONTROL APPARATUS TO CONTROL THE RAIN?
© 2001 United Feature Syndicate, Inc.
7/6/01
I...UH... DON'T HAVE ONE.
YOU CAN USE MINE. JUST RESET THE RANDOMIZER WHEN YOU'RE DONE.

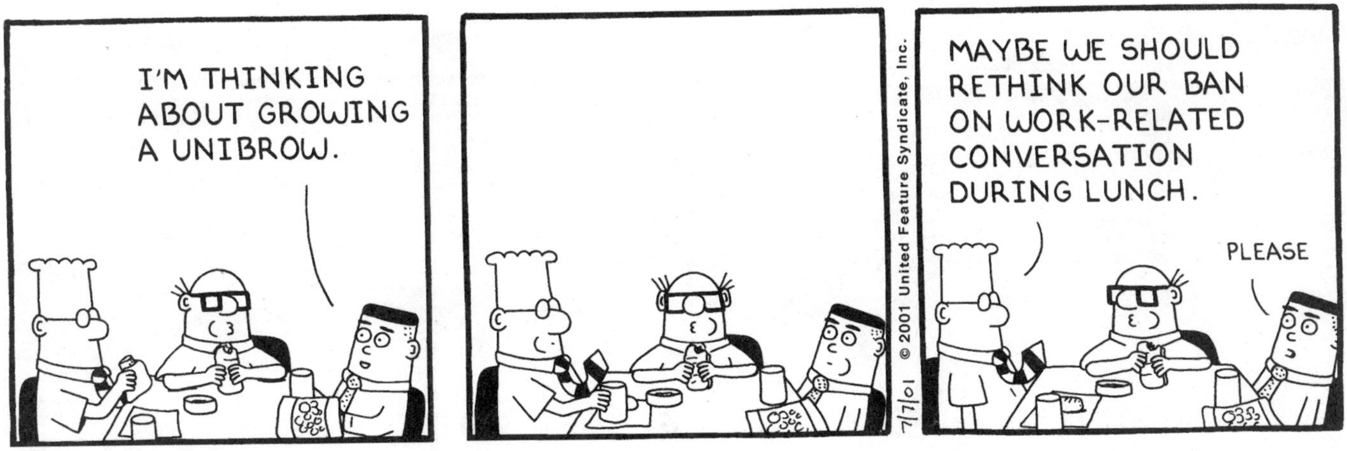
I'M THINKING ABOUT GROWING A UNIBROW.
© 2001 United Feature Syndicate, Inc.
7/7/01
MAYBE WE SHOULD RETHINK OUR BAN ON WORK-RELATED CONVERSATION DURING LUNCH.
PLEASE

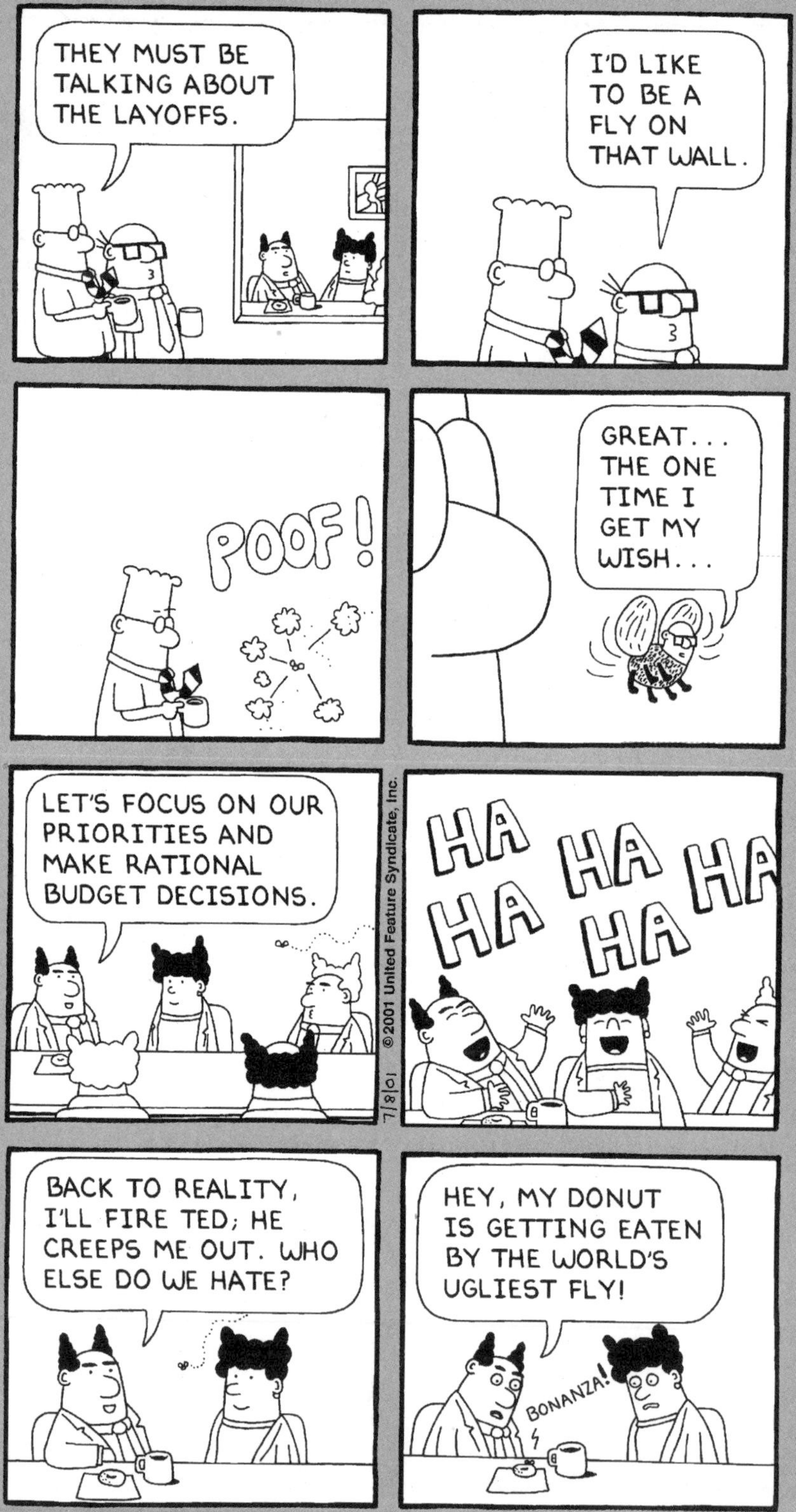
THEY MUST BE TALKING ABOUT THE LAYOFFS.
I'D LIKE TO BE A FLY ON THAT WALL.
POOF!
GREAT... THE ONE TIME I GET MY WISH...
LET'S FOCUS ON OUR PRIORITIES AND MAKE RATIONAL BUDGET DECISIONS.
©2001 United Feature Syndicate, Inc.
7/8/01
HA HA HA HA HA HA
BACK TO REALITY, I'LL FIRE TED; HE CREEPS ME OUT. WHO ELSE DO WE HATE?
HEY, MY DONUT IS GETTING EATEN BY THE WORLD'S UGLIEST FLY!
BONANZA!

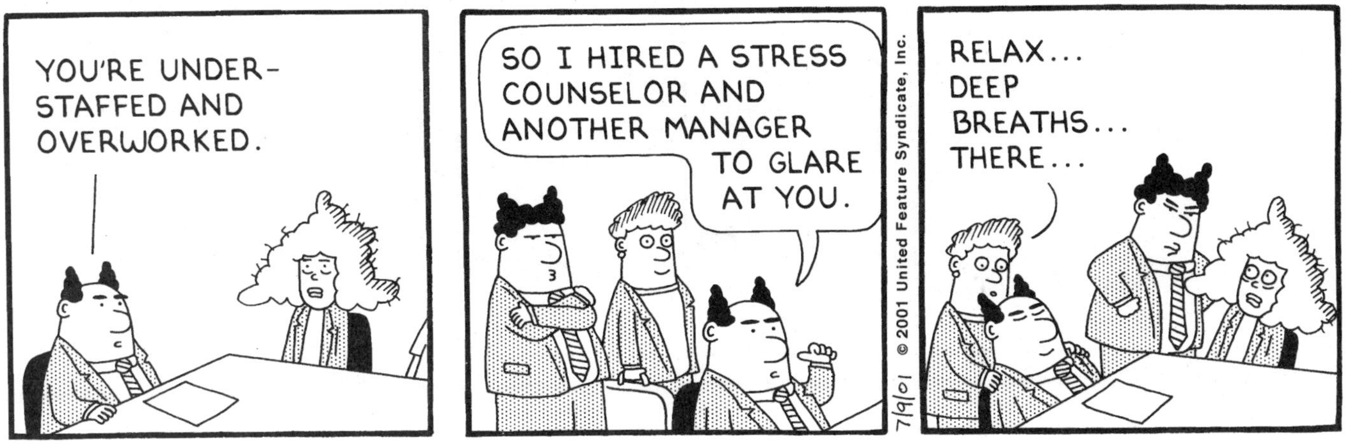
YOU'RE UNDER-STAFFED AND OVERWORKED.
SO I HIRED A STRESS COUNSELOR AND ANOTHER MANAGER TO GLARE AT YOU.
7/9/01 © 2001 United Feature Syndicate, Inc.
RELAX... DEEP BREATHS... THERE...

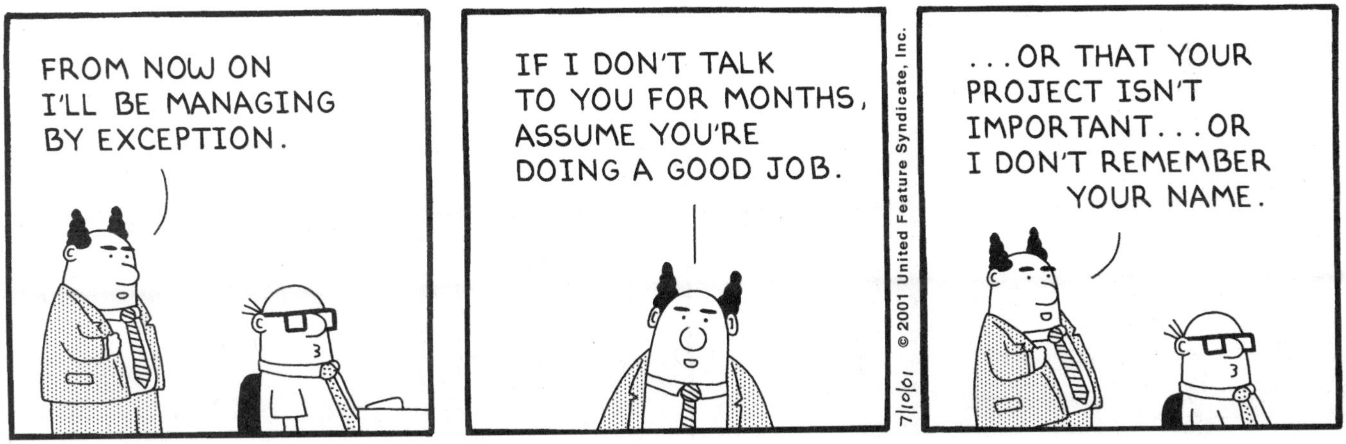
FROM NOW ON I'LL BE MANAGING BY EXCEPTION.
IF I DON'T TALK TO YOU FOR MONTHS, ASSUME YOU'RE DOING A GOOD JOB.
7/10/01 © 2001 United Feature Syndicate, Inc.
...OR THAT YOUR PROJECT ISN'T IMPORTANT...OR I DON'T REMEMBER YOUR NAME.

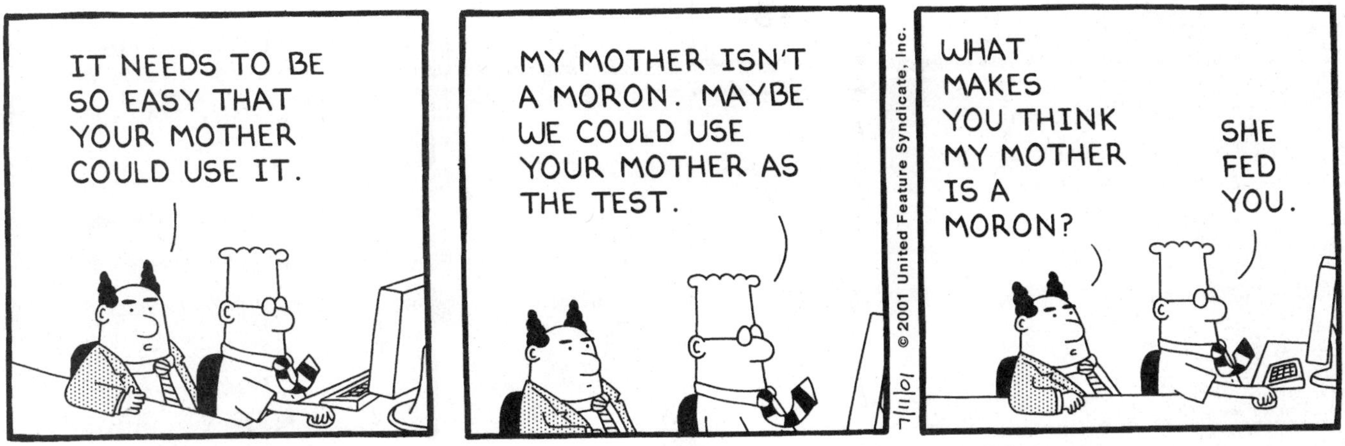
IT NEEDS TO BE SO EASY THAT YOUR MOTHER COULD USE IT.
MY MOTHER ISN'T A MORON. MAYBE WE COULD USE YOUR MOTHER AS THE TEST.
7/11/01 © 2001 United Feature Syndicate, Inc.
WHAT MAKES YOU THINK MY MOTHER IS A MORON?
SHE FED YOU.

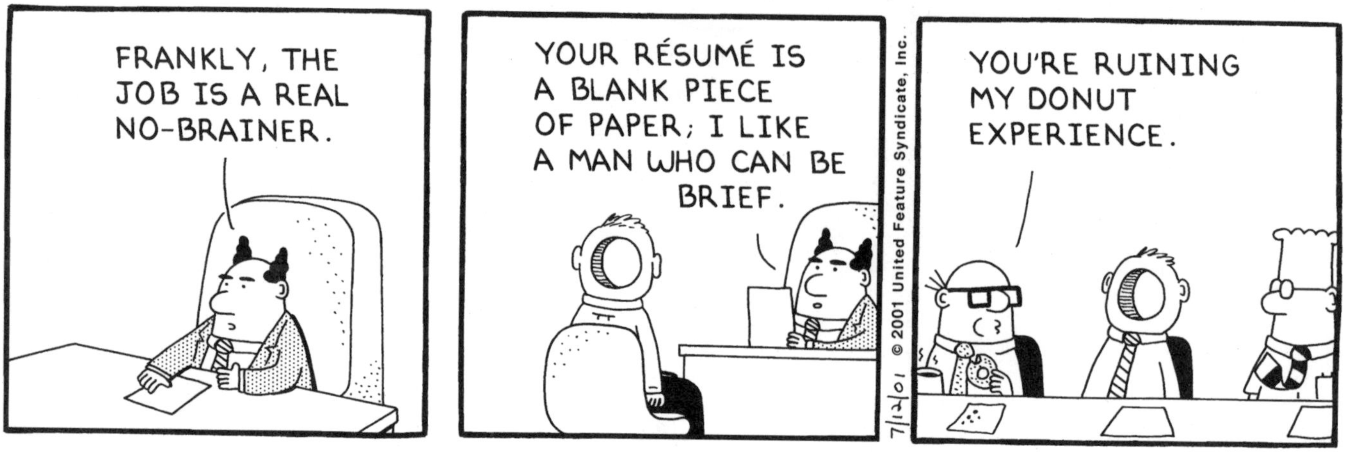
FRANKLY, THE JOB IS A REAL NO-BRAINER.
YOUR RÉSUMÉ IS A BLANK PIECE OF PAPER; I LIKE A MAN WHO CAN BE BRIEF.
7/12/01 © 2001 United Feature Syndicate, Inc.
YOU'RE RUINING MY DONUT EXPERIENCE.

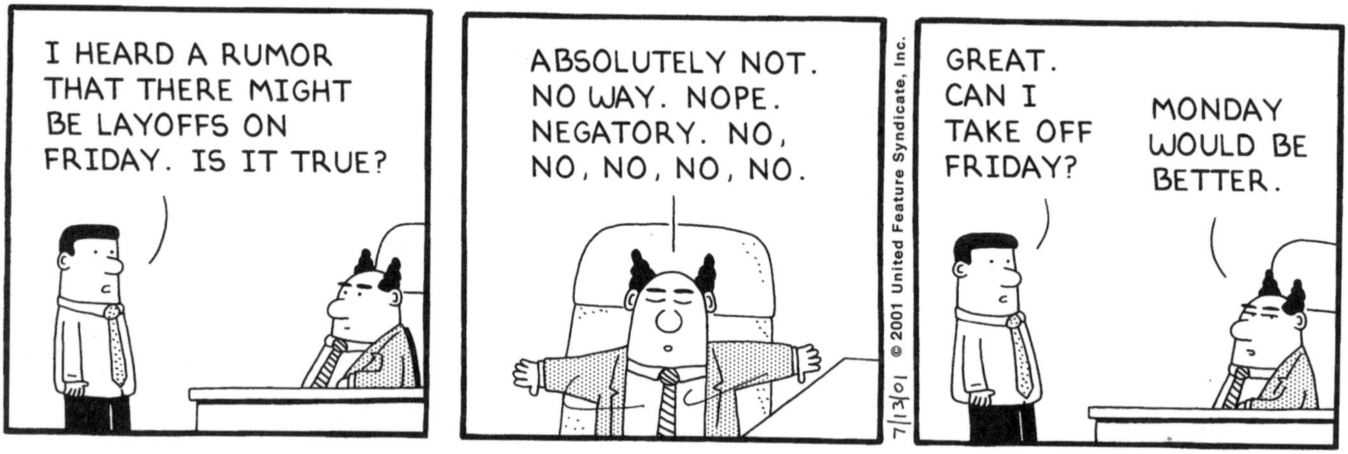
I HEARD A RUMOR THAT THERE MIGHT BE LAYOFFS ON FRIDAY. IS IT TRUE?
ABSOLUTELY NOT. NO WAY. NOPE. NEGATORY. NO, NO, NO, NO, NO.
7/13/01 © 2001 United Feature Syndicate, Inc.
GREAT. CAN I TAKE OFF FRIDAY?
MONDAY WOULD BE BETTER.

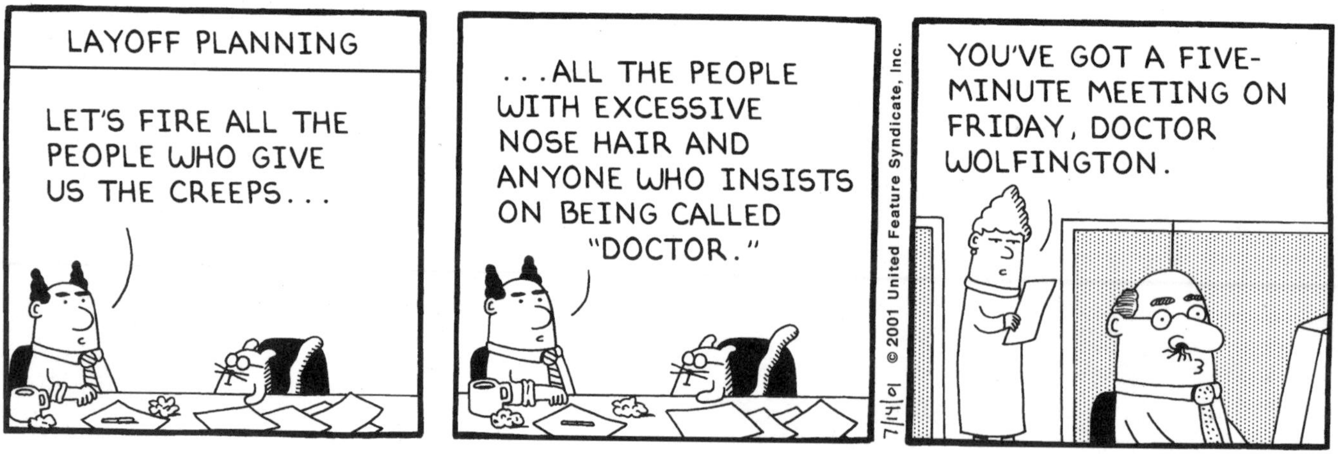
LAYOFF PLANNING
LET'S FIRE ALL THE PEOPLE WHO GIVE US THE CREEPS...
...ALL THE PEOPLE WITH EXCESSIVE NOSE HAIR AND ANYONE WHO INSISTS ON BEING CALLED "DOCTOR."
7/14/01 © 2001 United Feature Syndicate, Inc.
YOU'VE GOT A FIVE-MINUTE MEETING ON FRIDAY, DOCTOR WOLFINGTON.

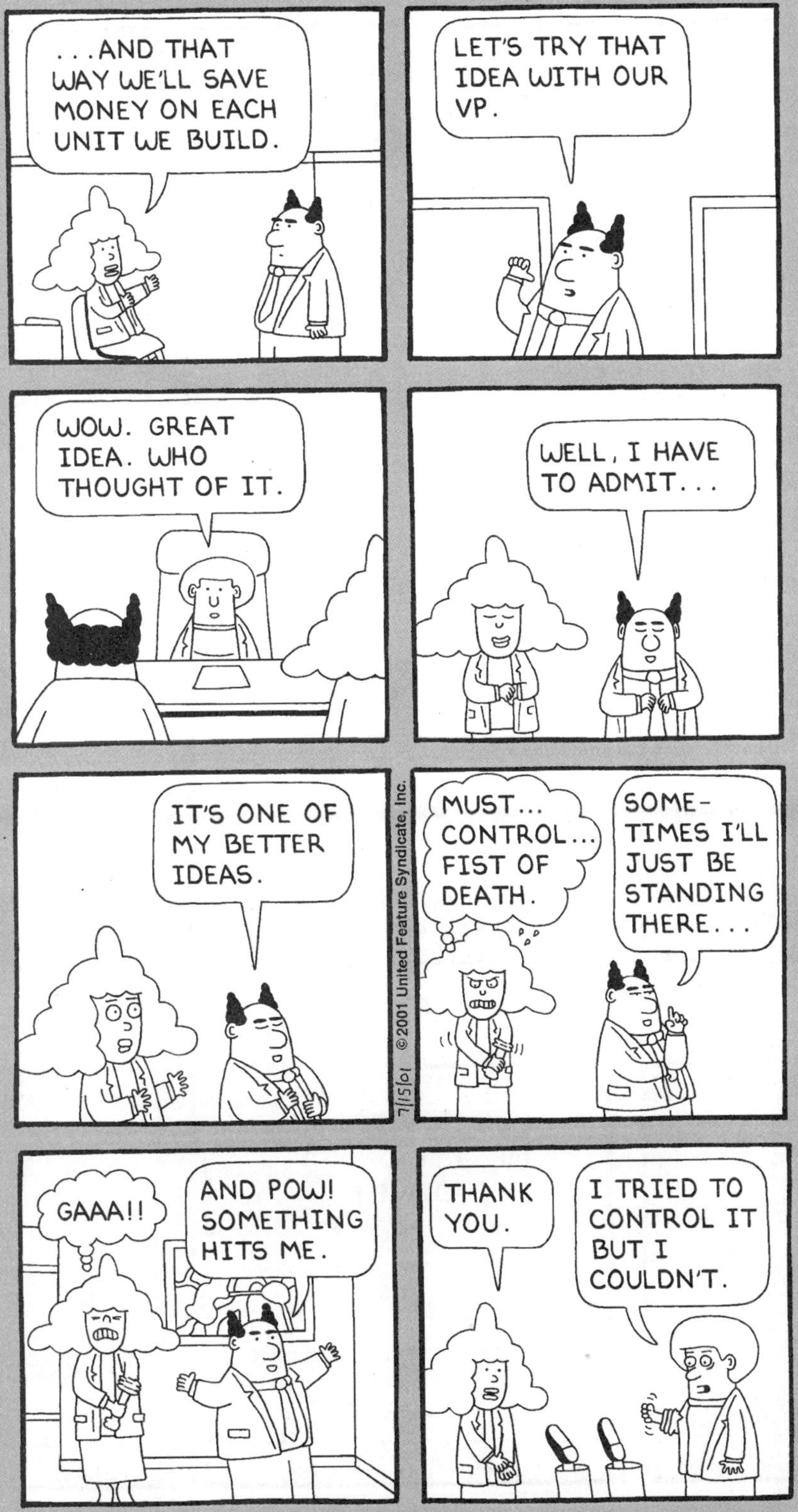
. . . AND THAT WAY WE'LL SAVE MONEY ON EACH UNIT WE BUILD.
LET'S TRY THAT IDEA WITH OUR VP.
WOW. GREAT IDEA. WHO THOUGHT OF IT.
WELL, I HAVE TO ADMIT . . .
IT'S ONE OF MY BETTER IDEAS.
©2001 United Feature Syndicate, Inc.
7/15/01
MUST... CONTROL... FIST OF DEATH.
SOME-TIMES I'LL JUST BE STANDING THERE . . .
GAAA!!
AND POW! SOMETHING HITS ME.
THANK YOU.
I TRIED TO CONTROL IT BUT I COULDN'T.

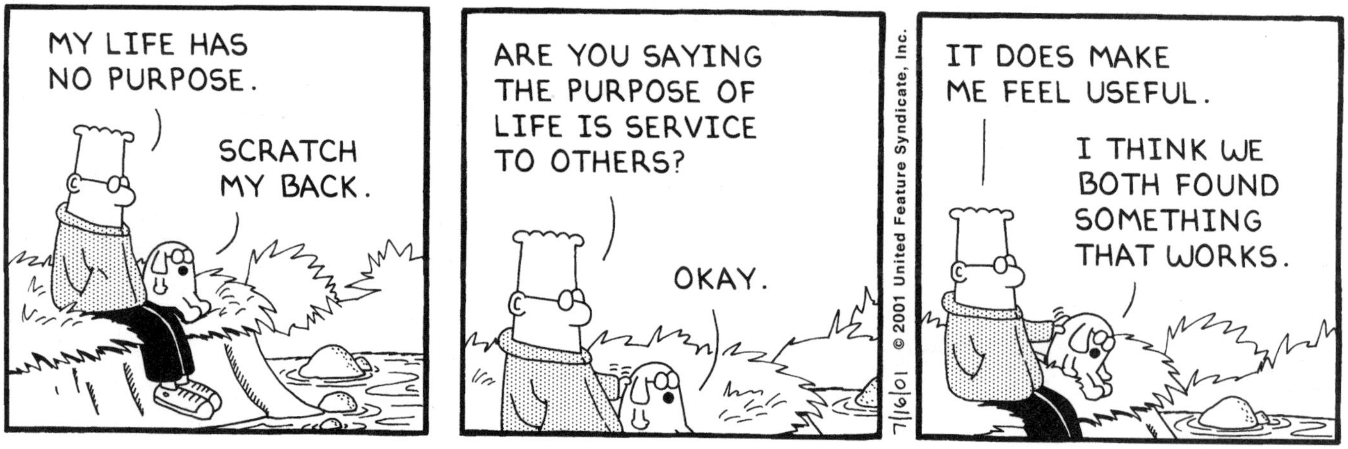
MY LIFE HAS NO PURPOSE.
SCRATCH MY BACK.
ARE YOU SAYING THE PURPOSE OF LIFE IS SERVICE TO OTHERS?
OKAY.
IT DOES MAKE ME FEEL USEFUL.
I THINK WE BOTH FOUND SOMETHING THAT WORKS.
7/16/01 © 2001 United Feature Syndicate, Inc.

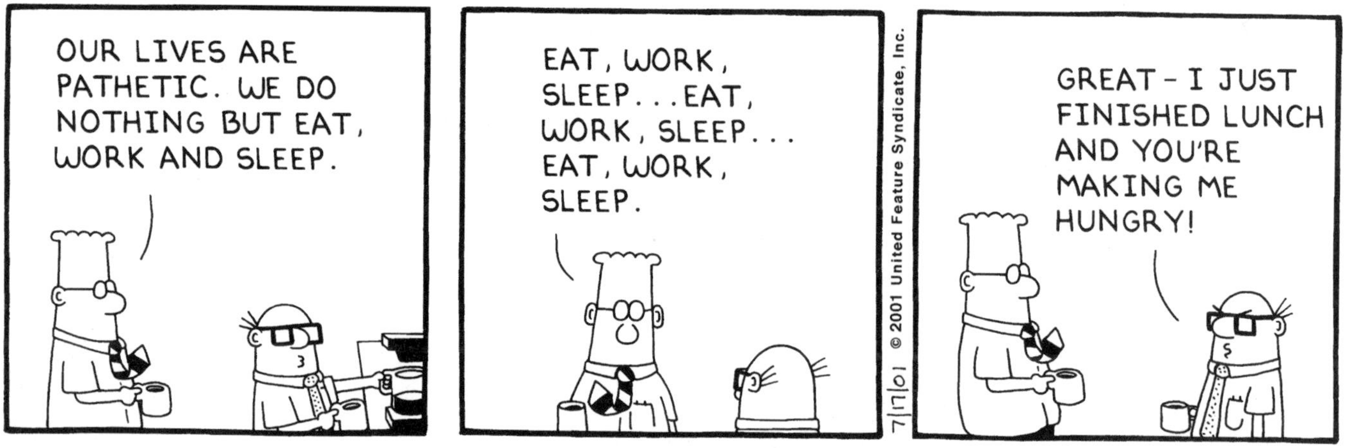
OUR LIVES ARE PATHETIC. WE DO NOTHING BUT EAT, WORK AND SLEEP.
EAT, WORK, SLEEP...EAT, WORK, SLEEP... EAT, WORK, SLEEP.
GREAT - I JUST FINISHED LUNCH AND YOU'RE MAKING ME HUNGRY!
7/17/01 © 2001 United Feature Syndicate, Inc.

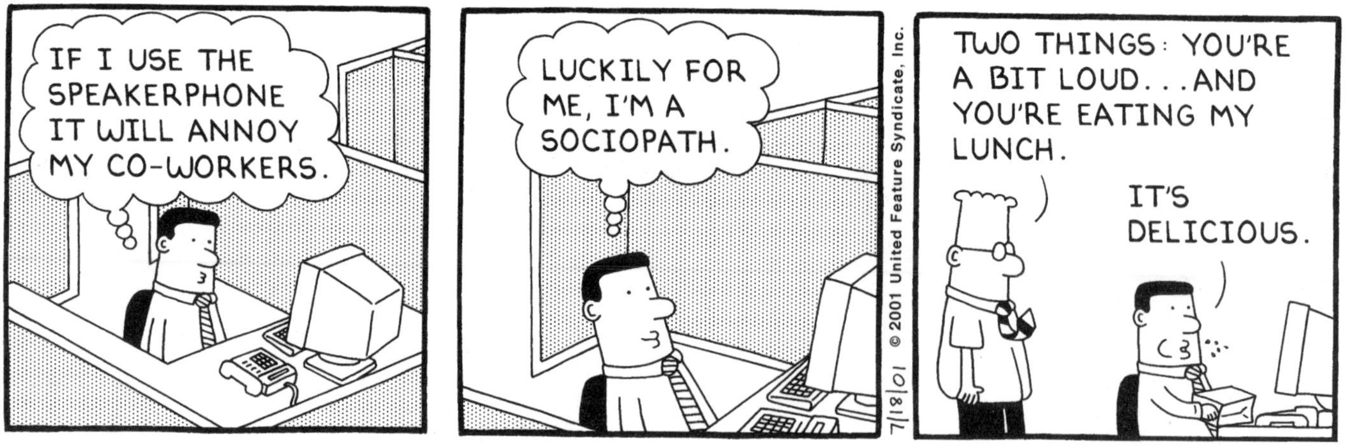
IF I USE THE SPEAKERPHONE IT WILL ANNOY MY CO-WORKERS.
LUCKILY FOR ME, I'M A SOCIOPATH.
TWO THINGS: YOU'RE A BIT LOUD...AND YOU'RE EATING MY LUNCH.
IT'S DELICIOUS.
7/18/01 © 2001 United Feature Syndicate, Inc.

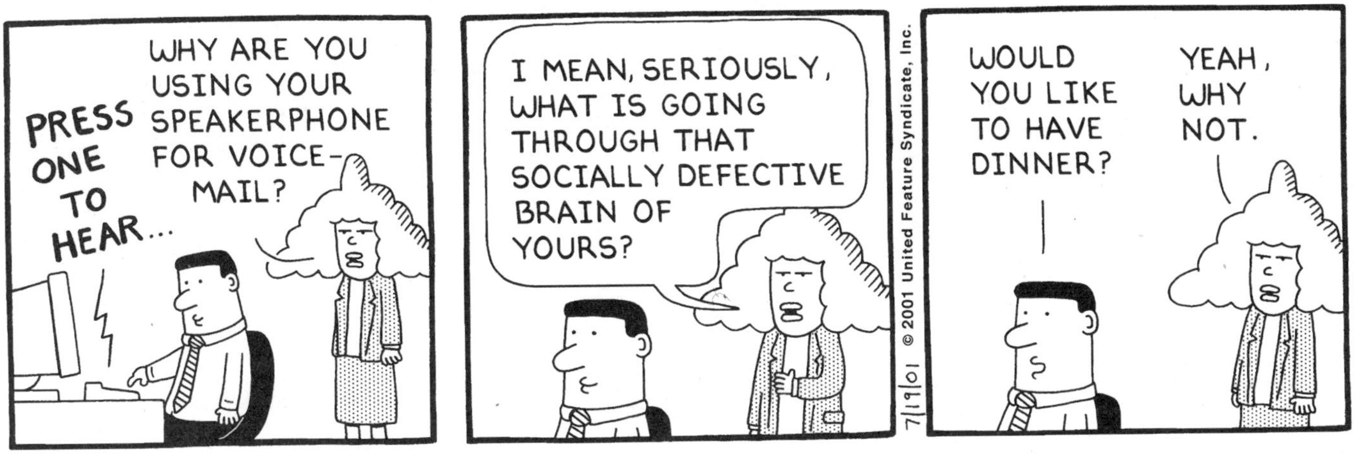
PRESS ONE TO HEAR...
WHY ARE YOU USING YOUR SPEAKERPHONE FOR VOICE-MAIL?
I MEAN, SERIOUSLY, WHAT IS GOING THROUGH THAT SOCIALLY DEFECTIVE BRAIN OF YOURS?
7/19/01 © 2001 United Feature Syndicate, Inc.
WOULD YOU LIKE TO HAVE DINNER?
YEAH, WHY NOT.

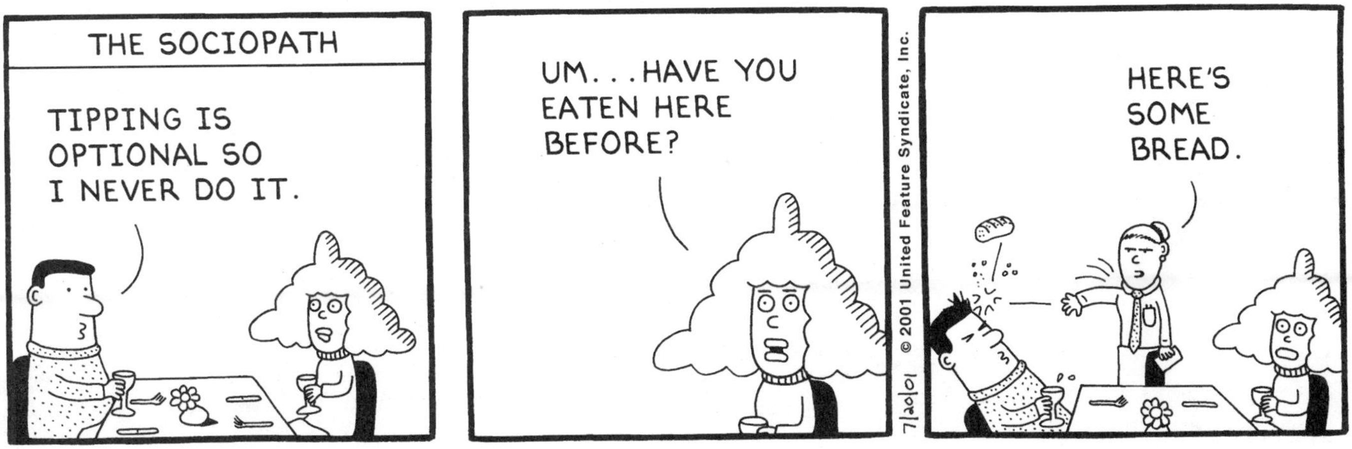
THE SOCIOPATH
TIPPING IS OPTIONAL SO I NEVER DO IT.
UM. . . HAVE YOU EATEN HERE BEFORE?
7/20/01 © 2001 United Feature Syndicate, Inc.
HERE'S SOME BREAD.

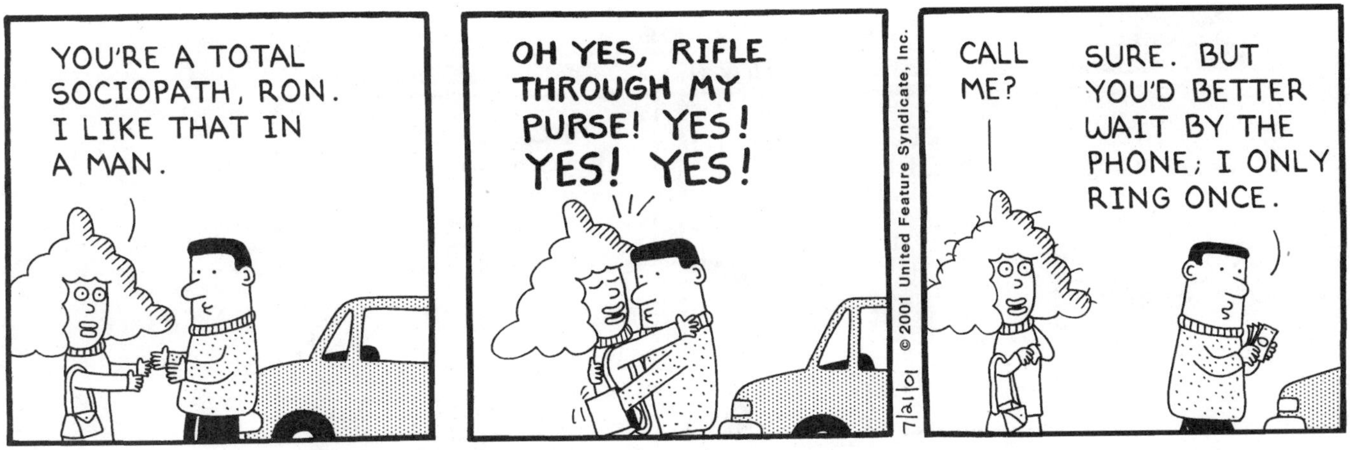
YOU'RE A TOTAL SOCIOPATH, RON. I LIKE THAT IN A MAN.
OH YES, RIFLE THROUGH MY PURSE! YES! YES! YES!
7/21/01 © 2001 United Feature Syndicate, Inc.
CALL ME?
SURE. BUT YOU'D BETTER WAIT BY THE PHONE; I ONLY RING ONCE.

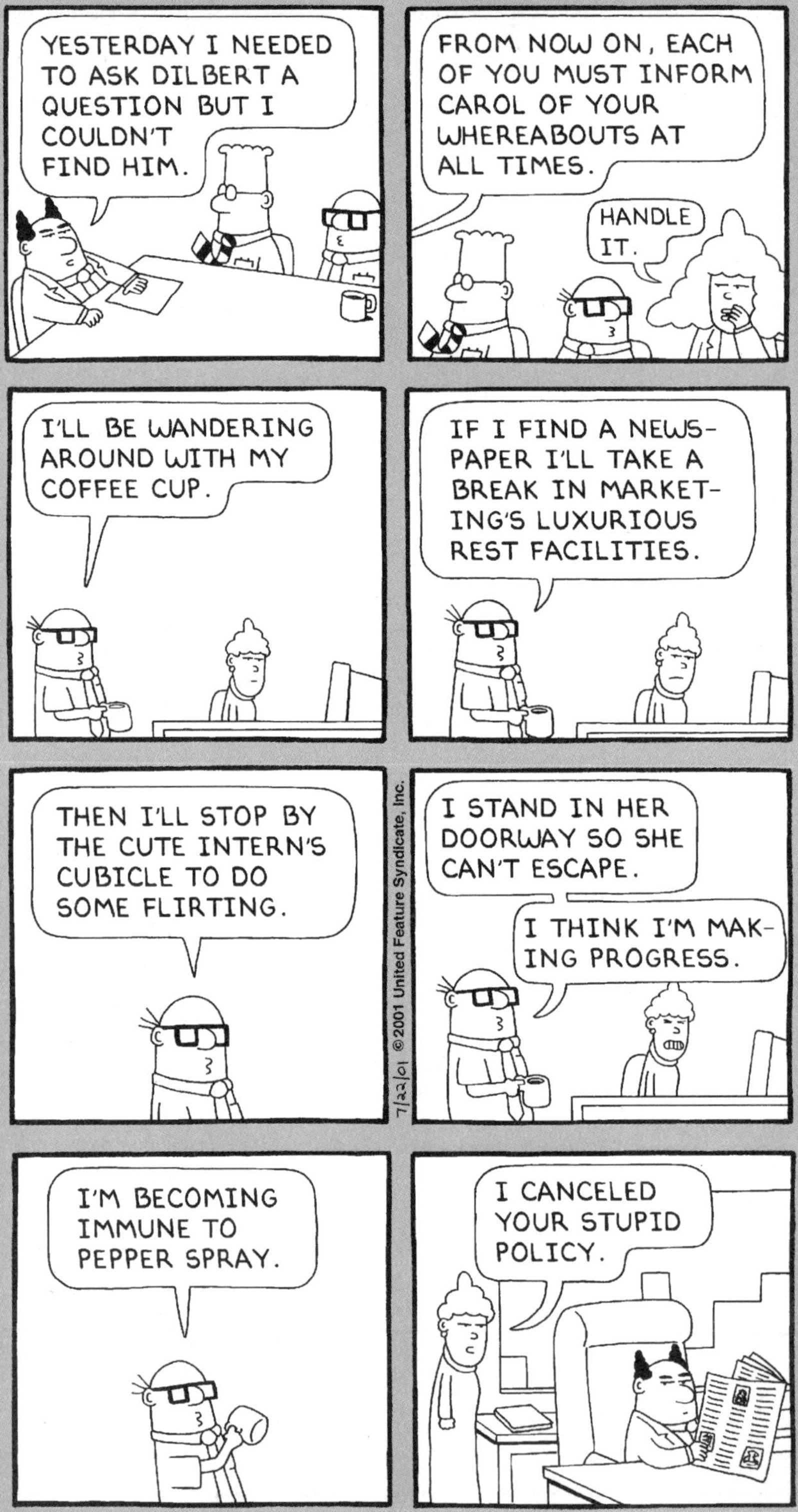
YESTERDAY I NEEDED TO ASK DILBERT A QUESTION BUT I COULDN'T FIND HIM.
FROM NOW ON, EACH OF YOU MUST INFORM CAROL OF YOUR WHEREABOUTS AT ALL TIMES.
HANDLE IT.
I'LL BE WANDERING AROUND WITH MY COFFEE CUP.
IF I FIND A NEWS-PAPER I'LL TAKE A BREAK IN MARKET-ING'S LUXURIOUS REST FACILITIES.
THEN I'LL STOP BY THE CUTE INTERN'S CUBICLE TO DO SOME FLIRTING.
7/22/01 ©2001 United Feature Syndicate, Inc.
I STAND IN HER DOORWAY SO SHE CAN'T ESCAPE.
I THINK I'M MAK-ING PROGRESS.
I'M BECOMING IMMUNE TO PEPPER SPRAY.
I CANCELED YOUR STUPID POLICY.

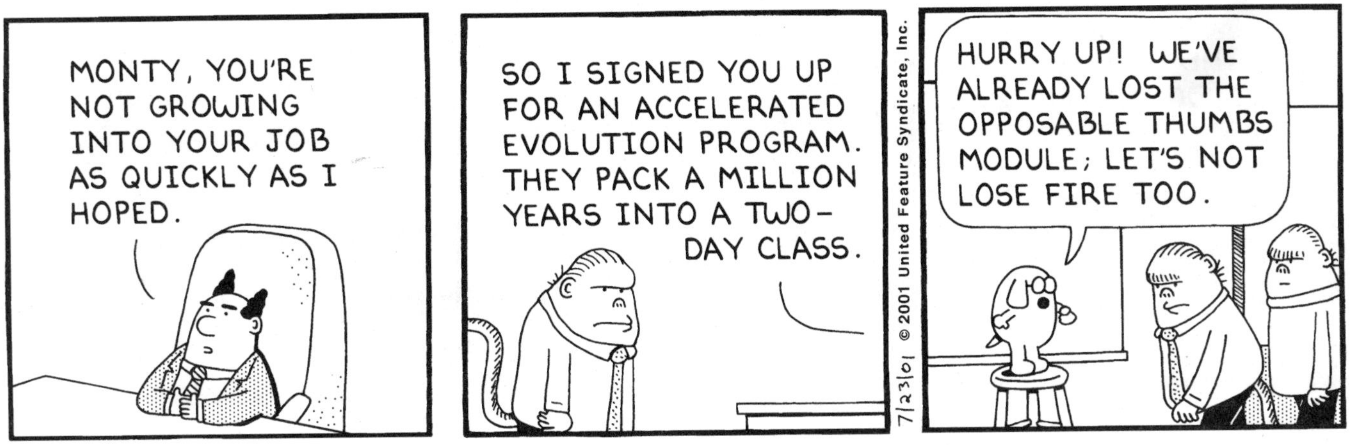
MONTY, YOU'RE NOT GROWING INTO YOUR JOB AS QUICKLY AS I HOPED.
SO I SIGNED YOU UP FOR AN ACCELERATED EVOLUTION PROGRAM. THEY PACK A MILLION YEARS INTO A TWO-DAY CLASS.
7/23/01 © 2001 United Feature Syndicate, Inc.
HURRY UP! WE'VE ALREADY LOST THE OPPOSABLE THUMBS MODULE; LET'S NOT LOSE FIRE TOO.

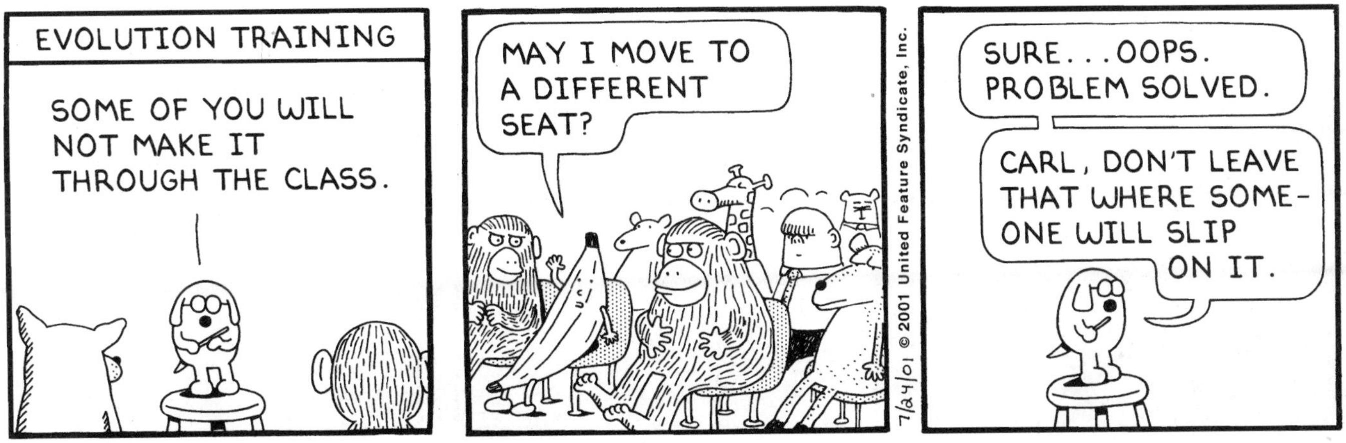
EVOLUTION TRAINING
SOME OF YOU WILL NOT MAKE IT THROUGH THE CLASS.
MAY I MOVE TO A DIFFERENT SEAT?
7/24/01 © 2001 United Feature Syndicate, Inc.
SURE... OOPS. PROBLEM SOLVED.
CARL, DON'T LEAVE THAT WHERE SOME-ONE WILL SLIP ON IT.

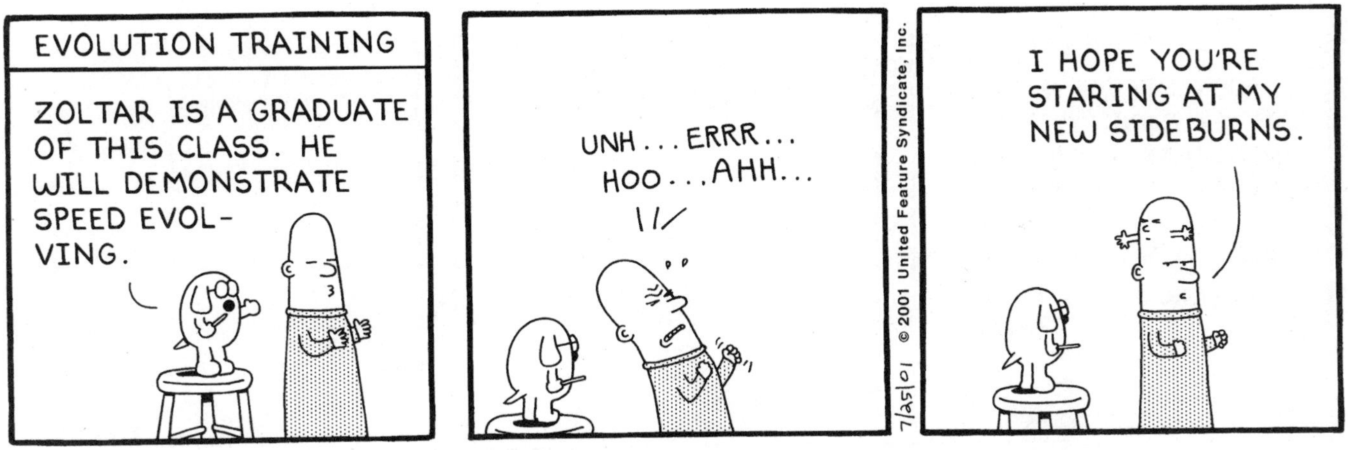
EVOLUTION TRAINING
ZOLTAR IS A GRADUATE OF THIS CLASS. HE WILL DEMONSTRATE SPEED EVOL-VING.
UNH... ERRR... HOO... AHH...
7/25/01 © 2001 United Feature Syndicate, Inc.
I HOPE YOU'RE STARING AT MY NEW SIDEBURNS.

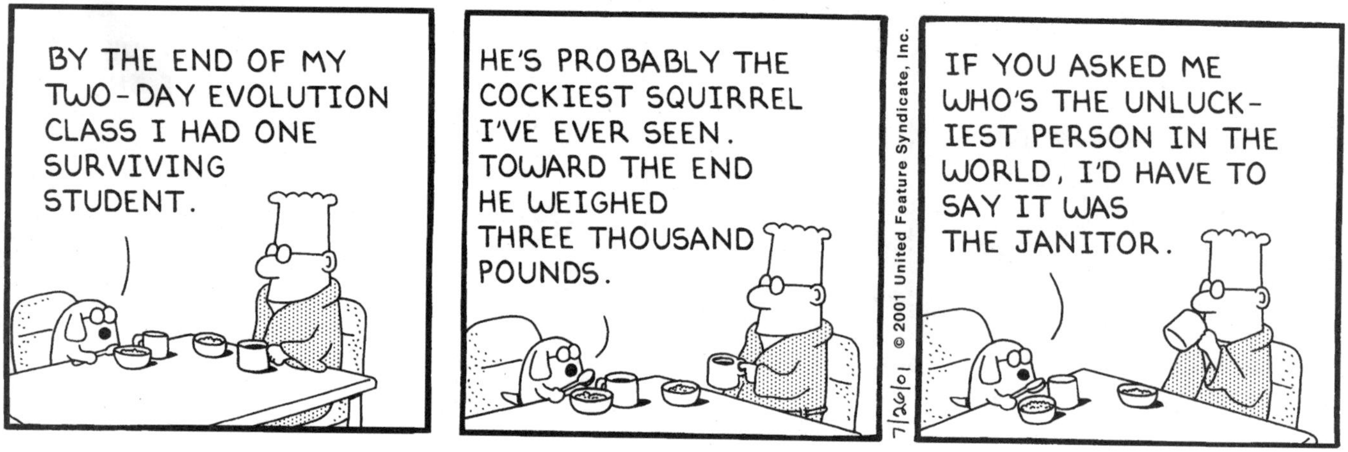
BY THE END OF MY TWO-DAY EVOLUTION CLASS I HAD ONE SURVIVING STUDENT.
HE'S PROBABLY THE COCKIEST SQUIRREL I'VE EVER SEEN. TOWARD THE END HE WEIGHED THREE THOUSAND POUNDS.
7/26/01 © 2001 United Feature Syndicate, Inc.
IF YOU ASKED ME WHO'S THE UNLUCK-IEST PERSON IN THE WORLD, I'D HAVE TO SAY IT WAS THE JANITOR.

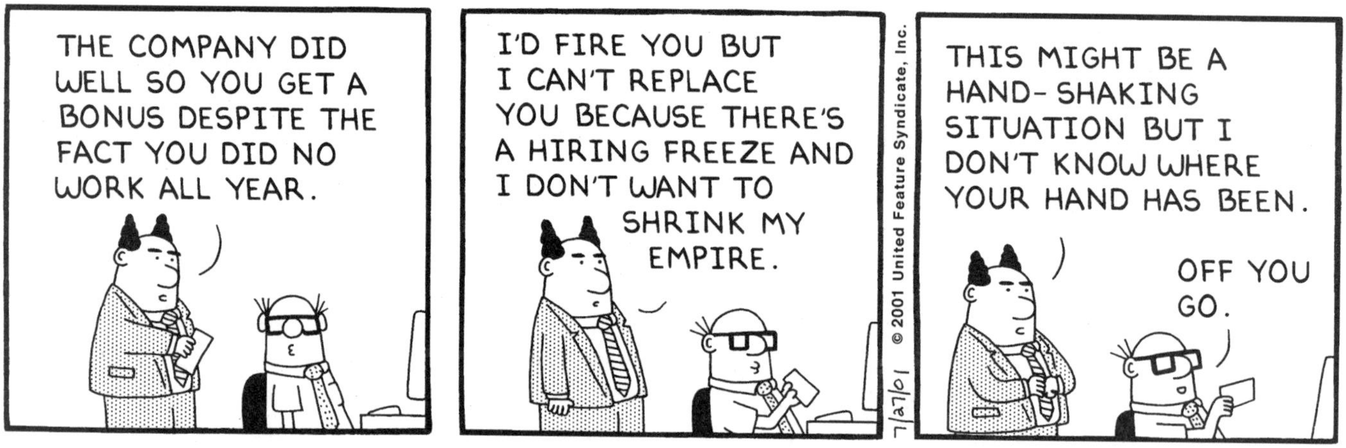
THE COMPANY DID WELL SO YOU GET A BONUS DESPITE THE FACT YOU DID NO WORK ALL YEAR.
I'D FIRE YOU BUT I CAN'T REPLACE YOU BECAUSE THERE'S A HIRING FREEZE AND I DON'T WANT TO SHRINK MY EMPIRE.
7/27/01 © 2001 United Feature Syndicate, Inc.
THIS MIGHT BE A HAND-SHAKING SITUATION BUT I DON'T KNOW WHERE YOUR HAND HAS BEEN.
OFF YOU GO.

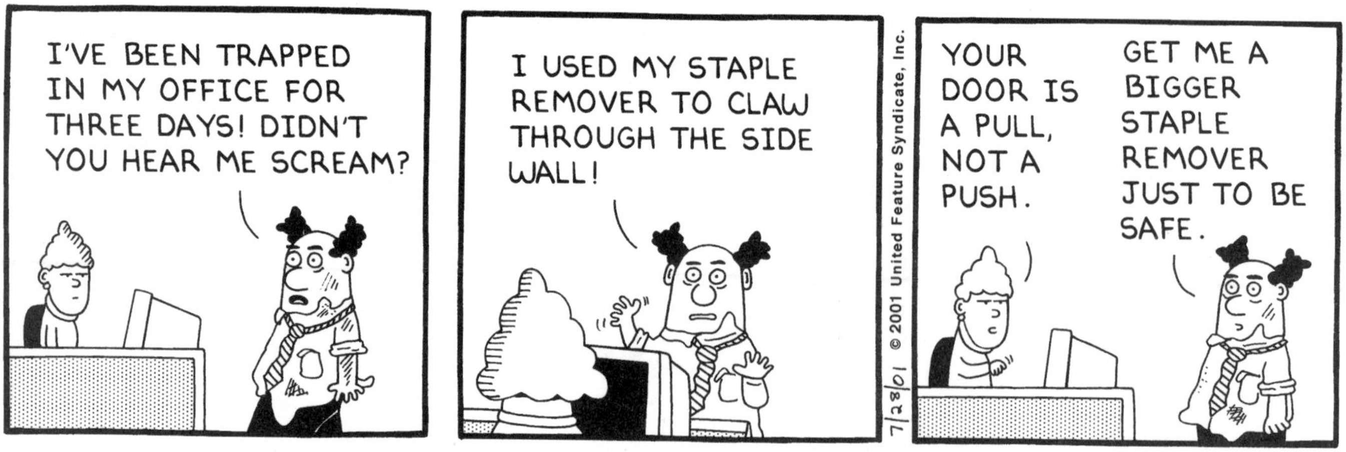
I'VE BEEN TRAPPED IN MY OFFICE FOR THREE DAYS! DIDN'T YOU HEAR ME SCREAM?
I USED MY STAPLE REMOVER TO CLAW THROUGH THE SIDE WALL!
7/28/01 © 2001 United Feature Syndicate, Inc.
YOUR DOOR IS A PULL, NOT A PUSH.
GET ME A BIGGER STAPLE REMOVER JUST TO BE SAFE.

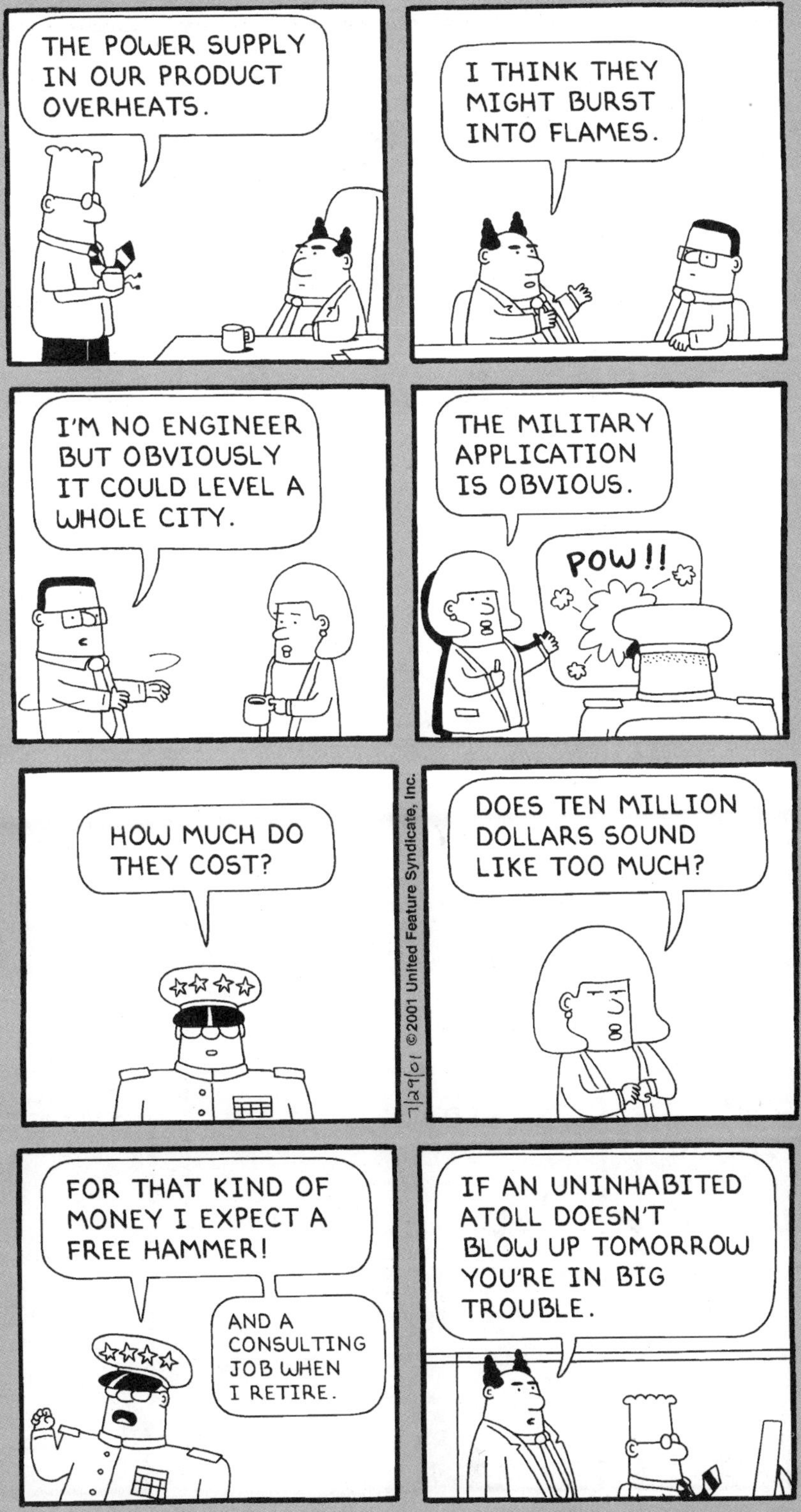
THE POWER SUPPLY IN OUR PRODUCT OVERHEATS.
I THINK THEY MIGHT BURST INTO FLAMES.
I'M NO ENGINEER BUT OBVIOUSLY IT COULD LEVEL A WHOLE CITY.
THE MILITARY APPLICATION IS OBVIOUS.
POW!!
HOW MUCH DO THEY COST?
DOES TEN MILLION DOLLARS SOUND LIKE TOO MUCH?
FOR THAT KIND OF MONEY I EXPECT A FREE HAMMER!
AND A CONSULTING JOB WHEN I RETIRE.
IF AN UNINHABITED ATOLL DOESN'T BLOW UP TOMORROW YOU'RE IN BIG TROUBLE.

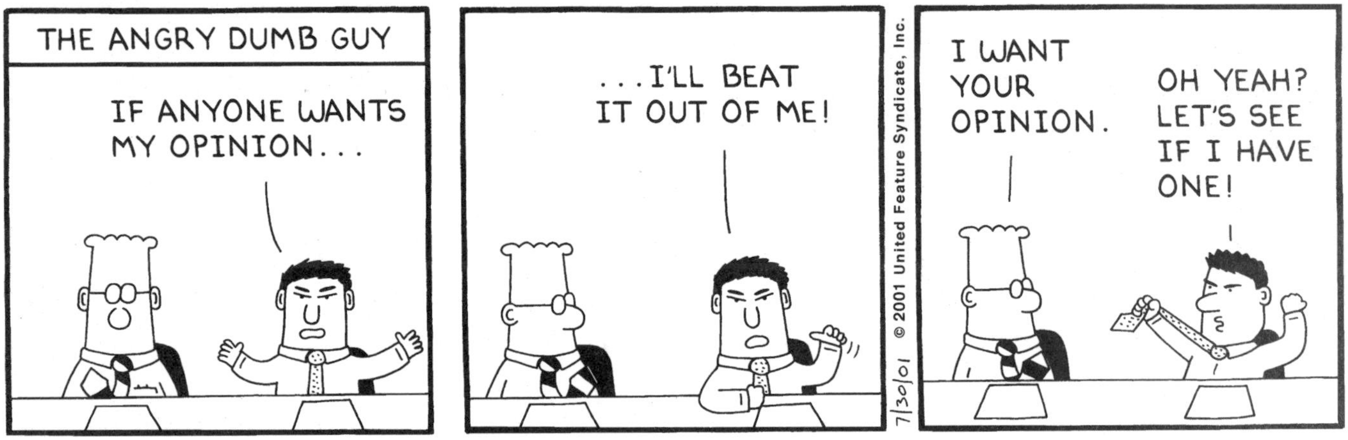
THE ANGRY DUMB GUY
IF ANYONE WANTS MY OPINION...
...I'LL BEAT IT OUT OF ME!
7/30/01 © 2001 United Feature Syndicate, Inc.
I WANT YOUR OPINION.
OH YEAH? LET'S SEE IF I HAVE ONE!

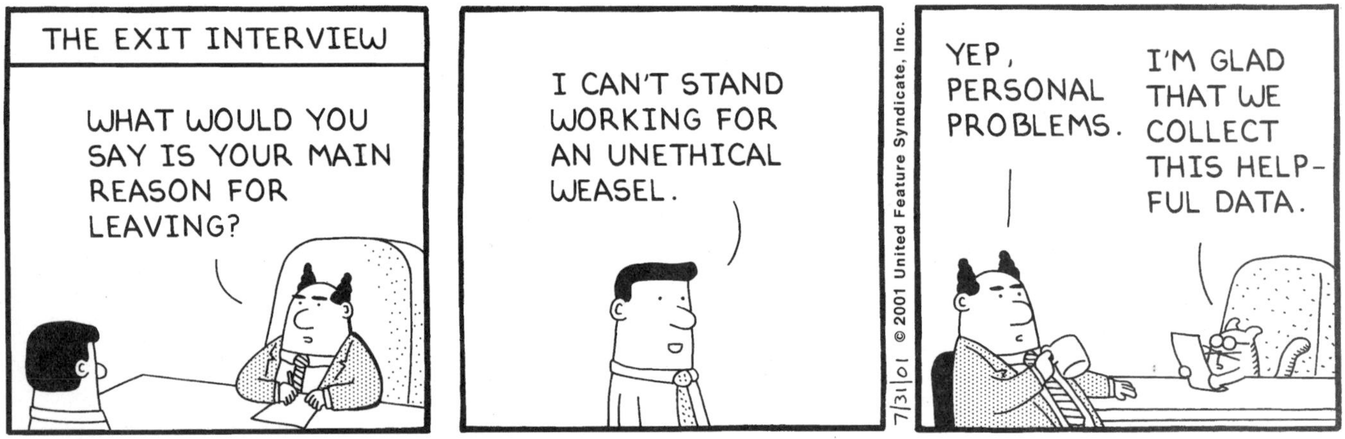
THE EXIT INTERVIEW
WHAT WOULD YOU SAY IS YOUR MAIN REASON FOR LEAVING?
I CAN'T STAND WORKING FOR AN UNETHICAL WEASEL.
7/31/01 © 2001 United Feature Syndicate, Inc.
YEP, PERSONAL PROBLEMS.
I'M GLAD THAT WE COLLECT THIS HELP-FUL DATA.

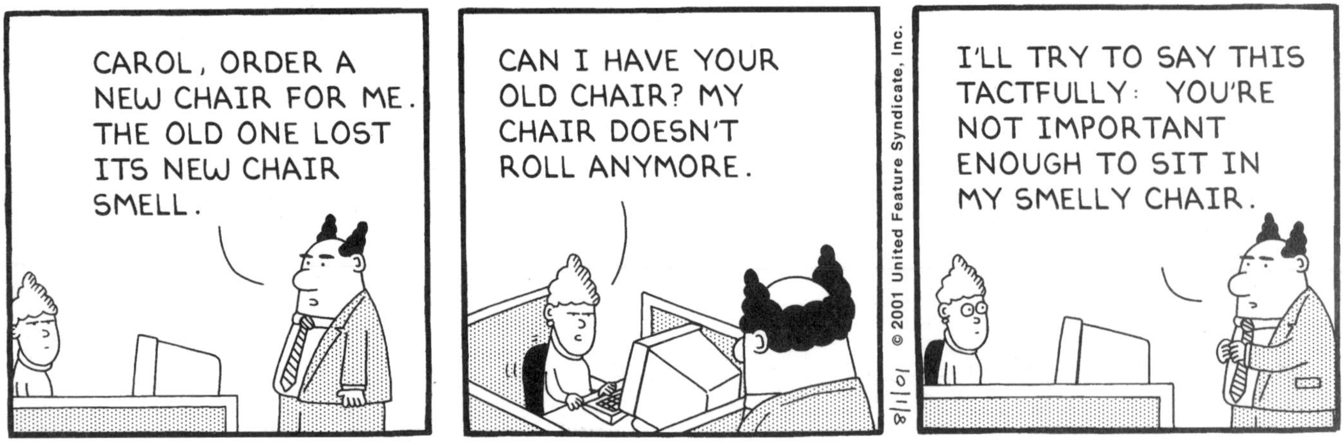
CAROL, ORDER A NEW CHAIR FOR ME. THE OLD ONE LOST ITS NEW CHAIR SMELL.
CAN I HAVE YOUR OLD CHAIR? MY CHAIR DOESN'T ROLL ANYMORE.
8/1/01 © 2001 United Feature Syndicate, Inc.
I'LL TRY TO SAY THIS TACTFULLY: YOU'RE NOT IMPORTANT ENOUGH TO SIT IN MY SMELLY CHAIR.

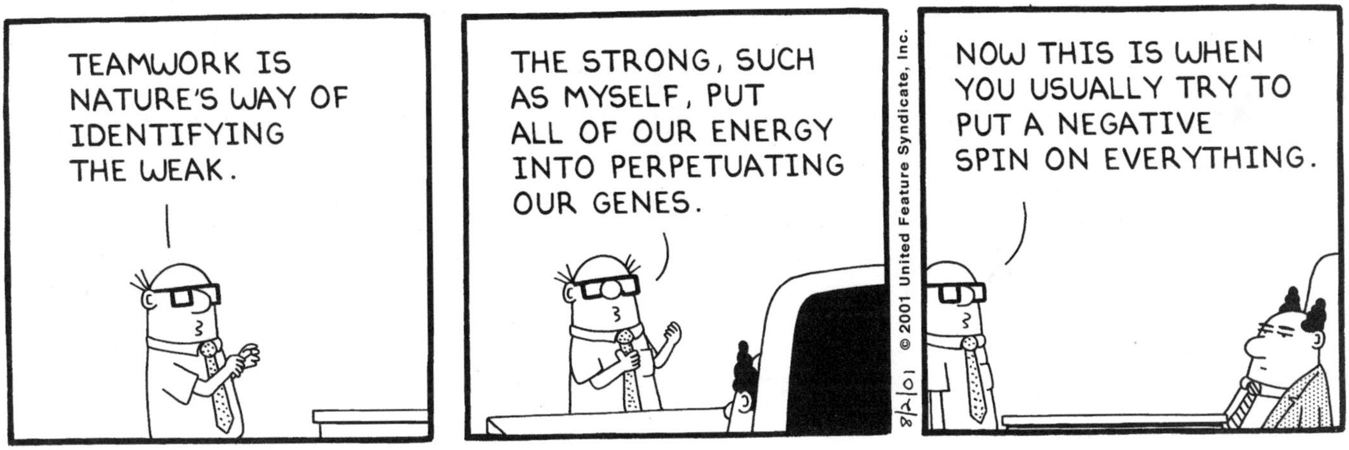
TEAMWORK IS NATURE'S WAY OF IDENTIFYING THE WEAK.
THE STRONG, SUCH AS MYSELF, PUT ALL OF OUR ENERGY INTO PERPETUATING OUR GENES.
8/2/01 © 2001 United Feature Syndicate, Inc.
NOW THIS IS WHEN YOU USUALLY TRY TO PUT A NEGATIVE SPIN ON EVERYTHING.

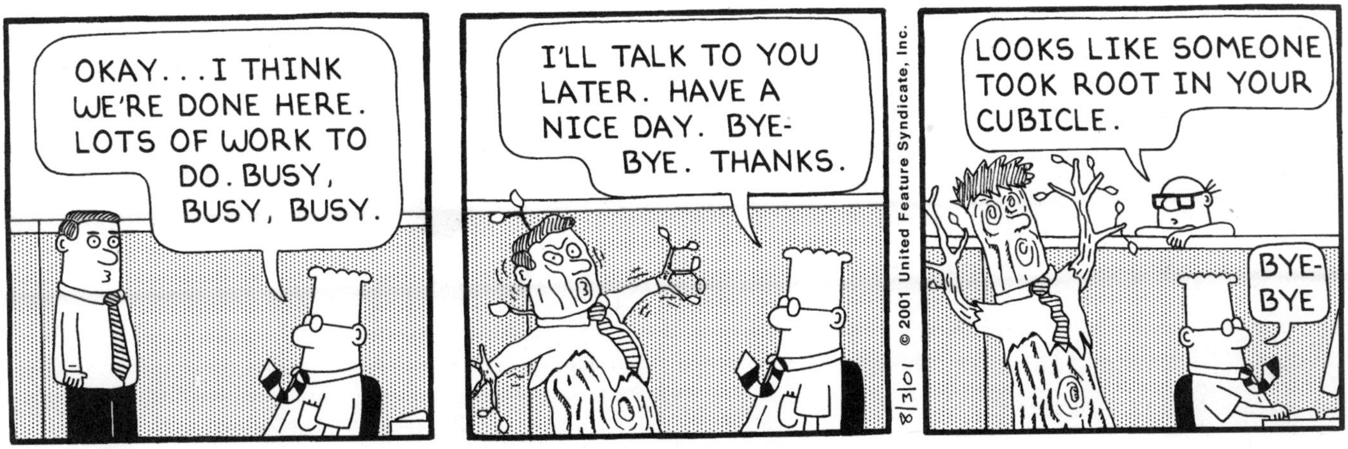
OKAY...I THINK WE'RE DONE HERE. LOTS OF WORK TO DO. BUSY, BUSY, BUSY.
I'LL TALK TO YOU LATER. HAVE A NICE DAY. BYE-BYE. THANKS.
8/3/01 © 2001 United Feature Syndicate, Inc.
LOOKS LIKE SOMEONE TOOK ROOT IN YOUR CUBICLE.
BYE-BYE

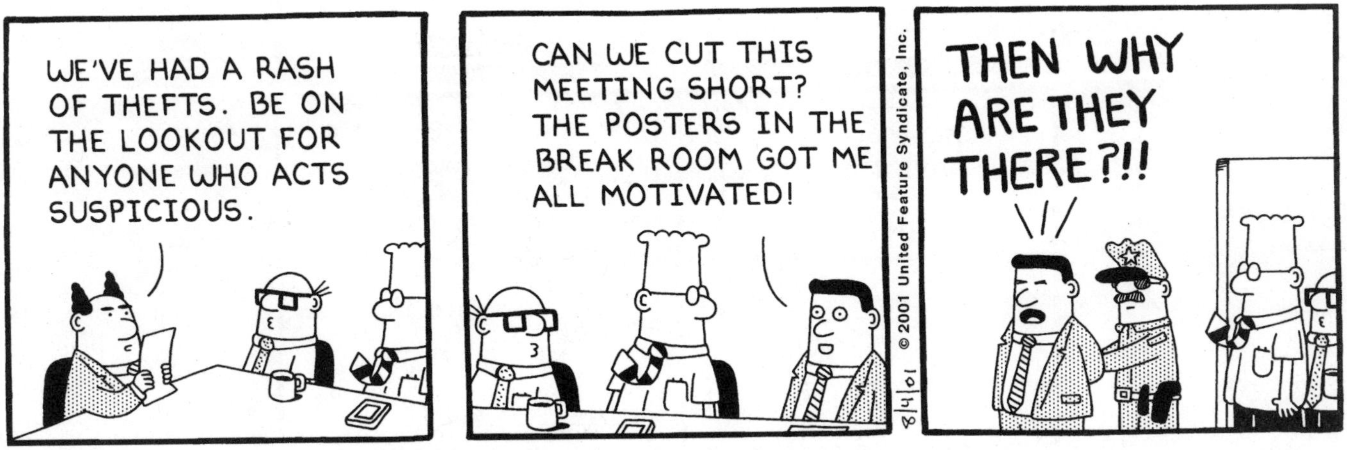
WE'VE HAD A RASH OF THEFTS. BE ON THE LOOKOUT FOR ANYONE WHO ACTS SUSPICIOUS.
CAN WE CUT THIS MEETING SHORT? THE POSTERS IN THE BREAK ROOM GOT ME ALL MOTIVATED!
8/4/01 © 2001 United Feature Syndicate, Inc.
THEN WHY ARE THEY THERE?!!

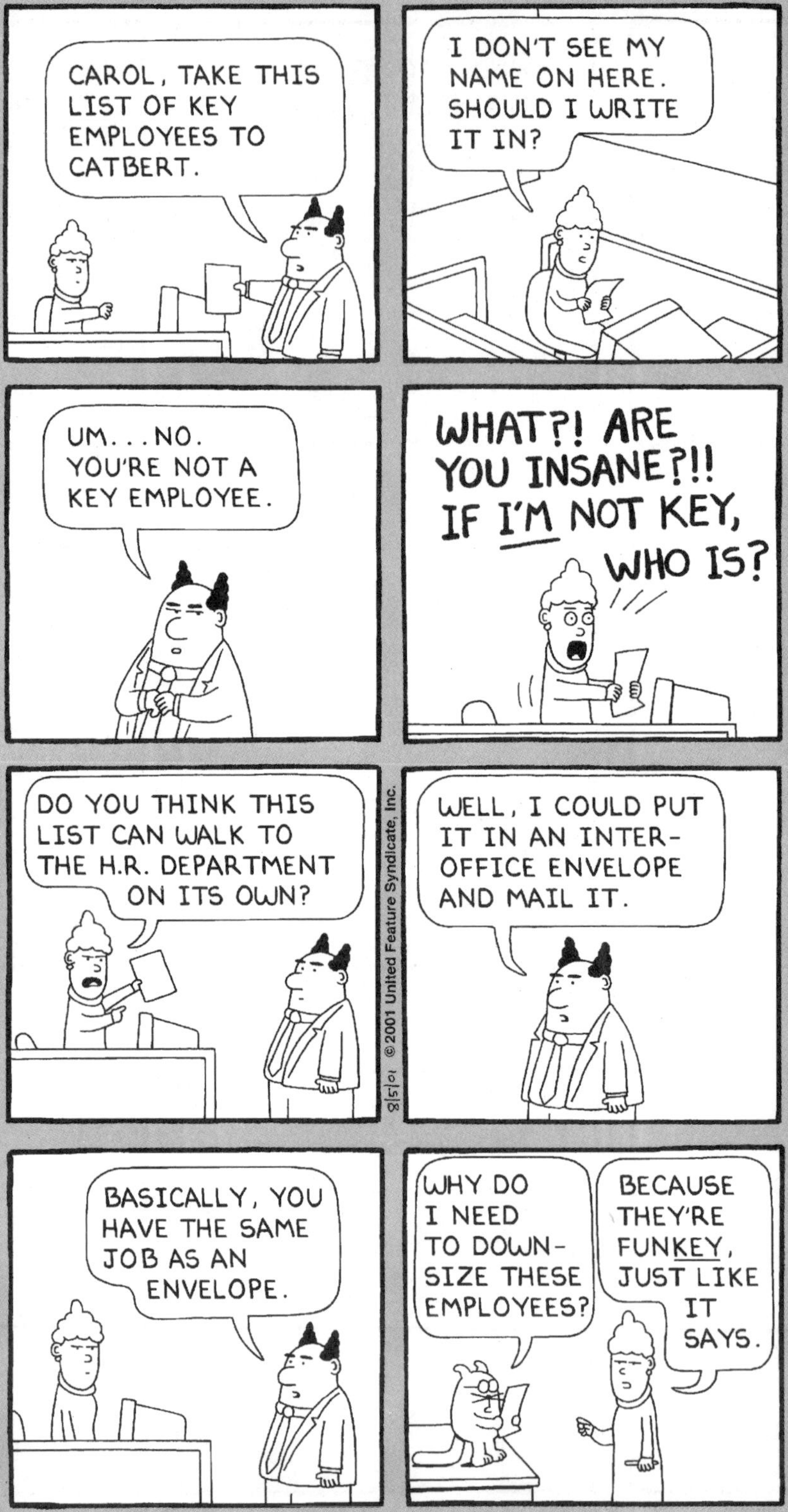
CAROL, TAKE THIS LIST OF KEY EMPLOYEES TO CATBERT.
I DON'T SEE MY NAME ON HERE. SHOULD I WRITE IT IN?
UM...NO. YOU'RE NOT A KEY EMPLOYEE.
WHAT?! ARE YOU INSANE?!! IF I'M NOT KEY, WHO IS?
DO YOU THINK THIS LIST CAN WALK TO THE H.R. DEPARTMENT ON ITS OWN?
WELL, I COULD PUT IT IN AN INTER-OFFICE ENVELOPE AND MAIL IT.
BASICALLY, YOU HAVE THE SAME JOB AS AN ENVELOPE.
WHY DO I NEED TO DOWN-SIZE THESE EMPLOYEES?
BECAUSE THEY'RE FUNKEY, JUST LIKE IT SAYS.
8/5/01 © 2001 United Feature Syndicate, Inc.

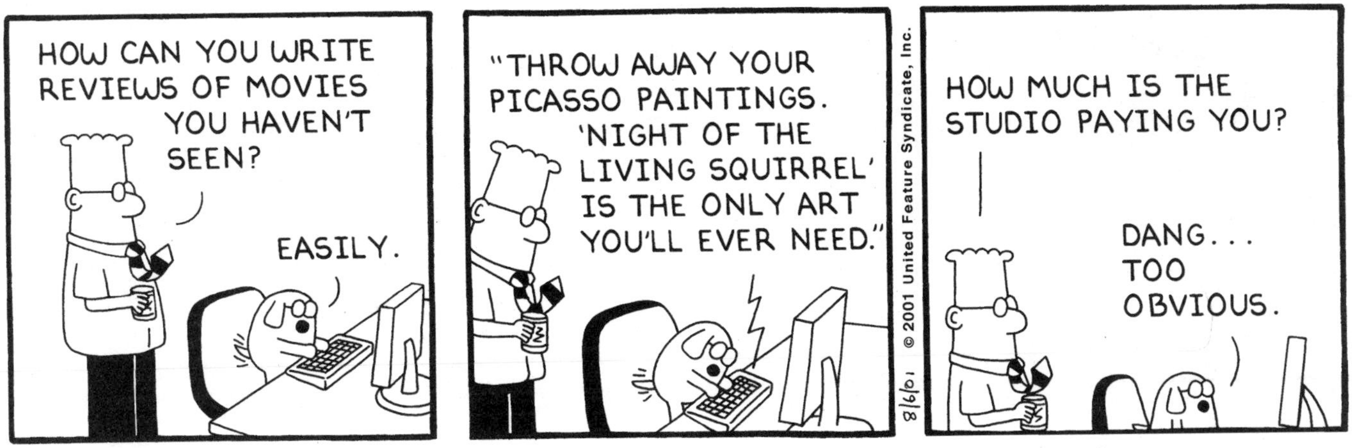
HOW CAN YOU WRITE REVIEWS OF MOVIES YOU HAVEN'T SEEN?
EASILY.
"THROW AWAY YOUR PICASSO PAINTINGS. 'NIGHT OF THE LIVING SQUIRREL' IS THE ONLY ART YOU'LL EVER NEED."
8/6/01 © 2001 United Feature Syndicate, Inc.
HOW MUCH IS THE STUDIO PAYING YOU?
DANG... TOO OBVIOUS.

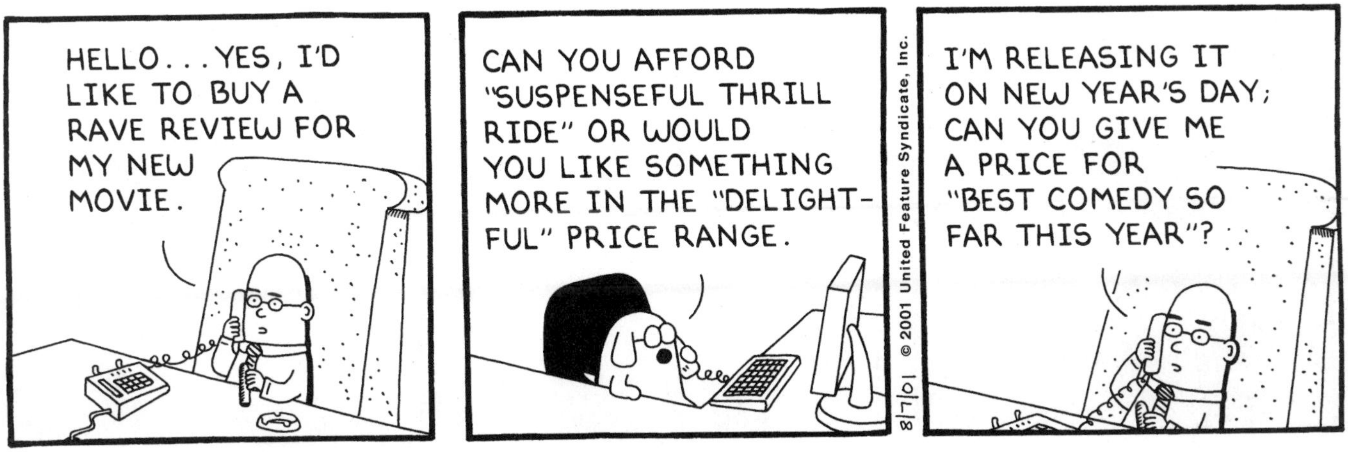
HELLO...YES, I'D LIKE TO BUY A RAVE REVIEW FOR MY NEW MOVIE.
CAN YOU AFFORD "SUSPENSEFUL THRILL RIDE" OR WOULD YOU LIKE SOMETHING MORE IN THE "DELIGHTFUL" PRICE RANGE.
8/7/01 © 2001 United Feature Syndicate, Inc.
I'M RELEASING IT ON NEW YEAR'S DAY; CAN YOU GIVE ME A PRICE FOR "BEST COMEDY SO FAR THIS YEAR"?

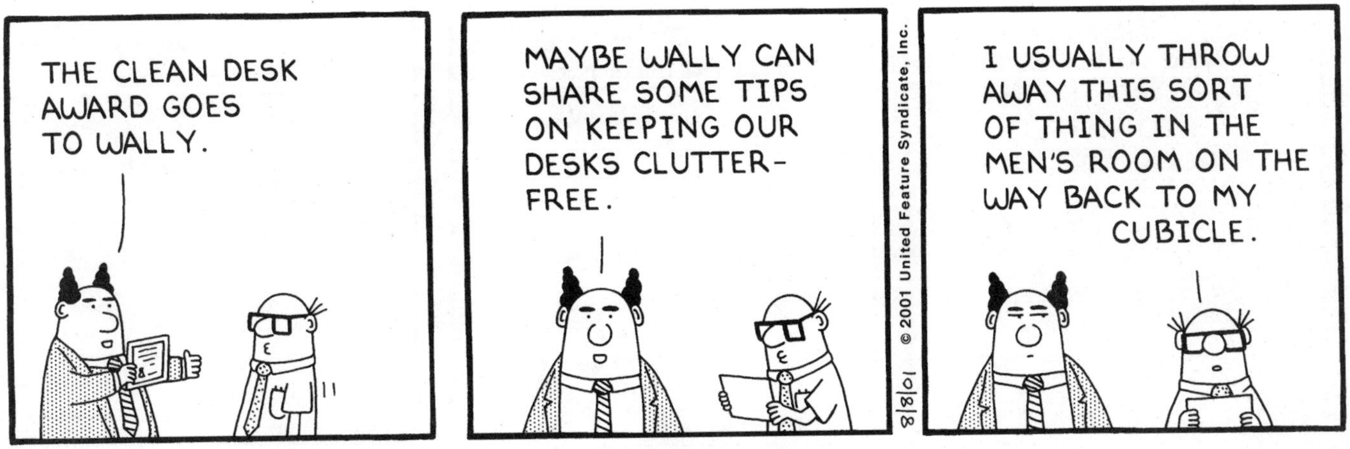
THE CLEAN DESK AWARD GOES TO WALLY.
MAYBE WALLY CAN SHARE SOME TIPS ON KEEPING OUR DESKS CLUTTER-FREE.
8/8/01 © 2001 United Feature Syndicate, Inc.
I USUALLY THROW AWAY THIS SORT OF THING IN THE MEN'S ROOM ON THE WAY BACK TO MY CUBICLE.

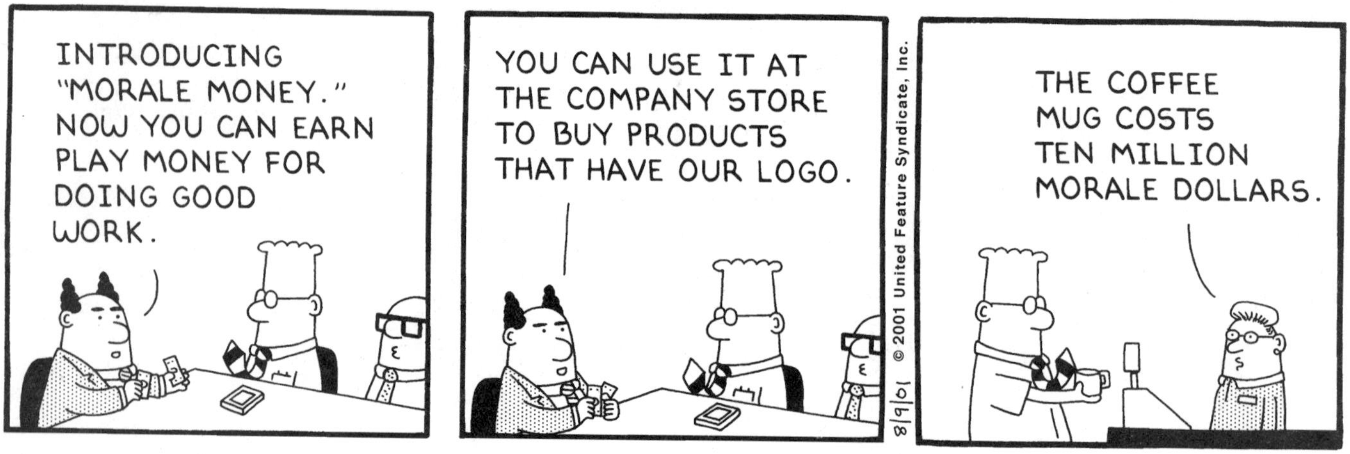
INTRODUCING "MORALE MONEY." NOW YOU CAN EARN PLAY MONEY FOR DOING GOOD WORK.
YOU CAN USE IT AT THE COMPANY STORE TO BUY PRODUCTS THAT HAVE OUR LOGO.
8/9/01 © 2001 United Feature Syndicate, Inc.
THE COFFEE MUG COSTS TEN MILLION MORALE DOLLARS.

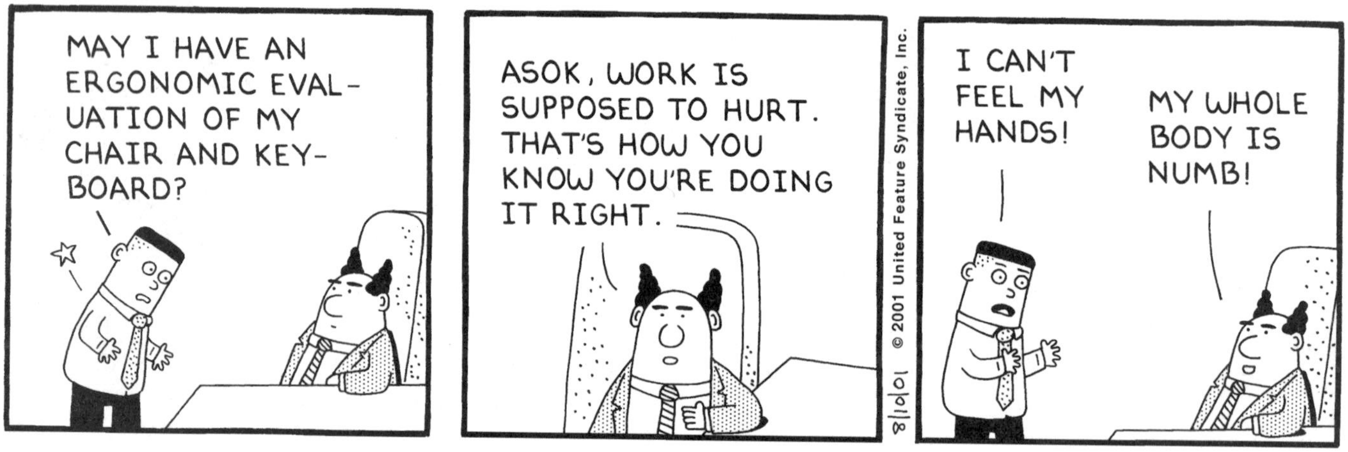
MAY I HAVE AN ERGONOMIC EVAL-UATION OF MY CHAIR AND KEY-BOARD?
ASOK, WORK IS SUPPOSED TO HURT. THAT'S HOW YOU KNOW YOU'RE DOING IT RIGHT.
8/10/01 © 2001 United Feature Syndicate, Inc.
I CAN'T FEEL MY HANDS!
MY WHOLE BODY IS NUMB!

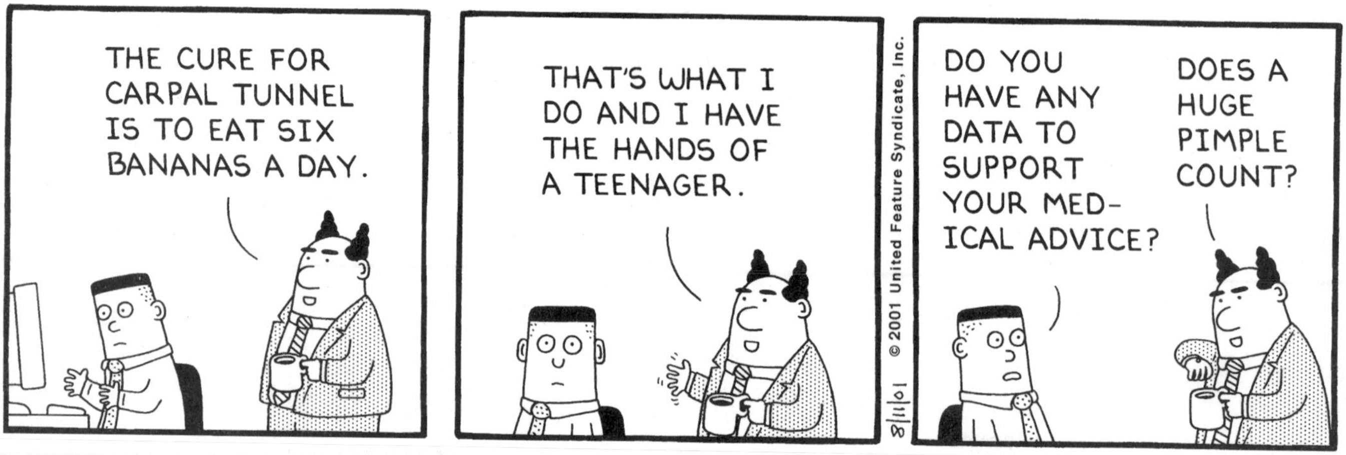
THE CURE FOR CARPAL TUNNEL IS TO EAT SIX BANANAS A DAY.
THAT'S WHAT I DO AND I HAVE THE HANDS OF A TEENAGER.
8/11/01 © 2001 United Feature Syndicate, Inc.
DO YOU HAVE ANY DATA TO SUPPORT YOUR MED-ICAL ADVICE?
DOES A HUGE PIMPLE COUNT?

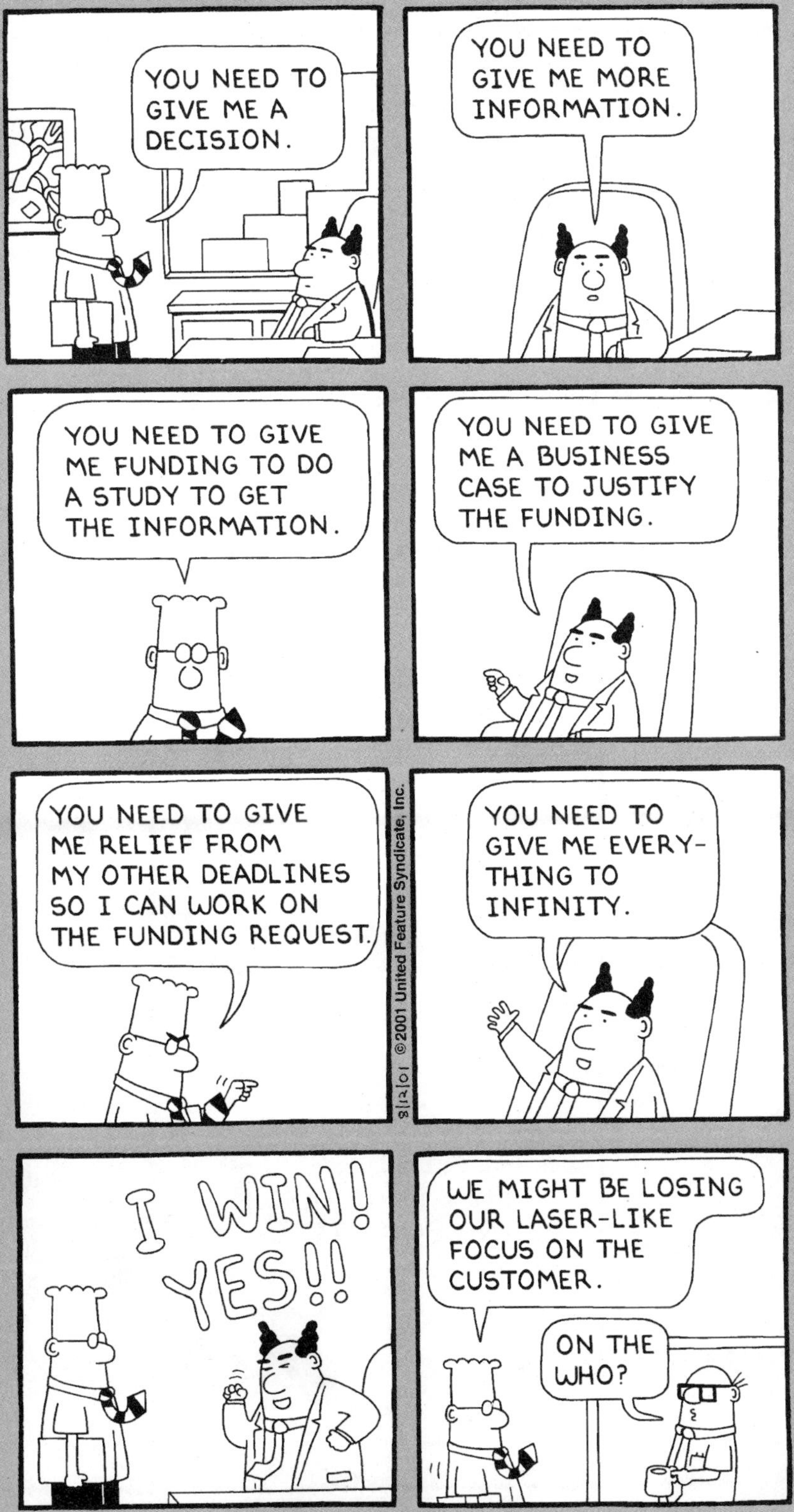
YOU NEED TO GIVE ME A DECISION.
YOU NEED TO GIVE ME MORE INFORMATION.
YOU NEED TO GIVE ME FUNDING TO DO A STUDY TO GET THE INFORMATION.
YOU NEED TO GIVE ME A BUSINESS CASE TO JUSTIFY THE FUNDING.
YOU NEED TO GIVE ME RELIEF FROM MY OTHER DEADLINES SO I CAN WORK ON THE FUNDING REQUEST.
YOU NEED TO GIVE ME EVERY-THING TO INFINITY.
8/12/01 ©2001 United Feature Syndicate, Inc.
I WIN! YES!!
WE MIGHT BE LOSING OUR LASER-LIKE FOCUS ON THE CUSTOMER.
ON THE WHO?

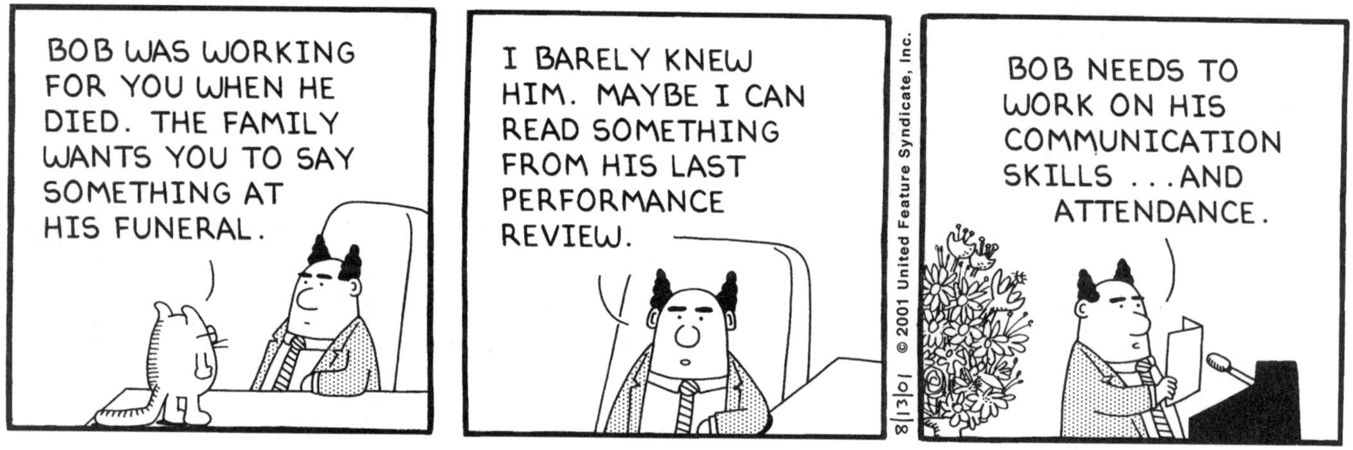
BOB WAS WORKING FOR YOU WHEN HE DIED. THE FAMILY WANTS YOU TO SAY SOMETHING AT HIS FUNERAL.
I BARELY KNEW HIM. MAYBE I CAN READ SOMETHING FROM HIS LAST PERFORMANCE REVIEW.
BOB NEEDS TO WORK ON HIS COMMUNICATION SKILLS . . . AND ATTENDANCE.
8/13/01 © 2001 United Feature Syndicate, Inc.

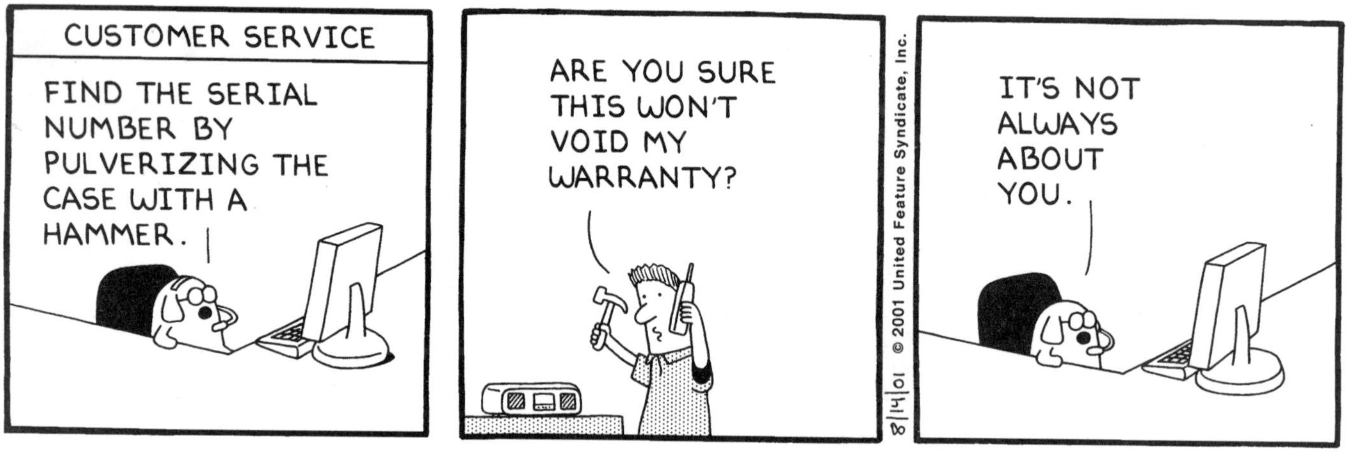
CUSTOMER SERVICE
FIND THE SERIAL NUMBER BY PULVERIZING THE CASE WITH A HAMMER.
ARE YOU SURE THIS WON'T VOID MY WARRANTY?
IT'S NOT ALWAYS ABOUT YOU.
8/14/01 © 2001 United Feature Syndicate, Inc.

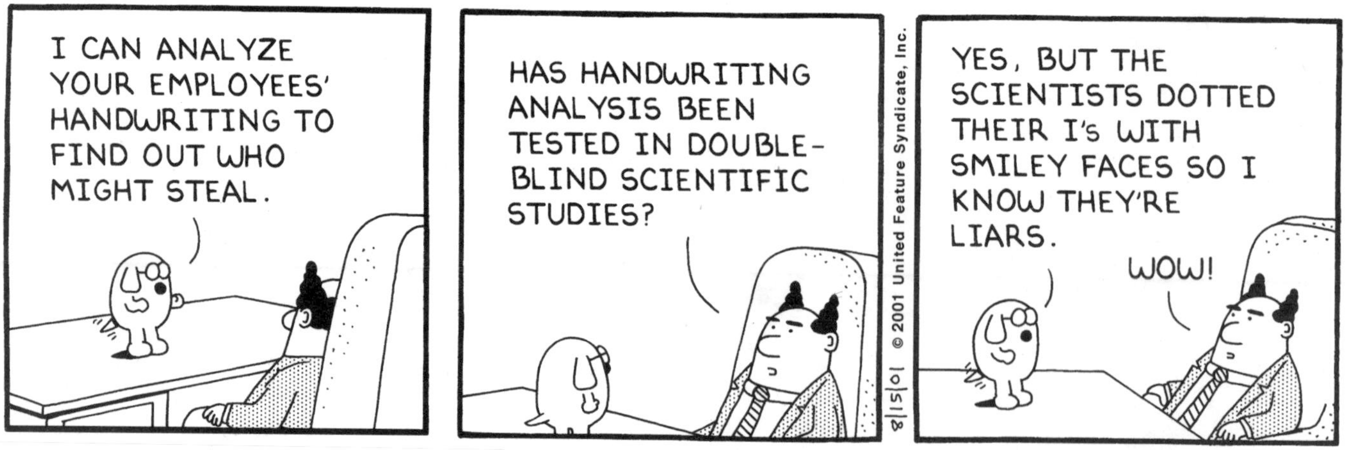
I CAN ANALYZE YOUR EMPLOYEES' HANDWRITING TO FIND OUT WHO MIGHT STEAL.
HAS HANDWRITING ANALYSIS BEEN TESTED IN DOUBLE-BLIND SCIENTIFIC STUDIES?
YES, BUT THE SCIENTISTS DOTTED THEIR I's WITH SMILEY FACES SO I KNOW THEY'RE LIARS.
WOW!
8/15/01 © 2001 United Feature Syndicate, Inc.

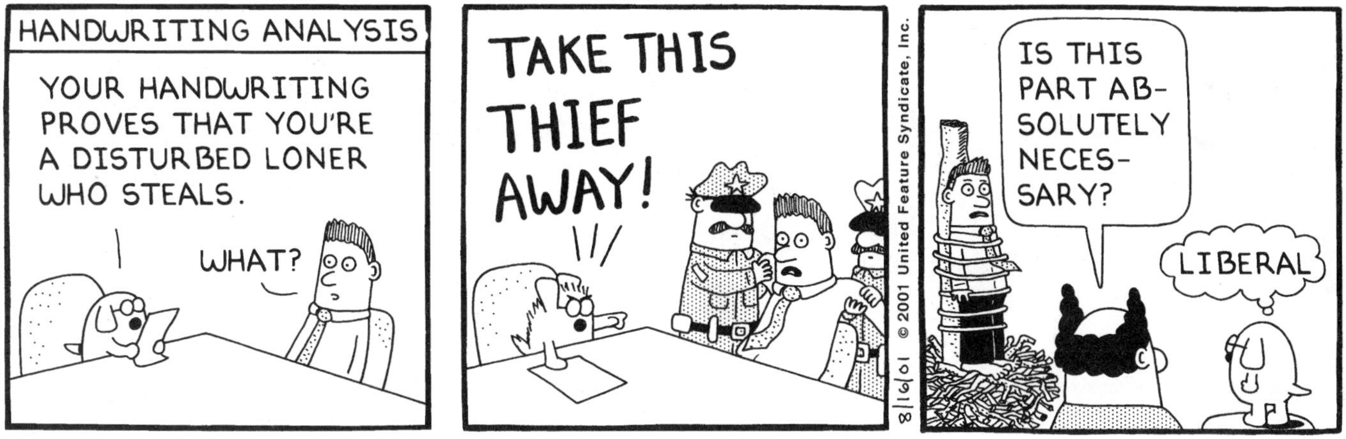
HANDWRITING ANALYSIS
YOUR HANDWRITING PROVES THAT YOU'RE A DISTURBED LONER WHO STEALS.
WHAT?
TAKE THIS THIEF AWAY!
8/16/01 © 2001 United Feature Syndicate, Inc.
IS THIS PART ABSOLUTELY NECESSARY?
LIBERAL

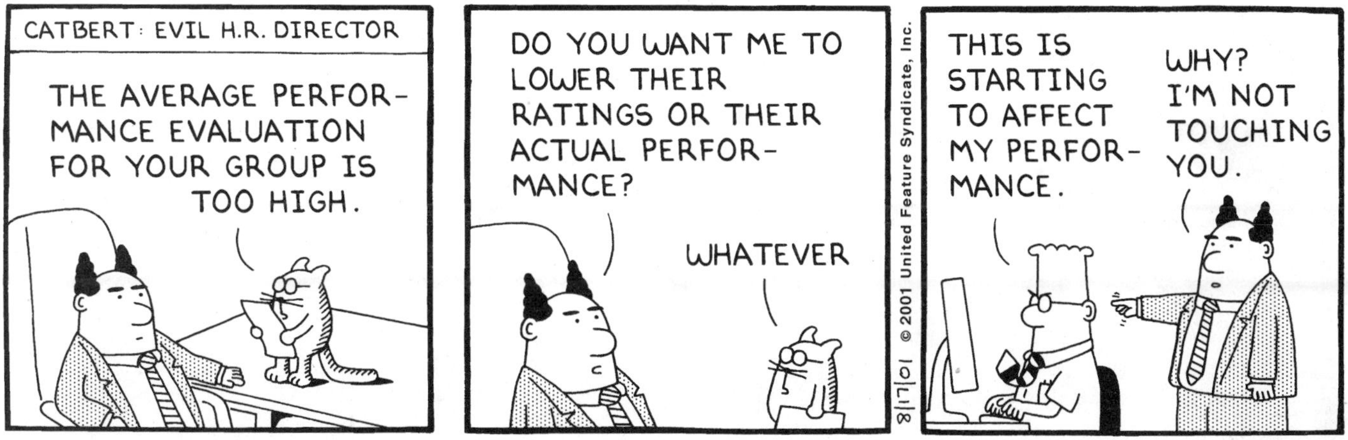
CATBERT: EVIL H.R. DIRECTOR
THE AVERAGE PERFORMANCE EVALUATION FOR YOUR GROUP IS TOO HIGH.
DO YOU WANT ME TO LOWER THEIR RATINGS OR THEIR ACTUAL PERFORMANCE?
WHATEVER
8/17/01 © 2001 United Feature Syndicate, Inc.
THIS IS STARTING TO AFFECT MY PERFORMANCE.
WHY? I'M NOT TOUCHING YOU.

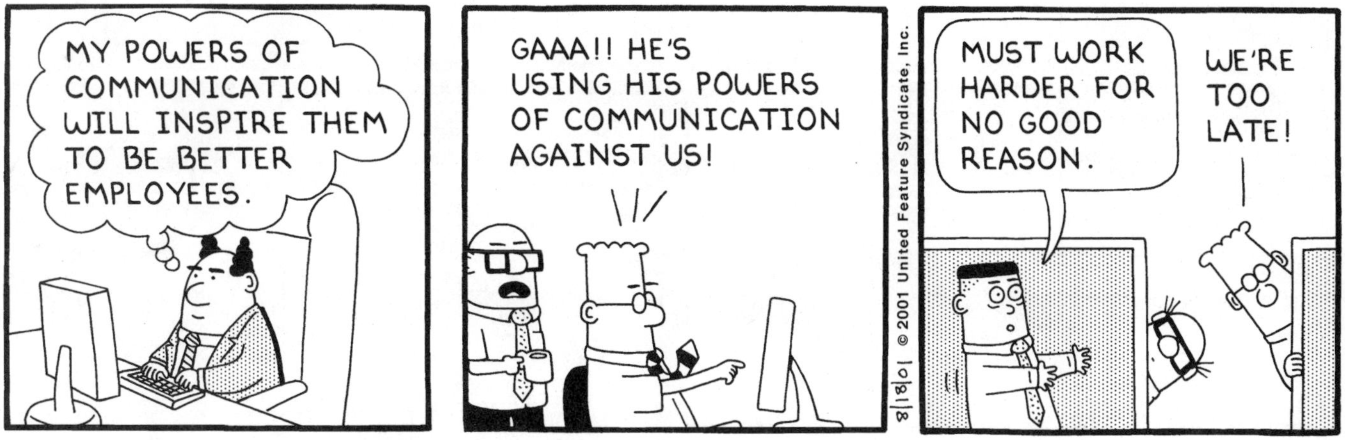
MY POWERS OF COMMUNICATION WILL INSPIRE THEM TO BE BETTER EMPLOYEES.
GAAA!! HE'S USING HIS POWERS OF COMMUNICATION AGAINST US!
8/18/01 © 2001 United Feature Syndicate, Inc.
MUST WORK HARDER FOR NO GOOD REASON.
WE'RE TOO LATE!

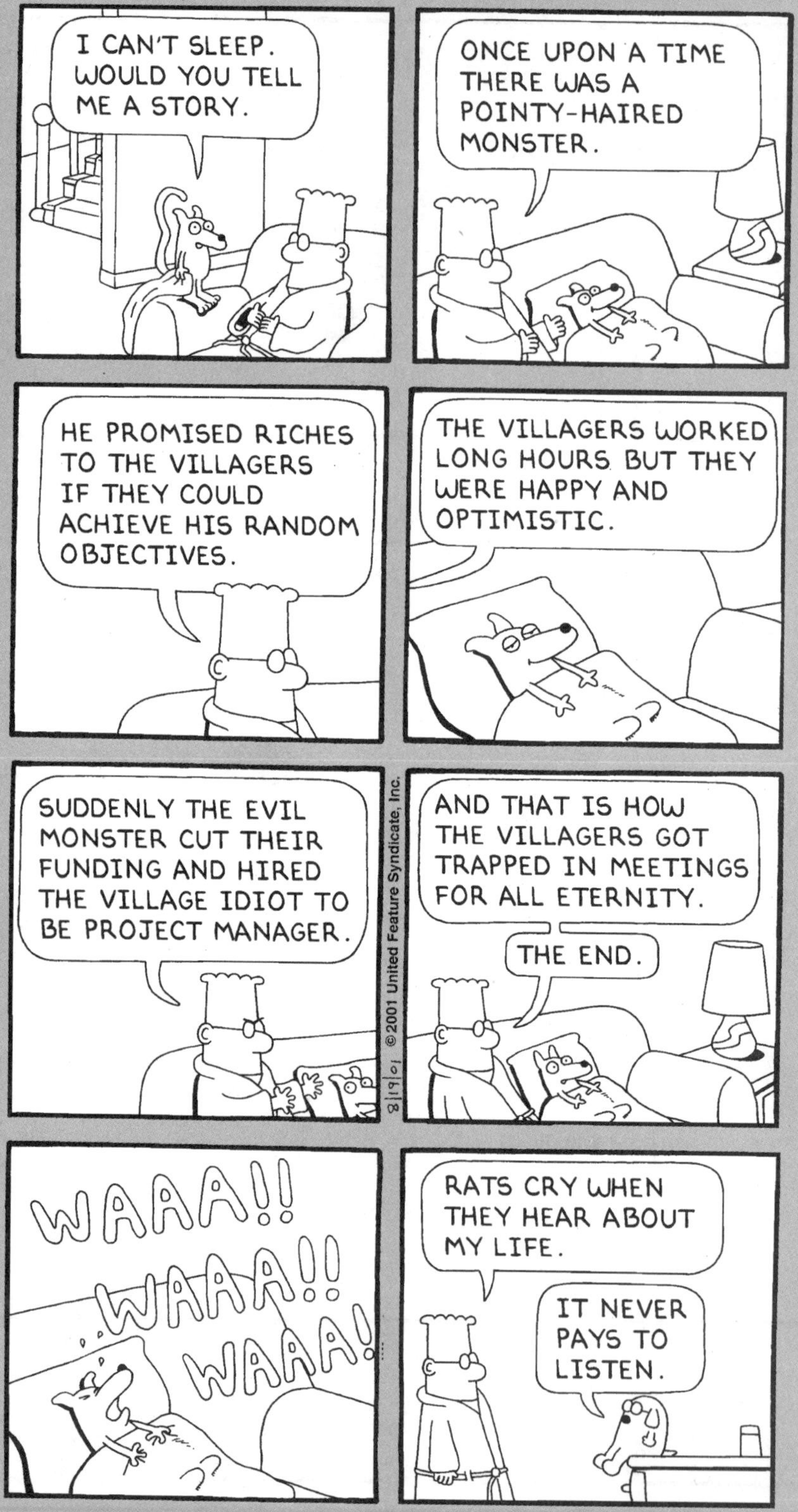
I CAN'T SLEEP. WOULD YOU TELL ME A STORY.
ONCE UPON A TIME THERE WAS A POINTY-HAIRED MONSTER.
HE PROMISED RICHES TO THE VILLAGERS IF THEY COULD ACHIEVE HIS RANDOM OBJECTIVES.
THE VILLAGERS WORKED LONG HOURS BUT THEY WERE HAPPY AND OPTIMISTIC.
SUDDENLY THE EVIL MONSTER CUT THEIR FUNDING AND HIRED THE VILLAGE IDIOT TO BE PROJECT MANAGER.
©2001 United Feature Syndicate, Inc.
8/19/01
AND THAT IS HOW THE VILLAGERS GOT TRAPPED IN MEETINGS FOR ALL ETERNITY.
THE END.
WAAA!!
WAAA!!
WAAA!
RATS CRY WHEN THEY HEAR ABOUT MY LIFE.
IT NEVER PAYS TO LISTEN.

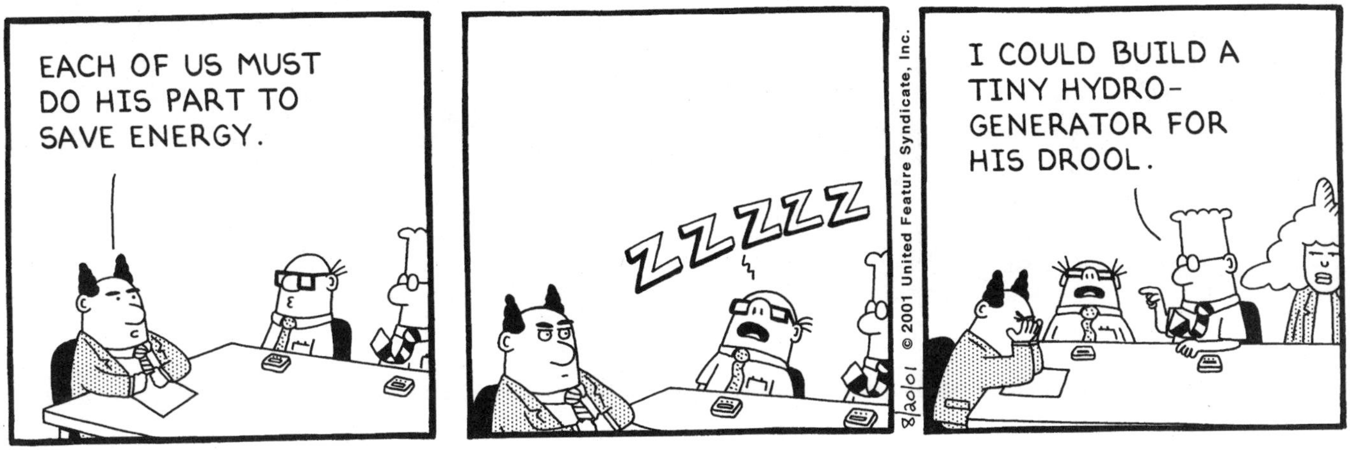
EACH OF US MUST DO HIS PART TO SAVE ENERGY.
ZZZZZ
8/20/01 © 2001 United Feature Syndicate, Inc.
I COULD BUILD A TINY HYDRO-GENERATOR FOR HIS DROOL.

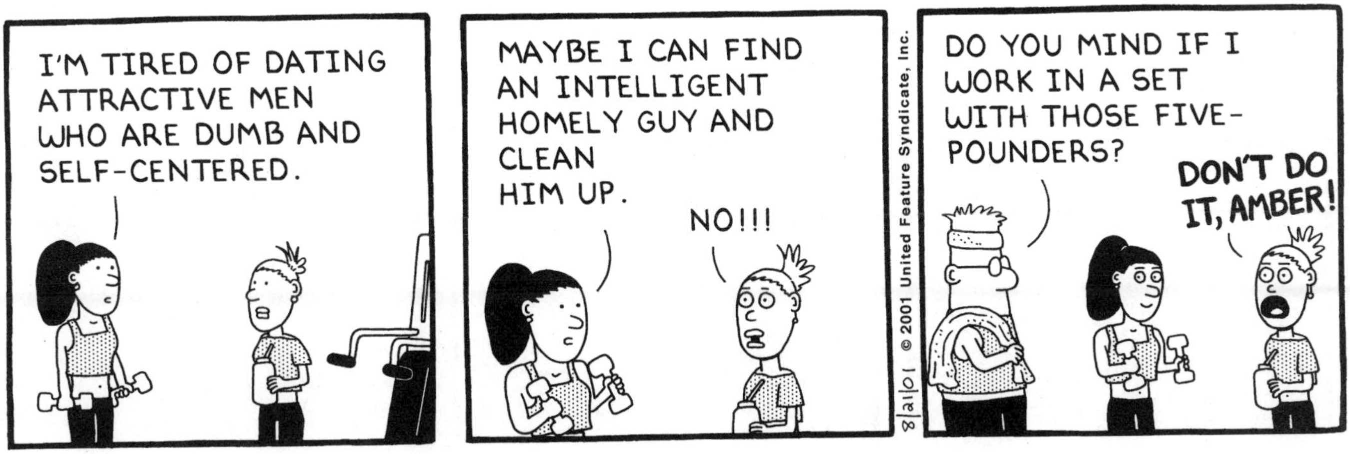
I'M TIRED OF DATING ATTRACTIVE MEN WHO ARE DUMB AND SELF-CENTERED.
MAYBE I CAN FIND AN INTELLIGENT HOMELY GUY AND CLEAN HIM UP.
NO!!!
8/21/01 © 2001 United Feature Syndicate, Inc.
DO YOU MIND IF I WORK IN A SET WITH THOSE FIVE-POUNDERS?
DON'T DO IT, AMBER!

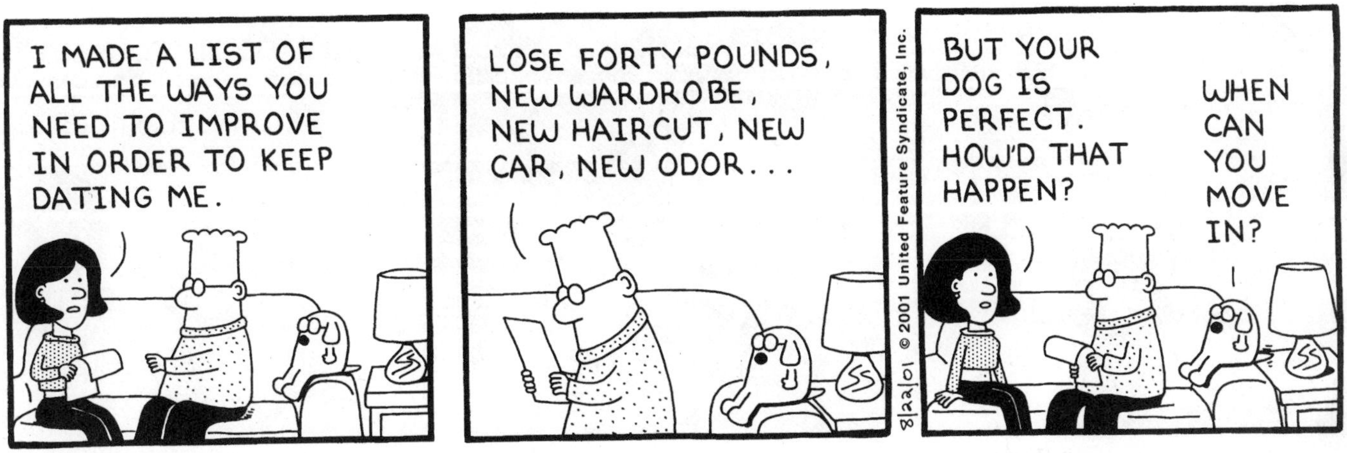
I MADE A LIST OF ALL THE WAYS YOU NEED TO IMPROVE IN ORDER TO KEEP DATING ME.
LOSE FORTY POUNDS, NEW WARDROBE, NEW HAIRCUT, NEW CAR, NEW ODOR...
8/22/01 © 2001 United Feature Syndicate, Inc.
BUT YOUR DOG IS PERFECT. HOW'D THAT HAPPEN?
WHEN CAN YOU MOVE IN?

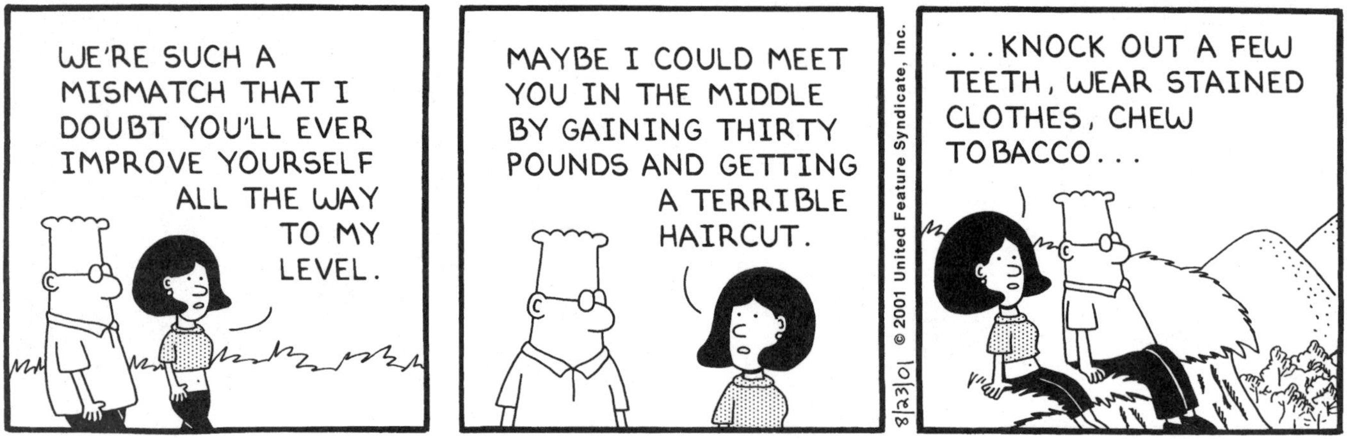
WE'RE SUCH A MISMATCH THAT I DOUBT YOU'LL EVER IMPROVE YOURSELF ALL THE WAY TO MY LEVEL.
MAYBE I COULD MEET YOU IN THE MIDDLE BY GAINING THIRTY POUNDS AND GETTING A TERRIBLE HAIRCUT.
8/23/01 © 2001 United Feature Syndicate, Inc.
...KNOCK OUT A FEW TEETH, WEAR STAINED CLOTHES, CHEW TOBACCO...

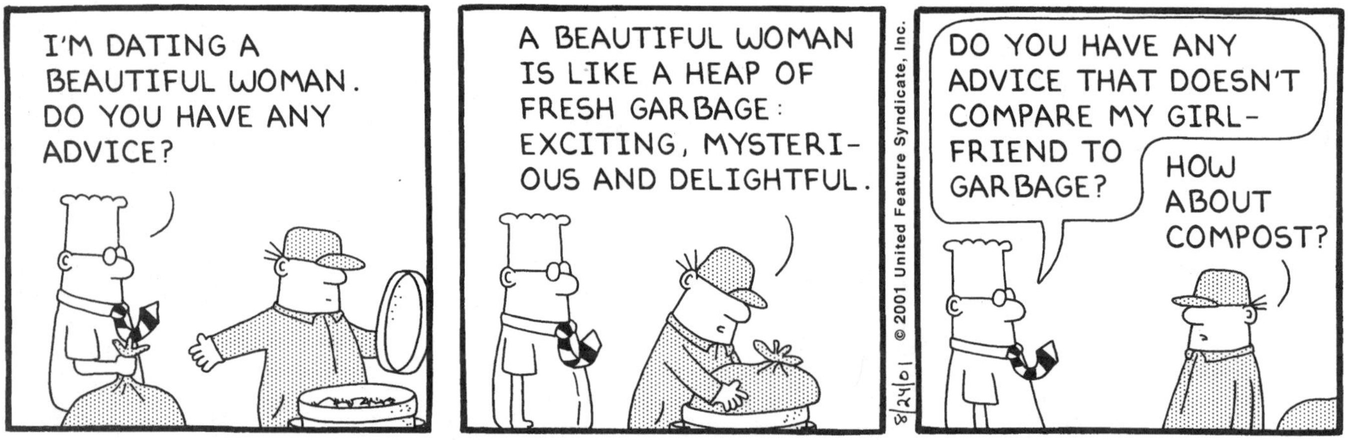
I'M DATING A BEAUTIFUL WOMAN. DO YOU HAVE ANY ADVICE?
A BEAUTIFUL WOMAN IS LIKE A HEAP OF FRESH GARBAGE: EXCITING, MYSTERIOUS AND DELIGHTFUL.
8/24/01 © 2001 United Feature Syndicate, Inc.
DO YOU HAVE ANY ADVICE THAT DOESN'T COMPARE MY GIRLFRIEND TO GARBAGE?
HOW ABOUT COMPOST?

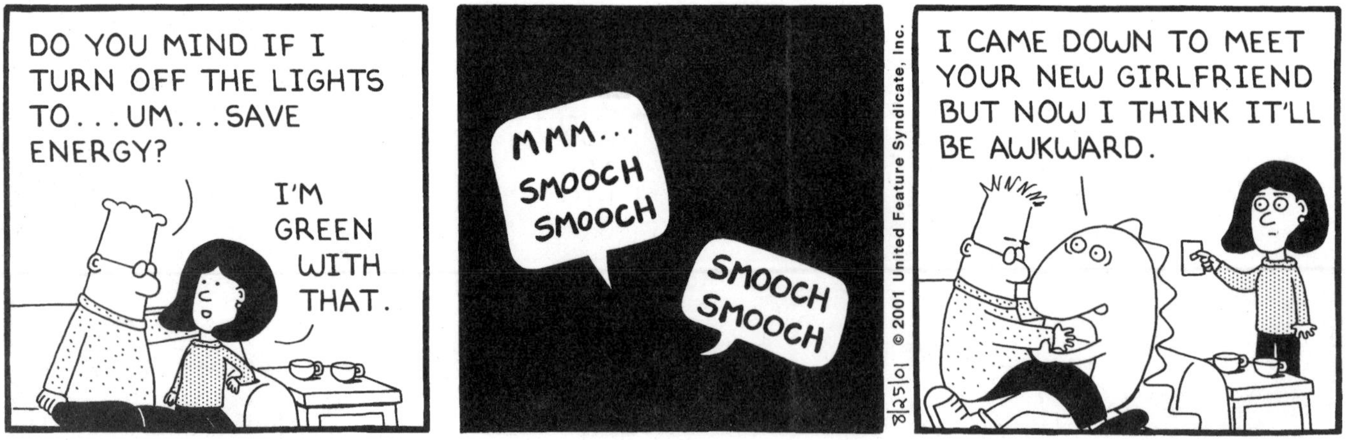
DO YOU MIND IF I TURN OFF THE LIGHTS TO...UM...SAVE ENERGY?
I'M GREEN WITH THAT.
MMM... SMOOCH SMOOCH
SMOOCH SMOOCH
8/25/01 © 2001 United Feature Syndicate, Inc.
I CAME DOWN TO MEET YOUR NEW GIRLFRIEND BUT NOW I THINK IT'LL BE AWKWARD.

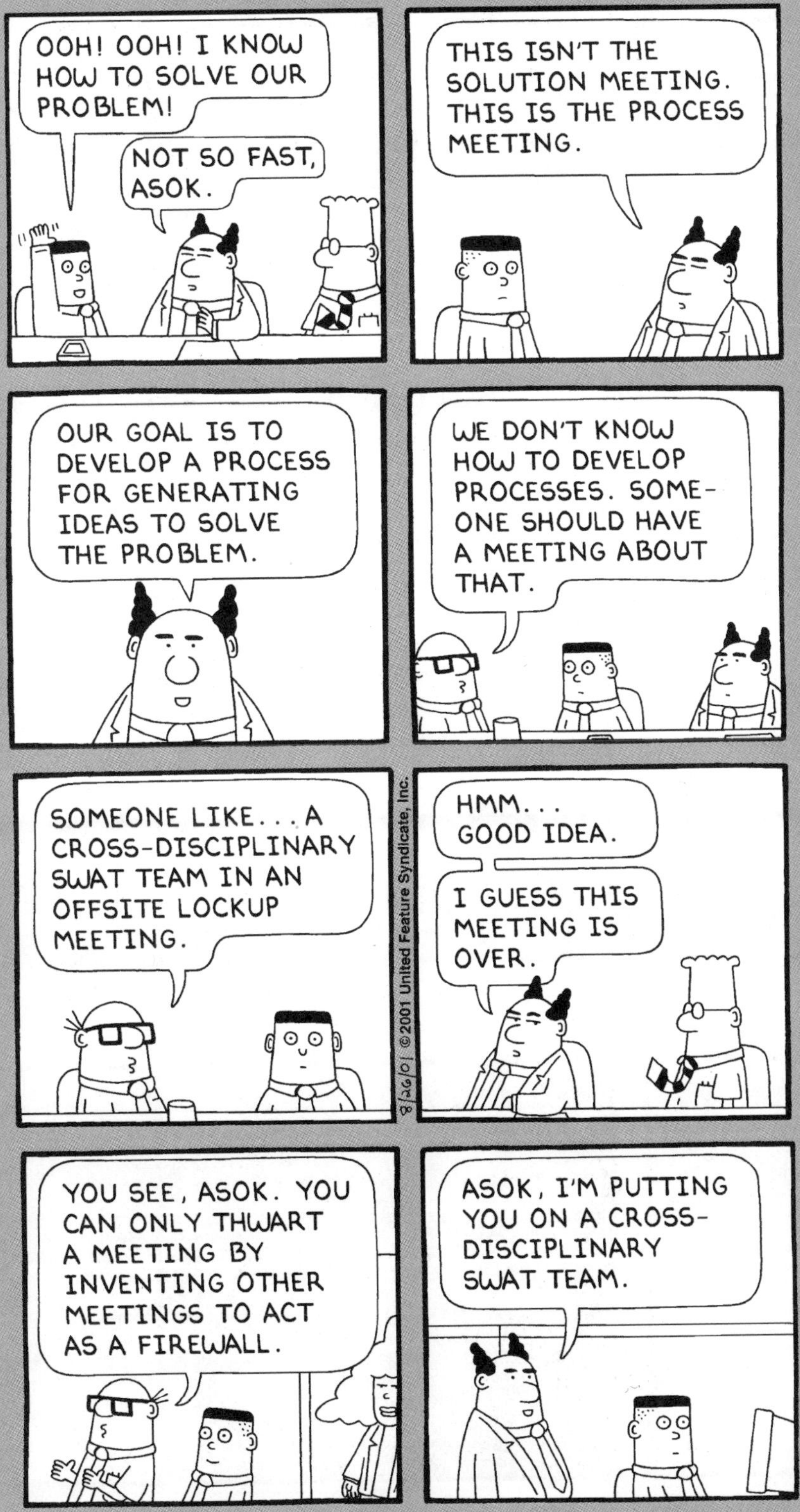
OOH! OOH! I KNOW HOW TO SOLVE OUR PROBLEM!
NOT SO FAST, ASOK.
THIS ISN'T THE SOLUTION MEETING. THIS IS THE PROCESS MEETING.
OUR GOAL IS TO DEVELOP A PROCESS FOR GENERATING IDEAS TO SOLVE THE PROBLEM.
WE DON'T KNOW HOW TO DEVELOP PROCESSES. SOME-ONE SHOULD HAVE A MEETING ABOUT THAT.
SOMEONE LIKE. . . A CROSS-DISCIPLINARY SWAT TEAM IN AN OFFSITE LOCKUP MEETING.
HMM. . . GOOD IDEA.
I GUESS THIS MEETING IS OVER.
YOU SEE, ASOK. YOU CAN ONLY THWART A MEETING BY INVENTING OTHER MEETINGS TO ACT AS A FIREWALL.
ASOK, I'M PUTTING YOU ON A CROSS-DISCIPLINARY SWAT TEAM.
8/26/01 ©2001 United Feature Syndicate, Inc.

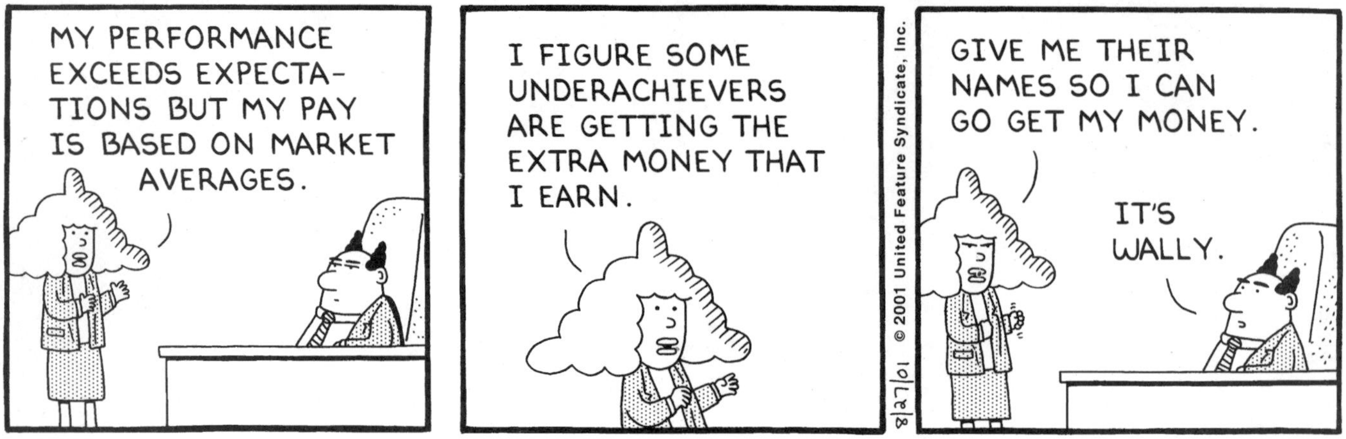
MY PERFORMANCE EXCEEDS EXPECTA- TIONS BUT MY PAY IS BASED ON MARKET AVERAGES.
I FIGURE SOME UNDERACHIEVERS ARE GETTING THE EXTRA MONEY THAT I EARN.
8/27/01 © 2001 United Feature Syndicate, Inc.
GIVE ME THEIR NAMES SO I CAN GO GET MY MONEY.
IT'S WALLY.

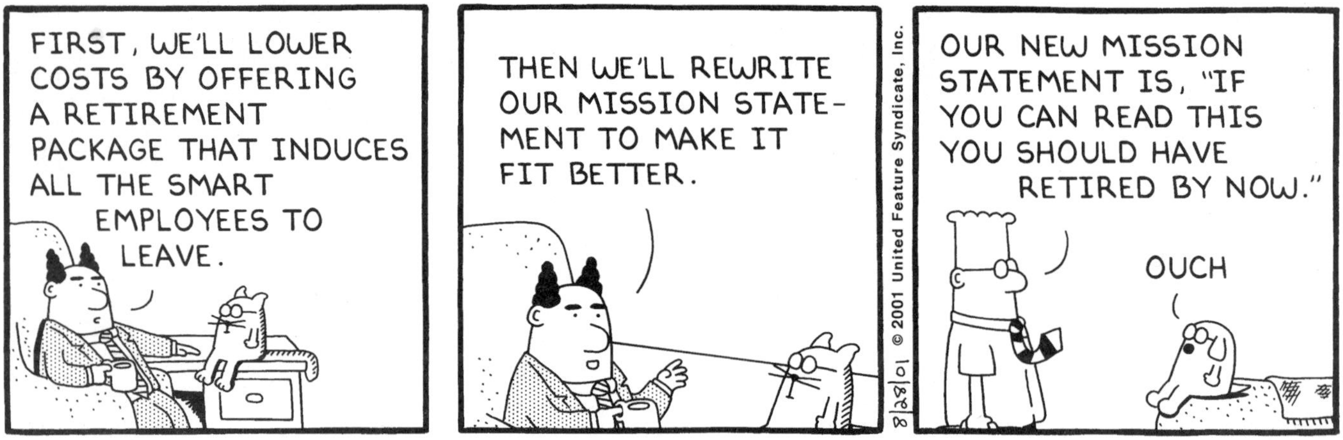
FIRST, WE'LL LOWER COSTS BY OFFERING A RETIREMENT PACKAGE THAT INDUCES ALL THE SMART EMPLOYEES TO LEAVE.
THEN WE'LL REWRITE OUR MISSION STATE- MENT TO MAKE IT FIT BETTER.
8/28/01 © 2001 United Feature Syndicate, Inc.
OUR NEW MISSION STATEMENT IS, "IF YOU CAN READ THIS YOU SHOULD HAVE RETIRED BY NOW."
OUCH

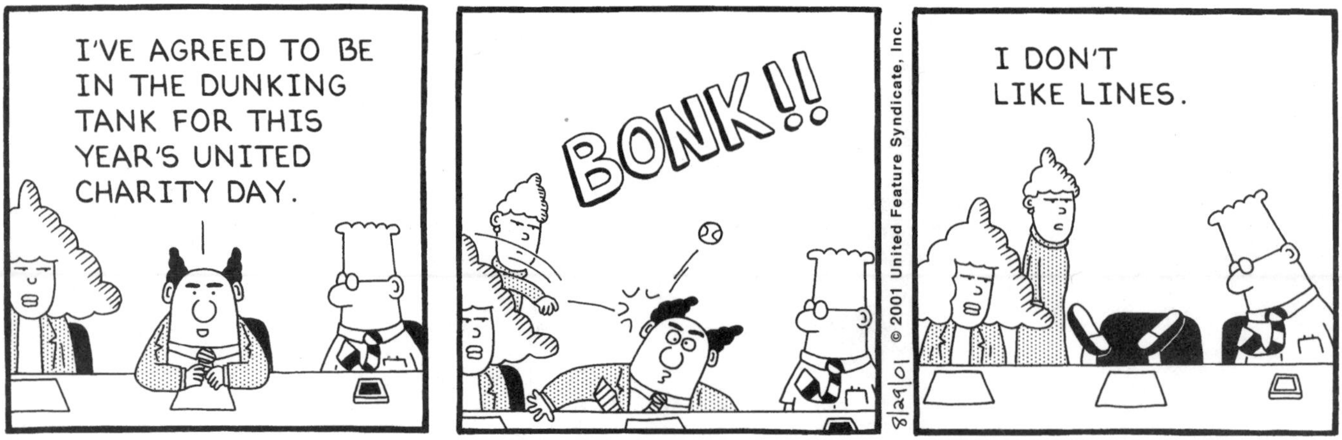
I'VE AGREED TO BE IN THE DUNKING TANK FOR THIS YEAR'S UNITED CHARITY DAY.
BONK!!
8/29/01 © 2001 United Feature Syndicate, Inc.
I DON'T LIKE LINES.

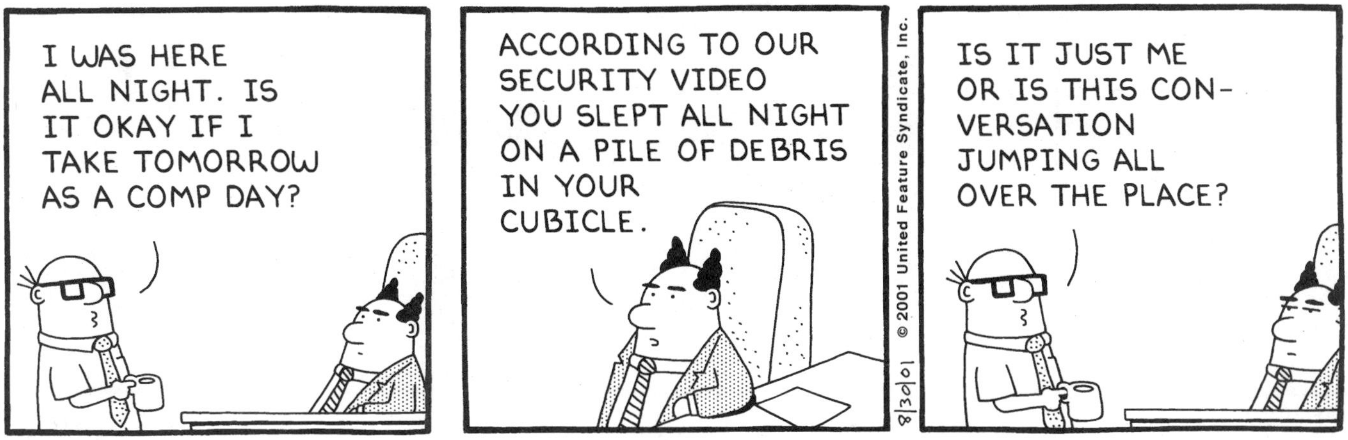
I WAS HERE ALL NIGHT. IS IT OKAY IF I TAKE TOMORROW AS A COMP DAY?
ACCORDING TO OUR SECURITY VIDEO YOU SLEPT ALL NIGHT ON A PILE OF DEBRIS IN YOUR CUBICLE.
8/30/01 © 2001 United Feature Syndicate, Inc.
IS IT JUST ME OR IS THIS CON- VERSATION JUMPING ALL OVER THE PLACE?

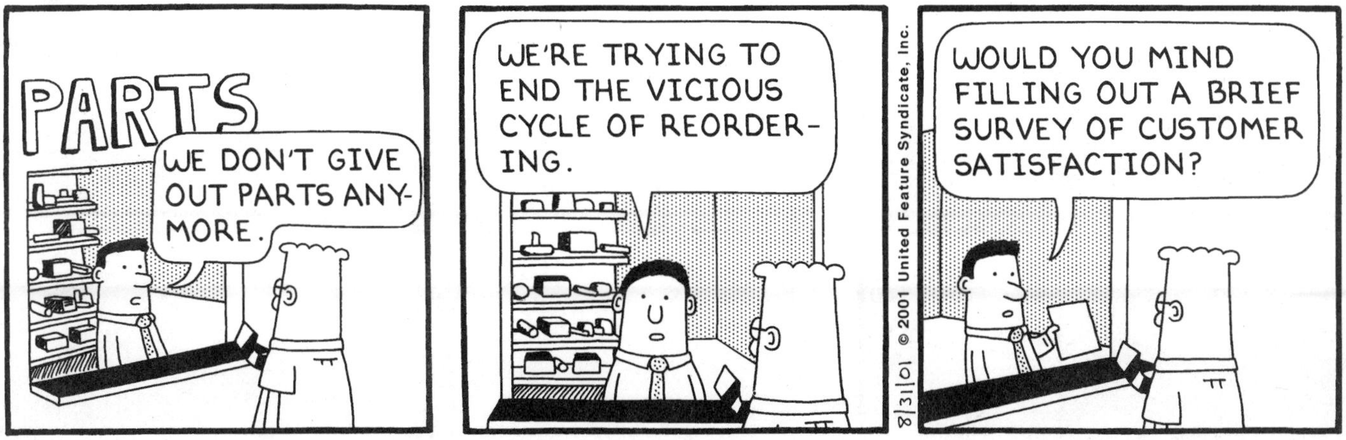
PARTS
WE DON'T GIVE OUT PARTS ANY- MORE.
WE'RE TRYING TO END THE VICIOUS CYCLE OF REORDER- ING.
8/31/01 © 2001 United Feature Syndicate, Inc.
WOULD YOU MIND FILLING OUT A BRIEF SURVEY OF CUSTOMER SATISFACTION?

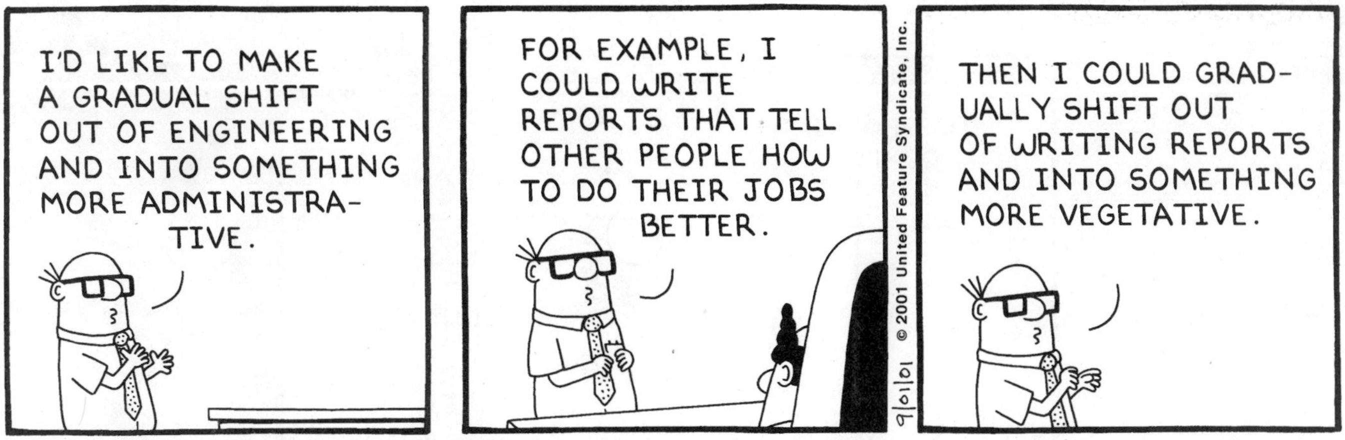
I'D LIKE TO MAKE A GRADUAL SHIFT OUT OF ENGINEERING AND INTO SOMETHING MORE ADMINISTRA- TIVE.
FOR EXAMPLE, I COULD WRITE REPORTS THAT TELL OTHER PEOPLE HOW TO DO THEIR JOBS BETTER.
9/01/01 © 2001 United Feature Syndicate, Inc.
THEN I COULD GRAD- UALLY SHIFT OUT OF WRITING REPORTS AND INTO SOMETHING MORE VEGETATIVE.

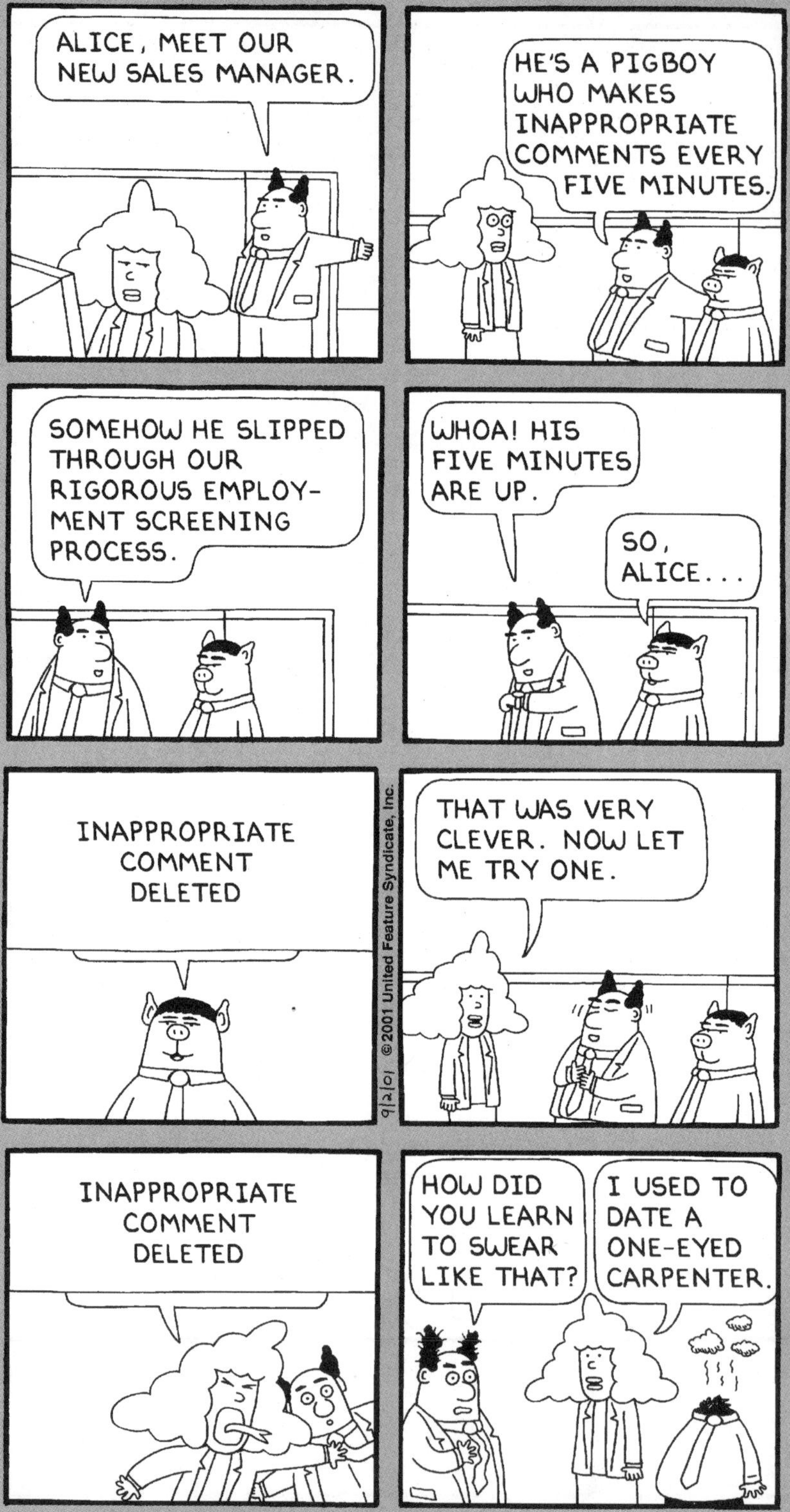
ALICE, MEET OUR NEW SALES MANAGER.
HE'S A PIGBOY WHO MAKES INAPPROPRIATE COMMENTS EVERY FIVE MINUTES.
SOMEHOW HE SLIPPED THROUGH OUR RIGOROUS EMPLOYMENT SCREENING PROCESS.
WHOA! HIS FIVE MINUTES ARE UP.
SO, ALICE...
INAPPROPRIATE COMMENT DELETED
THAT WAS VERY CLEVER. NOW LET ME TRY ONE.
INAPPROPRIATE COMMENT DELETED
HOW DID YOU LEARN TO SWEAR LIKE THAT?
I USED TO DATE A ONE-EYED CARPENTER.
9/2/01

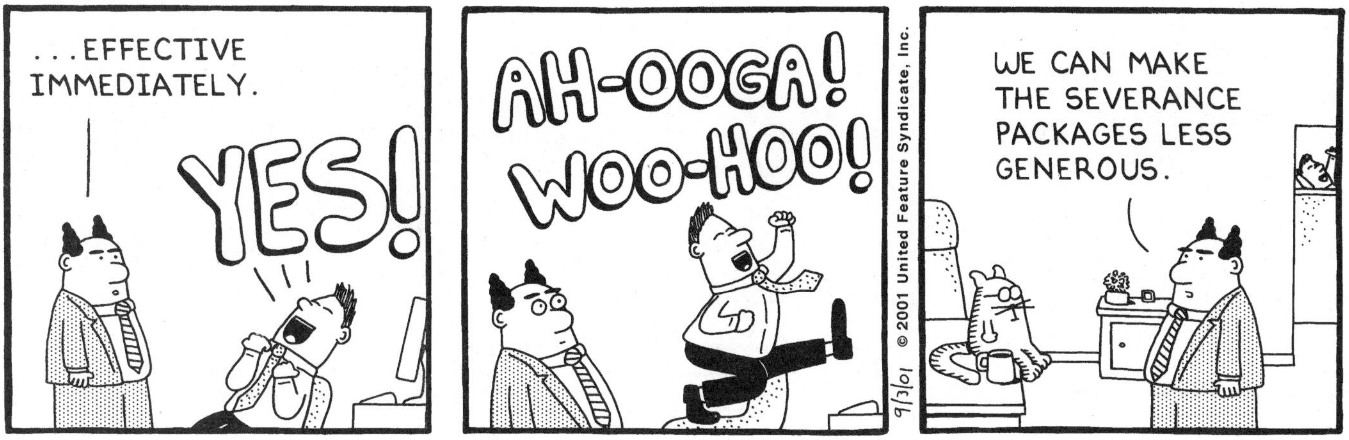
...EFFECTIVE IMMEDIATELY.
YES!
AH-OOGA! WOO-HOO!
9/3/01 © 2001 United Feature Syndicate, Inc.
WE CAN MAKE THE SEVERANCE PACKAGES LESS GENEROUS.

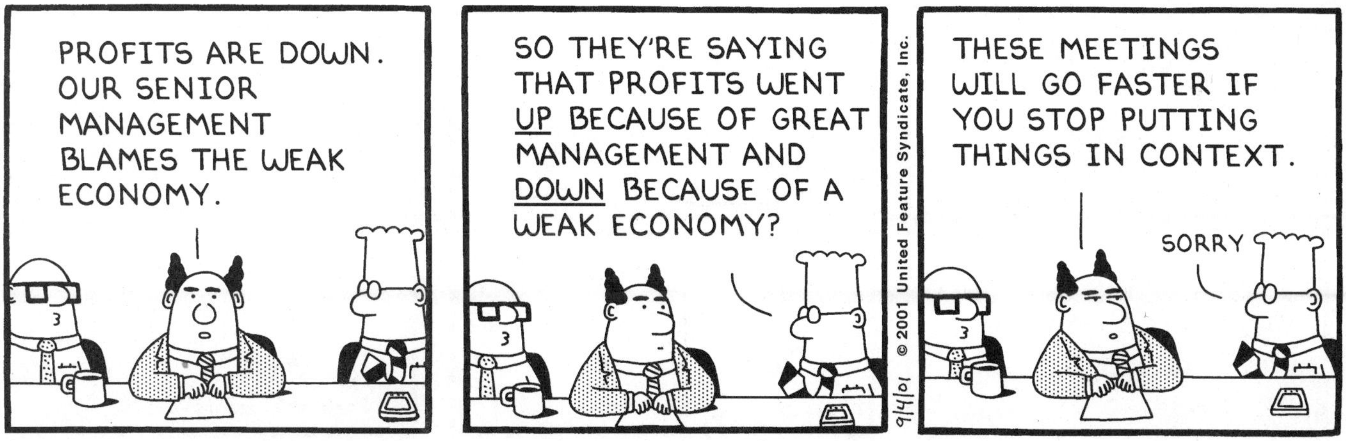
PROFITS ARE DOWN. OUR SENIOR MANAGEMENT BLAMES THE WEAK ECONOMY.
SO THEY'RE SAYING THAT PROFITS WENT UP BECAUSE OF GREAT MANAGEMENT AND DOWN BECAUSE OF A WEAK ECONOMY?
9/4/01 © 2001 United Feature Syndicate, Inc.
THESE MEETINGS WILL GO FASTER IF YOU STOP PUTTING THINGS IN CONTEXT.
SORRY

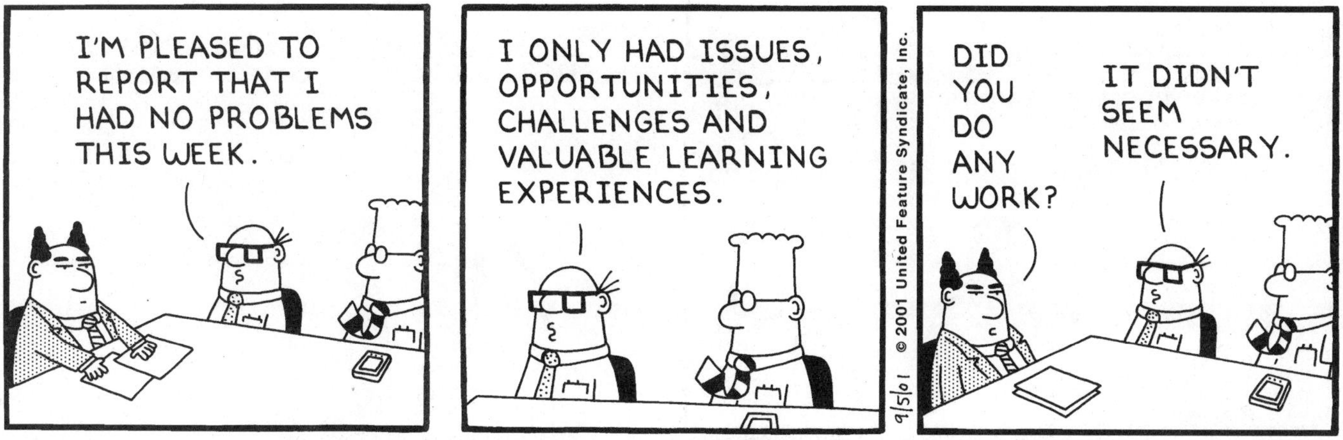
I'M PLEASED TO REPORT THAT I HAD NO PROBLEMS THIS WEEK.
I ONLY HAD ISSUES, OPPORTUNITIES, CHALLENGES AND VALUABLE LEARNING EXPERIENCES.
9/5/01 © 2001 United Feature Syndicate, Inc.
DID YOU DO ANY WORK?
IT DIDN'T SEEM NECESSARY.

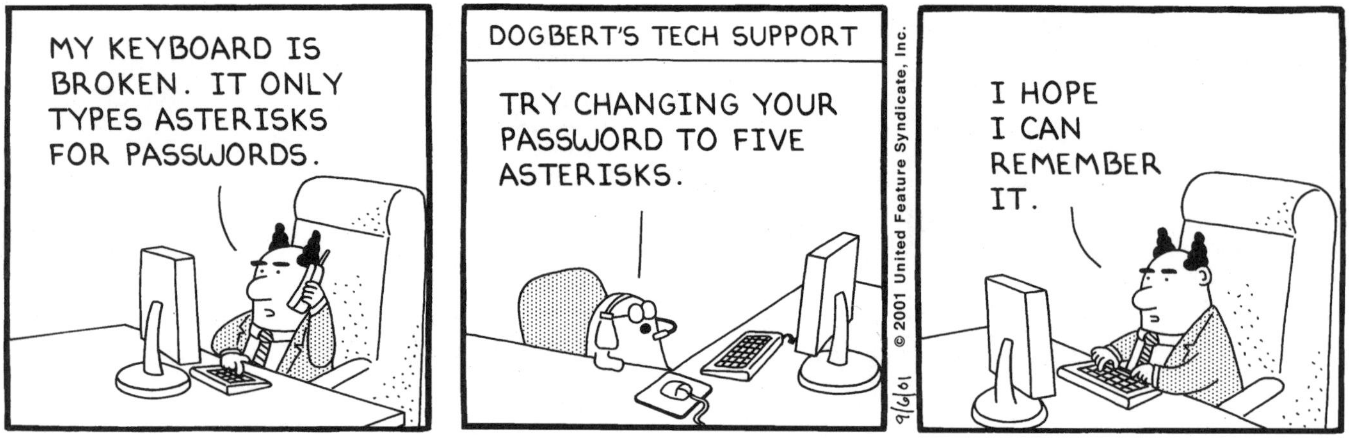
MY KEYBOARD IS BROKEN. IT ONLY TYPES ASTERISKS FOR PASSWORDS.
DOGBERT'S TECH SUPPORT
TRY CHANGING YOUR PASSWORD TO FIVE ASTERISKS.
9/6/01 © 2001 United Feature Syndicate, Inc.
I HOPE I CAN REMEMBER IT.

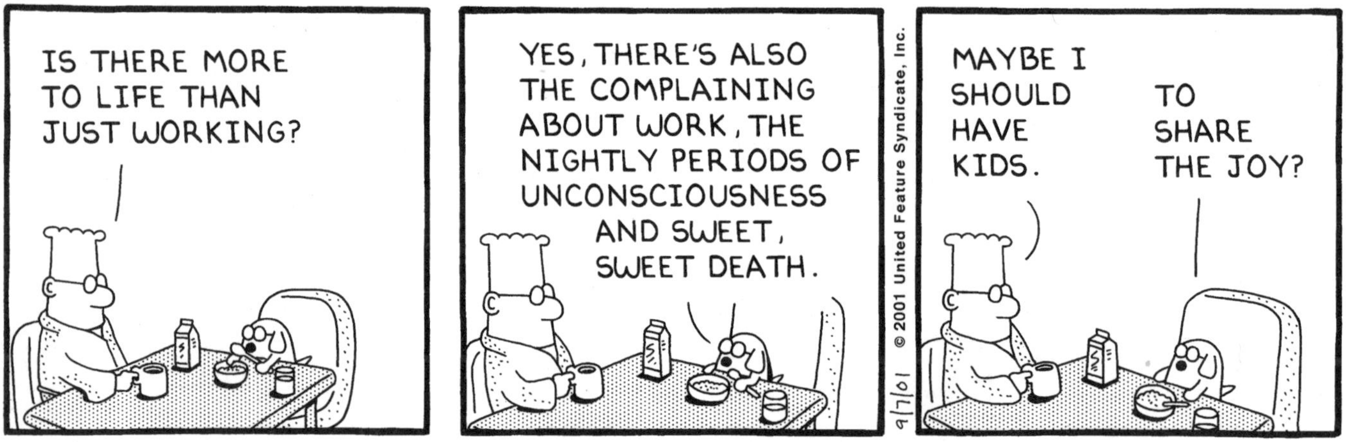
IS THERE MORE TO LIFE THAN JUST WORKING?
YES, THERE'S ALSO THE COMPLAINING ABOUT WORK, THE NIGHTLY PERIODS OF UNCONSCIOUSNESS AND SWEET, SWEET DEATH.
9/7/01 © 2001 United Feature Syndicate, Inc.
MAYBE I SHOULD HAVE KIDS.
TO SHARE THE JOY?

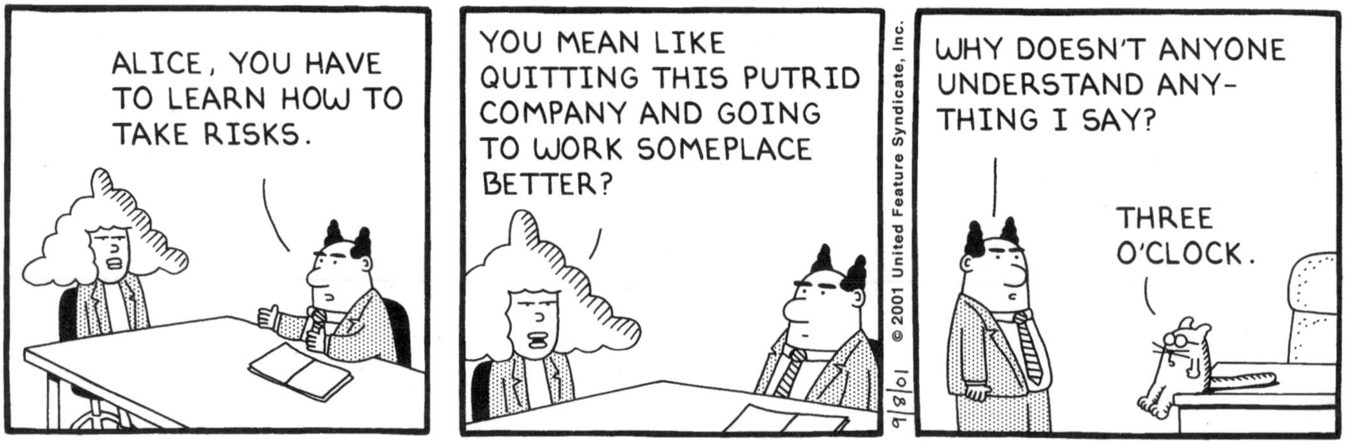
ALICE, YOU HAVE TO LEARN HOW TO TAKE RISKS.
YOU MEAN LIKE QUITTING THIS PUTRID COMPANY AND GOING TO WORK SOMEPLACE BETTER?
9/8/01 © 2001 United Feature Syndicate, Inc.
WHY DOESN'T ANYONE UNDERSTAND ANY-THING I SAY?
THREE O'CLOCK.

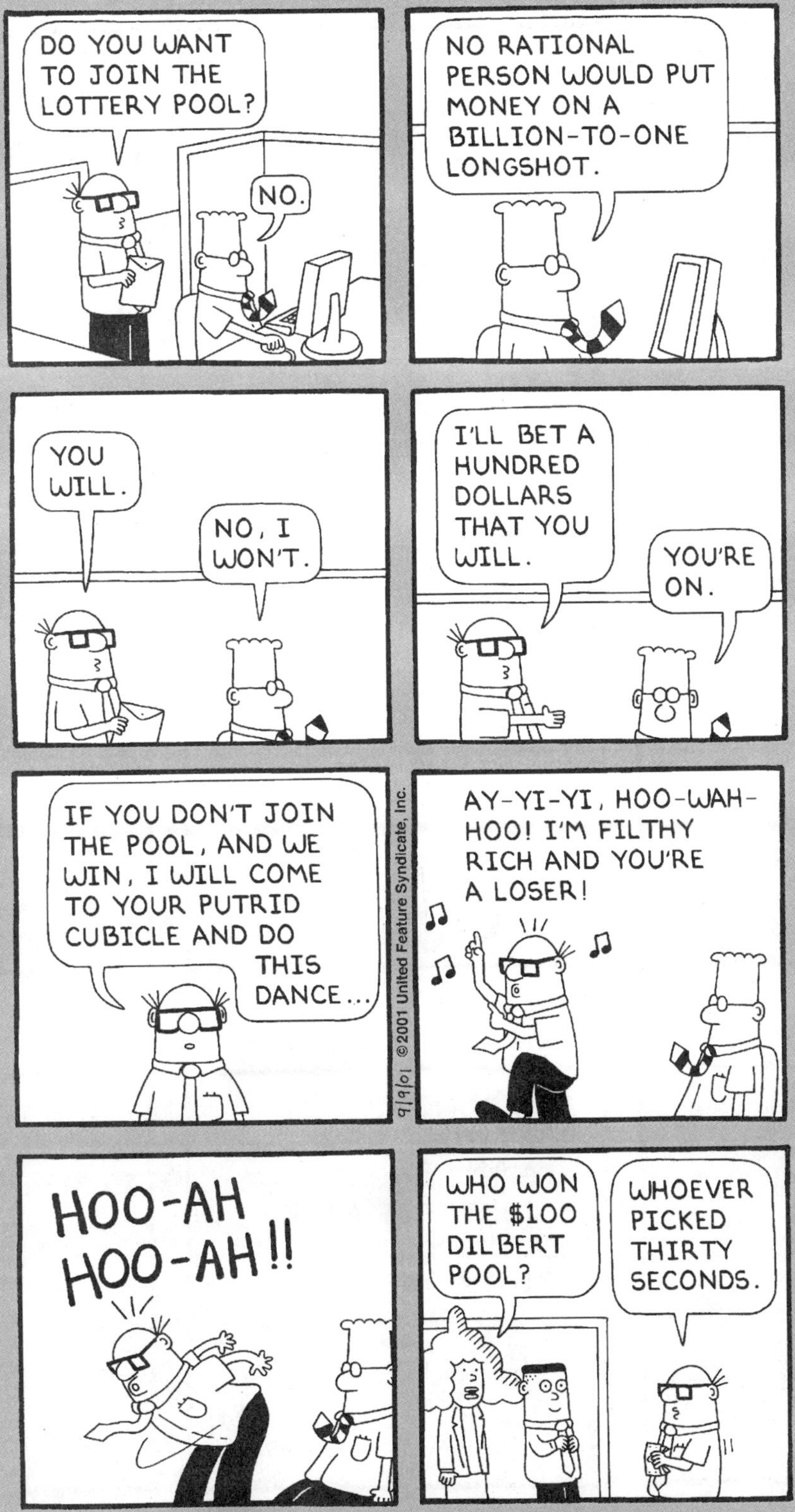
DO YOU WANT TO JOIN THE LOTTERY POOL?
NO.
NO RATIONAL PERSON WOULD PUT MONEY ON A BILLION-TO-ONE LONGSHOT.
YOU WILL.
NO, I WON'T.
I'LL BET A HUNDRED DOLLARS THAT YOU WILL.
YOU'RE ON.
IF YOU DON'T JOIN THE POOL, AND WE WIN, I WILL COME TO YOUR PUTRID CUBICLE AND DO THIS DANCE...
9/9/01 ©2001 United Feature Syndicate, Inc.
AY-YI-YI, HOO-WAH-HOO! I'M FILTHY RICH AND YOU'RE A LOSER!
HOO-AH HOO-AH!!
WHO WON THE $100 DILBERT POOL?
WHOEVER PICKED THIRTY SECONDS.

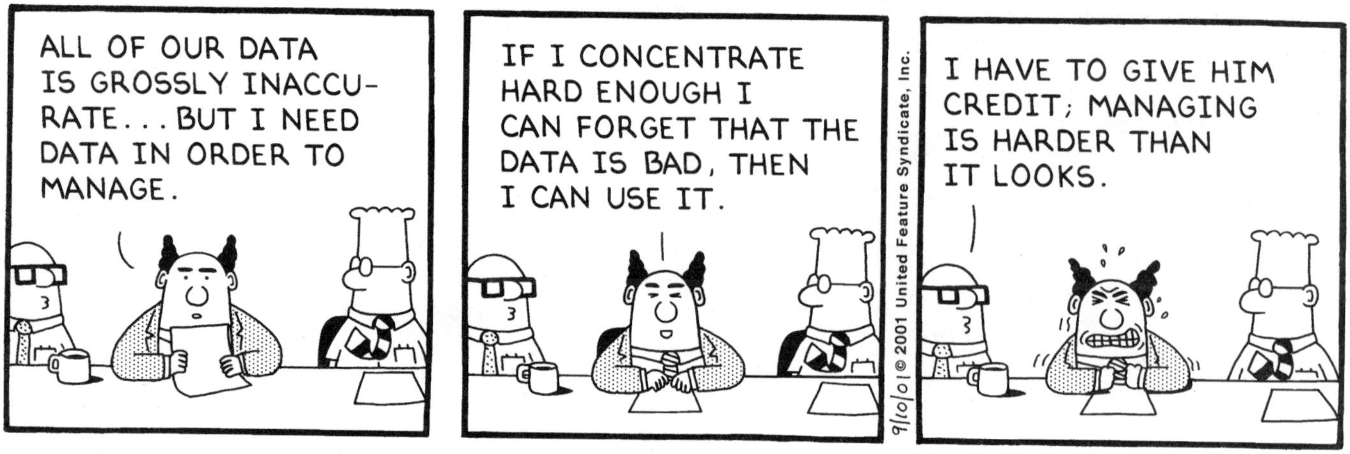
ALL OF OUR DATA IS GROSSLY INACCURATE. . . BUT I NEED DATA IN ORDER TO MANAGE.
IF I CONCENTRATE HARD ENOUGH I CAN FORGET THAT THE DATA IS BAD, THEN I CAN USE IT.
9/10/01 © 2001 United Feature Syndicate, Inc.
I HAVE TO GIVE HIM CREDIT; MANAGING IS HARDER THAN IT LOOKS.

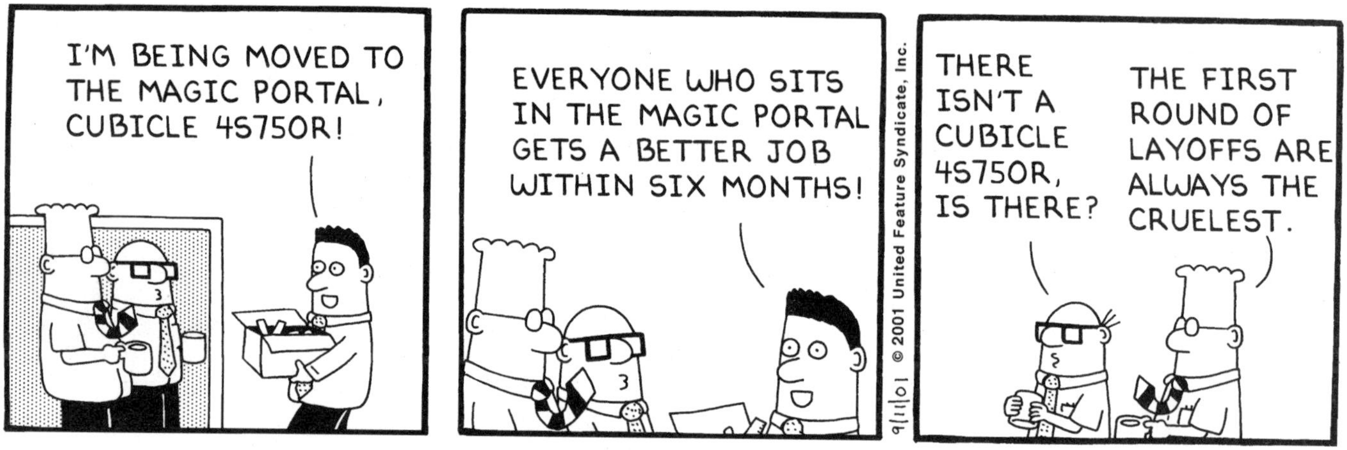
I'M BEING MOVED TO THE MAGIC PORTAL, CUBICLE 4S750R!
EVERYONE WHO SITS IN THE MAGIC PORTAL GETS A BETTER JOB WITHIN SIX MONTHS!
9/11/01 © 2001 United Feature Syndicate, Inc.
THERE ISN'T A CUBICLE 4S750R, IS THERE?
THE FIRST ROUND OF LAYOFFS ARE ALWAYS THE CRUELEST.

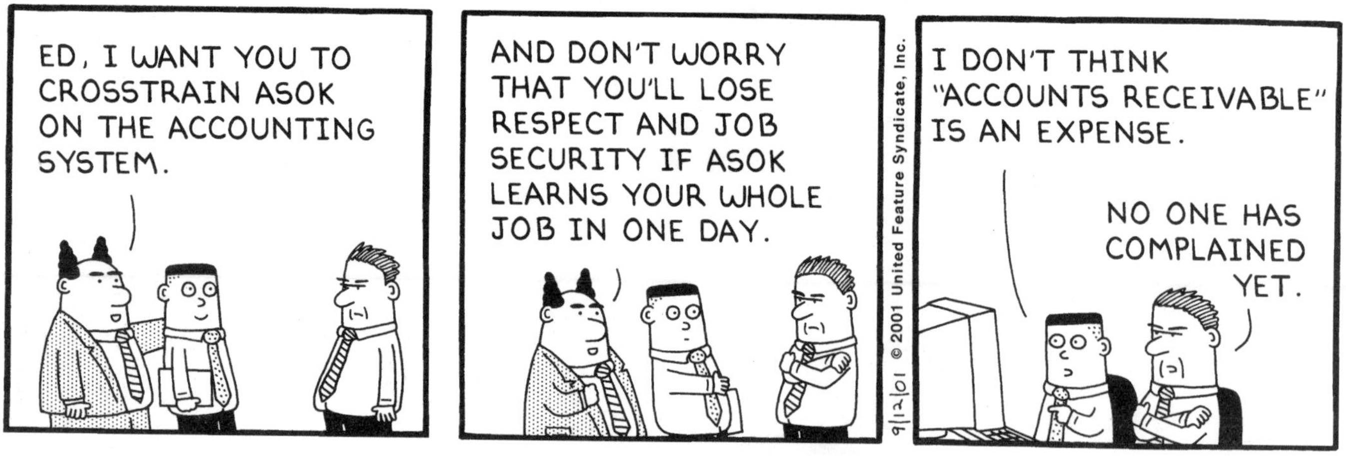
ED, I WANT YOU TO CROSSTRAIN ASOK ON THE ACCOUNTING SYSTEM.
AND DON'T WORRY THAT YOU'LL LOSE RESPECT AND JOB SECURITY IF ASOK LEARNS YOUR WHOLE JOB IN ONE DAY.
9/12/01 © 2001 United Feature Syndicate, Inc.
I DON'T THINK "ACCOUNTS RECEIVABLE" IS AN EXPENSE.
NO ONE HAS COMPLAINED YET.

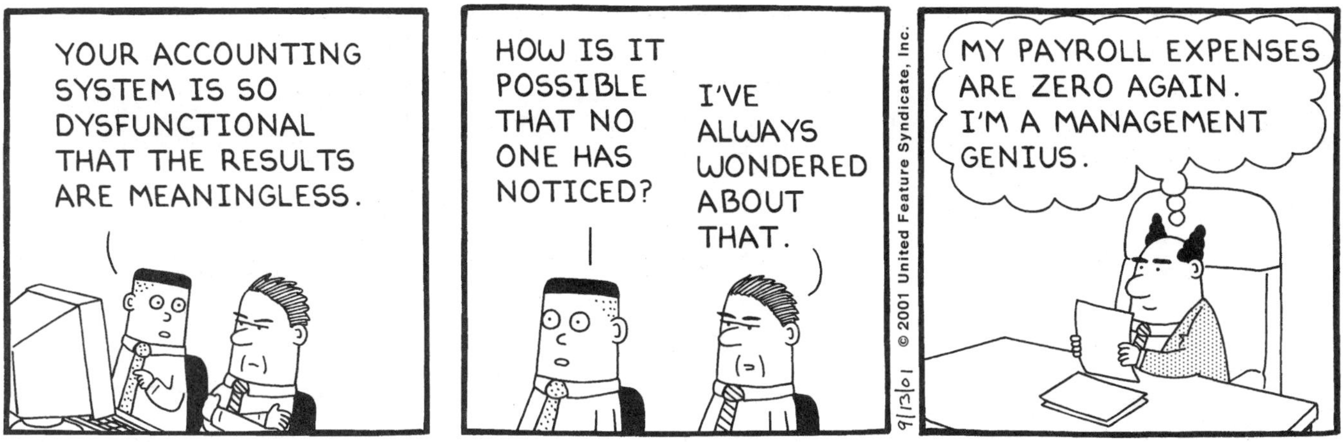
YOUR ACCOUNTING SYSTEM IS SO DYSFUNCTIONAL THAT THE RESULTS ARE MEANINGLESS.
HOW IS IT POSSIBLE THAT NO ONE HAS NOTICED?
I'VE ALWAYS WONDERED ABOUT THAT.
MY PAYROLL EXPENSES ARE ZERO AGAIN. I'M A MANAGEMENT GENIUS.
9/13/01

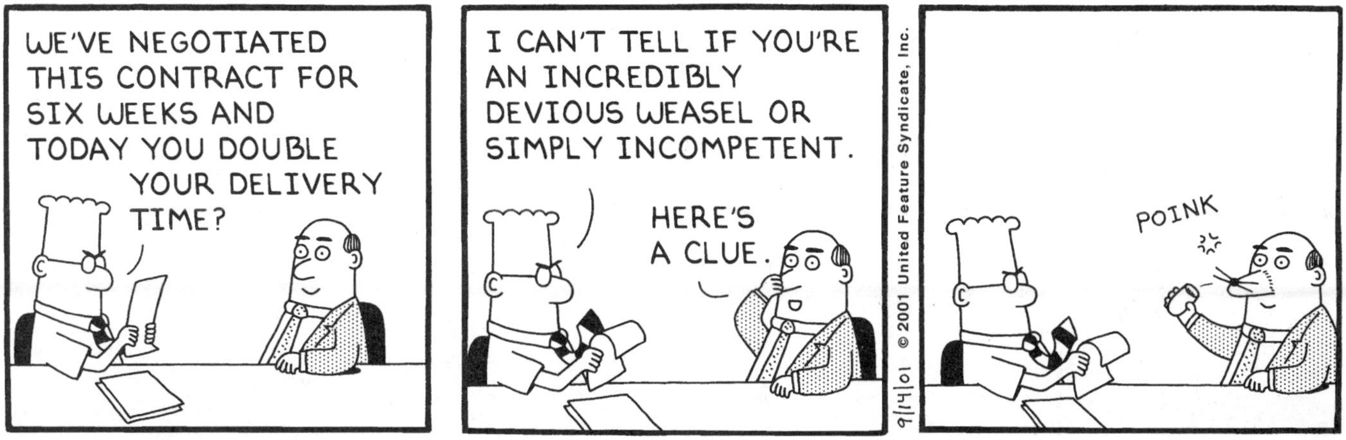
WE'VE NEGOTIATED THIS CONTRACT FOR SIX WEEKS AND TODAY YOU DOUBLE YOUR DELIVERY TIME?
I CAN'T TELL IF YOU'RE AN INCREDIBLY DEVIOUS WEASEL OR SIMPLY INCOMPETENT.
HERE'S A CLUE.
POINK
9/14/01

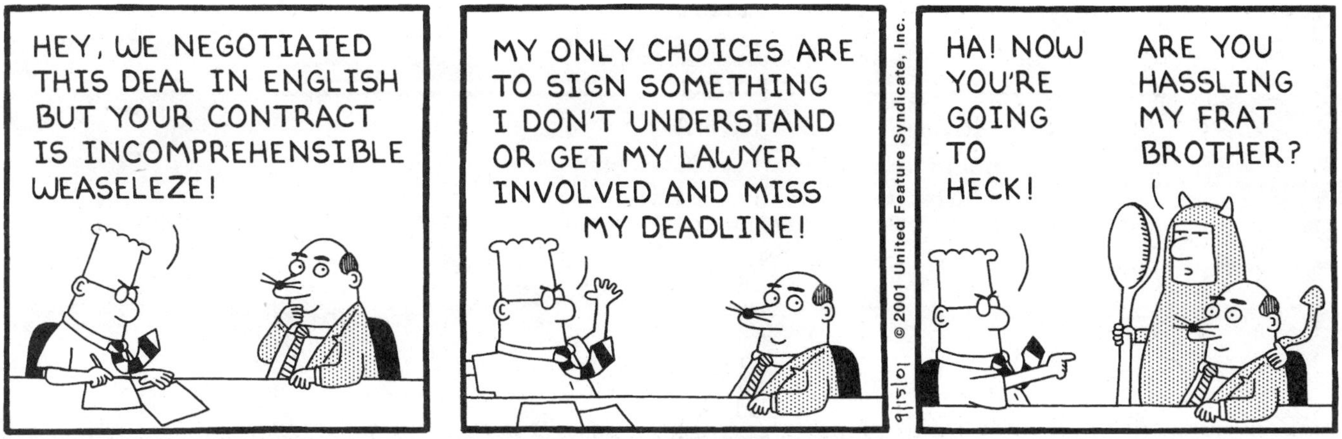
HEY, WE NEGOTIATED THIS DEAL IN ENGLISH BUT YOUR CONTRACT IS INCOMPREHENSIBLE WEASELEZE!
MY ONLY CHOICES ARE TO SIGN SOMETHING I DON'T UNDERSTAND OR GET MY LAWYER INVOLVED AND MISS MY DEADLINE!
HA! NOW YOU'RE GOING TO HECK!
ARE YOU HASSLING MY FRAT BROTHER?
9/15/01

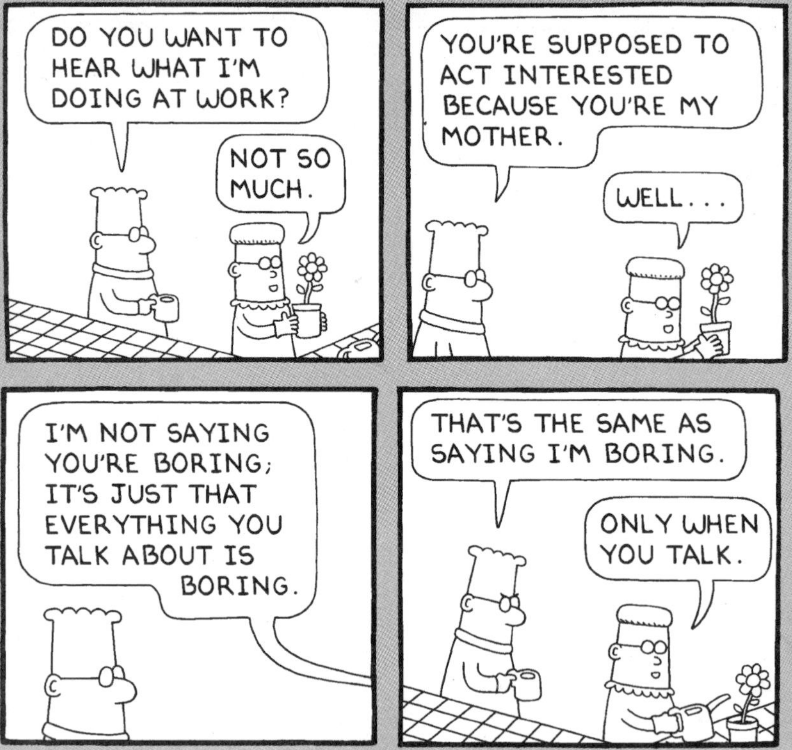
DO YOU WANT TO HEAR WHAT I'M DOING AT WORK?
NOT SO MUCH.
YOU'RE SUPPOSED TO ACT INTERESTED BECAUSE YOU'RE MY MOTHER.
WELL...
I'M NOT SAYING YOU'RE BORING; IT'S JUST THAT EVERYTHING YOU TALK ABOUT IS BORING.
THAT'S THE SAME AS SAYING I'M BORING.
ONLY WHEN YOU TALK.

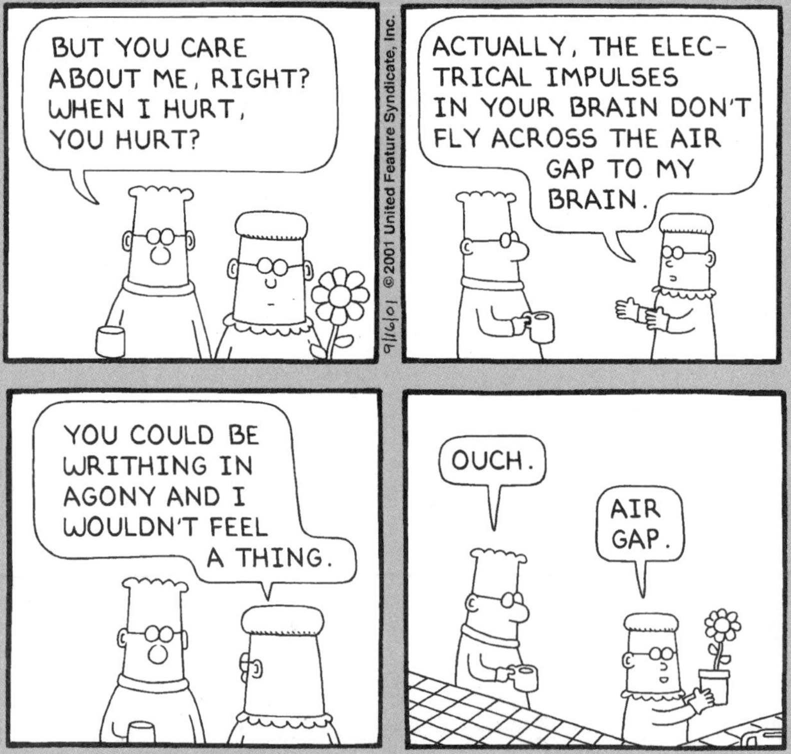
BUT YOU CARE ABOUT ME, RIGHT? WHEN I HURT, YOU HURT?
9/6/01 © 2001 United Feature Syndicate, Inc.
ACTUALLY, THE ELEC-TRICAL IMPULSES IN YOUR BRAIN DON'T FLY ACROSS THE AIR GAP TO MY BRAIN.
YOU COULD BE WRITHING IN AGONY AND I WOULDN'T FEEL A THING.
OUCH.
AIR GAP.

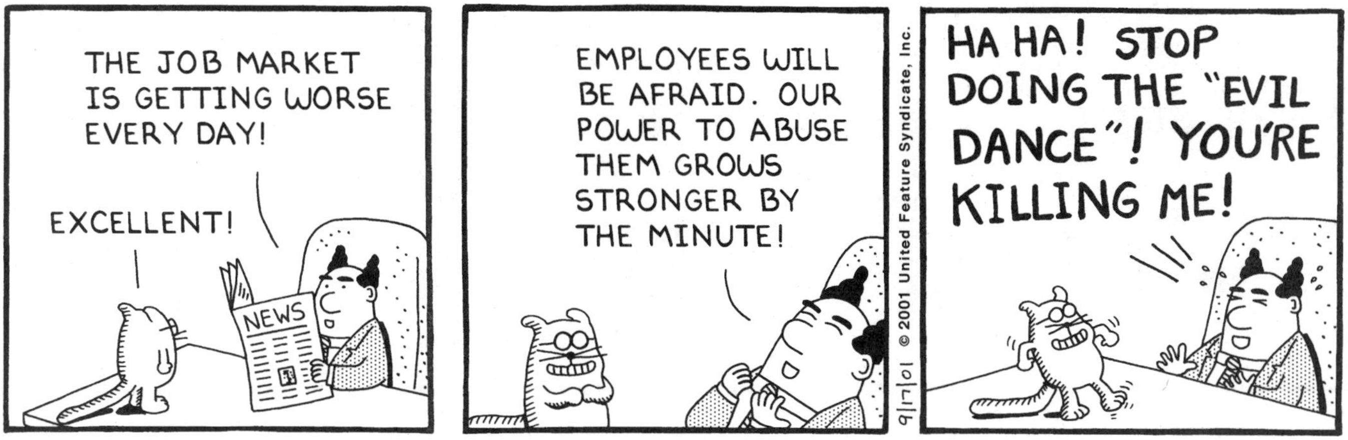
THE JOB MARKET IS GETTING WORSE EVERY DAY!
EXCELLENT!
NEWS
EMPLOYEES WILL BE AFRAID. OUR POWER TO ABUSE THEM GROWS STRONGER BY THE MINUTE!
9/17/01 © 2001 United Feature Syndicate, Inc.
HA HA! STOP DOING THE "EVIL DANCE"! YOU'RE KILLING ME!

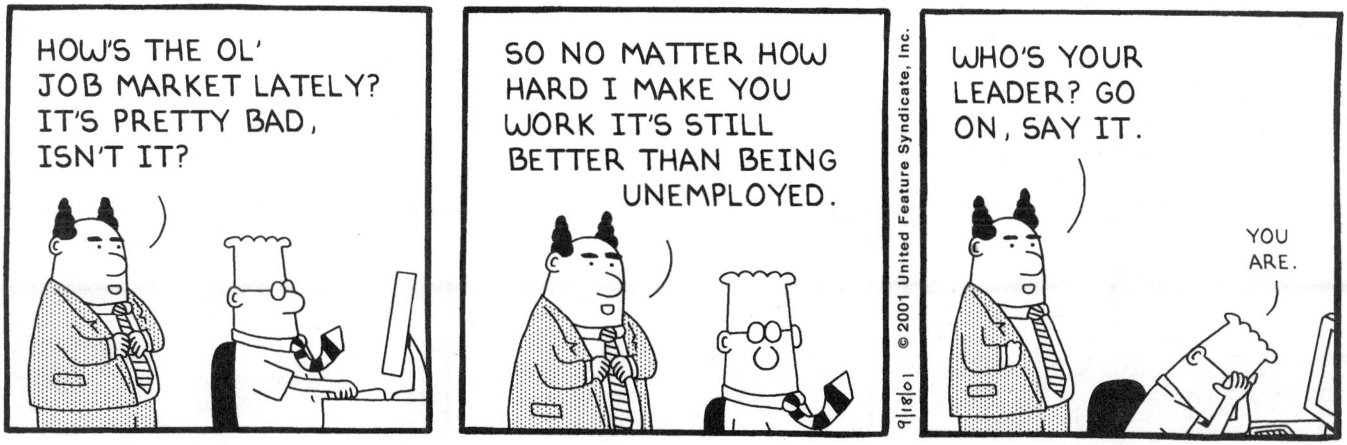
HOW'S THE OL' JOB MARKET LATELY? IT'S PRETTY BAD, ISN'T IT?
SO NO MATTER HOW HARD I MAKE YOU WORK IT'S STILL BETTER THAN BEING UNEMPLOYED.
9/18/01 © 2001 United Feature Syndicate, Inc.
WHO'S YOUR LEADER? GO ON, SAY IT.
YOU ARE.

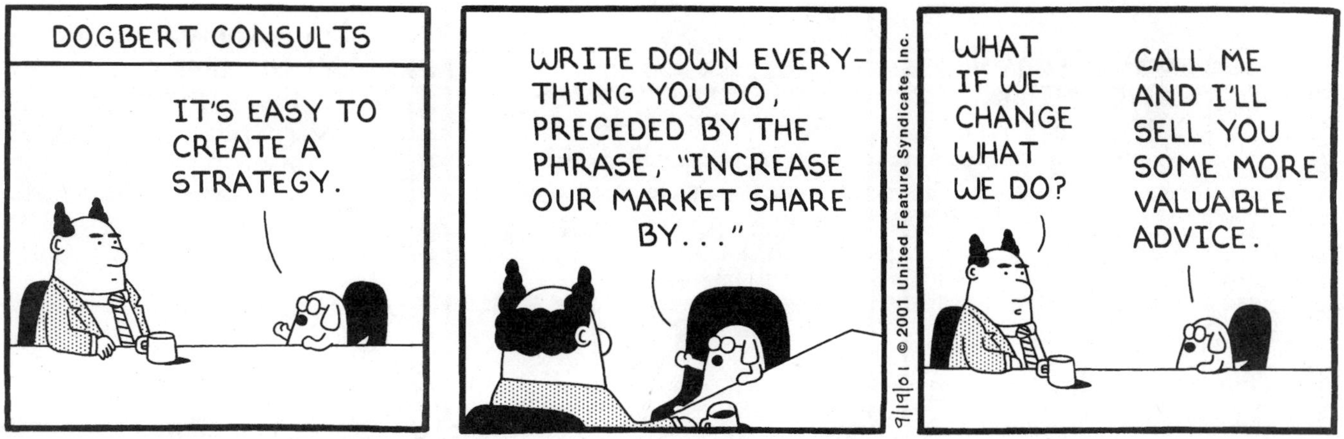
DOGBERT CONSULTS
IT'S EASY TO CREATE A STRATEGY.
WRITE DOWN EVERY-THING YOU DO, PRECEDED BY THE PHRASE, "INCREASE OUR MARKET SHARE BY..."
9/19/01 © 2001 United Feature Syndicate, Inc.
WHAT IF WE CHANGE WHAT WE DO?
CALL ME AND I'LL SELL YOU SOME MORE VALUABLE ADVICE.

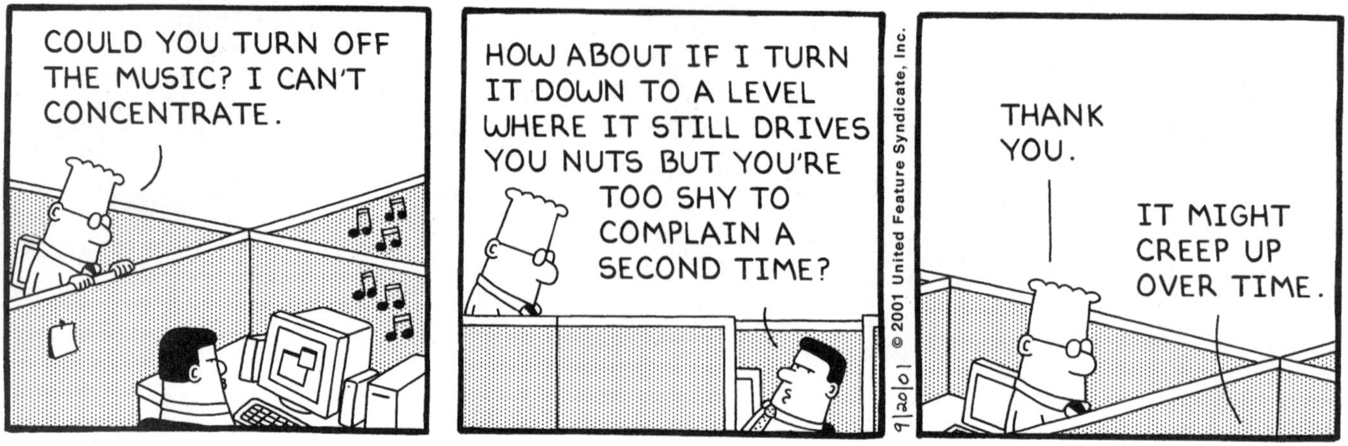
COULD YOU TURN OFF THE MUSIC? I CAN'T CONCENTRATE.
HOW ABOUT IF I TURN IT DOWN TO A LEVEL WHERE IT STILL DRIVES YOU NUTS BUT YOU'RE TOO SHY TO COMPLAIN A SECOND TIME?
9/20/01 © 2001 United Feature Syndicate, Inc.
THANK YOU.
IT MIGHT CREEP UP OVER TIME.

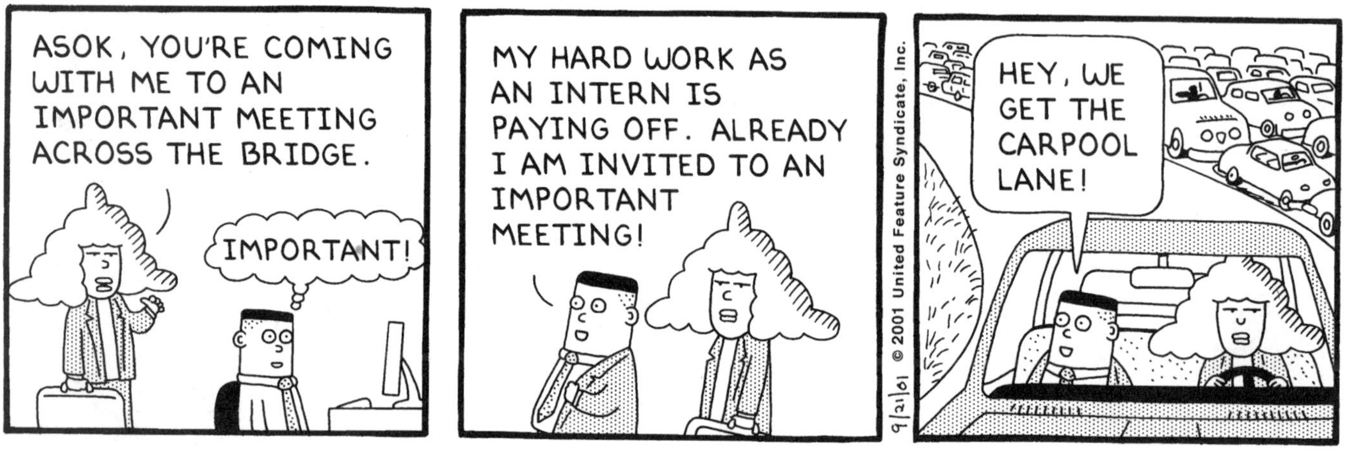
ASOK, YOU'RE COMING WITH ME TO AN IMPORTANT MEETING ACROSS THE BRIDGE.
IMPORTANT!
MY HARD WORK AS AN INTERN IS PAYING OFF. ALREADY I AM INVITED TO AN IMPORTANT MEETING!
9/21/01 © 2001 United Feature Syndicate, Inc.
HEY, WE GET THE CARPOOL LANE!

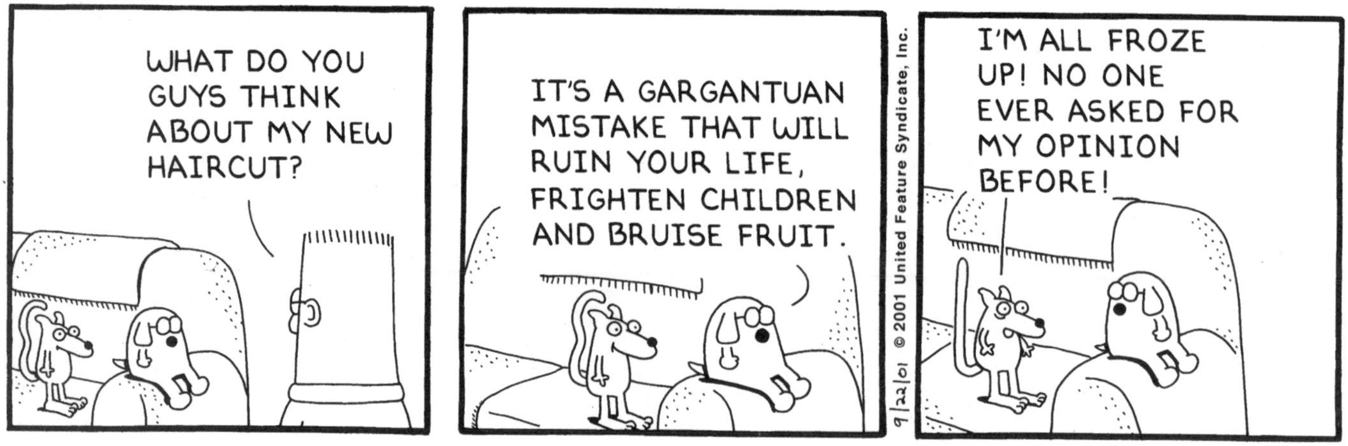
WHAT DO YOU GUYS THINK ABOUT MY NEW HAIRCUT?
IT'S A GARGANTUAN MISTAKE THAT WILL RUIN YOUR LIFE, FRIGHTEN CHILDREN AND BRUISE FRUIT.
9/22/01 © 2001 United Feature Syndicate, Inc.
I'M ALL FROZE UP! NO ONE EVER ASKED FOR MY OPINION BEFORE!

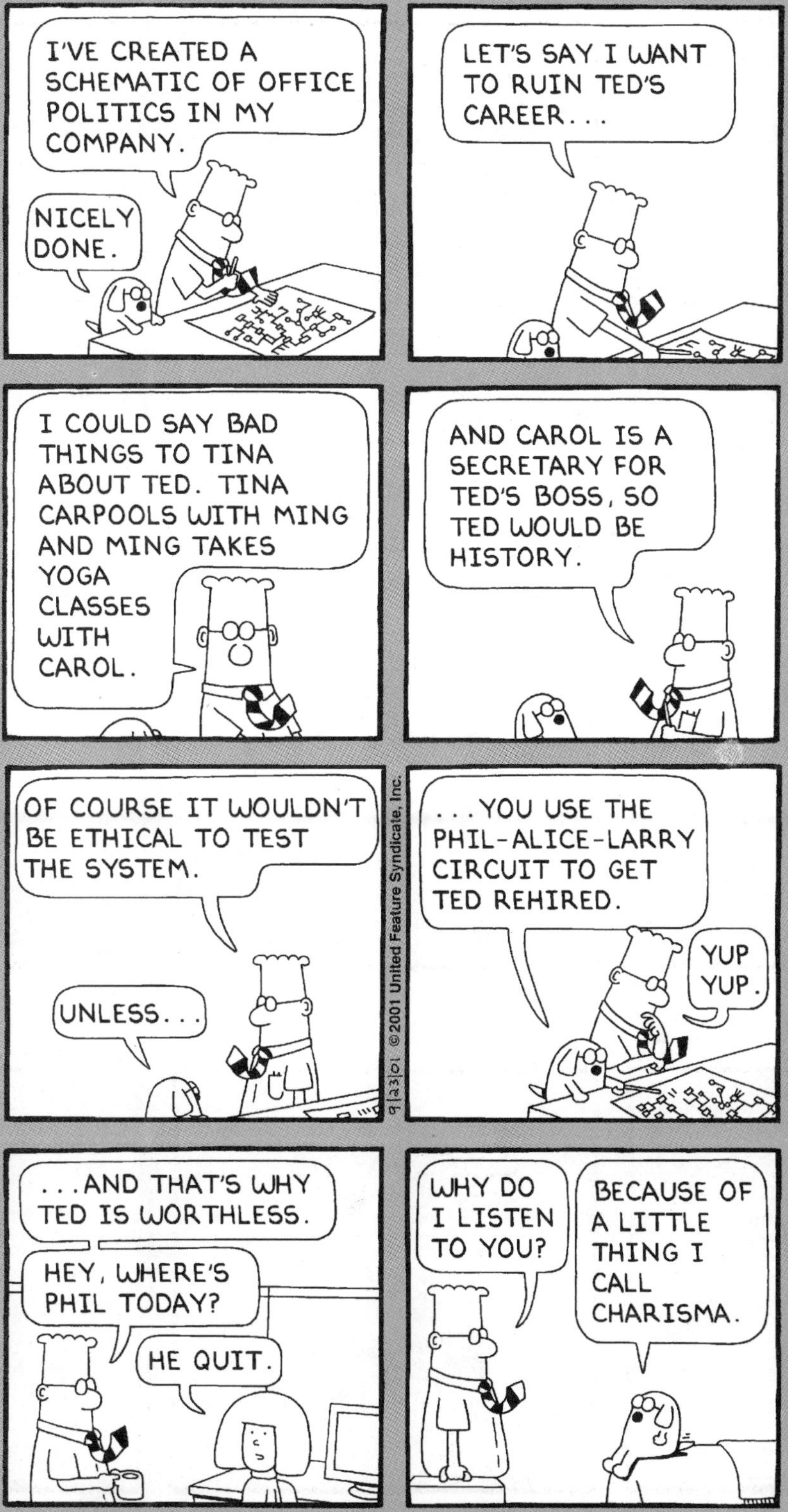
I'VE CREATED A SCHEMATIC OF OFFICE POLITICS IN MY COMPANY.
NICELY DONE.
LET'S SAY I WANT TO RUIN TED'S CAREER...
I COULD SAY BAD THINGS TO TINA ABOUT TED. TINA CARPOOLS WITH MING AND MING TAKES YOGA CLASSES WITH CAROL.
AND CAROL IS A SECRETARY FOR TED'S BOSS, SO TED WOULD BE HISTORY.
OF COURSE IT WOULDN'T BE ETHICAL TO TEST THE SYSTEM.
UNLESS...
...YOU USE THE PHIL-ALICE-LARRY CIRCUIT TO GET TED REHIRED.
YUP YUP.
9/23/01 © 2001 United Feature Syndicate, Inc.
...AND THAT'S WHY TED IS WORTHLESS.
HEY, WHERE'S PHIL TODAY?
HE QUIT.
WHY DO I LISTEN TO YOU?
BECAUSE OF A LITTLE THING I CALL CHARISMA.

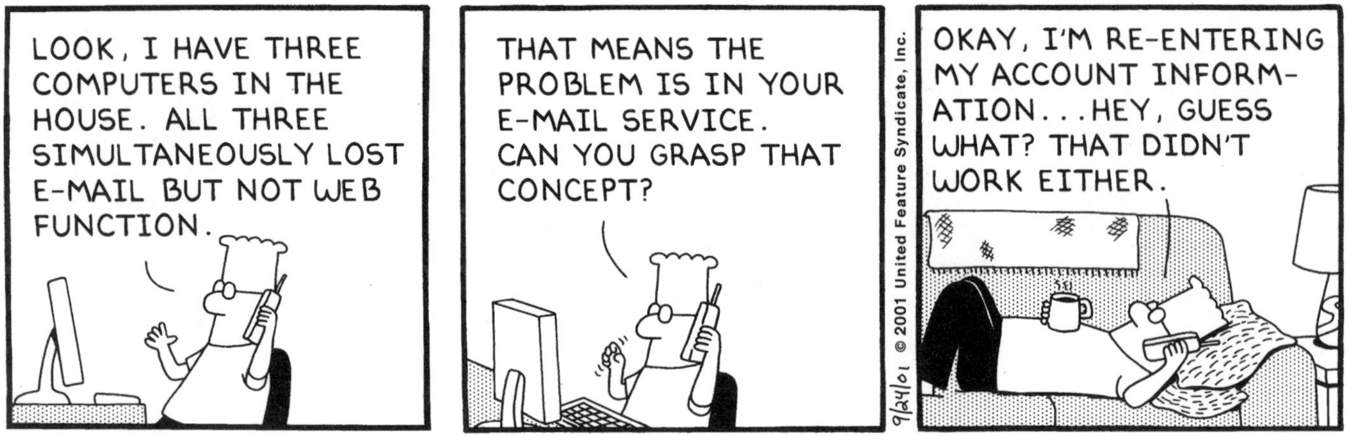
LOOK, I HAVE THREE COMPUTERS IN THE HOUSE. ALL THREE SIMULTANEOUSLY LOST E-MAIL BUT NOT WEB FUNCTION.
THAT MEANS THE PROBLEM IS IN YOUR E-MAIL SERVICE. CAN YOU GRASP THAT CONCEPT?
9/24/01 © 2001 United Feature Syndicate, Inc.
OKAY, I'M RE-ENTERING MY ACCOUNT INFORMATION...HEY, GUESS WHAT? THAT DIDN'T WORK EITHER.

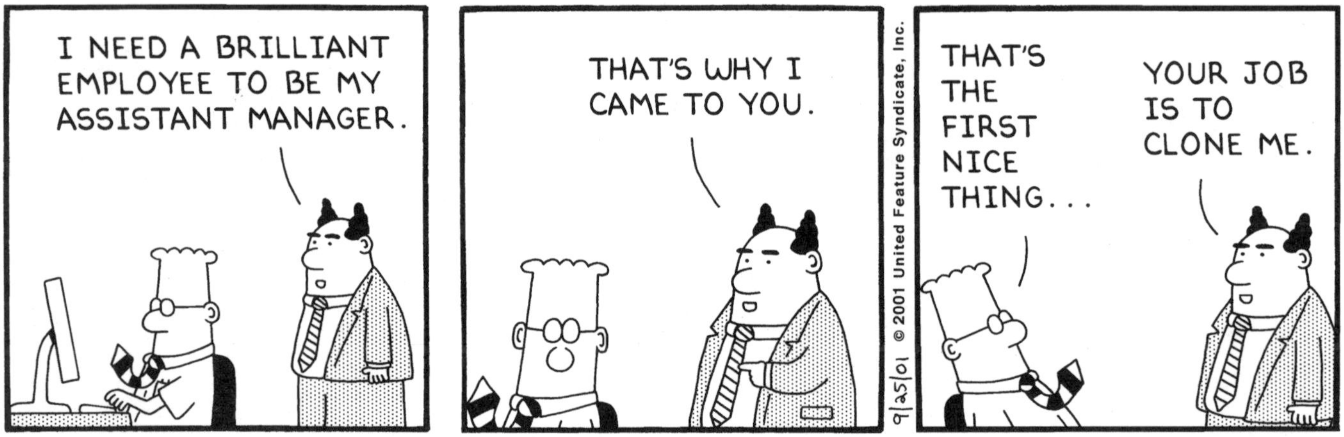
I NEED A BRILLIANT EMPLOYEE TO BE MY ASSISTANT MANAGER.
THAT'S WHY I CAME TO YOU.
9/25/01 © 2001 United Feature Syndicate, Inc.
THAT'S THE FIRST NICE THING...
YOUR JOB IS TO CLONE ME.

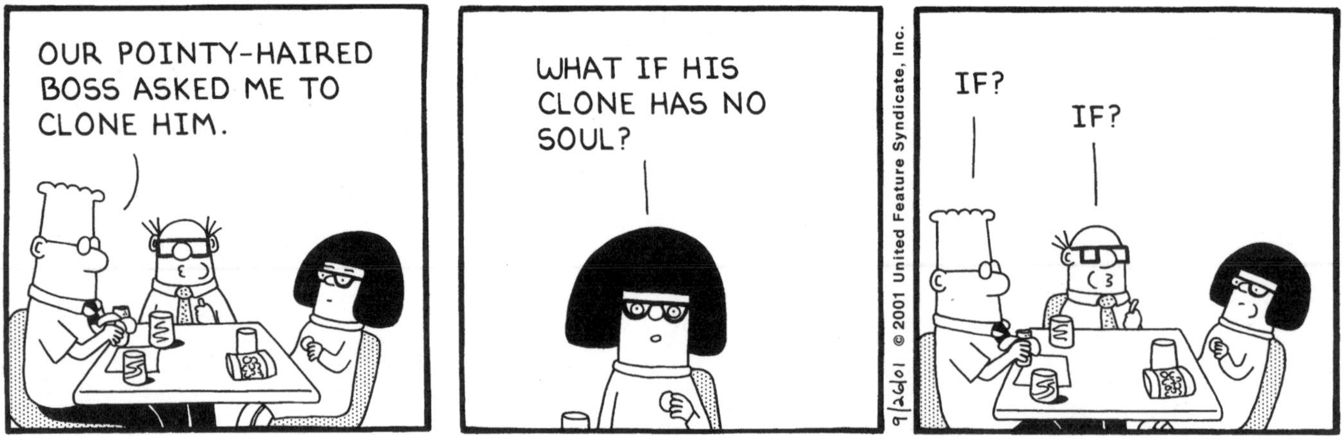
OUR POINTY-HAIRED BOSS ASKED ME TO CLONE HIM.
WHAT IF HIS CLONE HAS NO SOUL?
9/26/01 © 2001 United Feature Syndicate, Inc.
IF?
IF?

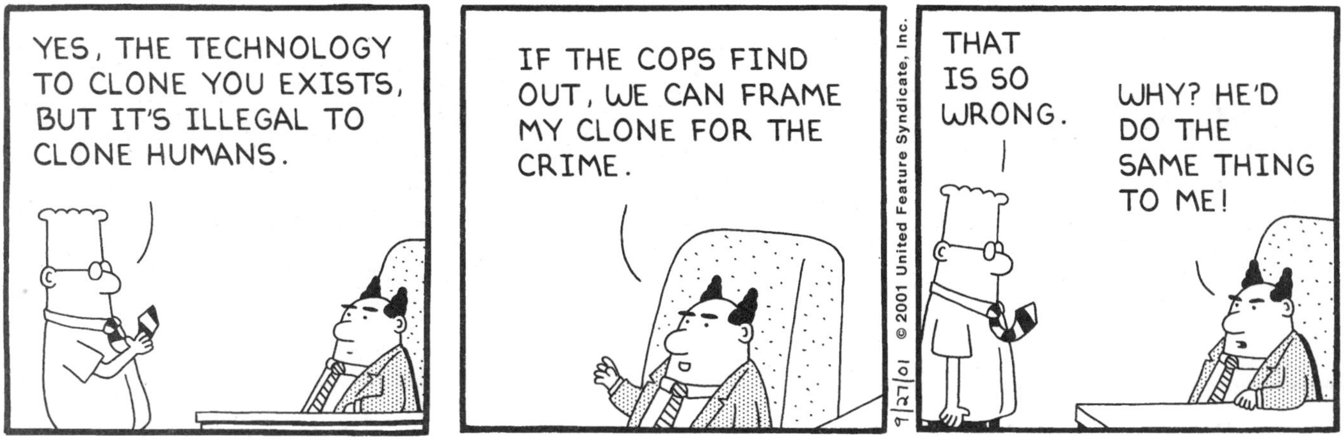
YES, THE TECHNOLOGY TO CLONE YOU EXISTS, BUT IT'S ILLEGAL TO CLONE HUMANS.
IF THE COPS FIND OUT, WE CAN FRAME MY CLONE FOR THE CRIME.
9/27/01 © 2001 United Feature Syndicate, Inc.
THAT IS SO WRONG.
WHY? HE'D DO THE SAME THING TO ME!

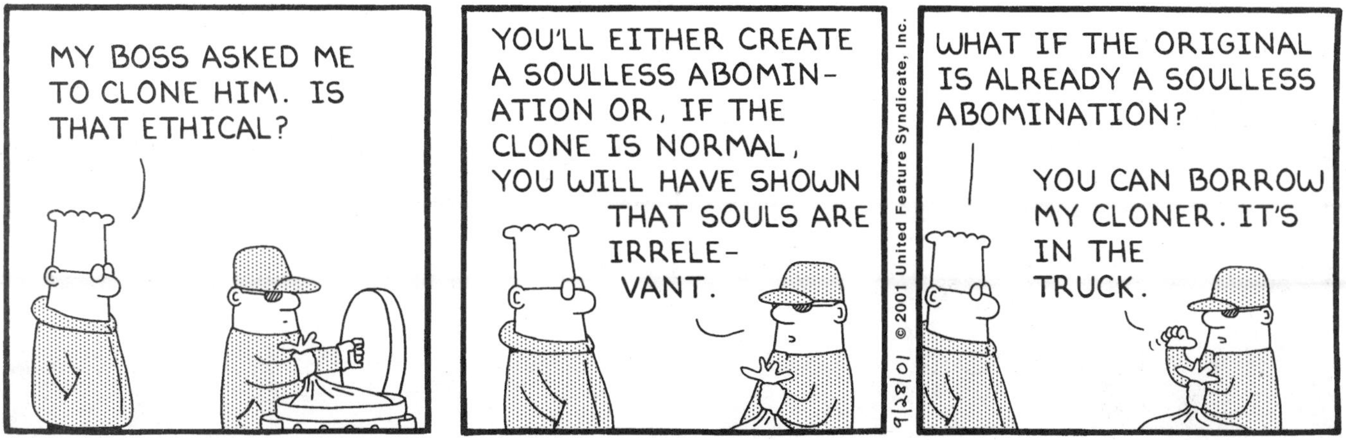
MY BOSS ASKED ME TO CLONE HIM. IS THAT ETHICAL?
YOU'LL EITHER CREATE A SOULLESS ABOMIN-ATION OR, IF THE CLONE IS NORMAL, YOU WILL HAVE SHOWN THAT SOULS ARE IRRELE-VANT.
9/28/01 © 2001 United Feature Syndicate, Inc.
WHAT IF THE ORIGINAL IS ALREADY A SOULLESS ABOMINATION?
YOU CAN BORROW MY CLONER. IT'S IN THE TRUCK.

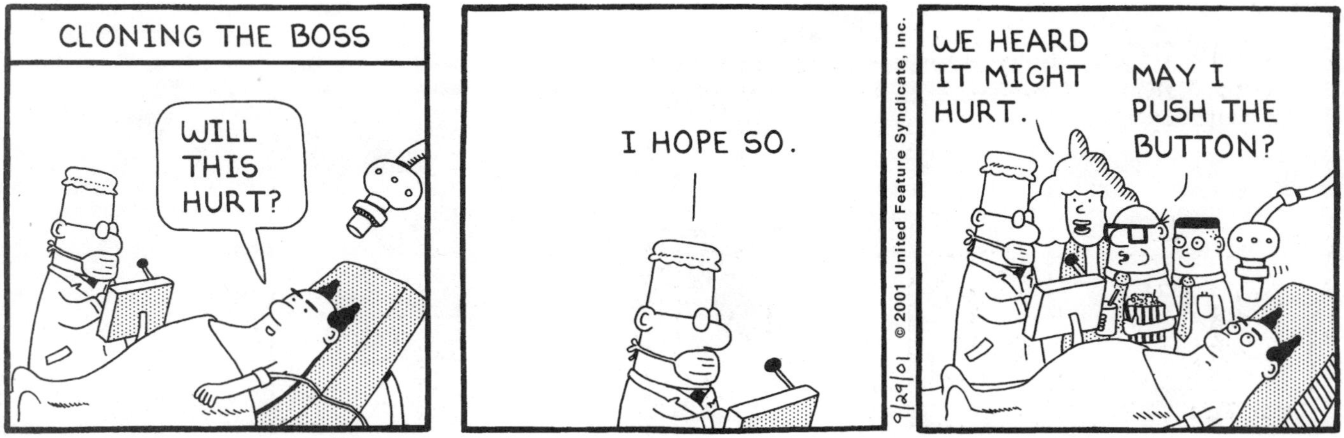
CLONING THE BOSS
WILL THIS HURT?
I HOPE SO.
9/29/01 © 2001 United Feature Syndicate, Inc.
WE HEARD IT MIGHT HURT.
MAY I PUSH THE BUTTON?

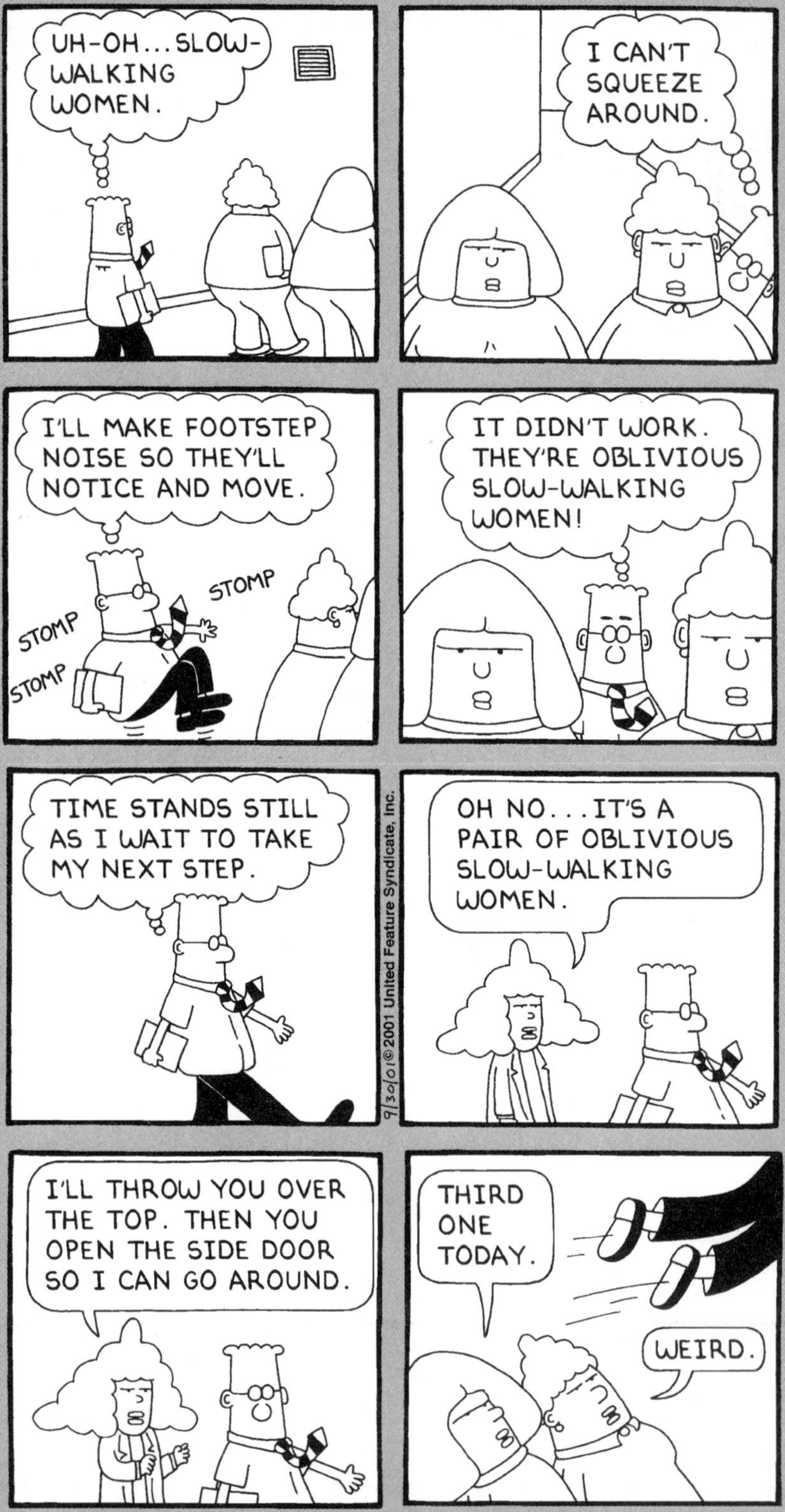

UH-OH... SLOW-WALKING WOMEN.
I CAN'T SQUEEZE AROUND.
I'LL MAKE FOOTSTEP NOISE SO THEY'LL NOTICE AND MOVE.
STOMP
STOMP
STOMP
IT DIDN'T WORK. THEY'RE OBLIVIOUS SLOW-WALKING WOMEN!
TIME STANDS STILL AS I WAIT TO TAKE MY NEXT STEP.
OH NO... IT'S A PAIR OF OBLIVIOUS SLOW-WALKING WOMEN.
I'LL THROW YOU OVER THE TOP. THEN YOU OPEN THE SIDE DOOR SO I CAN GO AROUND.
THIRD ONE TODAY.
WEIRD.
9/30/01 © 2001 United Feature Syndicate, Inc.

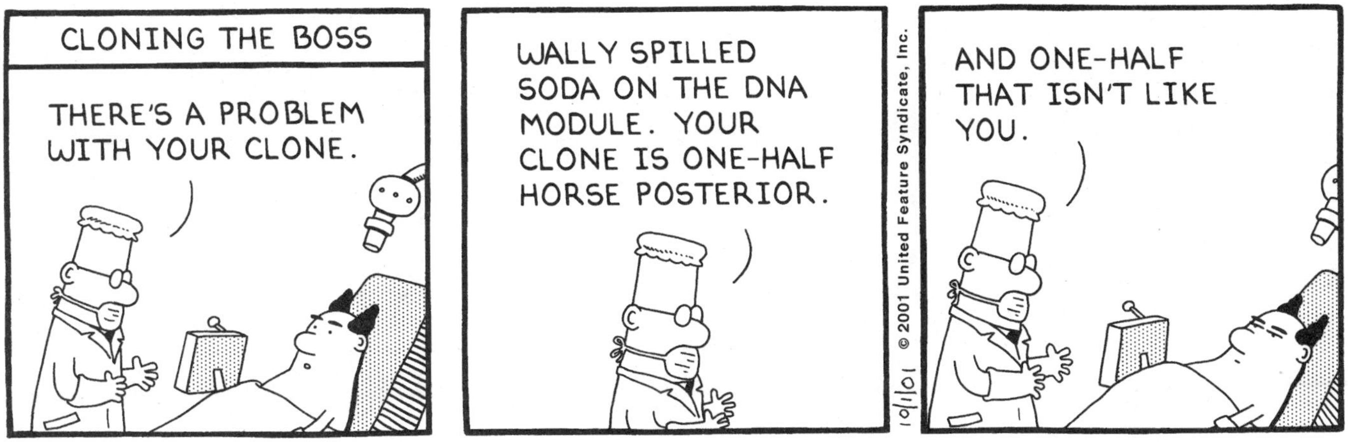
CLONING THE BOSS
THERE'S A PROBLEM WITH YOUR CLONE.
WALLY SPILLED SODA ON THE DNA MODULE. YOUR CLONE IS ONE-HALF HORSE POSTERIOR.
AND ONE-HALF THAT ISN'T LIKE YOU.
10/1/01 © 2001 United Feature Syndicate, Inc.

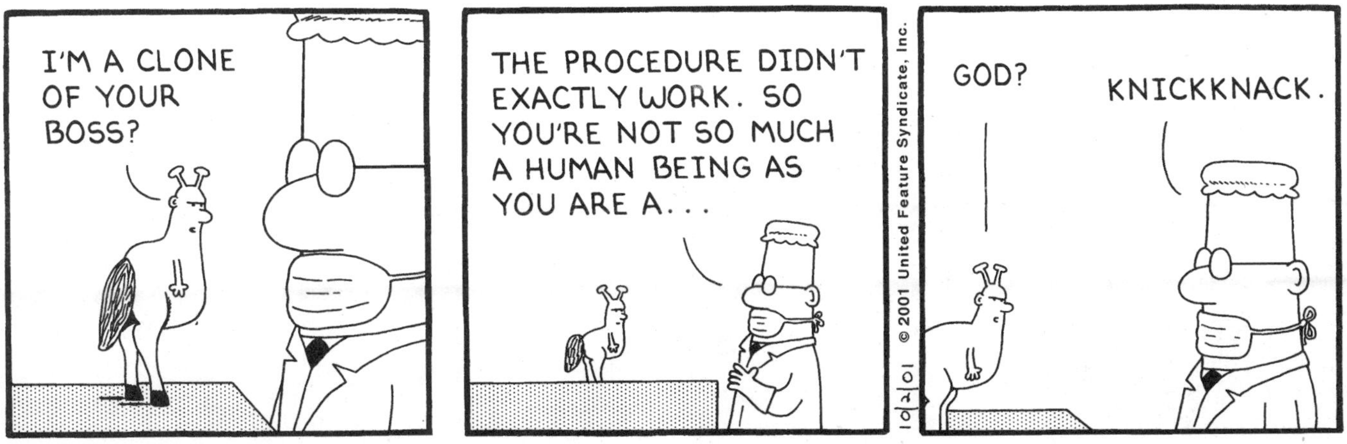
I'M A CLONE OF YOUR BOSS?
THE PROCEDURE DIDN'T EXACTLY WORK. SO YOU'RE NOT SO MUCH A HUMAN BEING AS YOU ARE A...
GOD?
KNICKKNACK.
10/2/01 © 2001 United Feature Syndicate, Inc.

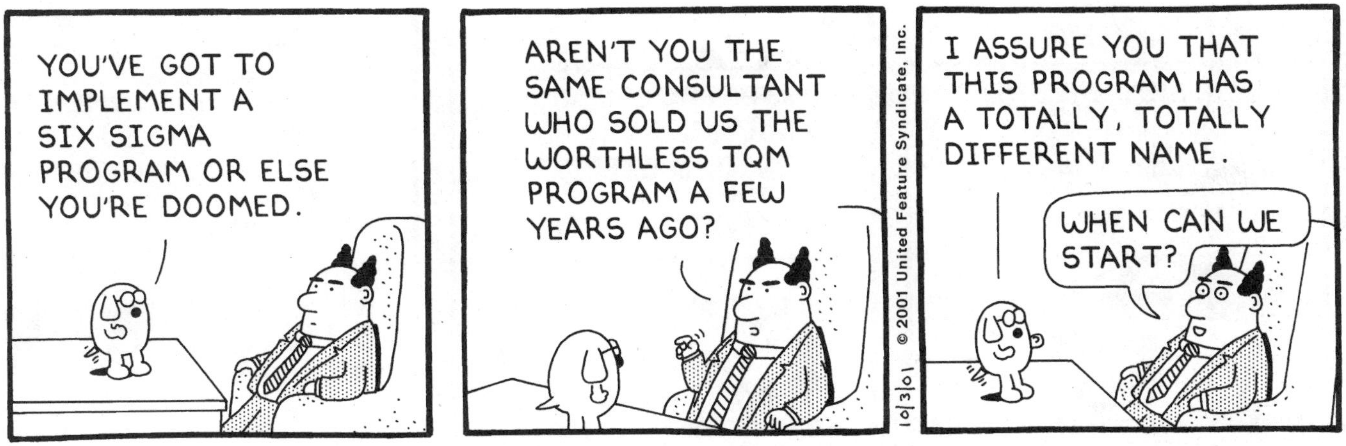
YOU'VE GOT TO IMPLEMENT A SIX SIGMA PROGRAM OR ELSE YOU'RE DOOMED.
AREN'T YOU THE SAME CONSULTANT WHO SOLD US THE WORTHLESS TQM PROGRAM A FEW YEARS AGO?
I ASSURE YOU THAT THIS PROGRAM HAS A TOTALLY, TOTALLY DIFFERENT NAME.
WHEN CAN WE START?
10/3/01 © 2001 United Feature Syndicate, Inc.

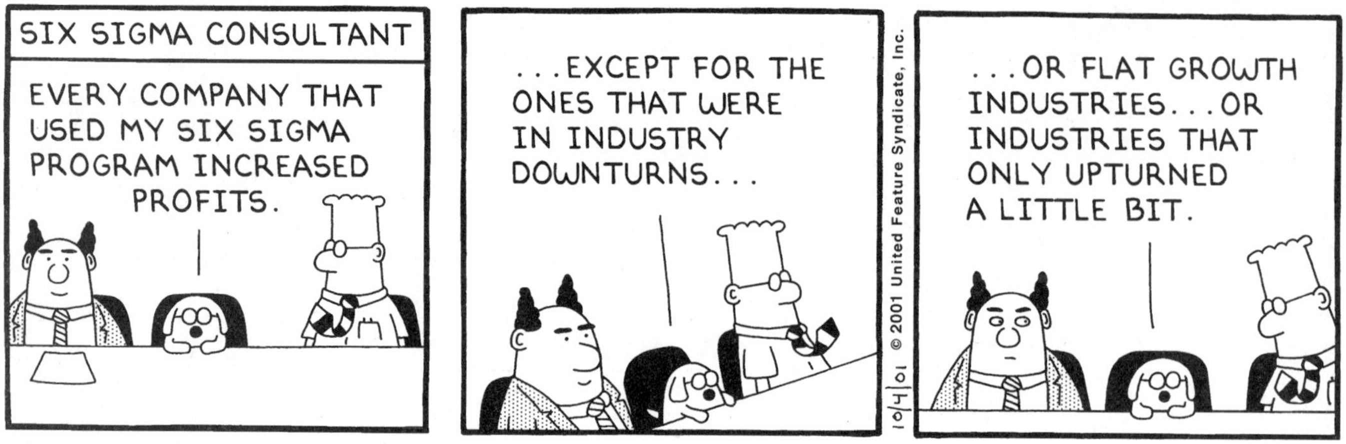
SIX SIGMA CONSULTANT
EVERY COMPANY THAT USED MY SIX SIGMA PROGRAM INCREASED PROFITS.
...EXCEPT FOR THE ONES THAT WERE IN INDUSTRY DOWNTURNS...
...OR FLAT GROWTH INDUSTRIES...OR INDUSTRIES THAT ONLY UPTURNED A LITTLE BIT.
10/4/01
© 2001 United Feature Syndicate, Inc.

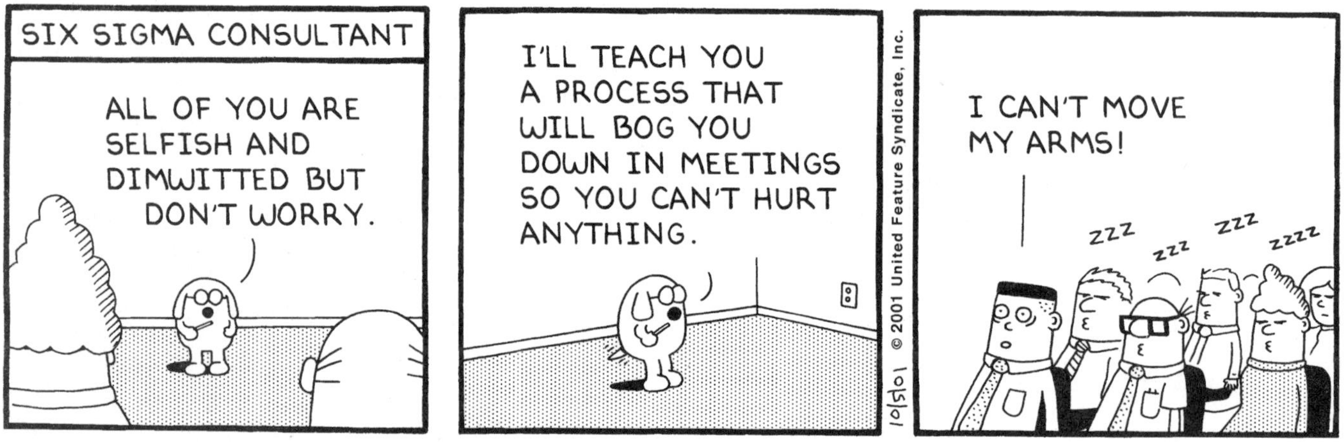
SIX SIGMA CONSULTANT
ALL OF YOU ARE SELFISH AND DIMWITTED BUT DON'T WORRY.
I'LL TEACH YOU A PROCESS THAT WILL BOG YOU DOWN IN MEETINGS SO YOU CAN'T HURT ANYTHING.
I CAN'T MOVE MY ARMS!
ZZZ
ZZZ
ZZZ
ZZZZ
10/5/01
© 2001 United Feature Syndicate, Inc.

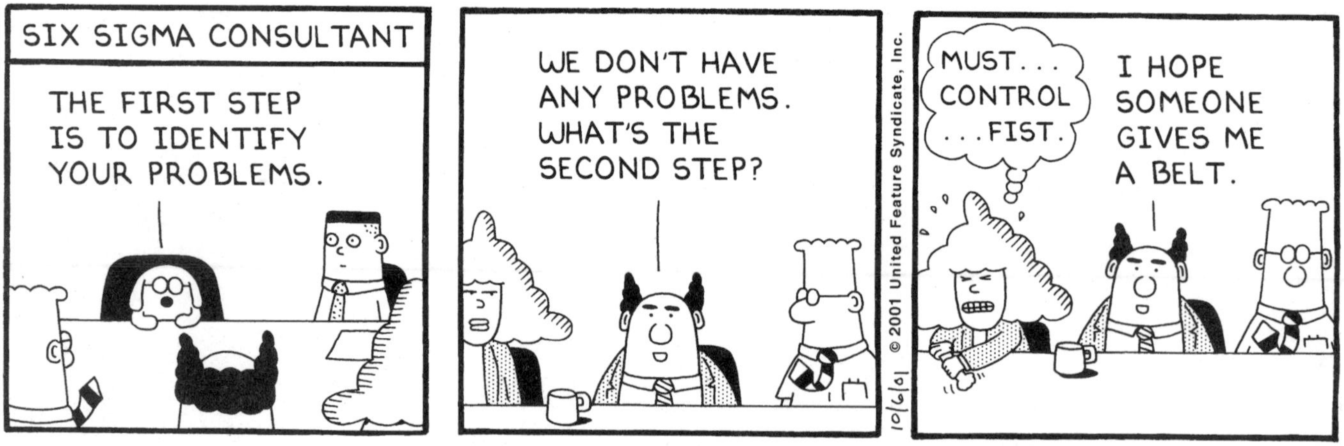
SIX SIGMA CONSULTANT
THE FIRST STEP IS TO IDENTIFY YOUR PROBLEMS.
WE DON'T HAVE ANY PROBLEMS. WHAT'S THE SECOND STEP?
MUST... CONTROL ...FIST.
I HOPE SOMEONE GIVES ME A BELT.
10/6/01
© 2001 United Feature Syndicate, Inc.

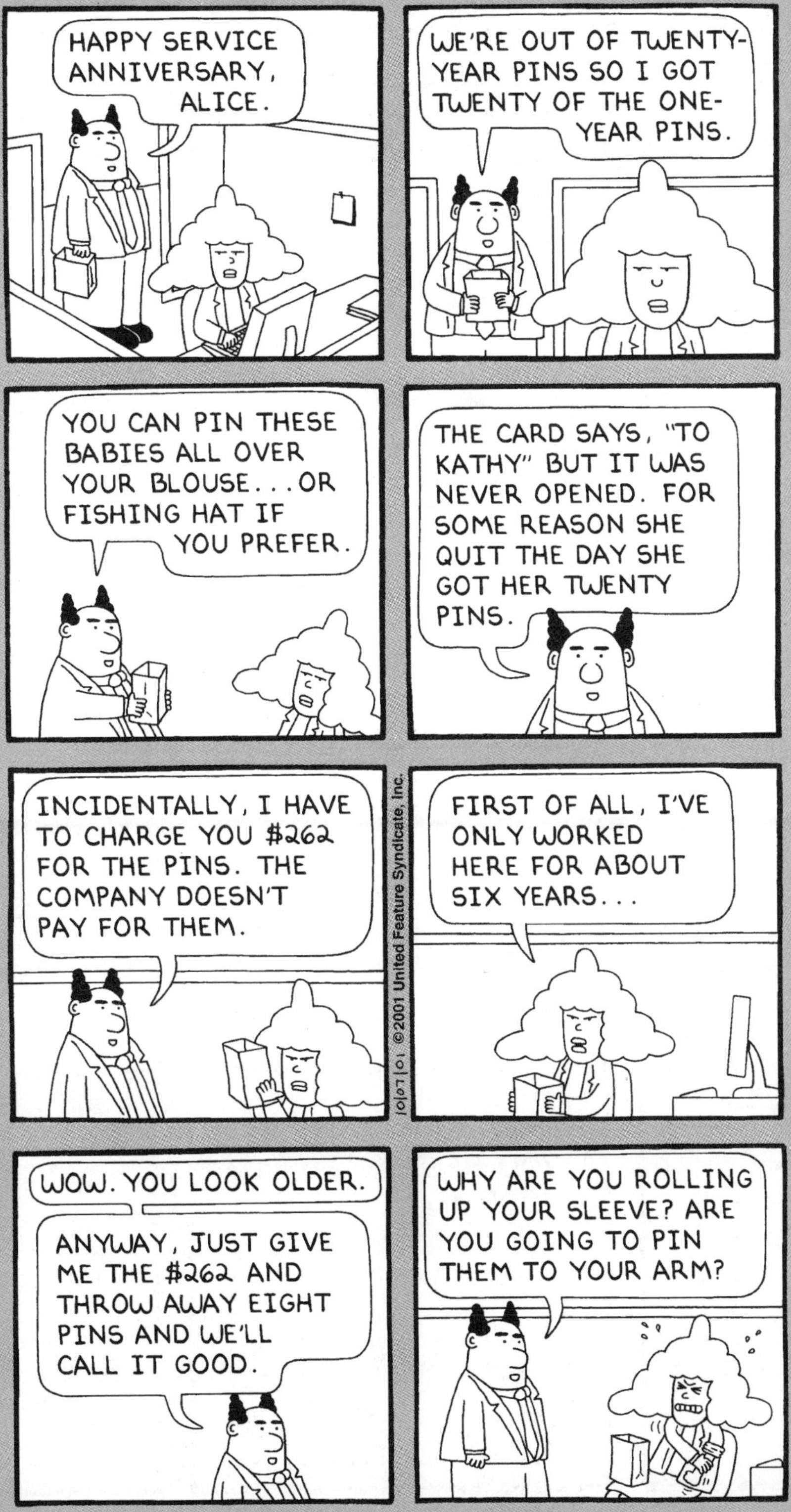
HAPPY SERVICE ANNIVERSARY, ALICE.
WE'RE OUT OF TWENTY-YEAR PINS SO I GOT TWENTY OF THE ONE-YEAR PINS.
YOU CAN PIN THESE BABIES ALL OVER YOUR BLOUSE...OR FISHING HAT IF YOU PREFER.
THE CARD SAYS, "TO KATHY" BUT IT WAS NEVER OPENED. FOR SOME REASON SHE QUIT THE DAY SHE GOT HER TWENTY PINS.
INCIDENTALLY, I HAVE TO CHARGE YOU $262 FOR THE PINS. THE COMPANY DOESN'T PAY FOR THEM.
FIRST OF ALL, I'VE ONLY WORKED HERE FOR ABOUT SIX YEARS...
WOW. YOU LOOK OLDER.
ANYWAY, JUST GIVE ME THE $262 AND THROW AWAY EIGHT PINS AND WE'LL CALL IT GOOD.
WHY ARE YOU ROLLING UP YOUR SLEEVE? ARE YOU GOING TO PIN THEM TO YOUR ARM?
10/07/01 ©2001 United Feature Syndicate, Inc.

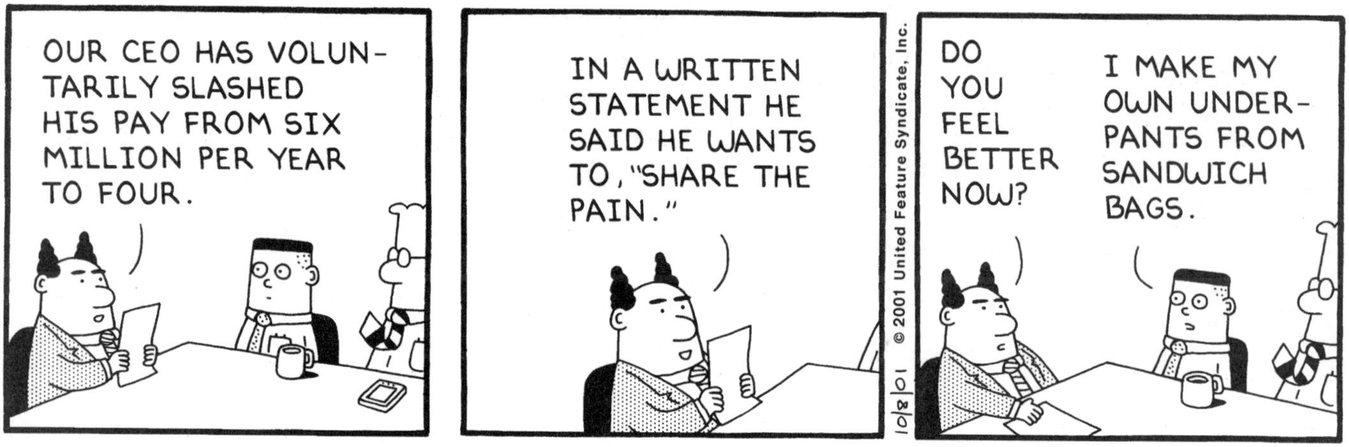
OUR CEO HAS VOLUNTARILY SLASHED HIS PAY FROM SIX MILLION PER YEAR TO FOUR.
IN A WRITTEN STATEMENT HE SAID HE WANTS TO, "SHARE THE PAIN."
DO YOU FEEL BETTER NOW?
I MAKE MY OWN UNDERPANTS FROM SANDWICH BAGS.
10/8/01 © 2001 United Feature Syndicate, Inc.

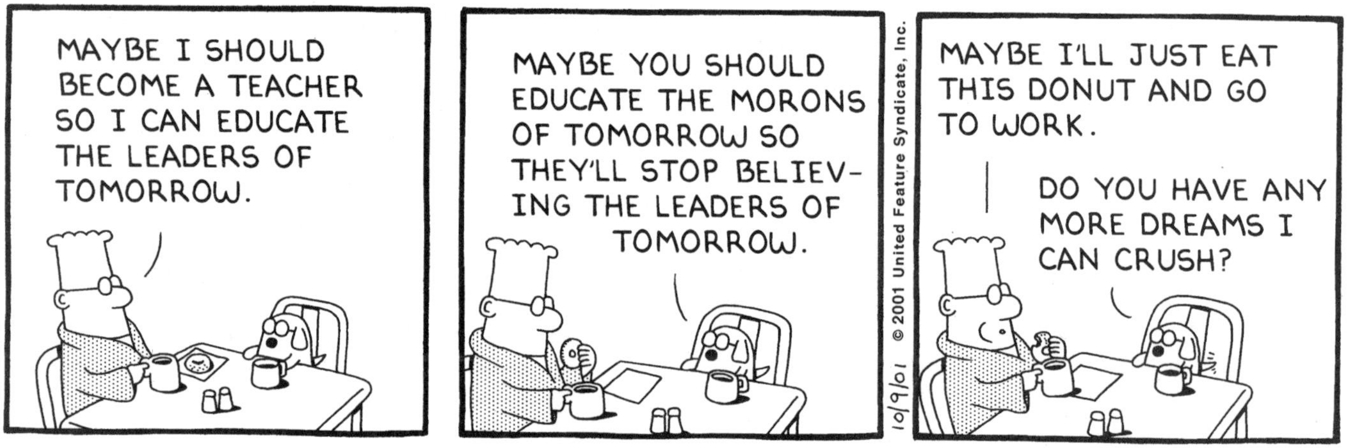
MAYBE I SHOULD BECOME A TEACHER SO I CAN EDUCATE THE LEADERS OF TOMORROW.
MAYBE YOU SHOULD EDUCATE THE MORONS OF TOMORROW SO THEY'LL STOP BELIEVING THE LEADERS OF TOMORROW.
MAYBE I'LL JUST EAT THIS DONUT AND GO TO WORK.
DO YOU HAVE ANY MORE DREAMS I CAN CRUSH?
10/9/01 © 2001 United Feature Syndicate, Inc.

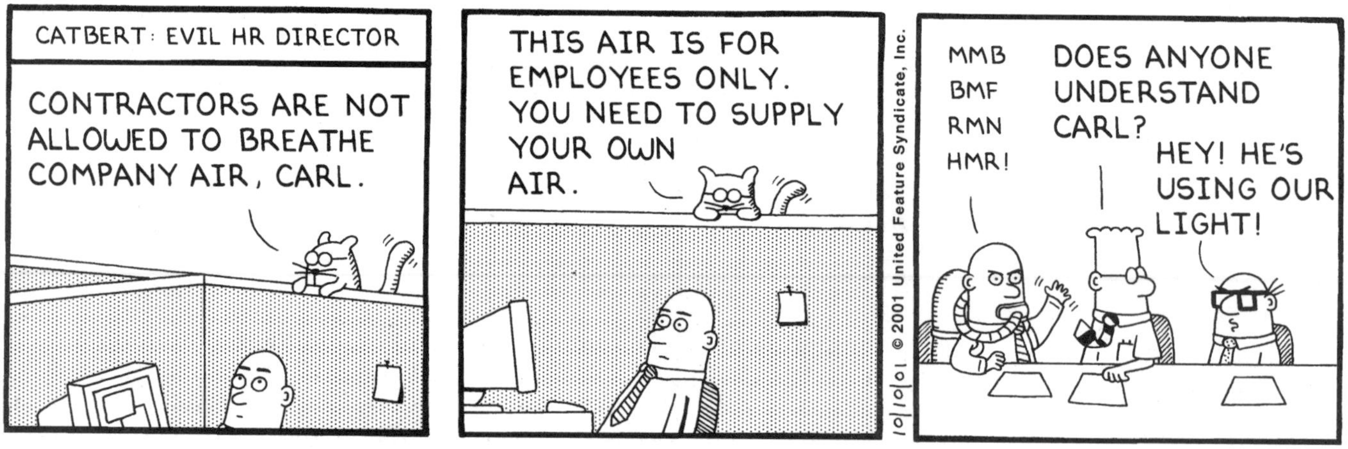
CATBERT: EVIL HR DIRECTOR
CONTRACTORS ARE NOT ALLOWED TO BREATHE COMPANY AIR, CARL.
THIS AIR IS FOR EMPLOYEES ONLY. YOU NEED TO SUPPLY YOUR OWN AIR.
MMB BMF RMN HMR!
DOES ANYONE UNDERSTAND CARL?
HEY! HE'S USING OUR LIGHT!
10/10/01 © 2001 United Feature Syndicate, Inc.

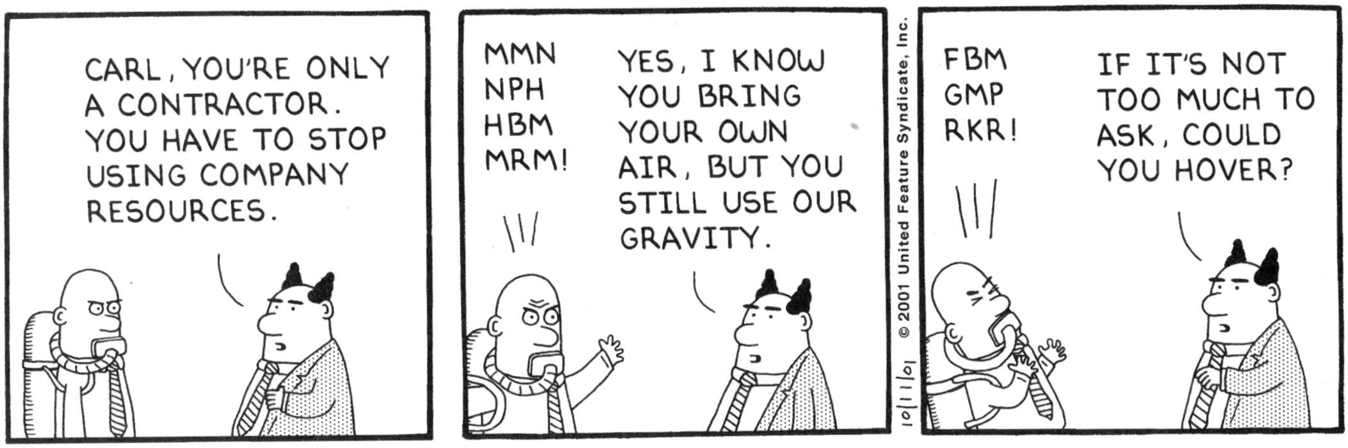
CARL, YOU'RE ONLY A CONTRACTOR. YOU HAVE TO STOP USING COMPANY RESOURCES.
MMN NPH HBM MRM!
YES, I KNOW YOU BRING YOUR OWN AIR, BUT YOU STILL USE OUR GRAVITY.
10/11/01 © 2001 United Feature Syndicate, Inc.
FBM GMP RKR!
IF IT'S NOT TOO MUCH TO ASK, COULD YOU HOVER?

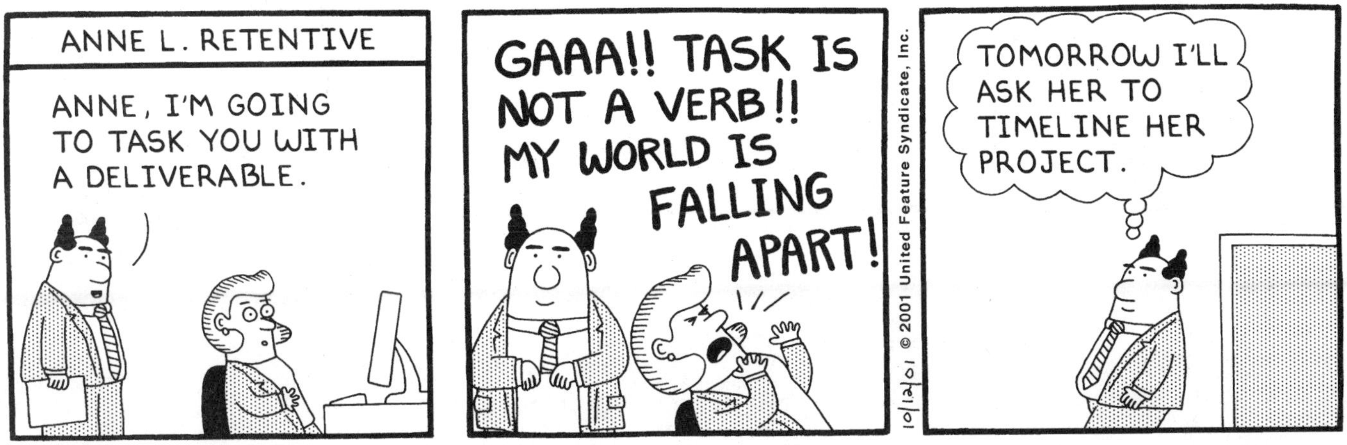
ANNE L. RETENTIVE
ANNE, I'M GOING TO TASK YOU WITH A DELIVERABLE.
GAAA!! TASK IS NOT A VERB!! MY WORLD IS FALLING APART!
10/12/01 © 2001 United Feature Syndicate, Inc.
TOMORROW I'LL ASK HER TO TIMELINE HER PROJECT.

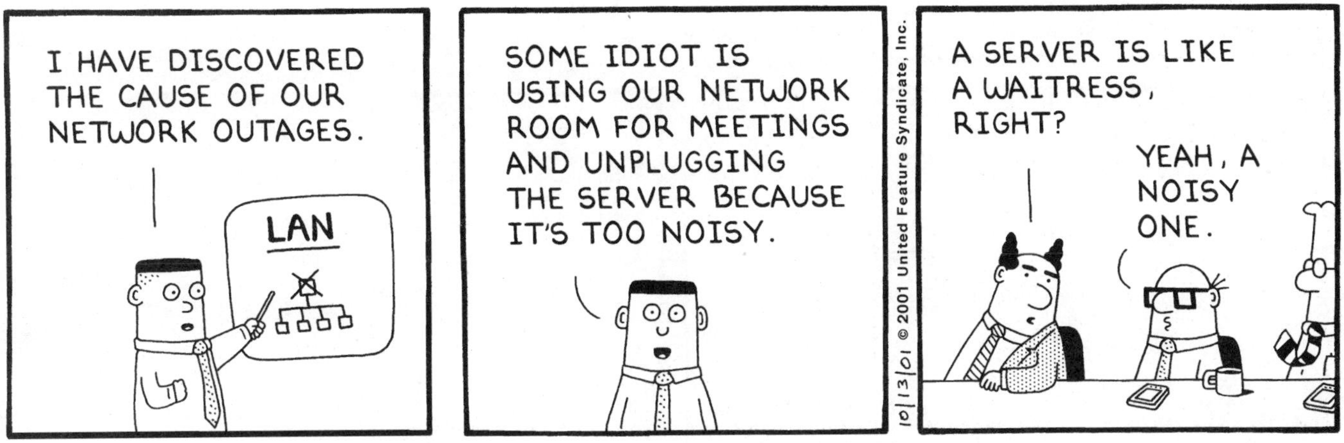
I HAVE DISCOVERED THE CAUSE OF OUR NETWORK OUTAGES.
LAN
SOME IDIOT IS USING OUR NETWORK ROOM FOR MEETINGS AND UNPLUGGING THE SERVER BECAUSE IT'S TOO NOISY.
10/13/01 © 2001 United Feature Syndicate, Inc.
A SERVER IS LIKE A WAITRESS, RIGHT?
YEAH, A NOISY ONE.

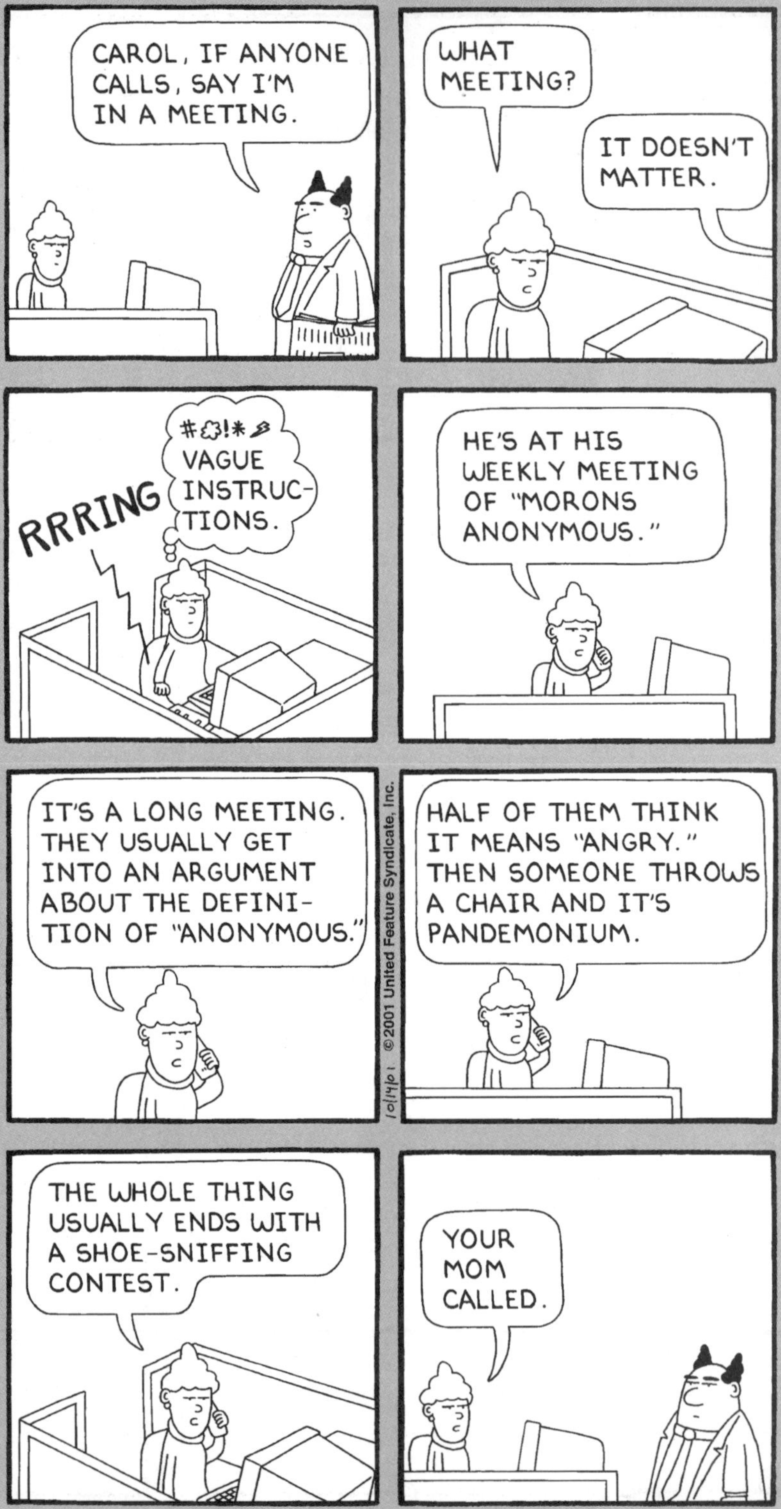
CAROL, IF ANYONE CALLS, SAY I'M IN A MEETING.
WHAT MEETING?
IT DOESN'T MATTER.
VAGUE INSTRUCTIONS.
RRRING
HE'S AT HIS WEEKLY MEETING OF "MORONS ANONYMOUS."
IT'S A LONG MEETING. THEY USUALLY GET INTO AN ARGUMENT ABOUT THE DEFINITION OF "ANONYMOUS."
HALF OF THEM THINK IT MEANS "ANGRY." THEN SOMEONE THROWS A CHAIR AND IT'S PANDEMONIUM.
THE WHOLE THING USUALLY ENDS WITH A SHOE-SNIFFING CONTEST.
YOUR MOM CALLED.
10/14/01 ©2001 United Feature Syndicate, Inc.

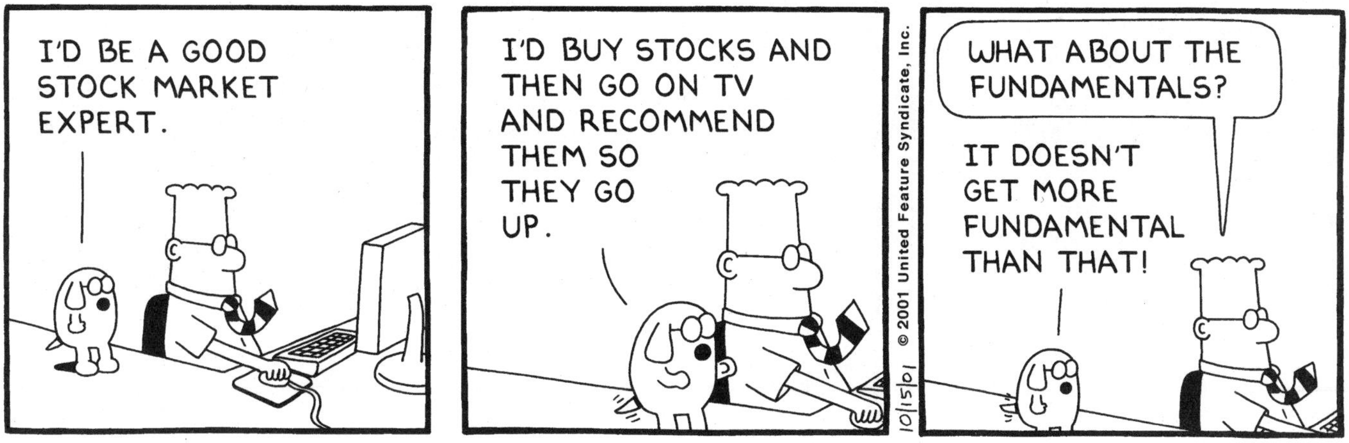
I'D BE A GOOD STOCK MARKET EXPERT.
I'D BUY STOCKS AND THEN GO ON TV AND RECOMMEND THEM SO THEY GO UP.
10/15/01 © 2001 United Feature Syndicate, Inc.
WHAT ABOUT THE FUNDAMENTALS?
IT DOESN'T GET MORE FUNDAMENTAL THAN THAT!

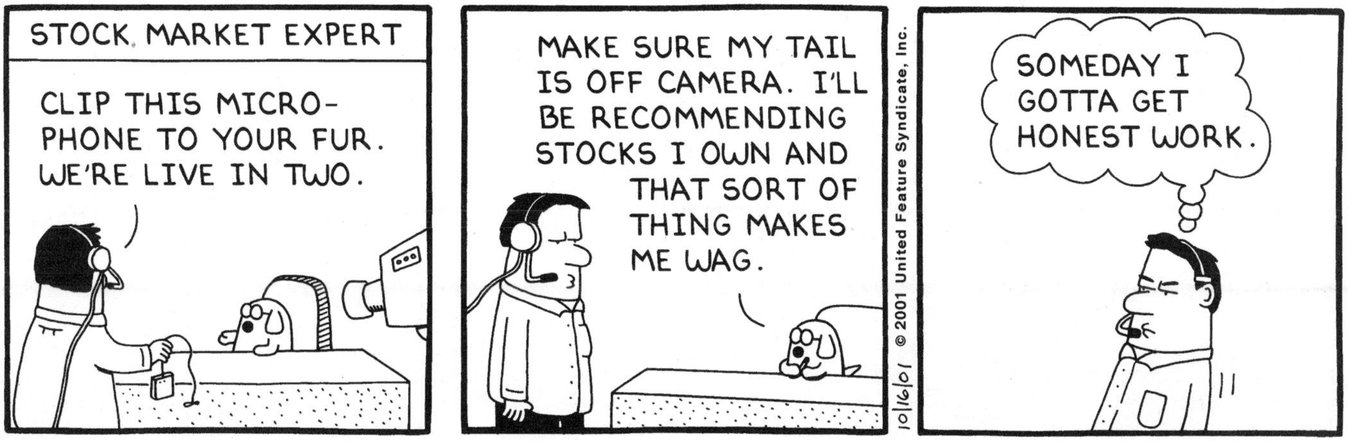
STOCK MARKET EXPERT
CLIP THIS MICRO-PHONE TO YOUR FUR. WE'RE LIVE IN TWO.
MAKE SURE MY TAIL IS OFF CAMERA. I'LL BE RECOMMENDING STOCKS I OWN AND THAT SORT OF THING MAKES ME WAG.
10/16/01 © 2001 United Feature Syndicate, Inc.
SOMEDAY I GOTTA GET HONEST WORK.

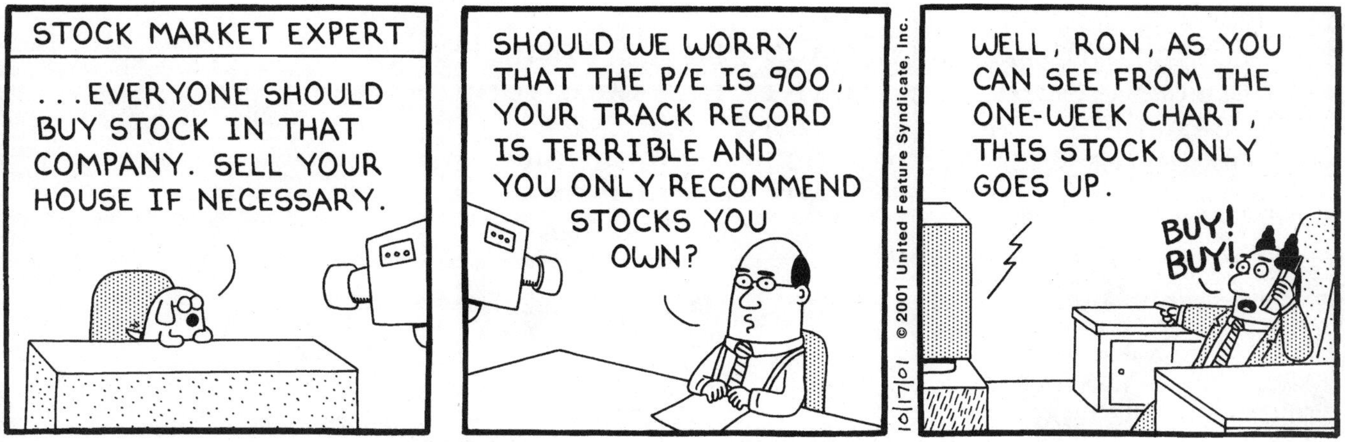
STOCK MARKET EXPERT
...EVERYONE SHOULD BUY STOCK IN THAT COMPANY. SELL YOUR HOUSE IF NECESSARY.
SHOULD WE WORRY THAT THE P/E IS 900, YOUR TRACK RECORD IS TERRIBLE AND YOU ONLY RECOMMEND STOCKS YOU OWN?
10/17/01 © 2001 United Feature Syndicate, Inc.
WELL, RON, AS YOU CAN SEE FROM THE ONE-WEEK CHART, THIS STOCK ONLY GOES UP.
BUY! BUY!

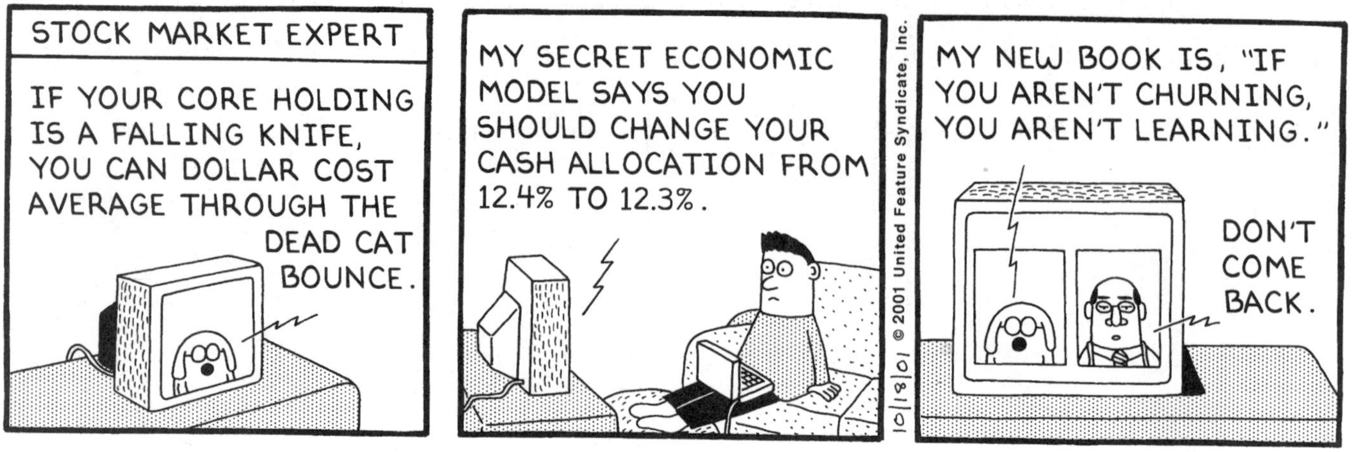
STOCK MARKET EXPERT
IF YOUR CORE HOLDING IS A FALLING KNIFE, YOU CAN DOLLAR COST AVERAGE THROUGH THE DEAD CAT BOUNCE.
MY SECRET ECONOMIC MODEL SAYS YOU SHOULD CHANGE YOUR CASH ALLOCATION FROM 12.4% TO 12.3%.
10/18/01 © 2001 United Feature Syndicate, Inc.
MY NEW BOOK IS, "IF YOU AREN'T CHURNING, YOU AREN'T LEARNING."
DON'T COME BACK.

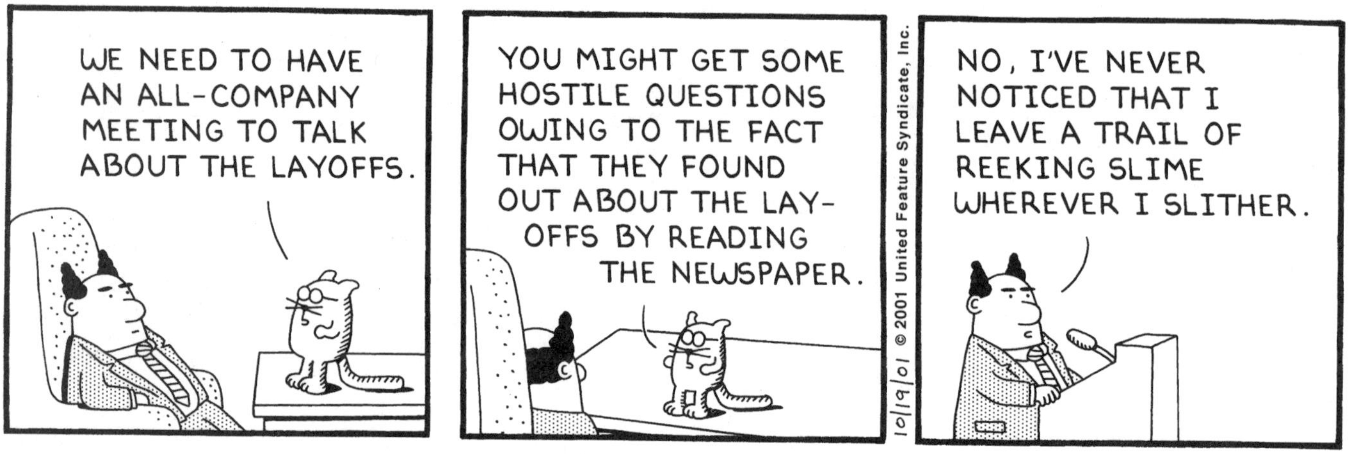
WE NEED TO HAVE AN ALL-COMPANY MEETING TO TALK ABOUT THE LAYOFFS.
YOU MIGHT GET SOME HOSTILE QUESTIONS OWING TO THE FACT THAT THEY FOUND OUT ABOUT THE LAY-OFFS BY READING THE NEWSPAPER.
10/19/01 © 2001 United Feature Syndicate, Inc.
NO, I'VE NEVER NOTICED THAT I LEAVE A TRAIL OF REEKING SLIME WHEREVER I SLITHER.

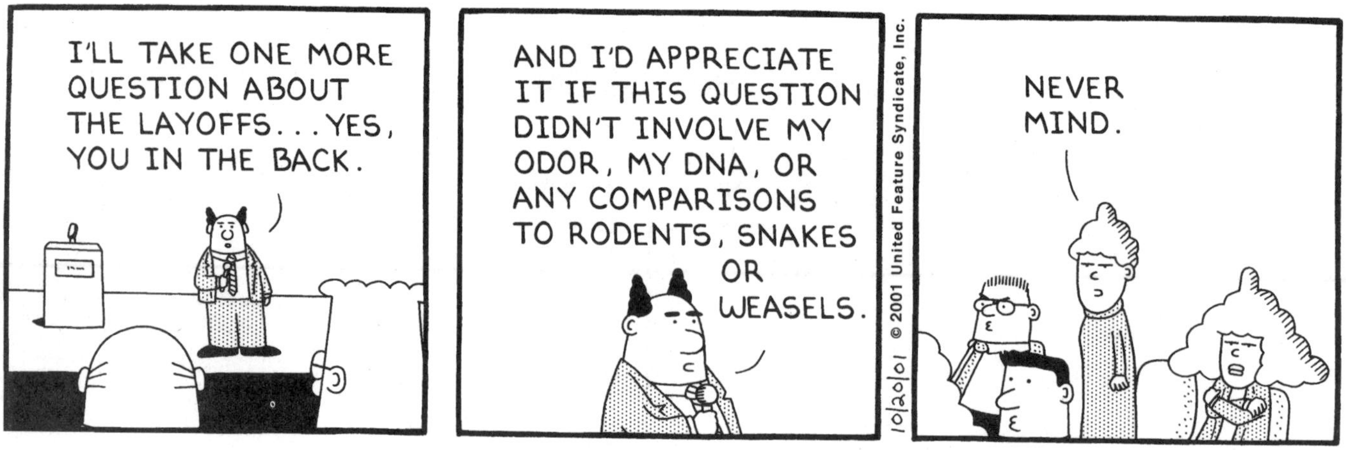
I'LL TAKE ONE MORE QUESTION ABOUT THE LAYOFFS... YES, YOU IN THE BACK.
AND I'D APPRECIATE IT IF THIS QUESTION DIDN'T INVOLVE MY ODOR, MY DNA, OR ANY COMPARISONS TO RODENTS, SNAKES OR WEASELS.
10/20/01 © 2001 United Feature Syndicate, Inc.
NEVER MIND.

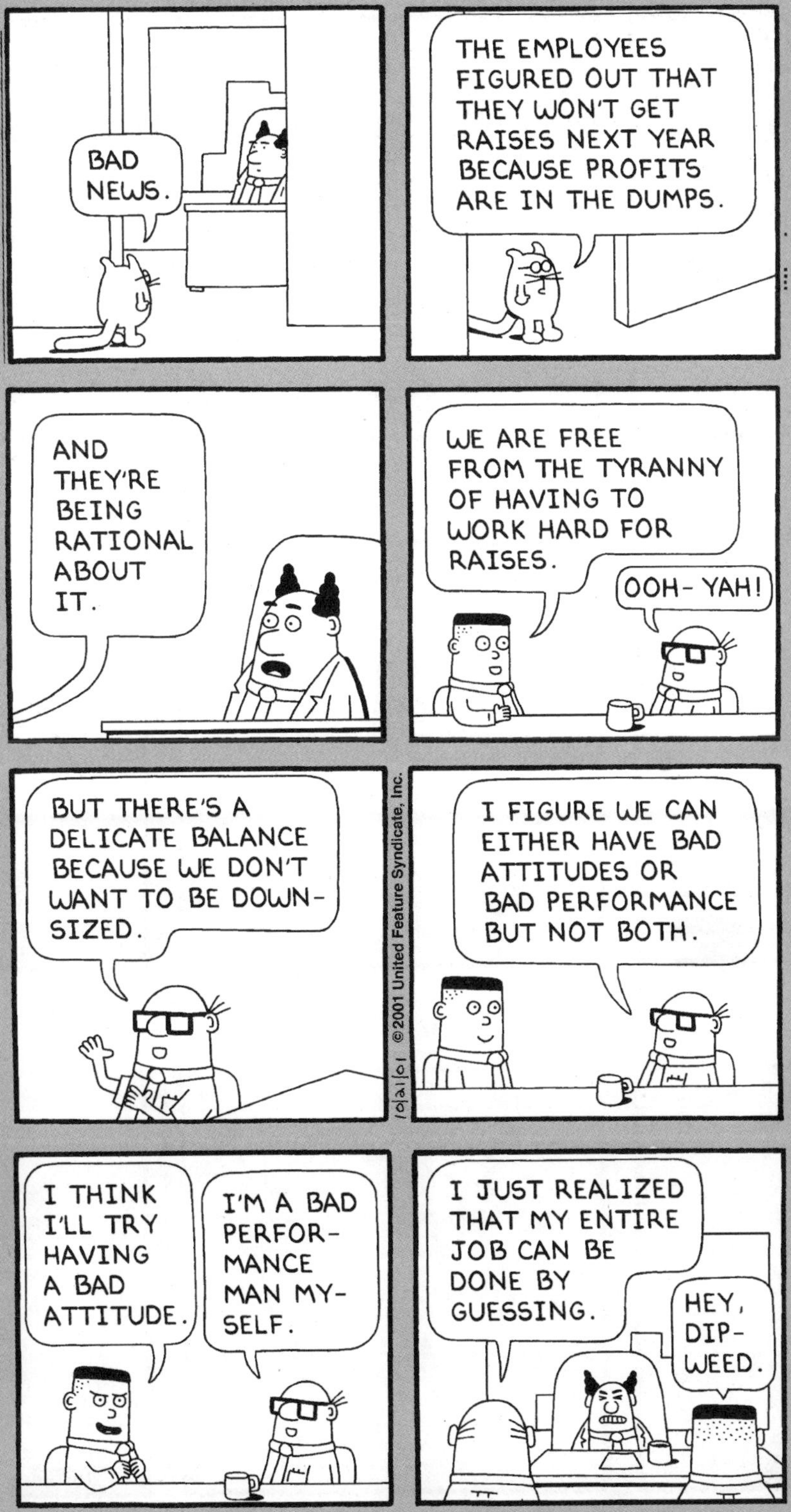
BAD NEWS.
THE EMPLOYEES FIGURED OUT THAT THEY WON'T GET RAISES NEXT YEAR BECAUSE PROFITS ARE IN THE DUMPS.
AND THEY'RE BEING RATIONAL ABOUT IT.
WE ARE FREE FROM THE TYRANNY OF HAVING TO WORK HARD FOR RAISES.
OOH- YAH!
BUT THERE'S A DELICATE BALANCE BECAUSE WE DON'T WANT TO BE DOWN-SIZED.
I FIGURE WE CAN EITHER HAVE BAD ATTITUDES OR BAD PERFORMANCE BUT NOT BOTH.
I THINK I'LL TRY HAVING A BAD ATTITUDE.
I'M A BAD PERFORMANCE MAN MYSELF.
I JUST REALIZED THAT MY ENTIRE JOB CAN BE DONE BY GUESSING.
HEY, DIP-WEED.

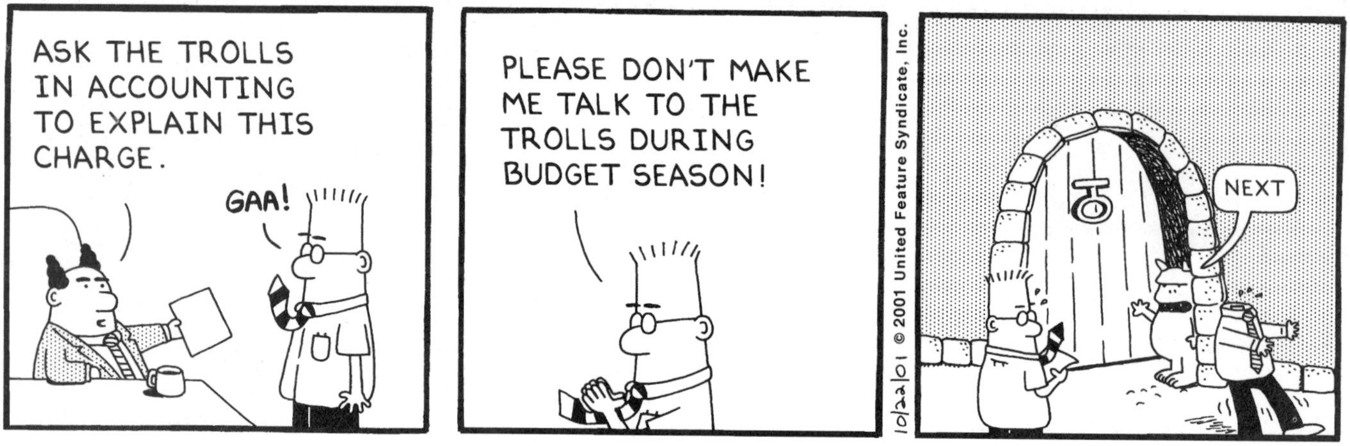
ASK THE TROLLS IN ACCOUNTING TO EXPLAIN THIS CHARGE.
GAA!
PLEASE DON'T MAKE ME TALK TO THE TROLLS DURING BUDGET SEASON!
10/22/01 © 2001 United Feature Syndicate, Inc.
NEXT

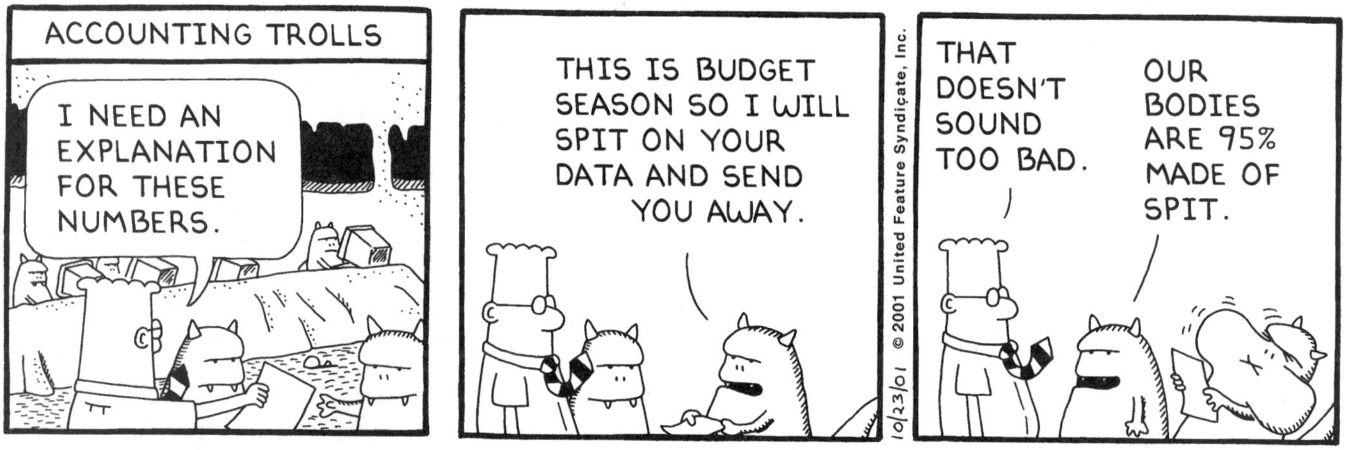
ACCOUNTING TROLLS
I NEED AN EXPLANATION FOR THESE NUMBERS.
THIS IS BUDGET SEASON SO I WILL SPIT ON YOUR DATA AND SEND YOU AWAY.
10/23/01 © 2001 United Feature Syndicate, Inc.
THAT DOESN'T SOUND TOO BAD.
OUR BODIES ARE 95% MADE OF SPIT.

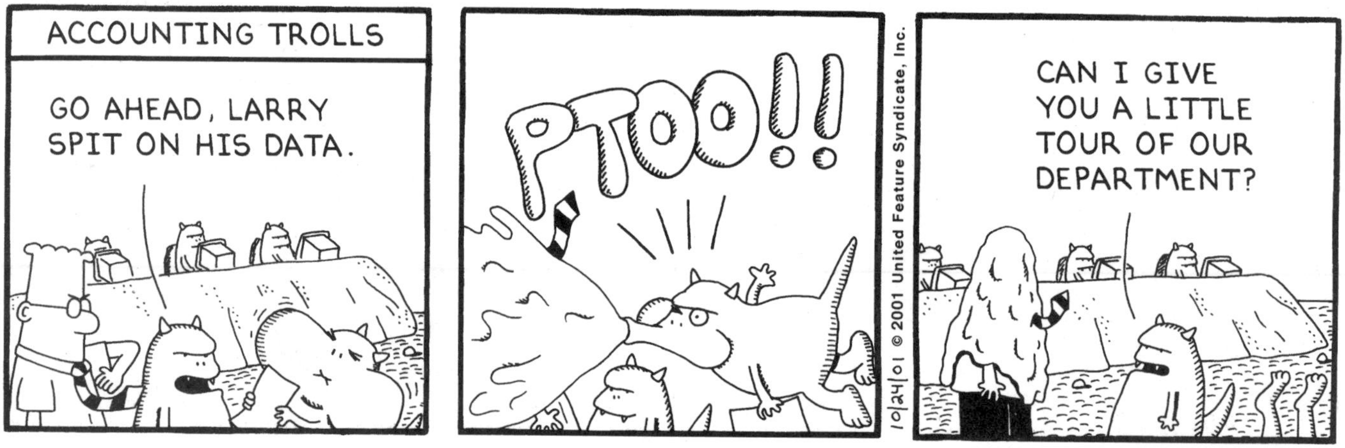
ACCOUNTING TROLLS
GO AHEAD, LARRY SPIT ON HIS DATA.
PTOO!!
10/24/01 © 2001 United Feature Syndicate, Inc.
CAN I GIVE YOU A LITTLE TOUR OF OUR DEPARTMENT?

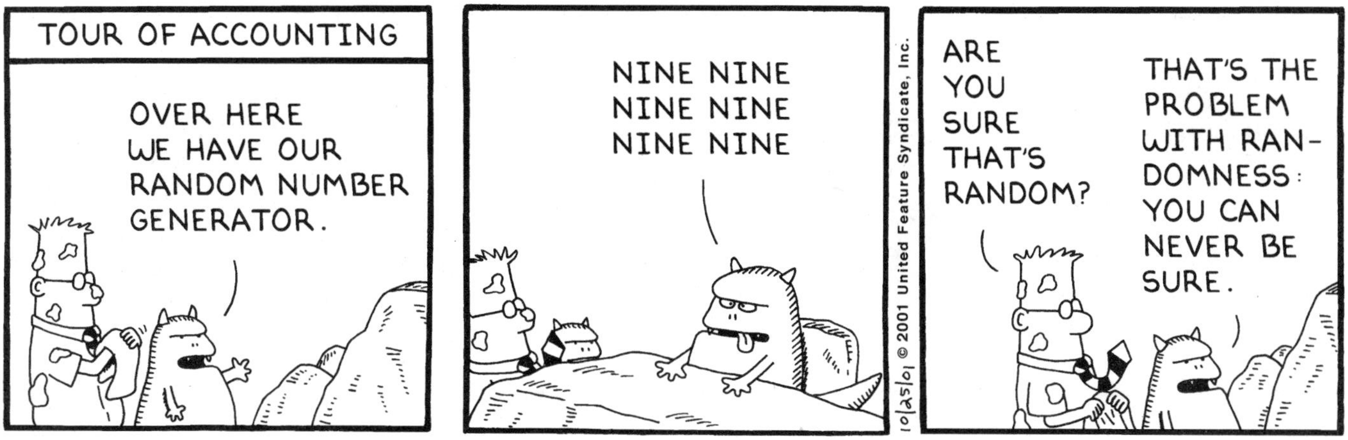
TOUR OF ACCOUNTING
OVER HERE WE HAVE OUR RANDOM NUMBER GENERATOR.
NINE NINE NINE NINE NINE NINE
ARE YOU SURE THAT'S RANDOM?
THAT'S THE PROBLEM WITH RANDOMNESS: YOU CAN NEVER BE SURE.
10/25/01 © 2001 United Feature Syndicate, Inc.

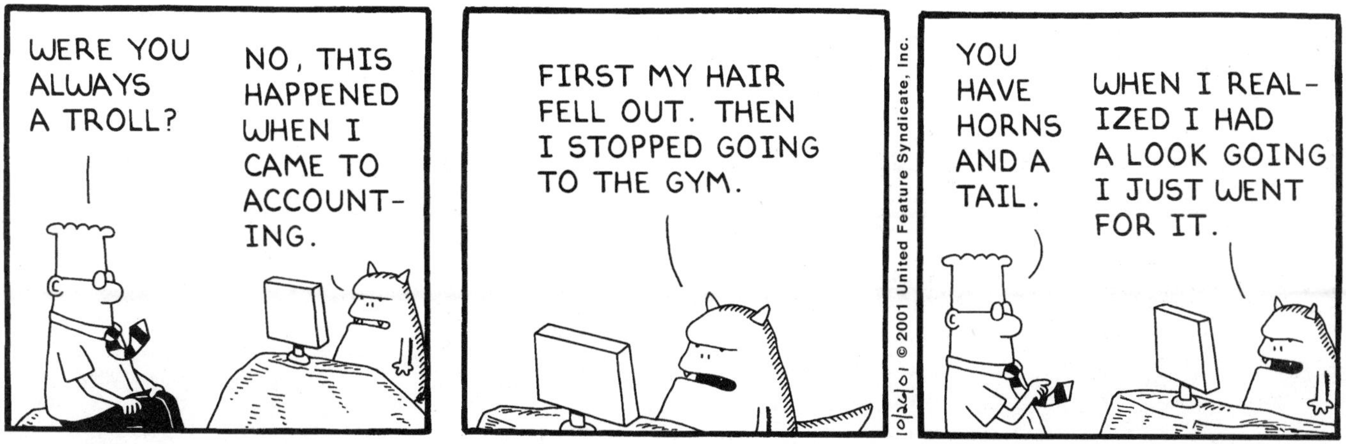
WERE YOU ALWAYS A TROLL?
NO, THIS HAPPENED WHEN I CAME TO ACCOUNTING.
FIRST MY HAIR FELL OUT. THEN I STOPPED GOING TO THE GYM.
YOU HAVE HORNS AND A TAIL.
WHEN I REALIZED I HAD A LOOK GOING I JUST WENT FOR IT.
10/26/01 © 2001 United Feature Syndicate, Inc.

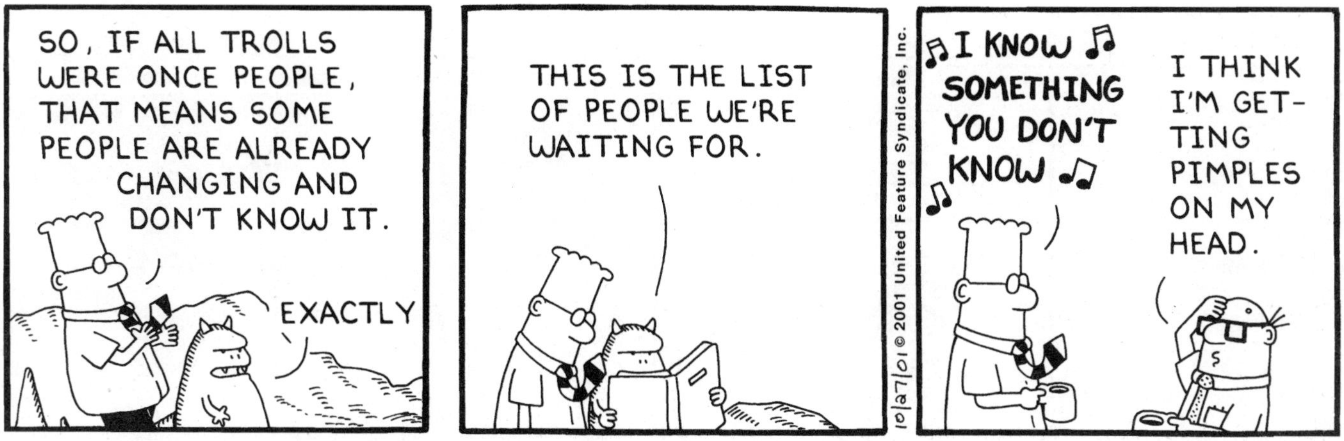
SO, IF ALL TROLLS WERE ONCE PEOPLE, THAT MEANS SOME PEOPLE ARE ALREADY CHANGING AND DON'T KNOW IT.
EXACTLY
THIS IS THE LIST OF PEOPLE WE'RE WAITING FOR.
♫ I KNOW ♫ SOMETHING YOU DON'T KNOW ♫
I THINK I'M GETTING PIMPLES ON MY HEAD.
10/27/01 © 2001 United Feature Syndicate, Inc.

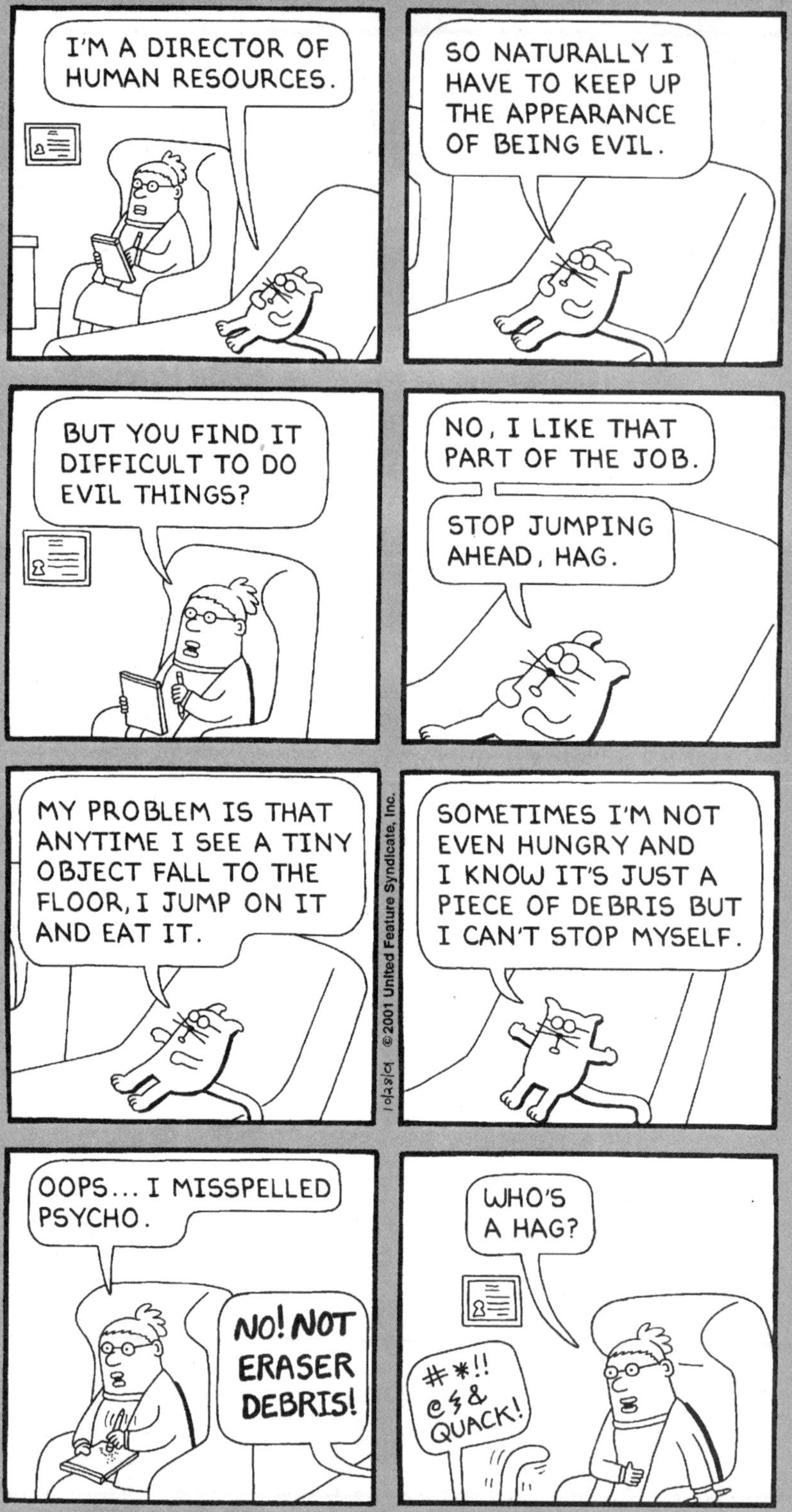
I'M A DIRECTOR OF HUMAN RESOURCES.
SO NATURALLY I HAVE TO KEEP UP THE APPEARANCE OF BEING EVIL.
BUT YOU FIND IT DIFFICULT TO DO EVIL THINGS?
NO, I LIKE THAT PART OF THE JOB.
STOP JUMPING AHEAD, HAG.
MY PROBLEM IS THAT ANYTIME I SEE A TINY OBJECT FALL TO THE FLOOR, I JUMP ON IT AND EAT IT.
SOMETIMES I'M NOT EVEN HUNGRY AND I KNOW IT'S JUST A PIECE OF DEBRIS BUT I CAN'T STOP MYSELF.
OOPS... I MISSPELLED PSYCHO.
NO! NOT ERASER DEBRIS!
WHO'S A HAG?
#*!! @$& QUACK!
10/28/01 © 2001 United Feature Syndicate, Inc.

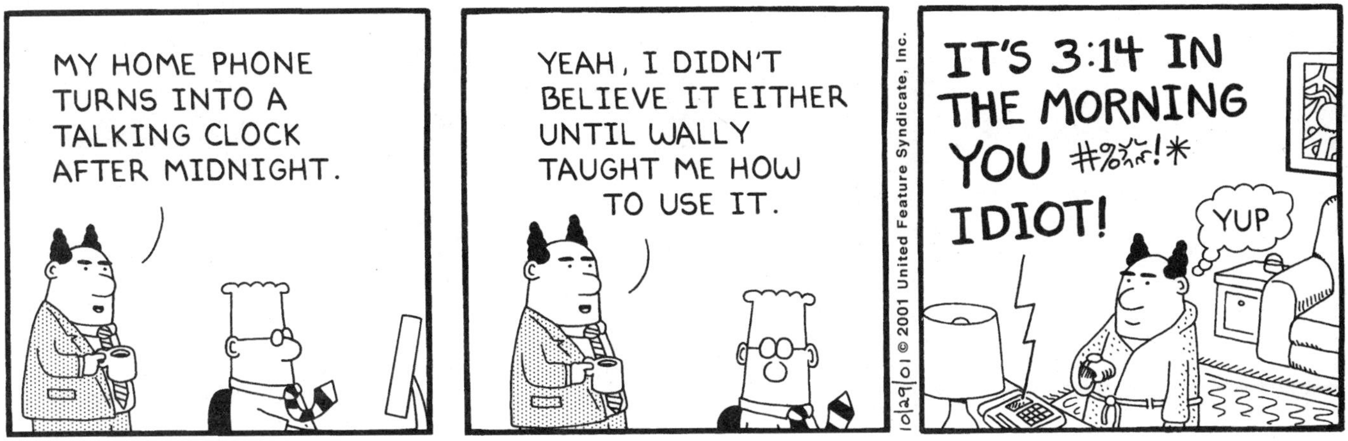
MY HOME PHONE TURNS INTO A TALKING CLOCK AFTER MIDNIGHT.
YEAH, I DIDN'T BELIEVE IT EITHER UNTIL WALLY TAUGHT ME HOW TO USE IT.
10|29|01 © 2001 United Feature Syndicate, Inc.
IT'S 3:14 IN THE MORNING YOU
IDIOT!
YUP

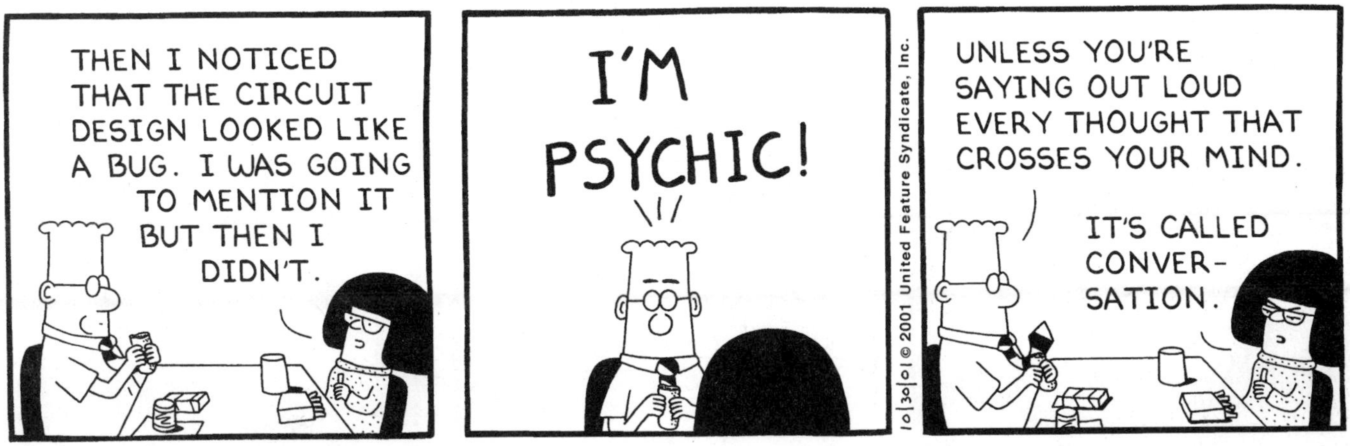
THEN I NOTICED THAT THE CIRCUIT DESIGN LOOKED LIKE A BUG. I WAS GOING TO MENTION IT BUT THEN I DIDN'T.
I'M PSYCHIC!
10|30|01 © 2001 United Feature Syndicate, Inc.
UNLESS YOU'RE SAYING OUT LOUD EVERY THOUGHT THAT CROSSES YOUR MIND.
IT'S CALLED CONVER-SATION.

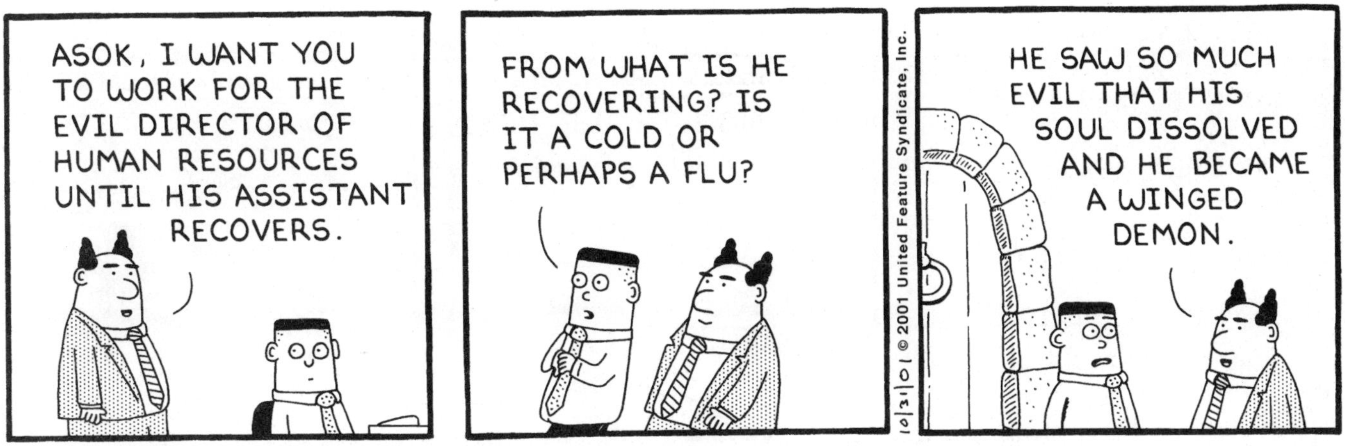
ASOK, I WANT YOU TO WORK FOR THE EVIL DIRECTOR OF HUMAN RESOURCES UNTIL HIS ASSISTANT RECOVERS.
FROM WHAT IS HE RECOVERING? IS IT A COLD OR PERHAPS A FLU?
10|31|01 © 2001 United Feature Syndicate, Inc.
HE SAW SO MUCH EVIL THAT HIS SOUL DISSOLVED AND HE BECAME A WINGED DEMON.

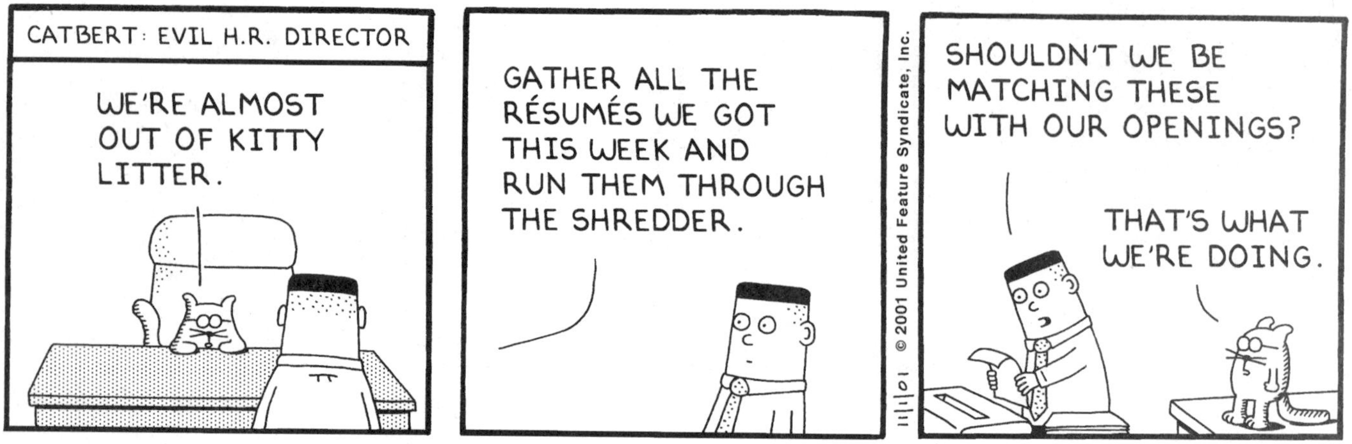
CATBERT: EVIL H.R. DIRECTOR
WE'RE ALMOST OUT OF KITTY LITTER.
GATHER ALL THE RÉSUMÉS WE GOT THIS WEEK AND RUN THEM THROUGH THE SHREDDER.
11/1/01 © 2001 United Feature Syndicate, Inc.
SHOULDN'T WE BE MATCHING THESE WITH OUR OPENINGS?
THAT'S WHAT WE'RE DOING.

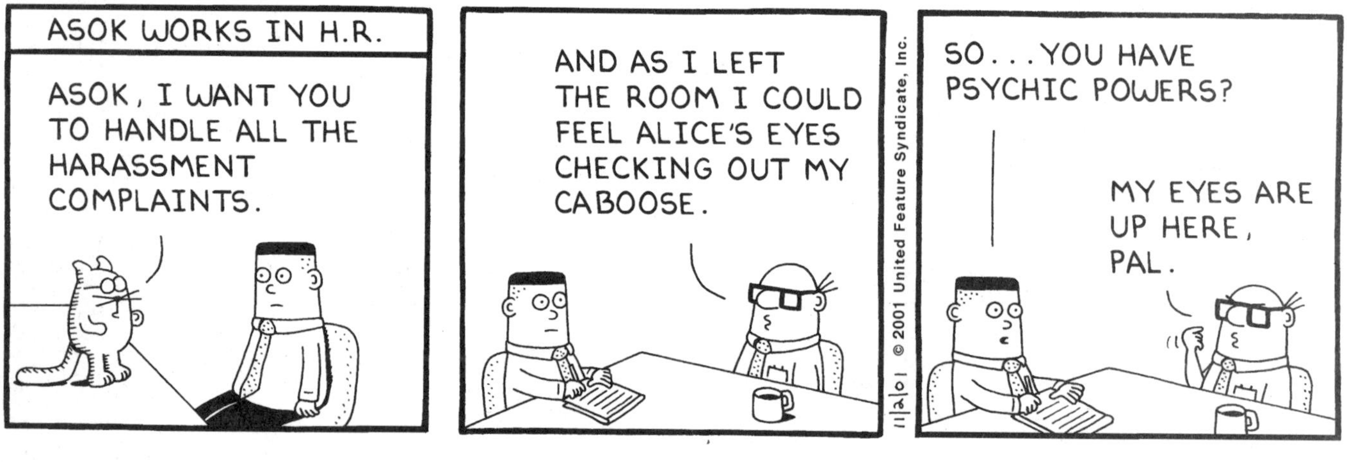
ASOK WORKS IN H.R.
ASOK, I WANT YOU TO HANDLE ALL THE HARASSMENT COMPLAINTS.
AND AS I LEFT THE ROOM I COULD FEEL ALICE'S EYES CHECKING OUT MY CABOOSE.
11/2/01 © 2001 United Feature Syndicate, Inc.
SO... YOU HAVE PSYCHIC POWERS?
MY EYES ARE UP HERE, PAL.

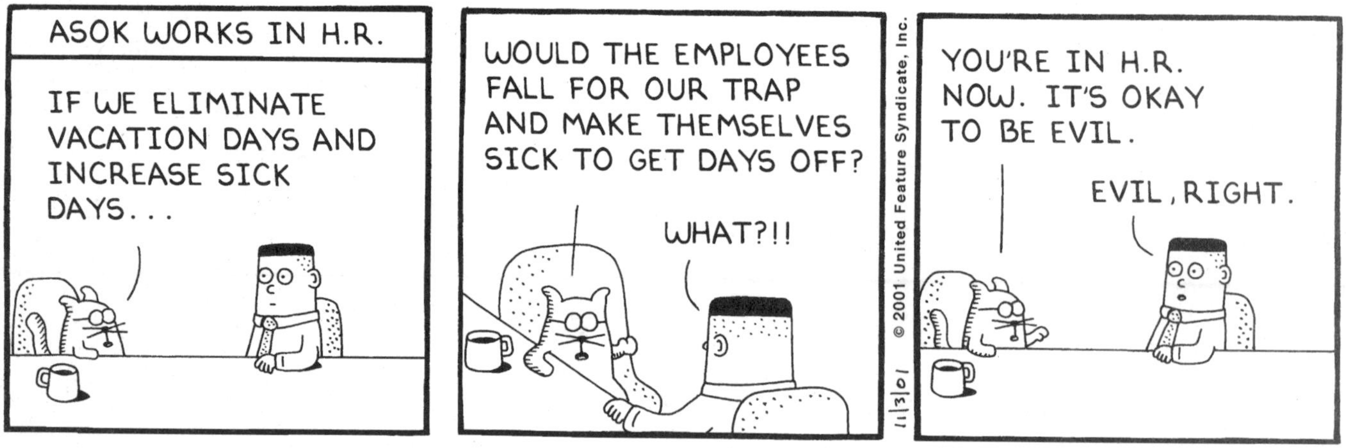
ASOK WORKS IN H.R.
IF WE ELIMINATE VACATION DAYS AND INCREASE SICK DAYS...
WOULD THE EMPLOYEES FALL FOR OUR TRAP AND MAKE THEMSELVES SICK TO GET DAYS OFF?
WHAT?!!
11/3/01 © 2001 United Feature Syndicate, Inc.
YOU'RE IN H.R. NOW. IT'S OKAY TO BE EVIL.
EVIL, RIGHT.

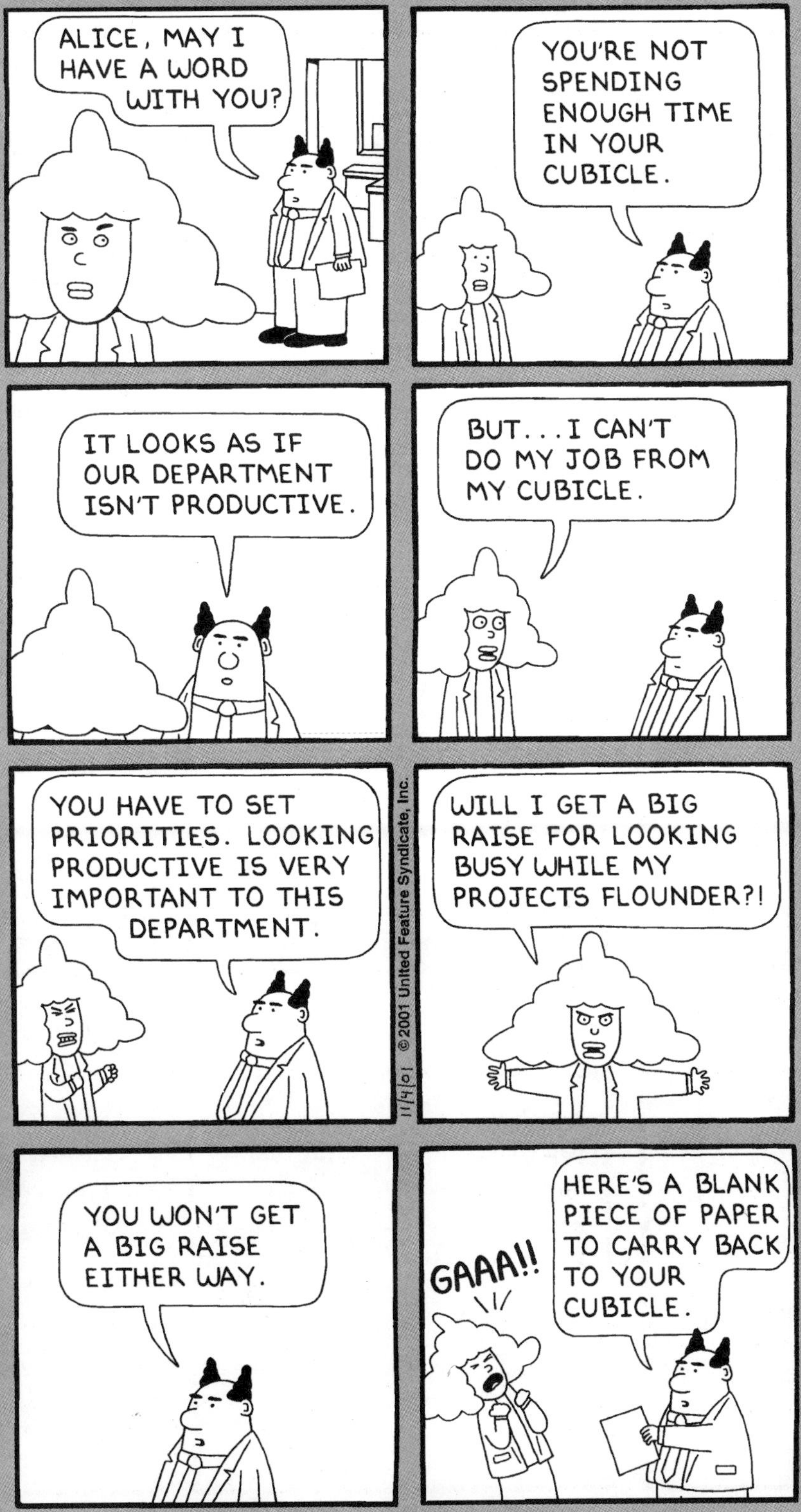
ALICE, MAY I HAVE A WORD WITH YOU?
YOU'RE NOT SPENDING ENOUGH TIME IN YOUR CUBICLE.
IT LOOKS AS IF OUR DEPARTMENT ISN'T PRODUCTIVE.
BUT. . . I CAN'T DO MY JOB FROM MY CUBICLE.
YOU HAVE TO SET PRIORITIES. LOOKING PRODUCTIVE IS VERY IMPORTANT TO THIS DEPARTMENT.
WILL I GET A BIG RAISE FOR LOOKING BUSY WHILE MY PROJECTS FLOUNDER?!
YOU WON'T GET A BIG RAISE EITHER WAY.
GAAA!!
HERE'S A BLANK PIECE OF PAPER TO CARRY BACK TO YOUR CUBICLE.
11/4/01 ©2001 United Feature Syndicate, Inc.

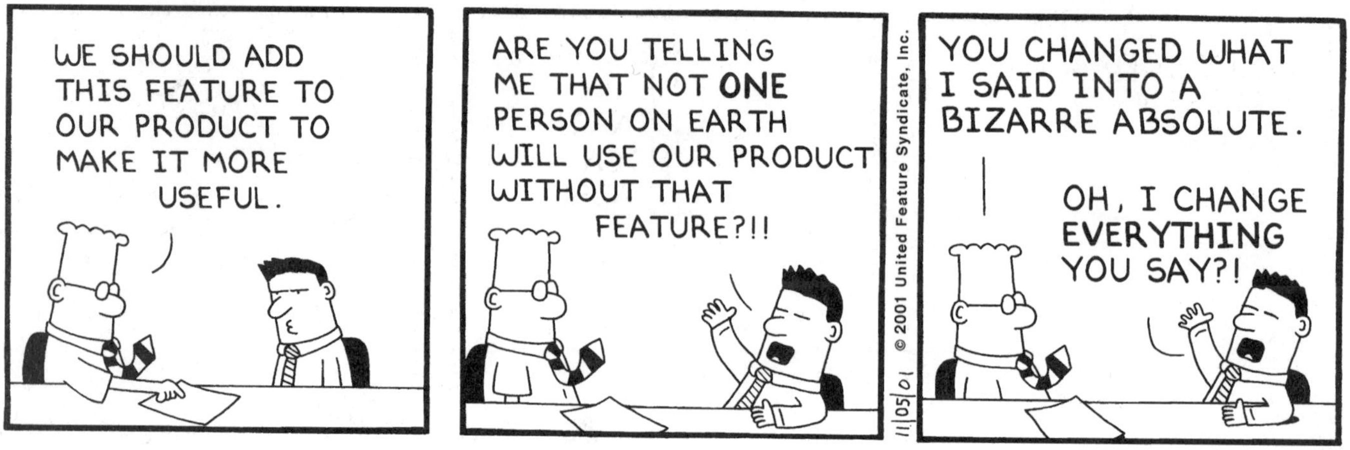
WE SHOULD ADD THIS FEATURE TO OUR PRODUCT TO MAKE IT MORE USEFUL.
ARE YOU TELLING ME THAT NOT **ONE** PERSON ON EARTH WILL USE OUR PRODUCT WITHOUT THAT FEATURE?!!
YOU CHANGED WHAT I SAID INTO A BIZARRE ABSOLUTE.
OH, I CHANGE **EVERYTHING** YOU SAY?!

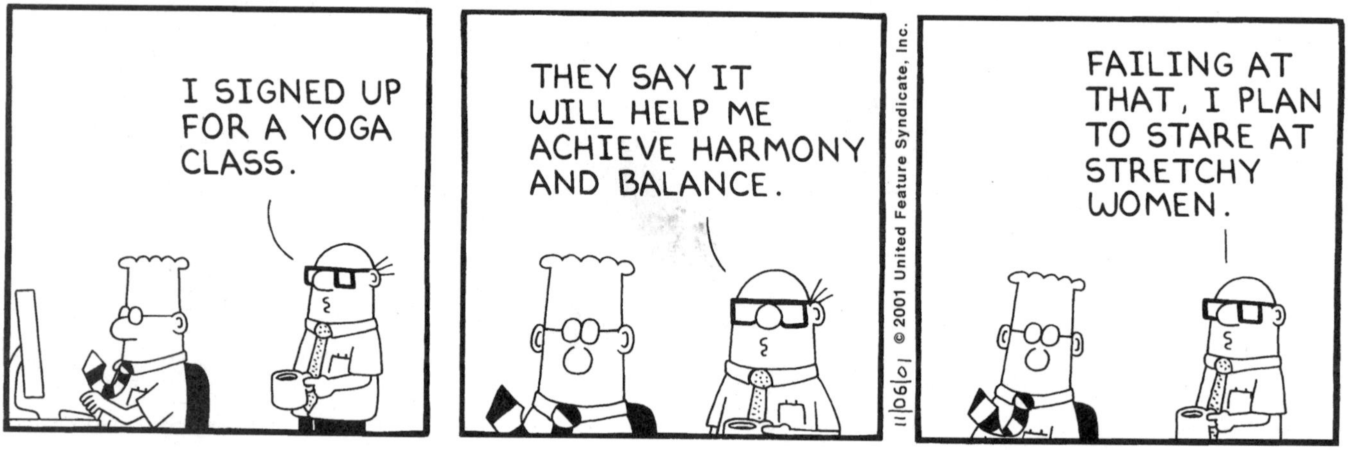
I SIGNED UP FOR A YOGA CLASS.
THEY SAY IT WILL HELP ME ACHIEVE HARMONY AND BALANCE.
FAILING AT THAT, I PLAN TO STARE AT STRETCHY WOMEN.

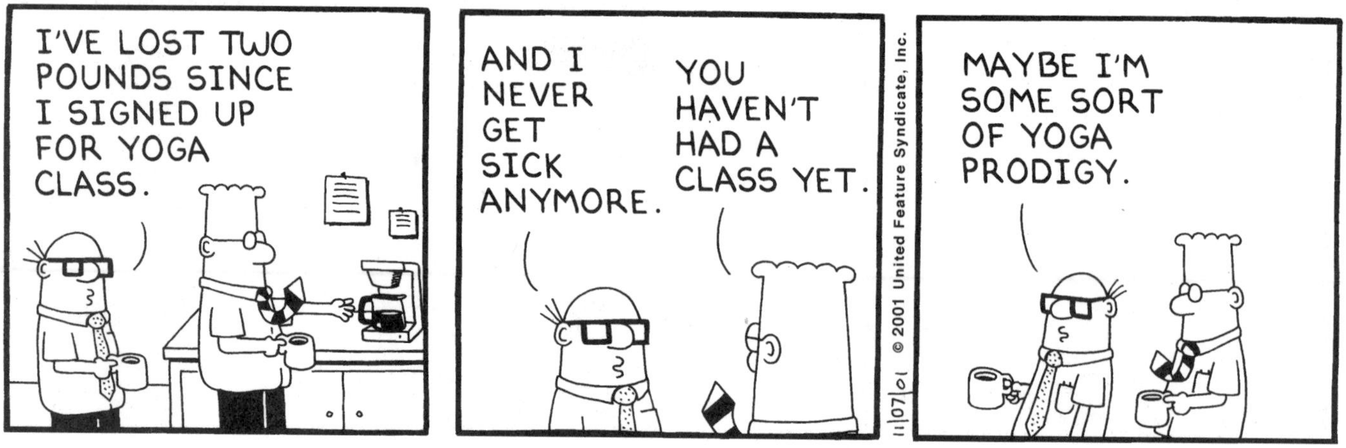
I'VE LOST TWO POUNDS SINCE I SIGNED UP FOR YOGA CLASS.
AND I NEVER GET SICK ANYMORE.
YOU HAVEN'T HAD A CLASS YET.
MAYBE I'M SOME SORT OF YOGA PRODIGY.

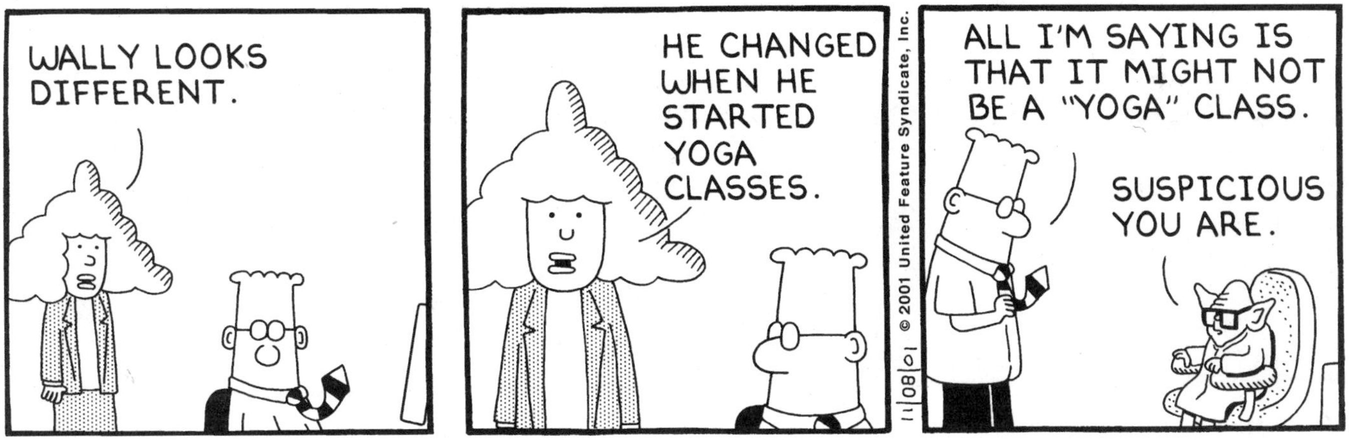
WALLY LOOKS DIFFERENT.
HE CHANGED WHEN HE STARTED YOGA CLASSES.
11/08/01 © 2001 United Feature Syndicate, Inc.
ALL I'M SAYING IS THAT IT MIGHT NOT BE A "YOGA" CLASS.
SUSPICIOUS YOU ARE.

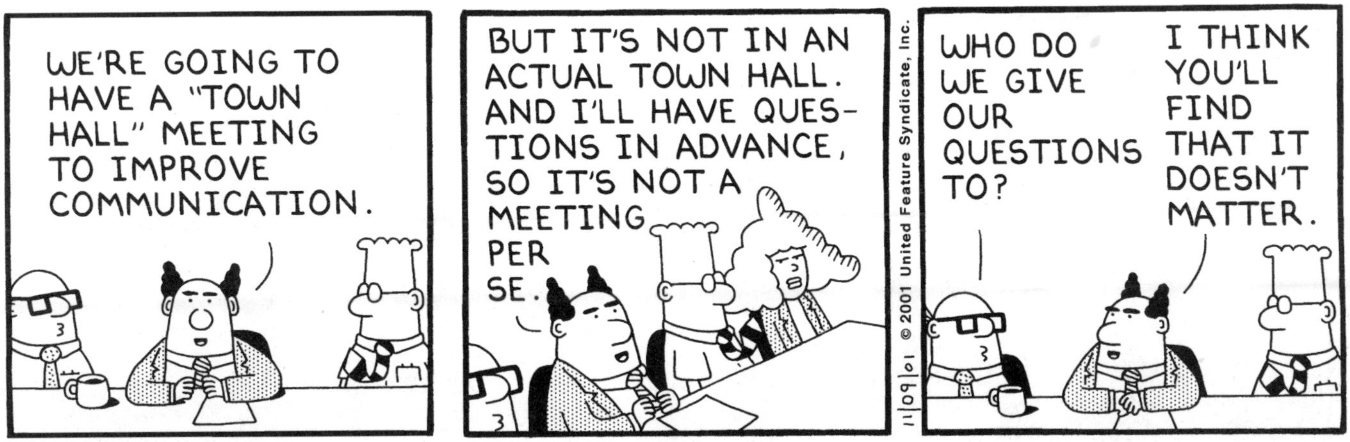
WE'RE GOING TO HAVE A "TOWN HALL" MEETING TO IMPROVE COMMUNICATION.
BUT IT'S NOT IN AN ACTUAL TOWN HALL. AND I'LL HAVE QUES-TIONS IN ADVANCE, SO IT'S NOT A MEETING PER SE.
11/09/01 © 2001 United Feature Syndicate, Inc.
WHO DO WE GIVE OUR QUESTIONS TO?
I THINK YOU'LL FIND THAT IT DOESN'T MATTER.

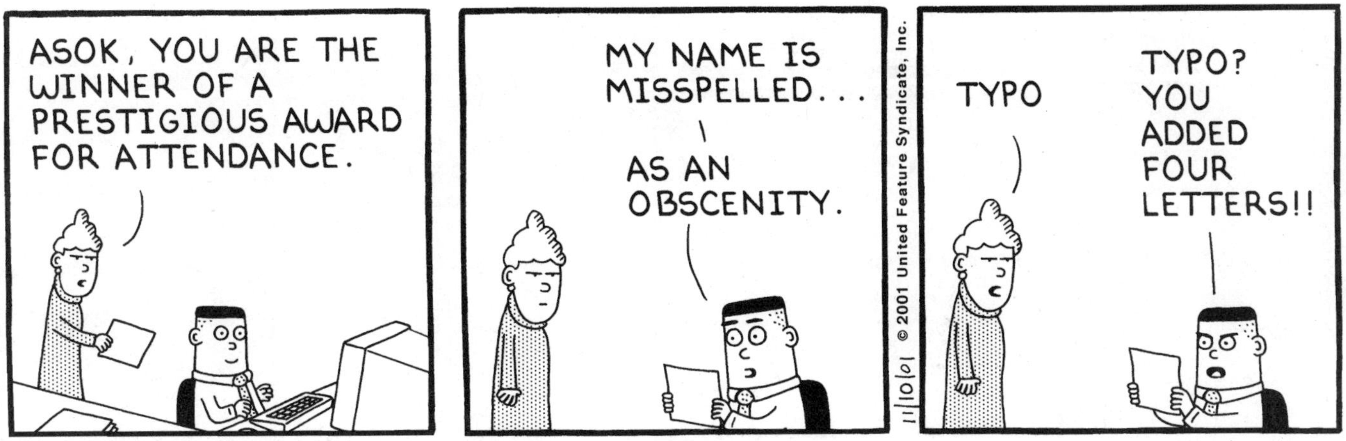
ASOK, YOU ARE THE WINNER OF A PRESTIGIOUS AWARD FOR ATTENDANCE.
MY NAME IS MISSPELLED...
AS AN OBSCENITY.
11/10/01 © 2001 United Feature Syndicate, Inc.
TYPO
TYPO? YOU ADDED FOUR LETTERS!!

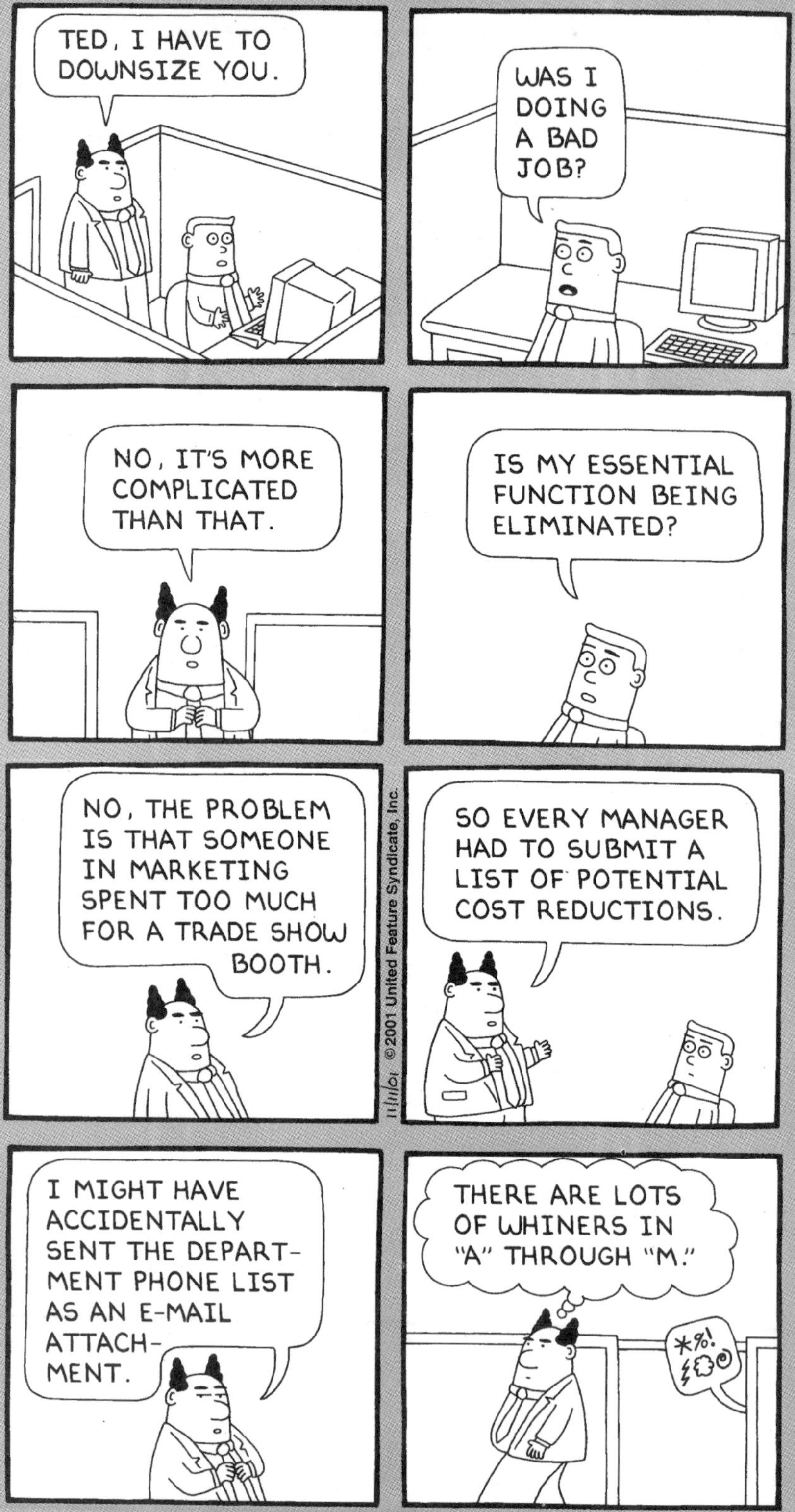
TED, I HAVE TO DOWNSIZE YOU.
WAS I DOING A BAD JOB?
NO, IT'S MORE COMPLICATED THAN THAT.
IS MY ESSENTIAL FUNCTION BEING ELIMINATED?
NO, THE PROBLEM IS THAT SOMEONE IN MARKETING SPENT TOO MUCH FOR A TRADE SHOW BOOTH.
SO EVERY MANAGER HAD TO SUBMIT A LIST OF POTENTIAL COST REDUCTIONS.
I MIGHT HAVE ACCIDENTALLY SENT THE DEPART-MENT PHONE LIST AS AN E-MAIL ATTACH-MENT.
THERE ARE LOTS OF WHINERS IN "A" THROUGH "M."
*%!
11/11/01 ©2001 United Feature Syndicate, Inc.